The
Cactus Hunters

The Cactus Hunters

DESIRE AND EXTINCTION IN THE
ILLICIT SUCCULENT TRADE

JARED D. MARGULIES

UNIVERSITY OF MINNESOTA PRESS
MINNEAPOLIS • LONDON

Cover design by Catherine Casalino
Cover art: The Natural History Museum / Alamy Stock Photo
Cover font: Diablitos, by Pablo A. Medina, based on *fileteado*, an Argentinian stylized lettering with floral ornamentation.

Portions of chapters 4 and 8 are adapted from "A Political Ecology of Desire: Between Extinction, Anxiety, and Flourishing," *Environmental Humanities* 14, no. 2 (2022): 241–64; copyright 2022 Jared Margulies; all rights reserved; reprinted by permission of the author, http://www.dukeupress.edu/. Portions of chapter 6 are adapted from "Korean 'Housewives' and 'Hipsters' Are Not Driving a New Illicit Plant Trade: Complicating Consumer Motivations behind an Emergent Wildlife Trade in *Dudleya farinose*," *Frontiers in Ecology and Evolution* 8: 604921. doi:10.3389/fevo.2020.604921; copyright 2020 Jared Margulies; all rights reserved; reprinted by permission of the author.

Excerpts from Alfred Lau's "Discovery at a Virgin Outpost" were originally published in *Cactus and Succulent Journal* 52, no. 5 (1980): 238–40; reprinted with permission.

All photographs and illustrations, unless otherwise specified, are by the author.

Published by the University of Minnesota Press
111 Third Avenue South, Suite 290
Minneapolis, MN 55401–2520
http://www.upress.umn.edu

ISBN 978-1-5179-1398-4 (hc)
ISBN 978-1-5179-1399-1 (pb)

A Cataloging-in-Publication record for this book is available from the Library of Congress.

Printed in the United States of America on acid-free paper

The University of Minnesota is an equal-opportunity educator and employer.

32 31 30 29 28 27 26 25 24 23   10 9 8 7 6 5 4 3 2 1

For my parents and Heeyoung

We have not yet lifted our eyes to the vaster horizons before us. We have not faced the almost terrifying challenge of the Plant.

—Ursula K. Le Guin, *The Author of Acacia Seeds*

There is a lot to say on the psychology of collecting. I am something of a collector myself.

—Jacques Lacan, *The Ethics of Psychoanalysis*

Contents

Contents

Preface

I was supposed to be studying the illegal trade in tiger bones. It was summer 2017, and I was preparing to move to the United Kingdom from Baltimore, Maryland, where I had finished my PhD, focused on wildlife conservation politics in South India. My new position was part of a research project examining the integration of biodiversity conservation and security through the illegal wildlife trade (IWT). Shortly after my dissertation defense, I came across an article about saguaro rustling and other cactus poaching in the U.S. Southwest that piqued my interest. *Strange,* I remember thinking.

Maybe if I hadn't been preoccupied by the health of a cactus sitting on my windowsill, this would have been the extent of my foray into the world of cactus and succulent plant trade and theft. Instead, something gripped me in this story of stolen saguaros and in the many articles I soon read about other kinds of cactus poaching. I began to wonder more about the cactus on my windowsill, how little I knew about it as a species, and how it came to be here. Something left me desiring to know more. Maybe things operating in the realm of the unconscious to which I do not have access could explain why I would choose to spend the next six years obsessively thinking about what makes succulents desirable and, in turn, how those desires reshape species futures. The mystery persists. But what is clear is that the work you hold in your hands is the product of embracing the throes of desire and others' desires becoming, in many ways, my own.

~

Two years later, I was in rural Czechia in the greenhouse of a man many have dubbed one of the most infamous cactus smugglers in the world. He is also considered one of the most knowledgeable experts on cacti in Europe. On a wet and gray fall day, he showed me thousands of propagated offspring of a Mexican cactus species so new to botanical knowledge that it was not yet included on Mexico's endangered species list. The plant, *Mammillaria bertholdii,* though familiar to serious cactus collectors, remains otherwise largely unknown. In Mexico, it is a naturally rare species with an exceedingly small habitat range in Oaxaca. There is no legal trade in this species (for reasons I describe later), and yet, at cactus and succulent expos around the world, it has been available for sale for years. This is a trade occurring, not in the shadowy corners of some black market, but out in the open, in person and online.

M. bertholdii is a strange-looking cactus. It features unusual spines that look like little, feathery amoebas (Figure 1). And it has a deep taproot, much larger than its tiny, aboveground stem. This water-storing taproot permits it to survive prolonged periods without rain in the Oaxacan drylands. It was officially "discovered" by the self-described German "cactoexplorer" Andreas Berthold in 2013. It was formally described in the botanical literature by another German, named Thomas Linzen.

Despite its status as new to science, seeds and small grafted stock of these rare plants were almost immediately available for sale online and at major cactus conventions in Europe. Given the species' relatively slow growth, individual plants and seeds were certainly smuggled out of Mexico years before it was ever described. Several years ago, grafted specimens of *M. bertholdii* purportedly sold for more than a thousand dollars per individual plant. The first seeds were available for approximately fifty dollars per packet of ten seeds from Czechia, quite likely offered by the man with whom

Figure 1. A grafted *Mammillaria bertholdii* held in the hand of a Czech cactus collector. The species' unusual pectinate spines resemble the teeth of a comb. Wild-growing plants of the species feature much less pronounced tubercles, where the plant instead lies nearly flat against the ground.

I was then standing. According to scientists and amateur botanists, the greatest threat the species faces is from poaching for international illegal trade.

Within the collector community, *M. bertholdii* quickly became a sensation. For the desirous collector, it checked all the boxes: new, rare in the wild, unusual shape, and featuring a massive magenta flower. But within a matter of years, the price fell to five to twenty-five dollars for grafted plants. The people who first stole *M. bertholdii* out of Mexico tell me they are responsible for this rapid price crash—that by providing cultivated plants and seed for the market, they were averting a rush of collectors seeking out wild-growing plants in Oaxaca. But all this was illegal and took place to the consternation of Mexican authorities. "If not for us, this plant might already be extinct in the wild, and yet we are made out as criminals," the Czech cactus dealer declared.

One collector would say later while discussing *M. bertholdii,* "Most of us will be quite happy with a cultured or grafted plant. But there will always be those who want the *real* thing." The research behind this book sets off from this mystery: why would succulent collectors, people who are so passionate about these plants—rare, endangered, or otherwise—seemingly love them into extinction through illicit acts? What propels the fantasy of searching for "the *real* thing," and at what costs? The unconscious is a space of play between dynamic, interacting, and often contradictory thoughts, ideas, and forces. The same proved true in researching and writing the multispecies stories that follow. They are full of obsessive characters, beguiling emotions, and complex alliances. "It is crazy to blame enthusiasts as people who don't love nature enough; portraying them as smugglers doesn't capture our obsession with nature," the Czech cactus smuggler later would tell me. In time I would come to learn something about this obsession: I was immune neither to the transference of these desires nor from developing caring relations with the collectors, botanists, and conservationists who permitted me to learn from them. But the smuggler also admitted that this obsession has at times proved disastrous for species that became objects of desire. "The collector community needs to be cultivated," he said with a wry smile.

This book is also a work of cultivation, a guide to collisions of botany, care, conservation, and desire as an effort to develop new insights about a serious set of problems affecting species around the world impacted by illicit and illegal trade. An engagement with the unconscious would prove vital to my efforts to explore how desire structures people–plant relations. In turning to matters of the unconscious, emotion, and desire, the text may strike some readers as surprisingly personal for a book on plant trade and trafficking. I stand by this choice to emphasize narrative, emotion, ambivalence, and my own subjectivity over distance and the performance of expert authority in the chapters that follow. I cannot entirely disentangle the succulent desires and emotional bonds I detail in the pages that follow from my own. I trust in this choice as a more helpful if still fallible and unfinished guide as together we explore this succulent subject.[1]

Abbreviations

ABS access and benefit sharing

AOPK Agentura Ochrany Přírody a Krajiny (Agency for Nature and Landscape Conservation) (Czechia)

BCSS British Cactus and Succulent Society

CBD Convention on Biological Diversity

CDFW California Department of Fish and Wildlife

CITES Convention on International Trade in Endangered Species of Wild Fauna and Flora

ČIŽP Česká Inspekce Životního Prostředí (Czech Environmental Inspectorate)

CNPS California Native Plant Society

CONABIO Comisión Nacional para el Conocimiento y Uso de la Biodiversidad (National Commission for the Knowledge and Use of Biodiversity) (Mexico)

CONANP Comisión Nacional de Áreas Naturales Protegidas (National Commission of Natural Protected Areas) (Mexico)

ESA U.S. Endangered Species Act

GARES Gyeonggido Cactus and Succulent Research Institute (South Korea)

IUCN International Union for Conservation of Nature

IWT illegal wildlife trade

PROFEPA Procuraduría Federal de Protección al Ambiente (Attorney General's Office for Environmental Protection) (Mexico)

SČSPKS Společnost Českých a Slovenských Pěstitelů Kaktusů a Sukulentů (Society of Czech and Slovak Cactus and Succulent Growers)

UNTOC United Nations Convention against Transnational Organized Crime

USDA U.S. Department of Agriculture

Introduction

Cactus, Be My Desire

The truth is cacti deserve their special cult, if only because they are mysterious.

—Karel Čapek, *The Gardener's Year*

Across sandstone flats near the side of a highway in Bahia, Brazil, is a sea of tiny cacti. A Candomblé altar is tucked into a thicket of scrub nearby—an assembly of gourd vessels, candles, and coin offerings. Dusk approaches as I crouch on a pockmarked slab of rock to look at scores of little cacti beneath my feet. My eye is drawn toward one. My traveling companions, a small group of mostly European, self-described "cactoexplorers," tell me this cactus the circumference of a dime is called *Discocactus zehntneri* subspecies *boomianus*. It's a long name for a very small plant. It isn't particularly distinct from other species in the genus I have seen, whose name comes from the Greek for "disc-cactus" owing to their flattened, round form. The species is named for Leo Zehnter, a Swiss botanist who spent several years living in Bahia. The subspecies name recognizes the Dutch botanist Boudewijn Karel Boom.

Many cacti are named like this, telling us more about the desires of European or American men than the plant as it is or the places it grows. The cactus before me is lime green and encased in a dense mat of long, flexible spines. Although it looks thirsty and

1

sunbaked, I am aware of just how dazzling these plants can become when living under less strenuous conditions. As a genus, *Discocactus* relies on nocturnal pollinators and puts out huge, stunning white blooms at night to attract them. Even more beautiful than their flowers, I'd argue, are their fragrances. Their scents are as rich and intoxicating as a gardenia or coffee blossom, as enveloping as perfume. But in cultivation, *Discocactus* species are difficult to keep alive, marking them as both rarities and prized by collectors. Collectors who can bring *Discocactus* species into flower are recognized by their peers as skillful caretakers.

Without warning, I am enticed by this plant beneath my feet. In a matter of seconds, I could uproot it with a penknife or even a coin. Surrounded by a population of plants in large clumps, I imagine plucking it from the rock, as if the cactus would prefer to slip into my shirt pocket. The state of the vegetation suggests it has hardly rained in months; a day or two left on bare roots in international transit likely wouldn't do this cactus much more harm. Adapted for survival in an extreme climate, the plant's *lootability* has evolved.

People the world over utilize and consume countless species as part of everyday life. But on the much narrower list of species that people desire as living companions—dogs and cats, monsteras and aloes, birds and reptiles—few species are so easy to illicitly grasp, so lootable, as many cactus and succulent plants. Imagine the effort required to covertly steal a hundred-year-old oak tree with the intent to keep it alive rather than turn it into a pile of timber.[1] In contrast, a saguaro of the same age—that towering icon of the Sonoran Desert that can reach as much as fifty feet in height and weigh upward of six tons—is comparatively easier to pry from the ground. Its shallow roots, just inches deep yet radiating as far as the saguaro is tall, have evolved to quickly soak up summer monsoon rains, water that in turn is stored in the fleshy tissue of the plant's massive stem, which has evolved to swell in an accordion-like fashion. These pleats will contract again over time as the stored water is slowly used up in periods without rain. This adaptation to life in an extreme climate also facilitates the saguaro's extraction from the ground with just a shovel or two, a winch, and pickup truck (and a lot of burlap for protection).

Scientists include approximately twelve thousand species of plants in the category of "succulents."[2] Succulents are not a formal plant group, however, and succulents are found across a wide range of taxonomic orders, meaning the adaptation for succulent living evolved independently across the vegetal tree of life.[3] Though disagreement exists, we can say a succulent is a plant that possesses specialized tissue that offers temporary storage of water, enabling the plant to be "temporarily independent" from an external water supply and maintain metabolic activity when roots are no longer able to obtain water.[4] So, although all cacti fit this general succulent description, not all succulents are cacti.

Between fifteen hundred and two thousand agreed-upon species fall within the Cactaceae family, though the exact number varies between sources. Whereas succulence is a descriptor of a kind of vegetal adaptation, cacti are part of a family with a shared evolutionary history. Nearly all cacti have spines (not thorns), which are highly modified leaves that evolved to help the plant reduce water loss through evapotranspiration. These spines both protect the plant from herbivory and also help with water retention by reducing airflow around the plant and providing shade. Another important feature of cactus plants is what is called an areole, a kind of modified bud where both spines and flowers emerge from the plant. Areoles often look like little fuzzy buttons or dots evenly spaced along a cactus stem. In the absence of true leaves, the photosynthetic part of the cactus plant is the stem (Figure 2). Despite their common ancestry, cacti compose an extremely diverse family that continues to radiate and evolve. Some, like the saguaro, are measured in tons and meters, whereas other cacti may be decades old and never grow larger than a thumbnail. Some are exceedingly hairy, others are woolly, while others are smooth, tropical epiphytes. Some are paddle shaped, while others grow into sprawling clumps. Some cacti spend nearly their entire lives underground, and some cacti don't really look like cacti at all.[5]

Despite this great diversity of form, shape, and size, the lootability of succulents denotes how so many cacti and other succulents have evolved to living in extreme environments that enlace with human drives to obtain them. The live and illegal shipment of a baby tiger or parrot, whose value for an exotic pet keeper is in the animal's living status, is not so amenable to the kind of transit to which many succulents are subjected.[6] The lootability of succulent life tells us something about how vegetal adaptive strategies for survival might *grip* human desires. Lootability signals not only the capacity of certain succulents to survive theft but how the capacity to do so may constitute part of their enticement as objects of desire and the pleasure found in the taking.

The saguaro pried from the ground resonates with my overall approach to thinking with desire and human–plant relations in what follows: as an interactive entanglement of the human psyche in and through the environment and other organisms with great consequence for an array of species. This approach follows from what Anna Secor and Virginia Blum describe as a "psychotopological" approach to the psyche, where "material spaces and psychic processes shape one another."[7] Topology, in French psychoanalyst Jacques Lacan's terms, *is* the structure of the unconscious: a qualitative geometry linking the unconscious with the subject's world, in which the physical space and literal distances between places, species, and collections (for instance) do not matter so much as the *relation* of connections that bind them. Concerning ourselves with what enjoins the psyche with the environment is an encounter with Lacan's idea of *extimacy*. Extimacy enjoins the exterior with

Figure 2. Botanical illustration of *Mammillaria elephantidens* (today considered *Coryphantha elephantidens*) from Charles Lemaire's *Iconographie descriptive des cactées, ou, Essais systématiques et raisonnés sur l'histoire naturelle, la classification et la culture des plantes de cette famille* (Illustrations from a descriptive iconography of cacti) (Paris: H. Cousin, 1841). In addition to the beautiful pale pink flowers, the image displays several of the key characteristics of members of the cactus family: spines emerging from the areole and cactus "wool" in the spaces between the plant's tubercles—the nodes or protrusions of the stem giving the plant its sculptural-like shape. The species gets its name from its imposing, "elephant tooth"–like spines. Illustration by Charles Lemaire. Courtesy the Biodiversity Heritage Library and Missouri Botanical Garden, Peter H. Raven Library.

intimacy; it means that the "exterior" is within us, and it also names the spatiality of the unconscious as expressed before us.[8] Thinking the unconscious with the cactus through extimacy helps give meaning to seeing the unconscious as in front of us—not hidden away from view but expressed in and through the world. To attend to where and how a cactus becomes affixed in the psychotopology of the unconscious is to put faith in desire as a mode of inquiry.

Of course, the stolen saguaro I describe does not live alone, nor only in the mind as a desirous fantasy, and it is just as likely it will die months later without significant care. Every story of illicit succulent life contains the storied lives of countless others. Saguaros evolved over millions of years with two pollinating bat species that rely on the saguaro's nectar for survival, while the gilded flicker and Gila woodpecker make their homes inside the saguaro's flesh and woody ribs. In time, owls and finches will move into these abandoned nests, while hawks hunt from the crooks of the saguaro's great arms and nest there as well. Dozens of species and human cultures rely on their large fruits, which split open to reveal thousands of protein-rich seeds. For the Tohono O'odham, Yaqui, Piipaash, and other O'odham nations that call the Sonoran Desert home, saguaros command deep reverence (for the Tohono O'odham, as literal kin), alongside providing an important source of nutrition. If the saguaro were eventually looted to extinction (an unlikely scenario, thankfully), it would doubtfully leave this earth alone, its absence upending reciprocal relations with other species millennia in the making. Today, however, climate change may pose a far greater threat to the flourishing of the species.

But just about any other cactus is easier to thieve than a saguaro. And back in Bahia, I contemplated the consequences of cactus theft. Would it be so wrong if this tiny *Discocactus* were to live out its life in a pot elsewhere, free from the stresses of extreme drought? The cactus was surrounded by the dead remains of others, lives cut short by a particularly hot and dry season and worsening droughts attributed to climate change. In the end, of course, I did not steal it. Aside from Brazilian law, the International Union for Conservation of Nature (IUCN) lists this species as "near threatened" on the Red List, the most comprehensive global assessment tool determining the degree of endangerment for nearly 150,000 species. But experts assessing the species note that subspecies like *D. zehntneri* subspecies *boomianus,* restricted to a few small populations, are much more vulnerable to extinction than the species as a whole. The entire genus of *Discocactus* is also listed on the appendix of the Convention on International Trade in Endangered Species of Wild Fauna and Flora, or CITES for short. CITES is a multilateral convention regulating the trade in wild species either currently or deemed to be potentially impacted by international trade. According to its website, the primary aim of CITES is "to ensure that international trade in specimens of wild animals and plants does not threaten the survival of the species." Today, more than thirty-seven thousand species of plants and animals are listed by CITES, and most of these are plants (and most of these are orchids). As a CITES Appendix I genus—the strictest CITES appendix—the international trade in any *Discocactus* species is prohibited. Not only would taking and transporting this cactus abroad have been ethically wrong—which is another way to say illicit—it would have also been illegal.

Some people might be said to love cacti and succulents to death. They are some of the most heavily threatened species among internationally traded plants for ornamental collection. A variety of species in the *Dudleya, Aztekium,* and *Ariocarpus* genera in North America, alongside the Conophytum family and *Lithops* genus in southern Africa (to name just a few examples), currently face intense illegal collecting pressure, and some face pressing extinction concerns. Over 75 percent of all cacti are experiencing population declines globally, and about one-third of all approximately fifteen hundred cactus species are threatened with extinction. *This makes cacti one of the most threatened taxa of life on the planet—inclusive of animals.* Nearly half of these threatened species are harvested for horticulture and private ornamental collections.[9] Climate change paints an even bleaker outlook for many of these species. The world regions with high succulent biodiversity and those expected to be most vulnerable to the impacts of climate change map tightly to one another.[10] For all the global recognition succulents receive as charismatic species, many face very precarious futures.

I smiled leaving the *Discocactus* out on the rocks that evening. But I wrote later in my notes about a feeling of creeping unease. On one hand, I felt immense pleasure in recognizing that increasing encounters had taught me to be affected by these wonderful plants. On the other, I could not shake the sense that this desire to possess was rooted in something else, something with both an uneasy history and a deeper urging predating my experiences in that place.[11] A new link in the "psychotopology" connecting me to place and species in a moment in time was forged; I was marked by the cactus and yet urged on by a desirous repetition for something *else*. Walking away, I was left with the firm conviction that had I taken the cactus, my desire would have only pointed toward pursuing another. The drive for a kind of satisfaction, while perhaps temporarily pleasing or fulfilling, would wither, sending me to seek out another. In this context, as rewarding as a work like Michael Pollan's *The Botany of Desire* is for thinking about the emergent passions of people for plants, Pollan does not go far enough in asking why people plant apple trees or go bonkers for tulips. This is because he does not ask what makes desire possible—in other words, how one becomes a desiring subject and keeps on desiring more.[12]

Cosmopolitan Cacti and Other Succulent Stories

The roots of plants belie their tendency to move. Though many of the plants featured in this book are exceptional for their highly restricted habitat ranges—a hillside in Brazil, a single valley in Oaxaca, Mexico, or a small island in the Pacific—they also lead cosmopolitan lives. Consider a cactus unique for rooting to the branches of trees in the tropical forests of the Mata Atlântica in southeastern Brazil. In contrast with the humanlike silhouette of the saguaro, this cactus is all lush and limbs, a toppling bouquet of flat, segmented stems with an abundance of pink and white flowers. The species is formally classified as endangered by conservation scientists, confined to a small geographic region fragmented by the megacities of São Paolo and Rio de Janeiro. It is also threatened by people who wrest it, plant by plant, for its ornamental value. But consider a million genetically identical clones whose origins are rooted in this species, circulating in barcoded plastic pots around the world. Maybe one is even sitting nearby as you read this. It is arguably one of the most "successful" succulents on the planet, if success is measured in abundance of individuals alone. You might know this plant as the Christmas or Thanksgiving cactus, favored for its brightly colored flowers that bloom in late autumn and winter in the northern hemisphere, compared to April or May in Brazil.

Veering toward extinction and in bloom the world over—this is one of many things that make the lives of plants good to think with; their roots and shoots extend in surprising directions. In the process, they connect seemingly disparate geographies. But some would argue that the species known to scientists as *Schlumbergera orssichiana* has nothing to do with the Christmas cactus you bought at the supermarket, that the latter is only the commodified, ghostlike apparition of *S. orssichiana*. Nearly all commercially available Christmas cacti are hybrid crosses of multiple *Schlumbergera*

9

species; really, your plant is the composition of multiple species achieved through thousands of genetic crosses to coax out desirable traits. A veritable monstrosity of managed species comingling is sitting on your windowsill. Plant breeders and cultivators might say that their hybrids hold no relation whatsoever to wild *Schlumbergera* species. Instead, I would suggest that these plants *are* related, even if the biological and social ties that connect them grow more distant year by year.

Attention to relation and difference in excavating the histories that bind these plants is an important corrective to conventional natural histories. It creates more space for the human within non-human stories, while allowing for learning about how the nonhuman world both affects and transforms the human.[13] It presents a prompting to think carefully about "more-than-human" care, a topic that has received notable attention and theorization in recent years.[14] Connecting matters of care with commodification is to stay close to the tensions they express, as opportunities to stretch and probe their meaning. I extend this dialectical approach to thinking about care for cacti and other succulents in this book to make a similar—though perhaps more controversial—argument about species collection and wildlife conservation. Rather than approaching them as antithetical practices, I argue they should be understood as rooted in shared human experiences, desires, fantasies, and anxieties that continue to shape the fate of much of the nonhuman world. These subjects touch on divergent and disparate fields of study from psychoanalysis to botany to political ecology. I read, think, and do translational work across these fields to say something about the connections between them. I did not seek out this subject because I was searching for a topic that might bring these areas of intellectual thought together. This is anything but a story of a hammer searching for a nail. Instead, this book exemplifies the work of desire in the research creation process: I became transfixed by the succulent subject; I was in the throes of its desire as my own.[15] Through this work, I found that the succulent subject is not just good to think with as a model transdisciplinary subject but that the succulent subject demands it.

A Political Ecology of Desire

This book is a political ecology of desire, and as such, I conceptualize the *production of desire* as a framework for psychoanalytic political ecologies. This means that an analysis of the political economy of environmental change is aided through turning to the unconscious and what propels the desiring subject forward in their search for satisfaction. The production of desire names how political economy shapes and adheres to psychic processes, and vice versa, with a recognition that doing so entails transformations of the living world with more-than-human (and psychic) consequence. Desire is not a one-way street; it works in multiple (topological) directions, between the conscious and unconscious, as well as in the "interior" of the self in relation to its expression in the wider world and the chains of signification through which unconscious thoughts are entwined. Our desires are never ours alone, but neither do desires adhere to just any random "object." Desire emerges between subject and object, but this does not mean we must deny the object of active capacity to work on us as well. The title *The Cactus Hunters* speaks to the aching search and yearnings expressed by all manner of subjects in this book for what they suppose they desire, ranging from cactus smugglers to law enforcement agents to passionate conservationists. Although academic debates rage on about whether nonhumans can or should be understood to "act" or have "agency" in coproducing the world, it is quite clear to me that they do. As unlikely a source as it might first seem, psychoanalysis offers some surprising insights into how it is that these "objects" shape desires in ways that can profoundly transform the world.

Broadly speaking, political ecology is the practice of studying and organizing around the production of environmental inequalities, human (in)access to natural resources, and the intersection of social justice and environmental concerns with close attention to questions of power and economy.[16] In joining "production" with desire, I am thinking about desire as an active force working in a world transformed by capitalist world ecologies and how central desire is to the reproduction of capitalism and the commodity form.[17] In the chapters that follow, I extend thinking about the place of desire in shaping environments and other species in a more-than-human world. I do so by bridging theories of lively or living capital (the commodified forms of these living plants) with matters of more-than-human care and key Lacanian psychoanalytic theories of desire, drives, anxiety, and fantasy.[18] In building my arguments, I draw on diverse scholarly works ranging from psychoanalytic geographies to more-than-human geographies, political ecologies of wildlife trade, and feminist theories of care.

Our social worlds have always been *more-than-human*. This phrasing is not a reminder that we inhabit an earth full of a diversity of life (there are simpler ways to say this) but that the human is not composed of the human alone.[19] In this vein of thinking, I pursue "arts of noticing" to make sense of the tangled connections we share with a dizzying array of life-forms, connections that are integral to composing what we call the human.[20] This shift in social research away from the atomistic human subject is an effort to decenter the fixity of humans as the only meaningful actors in social life. A turn to psychoanalytic theory may therefore strike some readers as strange, given its preoccupation with the distinctively human unconscious. To the contrary, I suggest that considering how "entangled" social research has become, it seems stranger still how comparatively little of the more-than-human literature engages with psychoanalytic thought.[21] It is as if our unconscious desires do not matter in composing the world as we encounter it, full of nonhuman life. If "human nature is an interspecies relationship," as Anna Tsing writes, why have scholars invested in asserting the presences of the many other species that compose this relationship ignored the material import of the unconscious as part of that story?[22] In the words of Donna Haraway, "we are in a knot of species coshaping one another in layers of reciprocating complexity all the way down."[23] But our unconscious selves aren't just along for this ride; they mediate the very meaning of the journey "all the way down."

With desire as my compass, I followed species caught up in illegal trades around the world and sought to understand the social, political, and economic dynamics and consequences of these succulent circulations. At the same time, I take seriously the charge to center plants as active subjects in the shaping of trades I followed. But what I found in granting attention to the material and unique constitutional capacities of succulents exceeded the domain of the vegetal world alone; I also encountered the ebb and flow of the unconscious with the world, the space of interactivity where mind and matter meet—life as a process and an unfolding event.

The Succulent Subject

Psychoanalytic geography has firmly established itself as both a vibrant subfield of geography and also one increasingly in conversation with other related fields, including political ecology.[24] There is a growing body of scholarship on how Lacanian psychoanalysis offers a great deal to advancing contemporary discussions of the environment.[25] My research is supported by this robust scaffolding linking the insights of psychoanalysis to how and why humans interact in their environments, with consequences for the ecologies and spaces we inhabit.

During my research with cactus collectors, one research participant described his community as "plant-people." One way to think about this book is as a dedication to that hyphen: what both connects and separates the collector from the plants that serve as objects of desire. There is an important distinction between the "object" we speak of in collection and the "object" in psychoanalysis, the latter of which, among other things, is "a point of imaginary fixation which gives satisfaction to a drive."[26] To understand what distinguishes these sorts of objects from one another, or how a cactus can become imbued with significations of other sorts of psychoanalytic objects, we need to engage with some key ideas of Lacanian psychoanalysis that will surface throughout the book.

The desiring subject in Lacanian thought is a split subject, brought into being through the world of language. Thinking the hyphen in *plant-people* with Lacan, we can think of the "succulent subject" as a split subject as well, one where the "split" leaves room for fantasies propelling the subject's drives toward other species as objects of desire. Fantasy, in Lacan's words, "is the support of desire."[27] Through fantasy, we recognize ourselves as subjects of lack, subjects forever obliged to seek out what Lacan calls "the Thing" *(das Ding)* we suppose is lacking within us. The Thing is the void that is at once exterior to us yet sits at the center of the subject's sense of self; it is this extimacy that centers our very being. Like many of Lacan's insights, it is a paradoxical and challenging one: it is this Thing's absence that is constitutive of us, yet we recognize it only through the sense of lack in its missing.[28] This lack keeps us always on the move, searching for desirable "objects" that might fill the void, as well as propelling us ever forward in search of the fantasy of imagined wholeness we see as lost in the very moment we emerged as desiring subjects (what Lacan describes as alienation). But as a fantasy, this lack can never be truly satisfied—there is no cactus, no person, no "object," that can substitute for the absence of the Thing.

There are, however, objects that become imbued with the aura of the Thing. At times, then, real "objects" in the world may take on greater psychoanalytic heft as objects of desire through fantasies that place them closer to the Thing. And, as objects of desire (and through what we will encounter later as Lacan's *objet a*), they keep us stubbornly on the track of desire as a perpetual search. As Mari Ruti summarizes, "as a result, we spend our lives trying to find substitutes for what we imagine having lost; we stuff one object of desire *(objet a)* after another into the void . . . in the hope that one day we can heal our wound (undo our alienation)."[29] To this end, certain (if at times, improbable) material objects in the world—a cactus, for instance—can come to matter in unconscious registers in very significant ways.

The drive I describe that encircles the absent Thing is not equivalent to desire, however, and I will return to the drives in a moment, as they are also important to how I came to understand collector practices with consequence for succulent plants. But returning first to desire, desire signals the quest for the fantasy of impossible unification of the subject with what they suppose has been lost in the "split" as they enter the symbolic realm. This separation for Lacan signifies an *ontological* lack, a separation that occurs as infants and structures being itself.[30] Lacan further recognizes this entrance into the symbolic order through the emergence of language. Once a person enters the symbolic order of language, things are never again as they were. In speaking, as much as words stand in for real-world things—the word *cactus* signifies what we imagine cactus plants to be—the things themselves become signifiers; they are imbued with other memories, yearnings, and fantasies. Everything is in part constituted by what is *not* there. As "real" as the real world remains, we also live within a world that is forever mediated by signification. This is why Lacan insists that the unconscious is "structured like a language."[31] As Todd McGowan describes, "the subject in the world of signification can never just eat an apple but eats instead what 'keeps the doctor away,' what is juicy and delicious, or what connotes original sin. . . . This excess attached to the apple produces a satisfaction for the subject that an apple by itself—an apple that isn't an 'apple'—can never provide for an animal that eats it."[32] At the same time, the "apple" that can never truly satisfy what it seems to promise speaks to desire as the desire for the fantasy of what we suppose the "Other" desires.

The Other is the master signifier of the symbolic order, the figure the subject identifies as social authority, the guide to normative morality, the law, God, and so on. It is through the Other that we encounter our own desires, which is why "our" desires are never "ours" alone.[33] It is for this reason that we have Lacan's famous axiom that "desire is the desire of the Other."[34] Subjects become desiring subjects by constantly, unconsciously, aiming for what they suppose the imagined Other desires. As McGowan explains, "we desire what we assume the Other desires because the Other desires it and because we want to attract the desire of the Other. It is in these two senses that our desire is always the desire of the Other."[35]

But as I said, the work of desire and the drives are not equivalent. As I detail across chapters 1–3, attention to both desire and the drives is important for understanding the repetitive quest of cactus and succulent collectors to pursue "objects" for their collections. In Lacan's formulation, on the other side of desire are the subject's drives, the pursuit of enjoyment through encircling (and never obtaining) the absent Thing. This contrasts with the kind of total satisfaction imagined in desire, which remains forever out of reach in the unattainable "Other" and what we suppose are their desires.[36] Desire and drive are related through the subject's quest for enjoyment as they encircle the Thing, on one hand, and the compulsion to constantly seek out what we imagine to be lacking as our desire. "In other words," as Ruti explains, "the gap between the Thing as the (non)object that causes our desire and the objects *(objets a)* that our desire discovers in the world is why we are never entirely satisfied."[37] Paul Kingsbury and Steve Pile explain the drives further and point us in the direction of understanding the sorts of pleasure found through them: "the drives derive satisfaction by encircling or missing their object. Thus the drives are associated with activities that are excessive, repetitive, and potentially destructive."[38] They "exert a menacing and constant pressure on the psychoanalytic subject."[39]

In constantly failing to reach a totalizing satisfaction, what the subject instead encounters in the "gap" between the Thing and objects of desire is an excessive, painful pleasure, or what remains untranslatable in English as *jouissance. Jouissance* is one of Lacan's most profound insights for psychoanalysis. As Kingsbury writes, "a Lacanian geography shorn of the concept of jouissance is as curbed as a Foucauldian geography deprived of the concept of power."[40] It is through *jouissance,* this aching kind of pleasure brought about in the failure to obtain satisfaction, that we can see how repetitive failure *is* a kind of pleasure, yet also a pleasure we cannot shake or rid ourselves of entirely. As Joan Copjec clarifies on this repetition, Freud "interprets repetition as the invariable characteristic of the drives that fuel life. The being of the drives, he claims, *is* the compulsion to repeat."[41] In repetition (and, consequently, the experience of *jouissance*), the drives reveal their primary psychic expression in always aiming without attaining.[42] *Jouissance* will emerge in this book in various moments, such as "delighting" in the unique yet painful confrontation of species extinction as a singular encounter with rarity (chapter 4) and in a moment of reveling in the unexpected discovery of a cactus thought to be extinct, yet only to recognize that its presence still likely signals species obliteration (chapter 2).

We will also encounter how repetitive behaviors that produce expressions of *jouissance* are perfectly latched on to by capitalism and the commodity form (here in the form of commodified succulents). Capitalism exploits the fantasy of a radically singular satisfaction by introducing objects in the form of desirable commodities that would *appear* to be the one thing that might bring us some satisfaction but always fails to do so. Yet, perversely, this failure of the commodity to deliver total satisfaction is itself a form of *jouissance* and thus enables the repetition of pleasurable failure through the introduction of yet more commodities that might be the one true object of desire but, of course, never are. In this way, capitalism hijacks desire. And so, as good desiring capitalist subjects, we search on and on for the next object to stuff into the void. The insights of McGowan show how a Lacanian psychoanalysis of the commodity form is so necessary for understanding the psychic staying power of capitalism. And, as I detail in chapter 7, the aesthetics of lively succulent commodities can hold powerful sway over the desiring subject and their fantasies.[43]

Although I have only just introduced in a very cursory way some concepts of Lacanian thought, they help to foreground how the search for enjoyment might then encounter—and at times be enhanced by—the entrance of the illicit as a conceptual framing of norms and behaviors of social acceptability as another set of barriers that delay, and at times amplify, the pleasures of *jouissance*. Whether through the "rogue" status some cactus smugglers "enjoy," the "naughty" habits of collectors who occasionally "pinch a seed or plant" with little repercussion, or collectors who revel in their self-identification as the "bad boys" of the cactus world, the proximity of the illicit held forth enjoyment for many research participants. As much as this book is focused on the very pressing matter of species extinction and biodiversity loss resulting from illegal trade, I nevertheless encountered a great deal of enjoyment in the process of pursuing this research. These psychoanalytic insights are very important to the story of illicit succulent life.

Set against the backdrop of inequitably experienced planetary-scale challenges like climate change, pervasive pollution, and biodiversity loss, the illicit trade in cactus and succulent plants may seem a very small thing. But lessons of greater scale—about extinction, more-than-human care, and the politics of illegal wildlife trade

(IWT)—also come into focus through these plants. My journey into the unconscious and the lives of succulent plants is a traveled one, spanning multispecies ethnographic research across seven countries on four continents, dozens of species of plants, and more than one hundred interviews with law enforcement officers, cactus collectors, botanists, conservationists, commercial succulent dealers, and, yes, succulent poachers. Some of these stories begin in specific locations, while some might begin anywhere, like in the search bar of an internet browser, where cactus seeds from Mexico are sold by Hungarian dealers to buyers in the United Kingdom through a U.S.-based web auction portal. "The unconscious," Lacan wrote, "is outside," but crucially, as Kingsbury and Pile explain, "the unconscious is also communicative."[44] My commitment in the last instance has always remained with the plants at the heart of

Figure 3. The large budding purple flowers of a *Pilosocereus* cactus after a short rain. The genus earns its name for being an especially "hairy" torch cactus. A collector with a camera inspecting plants can be seen in the background.

this book and the ecologies they inhabit and that people inhabit with them. "Psychoanalysis affirms a radical incorporation and openness toward the extraordinary diversity that is life and the world."[45] Psychoanalytic thought, I think, therefore has a part to play in enacting another politics and ethics rooted in desire, one with great consequence for the more-than-human world.[46] I hope that in relating my journey into a more succulent life, I successfully convey some of the joys and pleasures I came to know in learning about and traveling with these plants as fellow inhabitants of the earth (Figure 3). Like many stories of small things, in tugging just a little on a thread—or, in this case, a root—entire worlds are revealed.

On Succulents I Did Not Follow

This book is restricted to studying the kinds of human–plant relations that emerge through collection of living ornamental plants and the consequences of these behaviors for the conservation of affected species. These practices are especially informed by Euro-American collecting habits. But of course, many other kinds of succulent consumption, as well as radically different forms of human–plant relations, exist. The Tohono O'odham, for instance, share very different kinds of relations rooted in kinship with saguaro cacti as people than the consumers driving their theft in the Sonoran Desert out of desire to reproduce the desert's aesthetics in their suburban Phoenix subdivisions. But Indigenous modes of relating to plants like the saguaro are so distinct (and distinctly important) from the kinds of "consumption" and botanical modes of relating found in the world of collection that they exceed the bounds of this work.[47] I also intentionally do not include the trade in peyote (*Lophophora* species of cacti) for their religious, medicinal, and mind-altering qualities. In a similar register, yet in relation to the theory I primarily deploy, I have had to carefully consider what place a turn to Lacanian psychoanalysis offers to political ecologies of environmental change today. This is even more important as long ignored, silenced, and marginalized voices and perspectives, alongside non-Euro-Western scholarly traditions, are finally moving from positions on the margins of political ecology toward its center, as Farhana Sultana has described.[48] Yet, in seeking out a body of theory equipped to disentangle succulent desires among passionate collectors, passions that in turn can drive IWT and even species extinctions, I found psychoanalysis to be a powerful form of theorizing well equipped for excavating what lies at the roots of these desires.

While I therefore do not share stories of other forms of succulent "consumption" in this book, the saguaro still serves as a useful warning about the harms both capitalism and state sovereignty can bring to bear on succulent life and the dangers we face in turning to matters of the illegal and illicit without a critical perspective. To counter the problem of saguaro poaching in the Sonoran Desert, the U.S. National Park Service made headlines in 2020 for microchipping saguaros, which have been illegally harvested for the landscape architecture trade for decades.[49] At the same time this was occurring, the U.S. Department of Homeland Security, ignoring the protestations of the Tohono O'odham Nation and conservation organizations, waived dozens of environmental protection laws to remove saguaros, among other protected species, to make way for the construction of an extended United States–Mexico border wall.

The saguaro paints a telling diptych of state power that can at once destroy or foster nonhuman life. It is an important reminder that what separates the legal and illegal tells us foremost about the wishes of the state to preserve its power, sovereignty, and economic benefits derived therein. This story also points us toward the important narrative politics of IWT that can be mobilized through species of interest and to great effect. As I turn to in the second half of this book through the story of *Dudleya farinosa*, even the topic of illegal plant trade can become a potent vehicle for reproducing harmful stereotypes and racist tropes that resonate through wildlife consumption practices and conservation, as well as serving as geopolitical fodder that places blame for IWT at the feet of some countries or cultures, while ignoring the same trades happening domestically.

In turning to stories of plants in an illicit key, it is important to avoid the tempting vortex of uncritical thought that presumes that what is legal is necessarily right and what is illegal is wrong. Furthermore, these matters of ethics—as opposed to law—are profoundly shaped by who or what is deemed worthy of care and concern. Even the smallest cactus, as we will see, can entangle an impressive array of actors with their own motivations and desires on either side of the law.

Let Our Roots Shoot Forth!

This book is written in such a way that it grows. I keep this sentiment of global connection, between people, economies, plants, and ecosystems, in mind, as it mirrors my method. Building on methodologies of "follow the thing," others have pursued the practice of "follow the species" to understand the webs of relations connecting species, geographies, and economies.[50] I followed a similar path, staying with species (both as an epistemic category and as shorthand for the actual plants they denote) in navigating both licit and illicit global commodity chains. The chapters of the book are broadly structured chronologically, along the same trajectory and timelines of my own learning.

Across the first four chapters of the book, I develop the concept of the production of desire as a way for thinking about the place of desire and the drives in transforming species, ecologies, and environments. Geographically, these chapters tack back and forth between locations in Europe, Brazil, and Mexico. In chapter 1, I orient readers to cultures and psychologies of cactus and succulent collection in the Euro-American tradition, drawing on ethnographic research I conducted as a budding member of a cactus and succulent society. I describe cactus and succulent collecting behaviors and motivations for engaging in these practices. The chapter provides an overview of who cactus and succulent collectors are, why they collect, and how forms of meaning and emotion emerge through caring for plants and other collectors. Chapter 1 also examines both gendered and geographic dimensions of cactus collecting. Continuing to build toward a theory of the production of desire, in chapter 2, I turn to matters of the illegal and illicit more explicitly through my participant observation in a "cactoexploration" trip with passionate collectors in Brazil. I detail by what means cactus and succulent trades register as illicit or illegal. In this chapter, I also confront the place of *jouissance* in collector activities as they seek out plants, as well as my own encounter with the cactus as "sublime object." Together, these two chapters offer insights about contemporary cactus and succulent collector habits and desires and how they intersect the illicit.

Building from my engagement with the illicit and illegal in chapter 2, in chapter 3, I turn back to Europe to story the emergence of one of the world's contemporary epicenters of illegal succulent trade. I narrate the history of Alberto Vojtěch Frič, an early Czech cactoexplorer and amateur anthropologist, as a central figure in the history of Czechoslovak cactus collecting as well as a crucial figure in structuring what I describe as the fantasy of the "Robin Hood conservationist" among Czech cactophiles. This historical turn offers an important temporal dimension to my research by considering how mental processes structuring collector behaviors interact with and can be amplified by the past and experiences of trauma. This chapter also describes most clearly the stakes and consequences of certain collecting behaviors and illegal trade practices for rare and endangered species conservation. Taking this theme of conservation and endangerment to its conclusion, in chapter 4, I share the story of a cactus on the literal edge of extinction. Through my encounter with *Arrojadoa marylanae* on a small mountain in Bahia, Brazil, I explore what underpins anxieties that disable response to extinction's threat. To do so, I present my own self-analysis of extinction anxieties as I encountered them. Anxiety, as we will see, is a force that interrupts the capacity to desire with consequences for enacting pathways out of dismal extinction futures wrought by global capitalism.

Whereas chapters 1–4 move from collection and desire to the edge of extinction through the consequences of capitalist development and collector practices, across the next three chapters, I give in-depth attention to an unfolding illegal international wildlife trade. I closely follow the species of two members of the succulent *Dudleya* genus as they transform from flourishing and lively organisms into illicitly traded global commodities. In chapter 5, I detail the rise of a new illegal trade in the California succulent species *D. farinosa*. Drawing on interviews and investigative research in California, I piece together this emergent trade and its primary actors, and I work to understand what would cause the sudden rise of a new form of IWT in a species that was easily and legally obtainable at the time the illegal trade began. The story of *D. farinosa* becomes an important opportunity to consider how and by what means desires affix to other species, in this case with grave consequences. Through *D. farinosa*, I also engage with questions about the structure of illicit commodity chains and networks, drawing on insights from the field of green criminology.

In chapter 6, I stay close to *D. farinosa* and a related species, *D. pachyphytum*, to take seriously the work of learning with plants to examine the import of the unconscious in structuring succulent desires. I draw on archival material and close vegetal observation to argue for how a multispecies research approach demands attending to the living species at the heart of these trades and to understand how the fate of one species could become entwined with another. By steering my research toward both the affinities and differences between these species, I was able to understand what bound disparate geographies between California and Mexico through collector desires, instantiating how the psychotypologies of collectors can produce durable connections linking species, geographies, and trades.

In chapter 7, I conclude the story of this new illegal trade in *Dudleya* by following the species and their illegal trade to South Korea. In turning to South Korean succulents, I engage most directly with the commodification of vegetal life. I do so through attention to the unconscious, economic, and aesthetic processes by which plants are made and unmade, in Rosemary-Claire Collard's words, as "lively capital" with resulting consequences for plants and people alike.[51] I engage with some of the harmful narrative politics of IWT and critique circulating myths about these trades that reproduce stereotypes of the "Asian super consumer" in IWT. This chapter also examines how cuteness, as a surprisingly powerful aesthetic, further shapes succulent transformations into lively capital. The chapter concludes with a discussion of the role of a single succulent smuggler in profoundly reshaping the trajectories of a number of species.

Synthesizing insights gained from the preceding chapters, chapter 8 develops an extended discussion of species, extinction, and the work of care to consider the stakes for enacting flourishing geographies. Bringing these themes together with desire and the unconscious, I consider the work of excavating the unconscious for enacting flourishing geographies as a horizon of pursuit through the embrace of desire. In concluding the book in chapter 8, I describe how sustaining human–plant bonds through desire can hold promise, rather than only peril, for succulent species futures.

⚡ 1 ⚡

On Collecting and
Caring for Cacti

*I had a friend once. He had a cactus. The same cactus sitting
on his windowsill for fifteen years. Then one day someone gave
him a second cactus. And within six months he had to move to
a bigger house with enough space for his cactus collection.*

—Lance, *The Detectorists*

Traveling down a dirt road in Minas Gerais, Brazil, in 2018 with an English gardener and a retired Belgian railroad worker, I asked them if they might elaborate on the differences between cactus and orchid collectors. "I don't know many, it's a totally different world," the gardener replied, then added, "But, when I was at horticultural college I did an essay on orchids. . . . I think in another life I might have been collecting orchids." I looked to the retired railroad worker for his thoughts. "Orchid collectors are *obsessive*," he replied. "But is there a difference between them and us? It's people who collect things. What's the difference between cactus collectors and people who collect stamps? They are both obsessions. It's in the nature of mankind to collect things. The only difference is stamps and coins you put on a shelf, but plants require care. You have to remember these are *living* things."

The difference between a cactus and a stamp collection may therefore depend on how you value a life that isn't human. Literatures on collecting cultures rarely take this distinction—life itself—into account, treating orchid collectors the same as coin collectors and treating the objects of these collections as simply "objects" as opposed to living beings. But what is a collector? What do they collect, and how does collecting matter for understanding what at the outset might seem a strange sort of IWT? Collecting, as much as it is about gathering (from the Latin *colligere*, "to gather together"), is also about difference, separation, and repetition. And as we will see, collections are as much a reflection of the collector as the objects composing the collection. It is these efforts to classify, arrange, and order—practices that closely mirror and at times overlap with similar efforts to know, understand, and distinguish in the fields of taxonomy or botany—that also begin to lead us toward concerns about species extinction and what it means to care well for nonhuman others. Before immersing ourselves in the world of illicit succulent life, we should understand who collectors are, what they collect, and what motivates their desires to possess and cultivate plants. I am therefore equally invested in exploring how collecting practices impinge on nonhuman life as in how cacti structure collections in ways that assert their status as living beings—and how this demands that collectors care.

Caring for Cacti

What caring for cacti indexes will always remain a species-specific activity. My perspective on more-than-human care advances from Joan Tronto and Bernice Fisher's now classic definition of care as "a species activity that includes everything that we do to maintain, continue, and repair our 'world' so that we can live in it as well as possible."[1] María Puig de la Bellacasa shows that to care is also to engage with the capacity to affect and be affected by others, human or otherwise. She writes that "a politics of care engages much more than a moral stance; it involves affective, ethical, and hands-on agencies of practical and material consequence."[2] But there is work to be done in learning the politics and ethics of engagement with vegetal worlds. Some plants demand more "hands-on" practices of care than others. Still others push us to think more creatively about what the "species" as a mode of caring signifies within the surprisingly mobile and fluid world of vegetal life, where tidy boundaries between cacti (for instance) as categorical entities are perhaps less discrete or enclosed than we might imagine.

It is no coincidence that much of the literature on more-than-human care stems from research in the garden, and it served me well in considering practices of cactus care. With its central focus on cultivating desirable plant relations, the garden is a site for studying how humans work to tend and care for plants and those beings with which they share helpful alliances.[3] The garden also reveals how caring creates conditions for—and demands—the exclusion of care for others in the work of cultivation. Cultivation also serves to reminds us that care for plants is an ancient (human) species activity. John Hartigan Jr. writes, "Anthropologists' notion of culture derives from an activity developed through and with plants: cultivation. *The historically recent usage of culture to identify that which is distinctively human is a metaphoric extension of this original meaning. . . .* With the weight of long-standing assumptions that humans are the core reference for 'culture,' it is easy to forget that its principal reference—originally and to this very day—is care for plants."[4] As I discuss in the chapter that follows, many of the practices with which geographers and others have experimented to attune to human–plant relations have emerged in studies of gardeners with the plants they tend to, which I extended to the study of succulent collection practices.

Most of the collectors whose stories and practices I detail in chapters 1 and 2 are not in the business of breaking national or

Figure 4. Nikolai Aristides described collections as "an obsession organized." A particularly beautiful and orderly collection of cacti, carefully tended, in a greenhouse in Czechia.

international trade regulations in the name of their hobby or for profit, as much as many of them deeply disagree with current mechanisms for regulating succulent trade. But attention to how cactus collecting engages caring activities in the greenhouse, out "in habitat," as collectors would describe it, and in the interactive space between the mind and the wider world is an important jumping-off point into more illicit terrain (Figure 4). The "psychotopologies" linking species, habitats, experience, and emotional ties between collectors and plants prove durable and resilient, instantiating the need for not just a more-than-human accounting of human–plant relations but psychoanalytic accountings as well. It is the urge to possess and covet, and how these activities are variously urged forward by unconscious drives, that foregrounds what it means to speak of illicit succulent life. This chapter begins our journey into a political ecology of desire through exploring how the many practices that together compose "collecting" bring pleasure to the collector in seeking satisfaction through desire.

On Collecting

Evidence of collecting activities dates back millennia, but collecting as a hobby has expanded dramatically in the past several centuries, and all the more so beginning in the twentieth century.[5] As just one measure of its contemporary prevalence, upward of 30 percent of North Americans partake in some form of collecting.[6] The widespread rise of consumer cultures across much of the world has facilitated collecting practices ranging from rare art and antiquities to mass-produced consumer goods like dolls and bottle caps. Collecting is understood as a distinct category of activity through its focus on the development of sets of selected objects. Importantly, collecting elevates the objects in a collection beyond their original or intended use.[7] "Thus a person who accumulates a variety of toasters but does not use them to make toast is a collector of toasters."[8] Unlike hoarding, a disorder recognized by the American Psychiatric Association, collecting is considered a benign behavior with a variety of mental and social health benefits, though as we will see, this is not to say collecting does not also hold a suite of possible harms.[9]

In *On Collecting,* material culture scholar Susan Pearce summarizes a variety of key thematic threads on collecting. She interprets collections as

> sets of objects, and, like all other sets of objects, they are an act of the imagination . . . a metaphor intended to create meanings which help to make individual identity and each individual's view of the world. Collections are gathered together for purposes which are seen by their possessors as

lifting them away from the world of common commodities into one of special significance, one for which "sacred" seems the right word.[10]

In transforming the mundane into the sacred, scholars provide different typologies for categorizing collectors. Relevant to the cactus and succulent collecting hobby is the two-category system proposed by Belk, who distinguishes between "taxonomic" and "aesthetic" collectors.[11] Collectors of cactus or succulent plants may display both kinds of collecting tendencies, even if, because of the nature of natural history collections, they often veer toward the taxonomic, especially in Euro-American contexts. Finer subcategories of collecting taxonomies exist as well. There are collectors who collect primarily in one genus of cactus but may also maintain additional subcollections of especially prized plants in other genera, just as there are collectors who structure their collections based on geographic region or plant morphology. Structuring and refining collections in these ways can also help collectors avoid the problem of running out of room for plants, a dilemma less commonly faced by collectors of bottle caps or coins.

Without entirely discounting early Freudian interpretations of collecting as a manifestation of anal-retentive tendencies developed during infancy and early childhood, there is a wide-ranging set of reasons why people choose to collect things.[12] A pragmatic list of motivations for collectors comes from Ruth Formanek, who categorized motivations into the following five broad categories: "(1) in relation to the self [i.e., personal enjoyment in acquisition, fulfillment of narcissistic tendencies, self-expression, learning], (2) in relation to other people [e.g., social value, camaraderie, friendships], (3) as preservation, restoration, history and a sense of continuity, (4) as financial investment and (5) as addiction."[13] As this chapter and the three that follow show, cactus and succulent collectors certainly derive meaning from all five of these categories.

In contrast to this broader system of categorization, Pearce identifies a total of seventeen possible motivations for collecting, ranging from leisure, aesthetics, sexual foreplay, and reinforcing gender identity all the way to achieving immortality.[14] The desire for immortality may strike readers as grandiose, but it has perhaps the greatest staying power among the more psychologically minded readings of collecting. This drive finds purchase with contemporary psychological ideas of terror management theory, which "posits that to manage the potential for terror engendered by the awareness of mortality, humans sustain faith in worldviews which provide a sense that they are significant beings in an enduring, meaningful world rather than mere material animals fated only to obliteration upon death."[15] As McIntosh and Schmeichel note, "monuments, children, or an impressive collection may all serve a symbolic immortality function."[16] The connections between life and death are prominent in how many scholars have interpreted meanings of collections. But just as a collection may "deaden" an object in a certain respect by removing it from its purposeful function (a spoon in a collection is not the same as a spoon in a bowl of soup), objects in collection are also given a new life through the people who instill them with a sense of their living selves. Even if collections represent the death of the "living" object, as we will see in the world of cactus collectors, collections enable the self to live on through them, wrested out of time in a desire for the eternal.[17]

Like death and memory, gender plays an important role in the story of collecting. Objects in collections are gendered, just as collectors play out and/or reinforce gendered roles through collecting. When I set out to study cactus and succulent collecting cultures, I did not anticipate how matters of masculinity would inform my research. It is not men alone who collect cactus plants—far from it. But in my research, I found that men were proportionally overrepresented among collectors who focused their interest only on cacti, and furthermore, it is more often men within the sphere of the cactus and succulent hobby who partake in activities that fall outside the bounds of law.[18] These trends generally mirror widespread patterns within collecting hobbies, especially in Euro-American cultures, in which certain kinds of collecting hobbies associated with more "scientific" efforts were characterized over time as more masculine than collections of consumer items, such as clothing or housewares. While more women than men may collect Christmas ornaments or chinaware, these collections are often not thought of by the women collecting them as such and are instead associated with consumption habits. These feminized practices contrast with the performance of more "serious" collecting undertaken by men pinning moths or sorting military medals. But there is nothing more serious about collecting guns or baseball cards than dollhouses, only that it is men who tend to collect the former and insist on their seriousness (Figure 5).[19]

The gendered profiles of who collects what have also changed over time in response to shifts in gender norms of the day. Some records suggest that during the earliest phase of growing cactus interest in the United States in the late 1800s, the hobby was dominated by women compared to men.[20] This trend mirrored the general popularity (and acceptability) of botany and floriculture as hobbies practiced by women in the United States and Europe at a time when few other "natural history" hobbies were considered acceptable for women to pursue.[21] But here in the present, whether in the halls of cactus club meetings or in collector greenhouses, time and again, I found myself inhabiting a world populated by a majority white, heterosexual, cis-male majority. A noteworthy bias here is that my primary research was centered in European and U.S. cactus and succulent collecting communities, which differ of course in their composition from those in Japan, China, or any number of South American countries. This is therefore not to suggest any sense of fixedness or rigidity structuring cactus collecting in relation to gender or sex, as much as the morphology of some

Figure 5. Two collectors looking at and talking about cacti. One (foreground) is guiding the other as well as the author through their personal collection.

cacti may lead us to wonder about the phallic shape of cacti.[22] In sum, my interest in the masculinities of cactus collecting cultures recognizes that performances of masculinity were part of the overall story of illicit succulent life as I encountered it through my predominately white and male interlocutors.[23]

Alongside my ethnographic research, these trends in who collects cacti were reinforced by social survey data I gathered. Of a total 441 responses to an online survey of cactus- and succulent collecting hobbyists primarily concentrated in the United States and United Kingdom that I conducted with colleagues in 2021, 86 percent of respondents self-reported as white, 62 percent reported their gender as male, and more than 70 percent of respondents were older than fifty years.[24] Although the majority of cactus and succulent collectors tend to collect both cactus and other succulent plants, 37 percent of self-identifying male respondents primarily collected cacti, compared with 20 percent who primarily collected other succulents, while in a reversal of this trend, 24 percent of self-reporting female respondents primarily collected cacti, compared to 36 percent who collected other succulents. Even if, at the turn of the twentieth century, cactus collecting was more popular among women than men in Europe and the United States, today cacti have been masculinized as tough, spiky, phallic, and resilient, while other succulents have similarly been feminized as soft, pinchable, and cute.[25] Collectors do not escape how their socializing into gendered roles and norms shapes collecting practices.

Men, Their Cacti, and Feelings

For all the performed toughness of cactus men and their cacti, both also exhibited displays of vulnerability and a proclivity for the sensuous. Few outside the hobby would guess that what most excites many a cactus collector is not necessarily cacti's imposing spines or unusual shapes, ranging from the geometrically sublime to the wonderfully monstrous. Instead, it is especially common to hear collectors speak of a much more infrequent *moment* that is shared between collector and plant. These fleeting if seasonally predictable times (though never assured!) were those when their cacti would flower.

Czech author Karel Čapek wrote in 1929, "I tell you, a mother's pride is nothing to the boasting and bragging of a cactus-man whose cactus has come into flower."[26] Collectors will wax poetic about their cactus blooms, describing preferences for "gorgeous pink" or "ruffled" *Echinopsis* hybrid flowers or dazzling displays of soft pink *Mammillaria* blossoms. They will speak in gentle tones about the delicate task of hand-pollinating their cacti with a soft-bristled paintbrush. If cacti are associated with a "tough" or "aggressive" exterior, another world awaits in speaking to men about their cacti in bloom and the care they provide to coax them into flower.

As an organ, flowers have a long cultural association with the feminine. The current associations of cacti with masculine qualities is suspended in these briefer moments in which many cacti will suddenly become adorned with a veritable crown of flowers or when an immensely large flower bursts forth from an areole studded with spines. That some collectors likened themselves to their cacti through these moments in which tough-looking plants revealed their "feminine side" was a window into understanding how collectors imbued their plants with meanings of the self and their navigation of prescribed gendered norms. If cacti have been gendered in contemporary contexts as "tough" or "manly," it is the moment these plants flower, and importantly, how this reshuffles collector speech about their plants and their relations to them, that signals the productive potential of queer theory for investigating the erotic within human–plant relations and in the collector greenhouse.[27] This ability to nurture cacti to flower also highlights the role of the flower as a physical manifestation of the collector's capacity to care well for their plants (Figure 6).

During an interview with a veteran collector and former coal miner in England, several threads on what motivated his collection emerged connecting the worlds of cacti, their flowers, gender, and memory. I asked this collector how he first became interested in cacti. "Well, my grandmother . . . she had a little rickety greenhouse, [she had] three cacti in there, three flowering *Echinopsis*. I was in charge of watching them. Got to love them. Got another greenhouse. . . . Then I left for work, chasing girls, family, what have you, but then when I had my mining accident, and I thought, what do I do for a hobby?" I asked the collector why he thought he liked cacti so much in particular, compared to other plants. "I've been told it's the shape," he explained. "Now the other thing I like, as I've gotten older, is the plant that survives in a hostile environment.

Figure 6. The delicate and ruffled pale pink flower of an *Ariocarpus retusus* in bloom as viewed from above in a private cactus collection in Czechia. The species is generally spineless and features a dense growth of wool and fuzzy areoles.

That's tough looking, so there is a bit of, dare I say there is a bit of macho-*ness* in it, it's a tough-looking plant, but then it flowers—and it's got *such* beautiful flowers, but how that [cactus] lives in an awful condition. Symmetrically they're beautiful, and then produce a flower that's stunning."

After a lengthy discussion about his collection and the various kinds of cacti he prefers, the conversation returned to his plants in relation to his grandmother. "Now, there is also an attachment . . .

that me granny got me into it. . . . So what's my favorite thing? *Echinopsis* [a popular genus of cacti]. Why? Because they are the plants I got into with me granny. . . . When they flowered—this ugly thing—that we got from the desert that were just *wondrous* to me, that could live in a desert, and then have this beautiful flower, scented, to attract the moths . . ." His thought trailed off. I was curious to know if he still had any of his grandmother's plants. "An *Aloe vera,*" he replied. "And it's had hundreds and hundreds of babies, and I take one or two every year to the show. And I always sell them for fifty pence to kids. What I really regret is the three original plants [from his grandmother], the *Echinopsis,* when I stopped growing them, and a man came, and I got a collection at me home, after my granny passed away. And my dad said, 'Are you gonna pack it in?' and I said, 'Well, I'm working now, it's difficult.' And so this man said I'll buy the lot, and I said, 'You can buy the lot except for these three plants.' They were [the three] big *Echinopsis* that flowered and were me granny's, and there were an attachment [for me]. And he said, 'No, I want those ones,' and I said, 'Hold up, me granny has had since she was forty or fifty years old.' And I forgot, but he was going to give me a hundred or eighty pounds, which was a lot of money in those days, and he said, 'I'll tell you what, I'll give you a hundred pounds just for those three.' So I—regretfully—thinking more about girls, I sold them, but I wished I hadn't because imagine what they would be like now, I don't know," he said with a shake of his head.

For this retired coal miner, his collection of plants was an extension of his self and his own navigation of masculinity, which was freighted with concerns about outward displays (much like his cacti) of toughness or "macho-ness." But within the relatively secure space of his greenhouse, he was able to acknowledge the tensions he felt about his masculinity expressed through the beautiful flowers he cultivated in these cacti.[28] His plants, particularly an *A. vera* that was his grandmother's, also held an important symbolic role

Figure 7. Morphologically, cacti feature both expressions of "toughness," such as the imposing cage of spines shown here, and expressions of softness and vulnerability, such as in the soft mat of wooly areoles on this *Echinocactus horizonthalonius* cultivar from a private collection.

in extending her memory into the present through his own work to care for it and to give away its "pups" to children. But clearly it was the missing *Echinopsis* that held the greatest sentiments of absence, doubled, as it were, through holding close significations of his grandmother. We can imagine, following Lacan, how the closer proximity of these cacti to the absent maternal figure of his grandmother places the genus of *Echinopsis*—which composes much of his collection—as nearer to the "Thing," the absence around which the subject is pulled in seeking *jouissance* through the drives.[29]

More broadly, as Belk put it, echoing the early American psychologist William James a century earlier, collections are part of the "extended self."[30] In approaching the Thing, we might also consider these cacti as part of the extimate self.

"Maybe I see myself in them a bit you know," the collector said later while touring his greenhouse and showing me a variety of small *Echinopsis*. He described to me the many flowers they would produce in a matter of months that belied their spiky exteriors I saw on the day I visited (Figure 7). He chuckled and smiled, acknowledging a tension in his own performance of masculinity. We stood in his greenhouse crammed to the seams with hundreds of small *Echinopisis* and *Tephrocactus* in a moment of touching vulnerability, just two men surrounded by lovingly tended plants.

Cacti as Objects of Psychoanalytic Heft

As living plants that require care, and especially as long-lived plants, many cacti have a capacity to connect and maintain lively connections between people—such as the collector and his grandmother—through the work of caring for plants that were formerly cared for by others. For men who collect cacti and succulents, as compared to female collectors, I found in my survey that plants more frequently held meaning in relation to a maternal figure.[31] Across my interviews with self-described "serious" male cactus collectors, many began with a story of receiving a plant or cutting from a maternal figure during childhood or early adolescence as an important first memory of becoming enticed by succulent plants. There are several ways, drawing on various schools of psychoanalytic thought, to interpret the position of cacti (or other succulents) as objects of symbolic meaning, and one need not deny the significance of another interpretation for another collector.

One tendency might be to interpret these plants as kinds of "transitional objects" in the vein of Winnicottian psychoanalysis.

Transitional objects are objects that function for infants as an "intermediate area of experience," as an object that is both "me" and "not-me." These are objects of possession that are in union with (i.e., not truly mentally external to) the infant and the oral erotogenic zone. This object serves as an important space of experience—the thumb rubbing against the blanky or teddy bear—symbolically linking the infant with "part-objects" (the breast, the penis) standing in for the infant's true object of desire, but also possibly fear or anxiety, in the mother or father figure. But following Donald Winnicott's own definition of transitional objects, at best, we can interpret cacti as holding meaning through "transitional phenomena" rather than strictly as true transitional objects.[32] For Winnicott, the transitional object emerges in early infancy (up to twelve months), and its symbolic function in the healthy progression of childhood is diffused through transitional phenomena as the child ages and "decathects" from the transitional object. As Winnicott explains, eventually the transitional object "loses meaning, and this is because the transitional phenomena have become diffused, have become spread out over the whole intermediate territory between 'inner psychic reality' and 'the external world as perceived by two persons in common,' that is to say, the whole cultural field."[33]

It is not hard to imagine how cacti—given their physical forms often resembling the shape of a breast, testicle, or penis—could stand in as "part-objects" in the tradition of Melanie Klein's object relations theory, through which these transitional phenomena are diffused through the extimacy of psychic life.[34] Transitional phenomena become the "playground," as Winnicott describes it, for childhood navigation of the self with the primary object of interpersonal import (mother or father figures), here through a "potential space" between maternal figure and child expressed in wider and more "diffuse" ranges of social experience. Considering the relations of the retired coal miner with his grandmother, we can see how these plants became a place for navigating in an adult and more diffused psychic environment the "to-and-fro" of the maternal figure being and not-being the object of desire at the center of the child's play.[35] We return to Lacan's notion of the Thing as an absence fundamental to the emergence of the desiring subject. As a psychoanalytic object, the cactus may encounter the Thing through the process of what he calls "sublimation," when ordinary objects may be "elevated to the dignity of the Thing." Put another way, sublimation alerts us to the "revelation of the Thing beyond the object."[36]

Practices of collecting also have much to say about the desire of the collector to live on past the threshold of death through the inscription of their memory into objects. Echoing terror management theory, for many collectors, as Elsner and Cardinal write, "the collection is the unique bastion against the deluge of time."[37] This desire to subvert death through collection plays an important psychological function for the cactus collector, but in ways that hold deeper meaning when we consider plants in collections not just as collectible objects wrested out of time but as living beings within distinctive forms of time or their own vegetal temporalities.

As much as the retired coal miner's story suggests how the performance and embodiment of masculinity can mediate cactus desires, or how as a transitional phenomenon his cactus collection might exist as a space of "play" through which relations with the mother figure are symbolically enacted, it also demonstrates how plants can provide important material comfort to collectors in navigating the life course. This includes the collector's own anticipated death and the deaths of others with whom they share emotional bonds. As John Forrester describes, writing about Freud's own famous antiquities collecting habit, "a collection can symbolize the battle of life within death, of life being infiltrated by death, of a space cleared for the expression of this battle by the objects the collector has chosen as his personal representatives."[38] Composed of living plants, cactus collections are not time capsules or mere repositories of memory; they extend the self through the lives of nonhuman others that go on. But crucially, unlike dolls or stamps or coins, cacti also live and die, even if, as forms of vegetal life, they live and die in different registers of being than humans do. This can also cause anxiety to emerge. As an elderly cactus collector in Czechia explained, "this old generation would like someone who would care about their collections later, to pass their plants on to, but many do not know who will take them." Through thinking with living succulent collections, we can see that while plants serve as embodied afterlives or memories of husbands and wives, grandmothers, or close friends, they are also entwined with the natural growth, death, and reproductive cycles of the plants whose memories resonate through them.

Of Plants Loved and Lost

In November 2018, I joined a group of four European, self-described male "cactoexplorers" in search of cacti in Brazil ranging from the rare to the relatively common to those yet even to be formally described in the botanical literature. The community of collectors who go out and enjoy visiting and photographing wild plants is a smaller but significant segment of the larger population of collectors whose primary activities center around maintaining cactus and succulent collections at home. While I will revisit this trip in greater detail in the next chapter, here I focus on what I learned about how men developed emotional bonds with and through plants.

One day on another long drive between cactus locations, I brought up questions of feelings about cacti, more specifically about what happens when they die, with two collectors in our rented SUV. I sat in the back seat, peppering them with questions as they looked out at the scenery of small agricultural fields and rolling mountains in the distance. "It can be sad to lose a plant if you've had it for a long time," the Belgian collector said. "It can also be sad when you buy a twenty dollar plant, and it dies five days later!" the British gardener responded, laughing. The Belgian continued, "Yes, but more when it's plants you care about. When I left my first wife, I also lost my greenhouse. . . . There is a French expression—*compagnon de route*—and I lost these plants and it made me sad."

The expression to which the Belgian collector turned is interesting for the variation of meaning enfolded within it: *fellow traveler, companion on the road of life.* As long-lived plants, he considered them as long-term companions that aged as he did. I could imagine the sadness brought on in their absence amid an already major life transition marked by the ending of an important relationship.[39] And yet, knowing something of the history of this collector, I was also aware of a more literal interpretation. He had traveled the world to encounter these plants but also to gather some of their seeds, which would travel back to Belgium where he would cultivate them. As his "traveling companions," these plants would also greet him every day as material reminders of comradely experiences of collecting trips with close friends and fellow "cactus hunters." They would also hold meaning through the time, attention, and care he provided over the years to help them thrive.

Our conversation turned to deeper meanings attached to plants. "When someone gives you a plant, it serves as a memory of them when they pass. So when the plant dies, it's sad because it feels like you are losing a part of them," the gardener added after some time, to which the Belgian nodded affirmatively. "What we are saying is we are sentimental old fools!" he laughed. As the Belgian collector explained, summarizing what made for a "good plant," "[It's] a good plant, old, well grown, and often one that has moved from one collection to another," he said. "That's why we have these lotteries to give away plants of people who have passed away," he added.

Unlike more Freudian-inflected literature on collecting, which would suggest that collectors abhor giving away part of their collection, the passing on of plants is actually embedded within the succulent collecting hobby.[40] If we were to pursue the cactus in collection as a kind of Freudian fetish object, an object that unconsciously stands in for what was seen as lacking in the maternal figure in early life (a.k.a. the phallus), then it might follow that the cactus as fetishistic object would be overdetermined with meanings of something lacking in the collector's early childhood development.[41] It is easy enough to presume that the phallic nature of many cacti would lead to their more obvious interpretation as fetishistic objects, but even here Freud cautions about presuming that objects with more physical phallic forms are necessarily more likely to become fetish objects.[42] Although it might be true that collectors are less likely to give away their prized plants *in life*— and if the plants are serving as fetish objects, this would certainly be the case—for many, if not most, collectors, it is a central practice to give away offsets and seeds of parent plants, as well as to swap plant material. Rather than reading the giving away of one's collected things as an act of self-castration (the collected item, for cultural theorist and philosopher Jean Baudrillard, at least, represented a narcissistic symbol of the ego), in the world of cactus and succulent plants, "giving away" one's collection is an act of *reproducing the self* through networks of social relations.[43]

Baudrillard wrote in *The System of Objects* that the collected object "is the thing with which we construct our mourning" by simultaneously representing our future death while permitting us to transcend it through possession. Through the object, we "succeed in dispelling the anxiety associated with absence and with the reality of death. Objects allow us to apply the work of mourning to ourselves right now, in everyday life, and this in turn allows us to live—to live regressively, no doubt, but at least to live."[44] Where Baudrillard illuminates an unconscious significance of collections, he does not attend to grappling with living beings as more than objects. Baudrillard has little to say about plants (or animals, except in regard to their sex) as adaptive organisms with active capacities and their own experiences of life's temporalities. It is through attention to these vegetal heterotemporalities that we can see that plants do not inhabit the same kinds of regimented, intergenerational forms of time as the animal world. As Michael Marder describes, plants inhabit worlds of life and death simultaneously.[45] Plants exceed the synchronous and sequential temporalities of individuals amid generations, as animals do. In other words, plants inhabit *phyto*-temporalities all their own, marked by their unique and excessive rendering of time through (often) indeterminate growth in space. Relating to plants will always involve degrees of distance exceeding the animal world composed through difference.

In addition to creating avenues of social exchange and gift giving, the practice of trading and sharing plant material establishes and extends genealogies of collectors, the most valuable of which are inscribed with additional value (monetary and otherwise) when they lead back to charismatic leaders of the hobby or original "field" acquisitions. As the Belgian explained, "one plant I won in a lottery, it's an original wild plant brought over in '64 or '65 by [Friedrich] Ritter.[46] It's an *Aztekium ritteri,* named after the man who named it," he said. "My neighbor told me the handwriting on the plant's original tag was the handwriting of Ritter. He told me this is probably the only legal *A. ritteri* in the world [outside of Mexico], as it was brought over before Mexican legislation banned their export." I return to these questions of illegality directly in the next two chapters, but important here is that this plant held exceptionally high value for the collector owing to its genealogy and legacy as attached to the people who had acquired and cared for it previously, especially Ritter, one of the most famous cactus experts of the twentieth century.[47]

Layers of meaning developed with plants through the lives of others can produce profound emotional connections between collectors and their cacti. Later, walking along with the Belgian amid a spectacular field of white quartz sand dotted with hundreds of bright green and round *Uebelmanni gummifera* cacti, I asked him if he thought about plants differently than the average layperson. He paused and replied with a shrug, "I've never really thought about it, I'm sorry." We stood there for a moment, and then his expression softened and a smile drew across his sunburned face. "Yes, actually I think, I think we [collectors] do think about plants differently. I'll give you an example. If you lose a plant that dies after twenty years, it isn't like if your child dies, but it is a similar feeling; it hurts, it is sad. So I think that is probably different from other people."

Comparing the death of a plant to the death of a child may strike readers as exaggerated, but other collectors offered similar stories of plant loves lost and the sadness and mourning that could follow. There was the Czech collector who told me of a particularly harsh winter when he lost more than one-third of his collection to frost and was so distraught that he let his entire collection die in remorse, unable to enter the greenhouse; or the frequent-enough event when a cactus passed down through three generations of growers would finally succumb to time or a disease, initiating a mourning period not just for the plant but again for the people whose memories the plant embodied; or when a collector's very first cactus died of old age decades after first taking it home as a boy, and he wept.[48] As these conversations suggest, in the world of collection, cacti are far more than what they seem, nor do they embody their own lives alone. Cacti may serve as objects of psycho-analytic significance, a "link" in chains of signification that both connect and also separate the collector from a maternal or paternal figure, a plug in the void as objects of desire, a fetishistic disavowal of that which is lacking, or a "playground" through which collectors navigate the extimacy of psychic life. The material being of cacti is imbued with the extended self but also with the afterlives of others with whom they share emotional bonds.

Cultivating Care for Cacti and for Others

Attention to the unconscious and emotional meanings sutured to plants helps us to understand what can underpin movements toward vegetal care in the first place. It is also to recognize the inadequate attention to matters of the unconscious in discussions of caring for nonhuman life and what sets in motion the development of care-*full* relations between people and plants through attention to the drives and desire.[49] What does it mean to speak of care for plants in the greenhouse in this light, and how does care for cultivated plants relate to care for the same species growing elsewhere as wild beings?

To study acts of more-than-human care with plants, I turned to the work of a number of scholars, especially geographers, who have written about cultivating person–plant relations in the garden. Hannah Pitt suggests three primary avenues for learning with plants in the garden: attention to motion and movement in the garden, participating in shared work and activities with gardeners, and employing visual methodologies like photography and videography. These techniques transferred well to my research with collectors both in the greenhouse and on trips to see wild-growing plants. In fact, the methods on which I leaned to center human–plant forms of care emerged quite naturally through my multispecies ethnographic work and participant observation; it was only later, during the writing stages of this process, that I came to see the clear symmetries between Pitt's suggestions and those that developed organically during fieldwork.[50]

First, Pitt suggests, learning is facilitated through "attending to motion." This meant encouraging interviews and conversations

Figure 8. On being shown plants in the greenhouse. A collector describes some of the unique traits and growing challenges of *Lithops* plants (commonly called living stones) to the author during a tour of a private collection in northern England. The author is later given a small *Lithops* by the collector. The author accidentally overwaters it one day three months later, and the plant becomes a soggy pile of dead tissue twenty-four hours later.

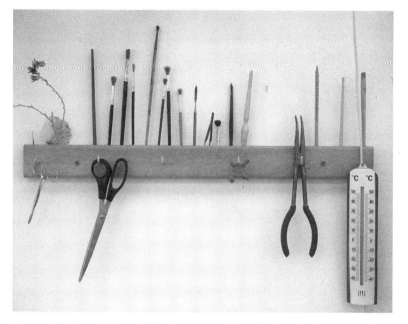

Figure 9. A few of the tools in the cactus collector's "care box": scissors, long and short tweezers for removing grit caught between spines, a scalpel, a thermometer to ensure that greenhouse conditions aren't too hot or too cold, pencils for marking labels, and paintbrushes for cleaning plants of debris and pollinating flowers.

about both cultivated and wild-growing plants to take place as much as possible, either in collector greenhouses as we walked around and talked or as we searched the landscape for species of interest. Walking and talking fosters conversations more spatially embedded in place, just as informed and prompted by one's shared surroundings full of signs and experience as the conversation emergent between us (Figure 8). "Ah, see how much fuller and plumped out the tubercles are when the plant is grafted to a good root stalk—you won't see a plant like this in habitat!" a collector explained one day, just as we were talking about the different traits plants can display in cultivated versus untended wild form.

In my visits to greenhouses in a variety of countries, I always enjoyed the inevitable moments in conversation when collectors were compelled to grab a pair of long tweezers to remove a dead leaf or rotate their plant pots a quarter turn to encourage even sun exposure and straight growth. I became used to the simple nod of the head as a sign of active listening while the collector's gaze would divert to inspecting their plants as they prowled for the unwanted presence of mites. Our conversations would continue, but their attention would be suspended within a wider view. The ability to read plants for signs of adequate drainage, air circulation, and light is not innate (what terrible damage the expression of being born with a "green thumb" has wrought on the plant kingdom!), nor are these necessarily the most difficult skills to cultivate. Instead, they are skills that develop slowly through attention: the ability to think in vegetal terms and temporalities as a sustained and care-full practice. In moving about, collectors were showing me how they cared (Figure 9).

Caring for Plants, Caring for Each Other

Caring for plants, and learning to care better, also brings collectors together socially. Like many hobby communities, collecting succulents serves a valuable social function, with membership organizations, conventions, and shows acting as a space where friendships and social bonds are made and sustained. It is frequently these human social bonds that often serve as a primary—or at least equally important—source of meaning compared to the kinds of human–plant relations that might appear to be at their center.[51] It was important not only to pay attention to how collectors forged ties through caring for those in their social networks but also to distinguish these forms of social care from what it means to care for plants. Here I sought to enact through a range of activities (in line with Pitt's second methodological suggestion) participating in collecting activities. This meant conducting participant observation in a variety of collector forums, including helping in the green-house with mundane tasks, practicing how to graft cacti, raising my own budding collection of plants (largely obtained as gifts from the many collectors I would meet), actively participating in multi-week cactoexplorations, and attending succulent club meetings and conventions.

In contrast with larger conventions, more regional shows might focus on a particular grouping of plants, such as a mesemb show I attended in Banstead, a small town on the outskirts of London. Mesembs (short for Mesembryanthemaceae, more recently reclassified as part of the Aizoaceae family) are a diverse grouping of succulents found in greatest abundance in South Africa and Namibia that includes the *Lithops* and *Conophytum* genera. These groups of plants have faced rapidly growing pressure in recent years due to illegal trade—South African officials are concerned some species have been collected to the point of extinction.[52] The event comprised collectors displaying their proudest examples of mesemb plants on folding tables in the town's community center. Judges awarded prizes to the best plants within specific genera. The event also featured a lecture by an expert mesemb collector, as well as a live auction. Just as I would come to learn that photography structured much of the time on collectors' trips to see wild plants, here, too, many attendees were armed with expensive digital cameras, working their way around the tables to take up-close and macro-scale shots of beautiful plants. I found myself moved into participating in the event in this way, examining plants and trying to capture some of the beauty of these resilient and long-lived species (Figure 10).

Despite the centrality of the plants in the community center, much of the hours-long event was taken up with collectors milling about and chatting with friends, grabbing a tea or coffee or something to eat at the community center kitchen. Heads darted up above the crowd, eyes on the lookout for anticipated arrivals. In

Figure 10. An up-close view of a *Lithops* plant (species unknown) at the Banstead Mesemb Show. Flowers are emerging from the nearly fused leaf pairs in the center of the plant. As some *Lithops* may grow into large clumps, it is hard to determine in a plant such as the one seen here if this is a grouping of many individual plants or in fact a growing clump of a single plant.

this way, the plants were at times secondary to the social activities of the day. While certainly vegetal care and concern were indirectly on display in Banstead, somehow, seeing hundreds and hundreds of tiny succulents sitting in individual plastic brown pots arranged on folding tables in a U.K. community center did not instill me with a sense of care-full vegetal relations at work. Rather, I left Banstead with a sense that as social creatures, these humans, while undoubtedly passionate about mesembs, were there for each other.

Socializing with Succulents

Especially in Europe and the United States, much of the hobby's community is sustained through regular meetings of local chapters of national cactus and succulent clubs. My entrée into the world of cactus and succulent collecting was entirely thanks to the generosity of the members of the Sheffield branch of the British Cactus and Succulent Society (BCCS). Although many passionate and dedicated collectors exist outside the membership of such clubs, especially younger collectors, these societies have long histories of collecting traditions that predate international trade conventions on endangered species, and older members were able to reflect on these different eras of collecting. And because of their longer histories, the cultures of collecting at the heart of my research were shaped by practices and preferences developed over time through these societies. Important as well, nearly all societies maintain an interest in conservation issues and even fund conservation projects related to cactus and succulent plants. My interest in these matters of trade, conservation, and illicitness was therefore appreciated by society members, even among those who disagree with many current trade regulations.

Over the course of two years, and in between fieldwork in a number of locations, I attended monthly evening meetings of the Sheffield BCCS branch. In a wooden second-floor hall presided over by a portrait of the Queen in the city center, chapter meetings began with announcements and updates from a club official about upcoming events, issues, and club needs, followed by the month's invited guest speaker. These speakers were mostly visitors from other BCCS chapters or members of the club themselves, who would give talks with slides on topics like "A Multitude of Marvelous Mesembs," "The North of Peru: A Cactoexploration," or "Agaves through the Ages." At other times, talks were more interactive and included demonstrations of a propagation technique or opportunity to inspect different grades of soil potting mixtures. As Pitt suggests (and drawing on the work of Tim Ingold), through being shown skills by experts, I was slowly inducted into their world through experience. As Pitt writes, "ethnography does not gather data but develops skills in perception and judgement so one can engage with the world."[53] In this case, I was being inducted into the world of succulent collection to learn to engage in cultivation and succulent care.

After forty-five minutes, the speaker would pause for a group tea and coffee break. On a typical evening, I would peruse the plants for sale with a cup of tea or biscuit in hand, then move toward the "show table" (typically a category, such as a particular genus or family) and observe as the week's appointed judge inspected plants. It was rarely obvious to me why one plant would win first prize compared to those winning second or third, but over time, my guesses improved. After a raffle was held and prizes dispersed (usually plants or books on plants), the meeting then resumed with the second half of the month's lecture. At its conclusion, members milled about and chatted before leaving or helped with putting folding chairs and tables away or doing the dishes. Often, I would walk the thirty minutes home with some cactus or succulent tucked into the crook of my elbow, trying to justify to myself this most recent acquisition, at times almost embarrassed at my inability to resist another plant.

Picturing Plants

Through these monthly meetings, I saw how collectors developed linkages between cultivating succulents in private collections with the world of wild plants living very far from northern England. Many monthly talks were opportunities for collectors who visited succulent habitats to share photographs and stories with other members curious to learn more about what these plants were like when not grown in plastic pots. In addition to serving as a vehicle for visual storytelling, photography enables collectors to partially satisfy the urge to "possess" desirable plants, (re)routed through the shutter of a camera lens. This sensibility mirrors the shift from trophy hunting to wildlife photography tourism and the sense that for many, especially in the Euro-Western tradition, the "proper" way to encounter nonhuman life is organized through an urge to capture, dominate, and possess.[54] I was surprised to learn how important photography was to many in the cactus and succulent collecting hobby.

Photography also served as an unexpected third method to engage with how collectors navigated urges both to possess and to care. Pitt describes how visual methods can be surprisingly attuned to the lifeworlds of plants, inclusive of still-image methods, photo-elicitation practices (using photographs or film to prompt collectors to talk about their experiences), automatic-photographic practices (e.g., time-lapse photography), and moving imagery. Mimicking collectors with whom I spent time, I purchased a macro lens so that I could take close-up images of plants and better appreciate their morphological features, as well as deepen my understanding of and engagement with collector behaviors. It was easy to get swept up in the joy of seeing the barely visible worlds of plants come into such sharp focus, to notice the patterning of cactus spination or intricacies of a flower in bloom. Zoomed-in optics provided an opportunity to appreciate the aesthetic and sensuous wonders of plants up close. This technique also tends to produce the notion of plants as individualized beings or, at even greater magnifications, a series of vegetal parts or abstracted forms. Macrophotography can minimize or erase the broader ecological contexts in which plants live (Figure 11).

There was also more occurring in psychic registers when looking closely at cacti. Later, while conducting research in Czechia, I discussed macrophotography with an advocate of the style. "The closer you go, the more intimate the details. . . . It creates this sense, I don't know how to describe it, like with a tiny cactus, and the bud opening, we say, 'This is sexual, it's just porn!'" he laughed, uncomfortably. "I'm just saying that as a joke, but maybe there is something to it, is it sexual arousal? I don't know what it is, it's [a] fascination, but I think it must be something physical even. . . . It's

Figure 11. Practicing macroscale photography with a flowering *Pilosocereus* cactus in Brazil. Macrophotography is powerful for its capacity to reveal the details of morphological features in plants that can be challenging to observe unaided by lenses.

really [an] addiction, to see and have the pleasure of seeing, it's part of the motivation to go to your collection every day." For this collector, these up-close images of vegetal organs and the desire to closely inspect plants elicited expressions of eroticized pleasure. His discomfort in describing it points to this pleasure as excessive, tinged with pain (or, here, painful recognition?), what in Lacanian terms we could call *jouissance*.[55]

Is the pleasure of seeing these images expressed as a fetish object in a Freudian sense, wherein the fetishist seeks out nongenital parts of the body or other objects, like a strappy shoe or a foot, as the displacement of desire through the fetish as a disavowal of what was seen as lacking in the maternal figure? Or reading the fetish more broadly with Lacan, is the fetish found in the language (rather than direct visual cues) used to speak of this eroticism, what links the cactus organ in a chain of signifiers to the disavowal of the lack of the Thing? Or turning to the object relations theory of Melanie Klein, we might also consider how the collector seeks out erotic pleasure through the "part-object" of the cactus's organs as a symbolic replacement of the breast, penis, and so on. Multiple readings are available to us of how these images of discorporate cactus organs might operate in the space of fantasy.

Staying with Lacan, the description provided by the collector fascinated with the eroticized cactus's organs offers a moment to ponder the subject's drives at play. I do not believe it is a coincidence that this occurs at the scale of the *up close,* in which the whole of the cactus as living, vegetal being is displaced by its constituent organs or "parts." This is a process of breaking down the living organism into something consumable. It would seem to reaffirm Karl Kraus's aphorism that "there is no unhappier creature under the sun than a fetishist who longs for a woman's shoe but has to make do with the whole woman."[56] Recognizing that this eroticized fantasy involves close-up images that break down the living organism into more objectifiable parts (part-objects) points us toward the cactus here as serving as an object of the drives, a lure, the photographs as a fantasy in the support of desire.[57]

It is worth briefly mentioning again the Lacanian distinction between what sits on the side of the drives and desire. On the side of the drives is the centripetal pull of the Thing—which is also where we find *jouissance* expressed most clearly. The Thing is paradoxically named, because far from naming some*thing* knowable, Lacan says, "the Thing is characterized by the fact that it is impossible for us to imagine it."[58] Where desire is found on the side of the big "Other" in the symbolic order, the Thing is the nonobject that structures the pleasure principle and what lies beyond it, signifying the fantasy of an impossible object as total source of *jouissance.* The drives, as Joan Copjec clarifies, have "no goal, but only an aim, this is because its object is no longer a means of attaining satisfaction, it is an end in itself; it is directly satisfying."[59] This encircling pull around the Thing is what makes *jouissance,* "as the aim of the drives," an irresistible lure despite the pain it causes—we know we can never fully "have it" because it would be too much, and it is precisely through never attaining it, instead always aiming for it, that we see *jouissance* most clearly expressed.[60] If there is an aching yearning, an awareness that something is too much, too good, too pleasurable, in looking at eroticized images of cacti, for instance, it is in the roundabout encircling of the Thing through the drives where we find ourselves irresistibly caught up in the pleasure of *jouissance.*

If playing with photography helped me engage with tools and practices of cactus and succulent collecting, as well as peek under the hood of what might lie "behind" cacti in the collector unconscious, moving imagery, namely, producing videos, allowed me to frame these plants within a wider, more interactive and ecological view. Moving imagery became a useful technique for asserting the presence of cacti not just as individual beings or fetishized objects in relation to collecting but as members of ecological assemblages. I began to capture short plant films. Revisiting them, I remain struck by a sense of wonder in how the presence of a variety of kinds of life interacting with succulents and their aboveground and belowground worlds becomes more apparent than when looking at the kinds of macrophotography that are especially popular in visualizing plants. Bees and flying insects whiz across the screen, tiny ants traverse the thick skin of a cactus or pollinate its open flower; a stunningly blue *Pilosocereus pachycladus* sways in the wind, its fine wisps of cornsilk-yellow hairs bending on invisible currents

Figure 12. *Pilosocereus pachycladus* in a wider view in Minas Gerais, Brazil. Film still from a short film of cactus hunting by the author. Absent are the rustling of the wind, the chirping of birds, the buzzing of insects, and the movement of cacti swaying in the wind.

(Figure 12). Attention to succulents as part of an ecology speaks to a more recent intervention by Sara Elton, who argues for a three-step methodology for studying what Fleming as well as Head and Atchison earlier described as getting with the "plantiness" of plants, or those traits and characters that make up what it is to be a plant.[61] Elton suggests that we can deepen our appreciation of the active capacities of plants through attention to plant-time, participating with plants, and scaling up attention to plants as part of interactive ecologies by recognizing difference in "plant ontologies" or the nature of being in plant life. To grant attention to plant ontology is to take notice that plant life is not well characterized through representing plants as individuals with discrete corporal forms like animal bodies. Rather, as Michael Marder writes, "a plant in its singularity is a collective being, a loose and disorganized assemblage."[62]

In contrast with macrophotography, in videography, I found myself drawn to centering the interactive relations these plants

Figure 13. A "cactoexplorer" has traversed thick brambles and endured bloody legs in the persistent drive for enjoyment just over the next hill. Film still from a short film of cactus hunting by the author.

share with others. Turning my lens more directly to human–plant encounters, I also used film (both still and moving) to capture the motion and movements of collectors as they searched for cacti. I watched as these men would ignore scrapes and cuts from thorny brambles and plod on with bloodied arms and legs to reach harder-to-find plants they so wished to see and photograph (Figure 13). Their greatest enjoyment often seemed to come out of these moments of minor sacrifice or pain; if the hunt were too easy, it would lose its potential as a source of pleasure. "Sometimes the achievement is having found the plant that is difficult to find. Here the enjoyment is how hard it is to get to, but then its abundance once you arrive," as one collector described as we marveled at a sea of *Uebelmannia gummifera* cacti before us.

Among collectors, photographing plants was also valued as an opportunity to inspect how plants look when growing in noncultivated, wild forms. "There is also enjoyment in seeing plants you have in your collections, but in the wild," as the collector went on to explain. The practice of "cactoexploration" contributed meaning to succulent collections back home through the opportunity to learn more about caring better for them, which in part was pursued through taking copious quantities of digital photographs of wild-growing plants.

One day while cactoexploring, we were looking for *Arrojadoa dinae,* a cactus endemic to southern Bahia and northern Minas Gerais. This small, thin cactus is especially appreciated by collectors for its unique and beautiful bicolor flowers, which are bright reddish orange with a distinctive yellow tip. The plants were not easy to spot; the rains that would coax these plants into their dramatically colored blooms were not due for two more months. As everyone searched on the off chance that a plant was in early flower, a collector explained that what drew him to the species, in addition to its beautiful flowers, was its ability to mimic its "wild" form while growing within the collector's greenhouse. "They look nice in pots, they will clump over time and look similar to how they do in habitat," he explained, while squatting down and peering through his camera viewfinder to take a photograph of a clump of *A. dinae* fanning out from the ground. For this collector, photographs would help inform his efforts to care for and cultivate his own collection of plants in ways that could mimic their wild forms.

While many collectors prefer to raise well-fertilized and blemish-free plants—an aesthetic only achievable in controlled conditions like a greenhouse—others prefer to cultivate plants in a style referred to as "hard grown." As one Czech collector explained to me about the importance to him of visiting wild-growing plants, "going to habitat, you see how they grow, only in habitat you understand their context. . . . In collection you see how they *can* grow, but only in nature do you see their complex conditions, *how* they grow, what they need." Hard-grown plants feature signs of sun bleaching, corking (when the base of the cactus becomes more woody, brown, and tough, which is also associated with older plants), a squatter or more compact appearance due to the administering of little water or fertilizer, and often the scars left by attacks by insects and other pests. In visits "to habitat," many collectors use photography as a reference for characteristics to attempt to replicate at home with their cultivated plants. "Some plants will look different in collection from habitat," another collector on my trip to Brazil explained. "For instance, [*Mammillaria*] *bertholdii* [the species I describe in the preface] looks completely different in collection versus habitat. . . . It's often the smaller ones that do that."

Referring to a day prior in which our group had spent hours taking photographs of several abundant populations of *Discocactus* plants in pure quartz sand, the British gardener and Belgian retired railroad worker excitedly discussed their enjoyment of seeing these plants growing wild. "When I close my eyes all I see is cacti!" the gardener said with a laugh. "I think walking through all of that quartz, it was almost like snow and felt so surreal." "And *Discocactus* are so hard to grow, so easy to overwater, and then here they were everywhere!" the Belgian replied. The collectors moved between talking about encounters with wild plants, the same species maintained in their collections, and what the plants demanded from them in terms of care. The sense of wonder conveyed in the experience of seeing flourishing fields of cacti was amplified through the contrast of the persistent struggle to keep cacti like *Discocactus* alive in cultivation in Europe. More than only painting a picture of divergent trajectories of life, these times observing and picturing wild-growing plants helped to inform collector practices of care for cultivated plants and what specific species required to thrive.

Caring for Vegetal Worlds in the Greenhouse and Beyond

In addition to the kinds of tendencies to possess, order, and arrange that are familiar to many forms of collection, plant collector drives are motivated by urges to care as a source of enjoyment, without suggesting that what it means to care is necessarily benign. As a collector explained, "the living thing gives back. . . . You mention[ed] flowers: to me they're the reward for you caring for them. An appreciation of your care as it were; I hate to say it, but self-affirmation." But perhaps more, flowers especially embody the living and ephemeral qualities of life, and time itself, a reminder to the collector of caring acts as well as the relations that bind them to their plants on shared journeys through time. Some cacti only bloom for one night the entire year. The fleeting flower in bloom holds a powerful presence in the mind of the collector both in and outside the greenhouse as a moment of meaningful connection with the forces of mortality that bind the living world.

As both living beings and objects in collections, cacti are full of feelings, it would seem. Rather than acting only as receptacle "objects" through which human emotions are contained or expressed, it is also through the liveliness of plants that feelings and affections emerge between collectors and the plants for which they care. But unlike true "objects," cacti resist the kinds of pure objectification that would enable dismantling them purely into constitutive parts as an act of narcissistic self-incorporation and projection or fetishization, even if the erotic dimensions of macrophotography speak to these tendencies. To say that insufficient attention has been paid in studies of more-than-human care to the unconscious in the distribution of care is to recognize that the collector's enjoyment found in caring is not simply an unselfish act of benevolence toward a nonhuman life. In caring, as the collector I mentioned earlier described, there is a form of "self-affirmation," an enjoyment tinged with narcissism of recognizing oneself, mirrored in the image of the plant that is cared for well. But as we have also seen, cacti can serve as repositories not only of the self but of memories of loved ones past. When a collector weeps at the death of a cactus or is kept up all night worrying about a mite infestation on a beloved plant, we must therefore ask what prompts this emotional response while recognizing that there is never only one answer at play. The meaning of collection will always index a series of interrelated desires.

Nevertheless, many collectors do care about the "care networks" that sustain succulent life. These care networks, a term I borrow from Anna Krzywoszynska, are the ecological webs inclusive of people that plants engage with, foster, and depend on to proliferate as flourishing beings beyond the greenhouse.[63] But caring does not apply evenness or any assurance of mutual flourishing. As Aryn Martin, Natasha Myers, and Ana Viseu write, "care is a selective mode of attention: it circumscribes and cherishes some things, lives, or phenomena as its objects. In the process, it excludes others."[64] The development of what we might call a cactus care ethic is therefore entirely dependent on how the collector comes to understand their conduct in relation to the assemblage of institutions and social networks that mediate what it means to care and care *"as well as possible."*[65] To care is not a purely human domain, and plants exhibit lively capacities that do work on collectors as well.[66] As much as the unconscious may structure collector behaviors and compulsions, which at times may result in acts of care, the plant also asserts its presence and makes demands on the collector. As stories of illicit succulent life will reveal, the purported "split" between the realm of the unconscious and the external world is far less distinctive than one might imagine: our mental selves are woven into the fabric of the wider world through which our unconscious is expressed. What we see instead more clearly is the split nature of the succulent subject, the split as brought forth through desire and the drives that set the subject on a desiring path with consequence for others.

In traversing the worlds of cultivated cacti and those plants variously flourishing or diminishing in the wider world, the experiences of collecting seed, photographing plants, and sharing in experiences with fellow collectors become bound up with plants in collection through memory and experience. But, unlike in the collecting of lifeless or "timeless" things, collecting cacti also *coproduces* memories and experiences with collectors that are themselves temporal. We would greatly impoverish the vitality and wonder of plants by placing them in the same category as stamps or coins, as collectible items on a shelf.[67] The lively status of cacti as collected objects stands apart from past studies of collecting cultures that look upon collections as the "unique bastion" against time itself. Plants live and die in entirely different registers of being.[68] Rarely in collection under caring hands and watchful eyes does a cactus simply *die*. A cactus can be passed down from one collector to the next through genetically identical offsets, just as one cactus can provide the seed material to share with dozens or hundreds of other collectors. A cactus may be dying from infection in one part of its body, only to have a skillful collector lop off a portion of its body to reroot it and begin again. In these many ways, succulent life can serve as a powerful vehicle for embodying emotions that build over a lifetime, just as they can carry on the memories of multiple generations of past carers that came before and the memories of place linking disparate and distant geographies.

Having introduced succulent collecting cultures and some of the care-full practices and activities that collecting entails, in the next chapter, I turn to how collecting cultures collide with the illicit and illegal. As important as it is to understand how collectors find meaning and pleasure in collecting, the drive to possess is not simply a benign compulsion or habit. Attention to collector drive is important for revealing how broader practices of commodification rework the living world into objectified forms subsuming life under capitalism. As we will see in what follows, capitalism brilliantly preys on unconscious desires, constantly reproducing itself and the commodification of life through the fantasy of the commodity that might deliver true satisfaction. As much as collectors may display adept skills of vegetal care in the greenhouse for individual plants, this does not preclude possibilities for causing great harm to the species in the name of doing so, nor of individual desires being co-opted by greater economic forces at work in the world. We will therefore come to see how desire and the illicit become entwined and, at times, amplified through one another.

⫷ 2 ⫸

Illicit Encounters with
Succulent Collectors

*Some people love illegality for its own sake. Men, more often
than women. It's men who make laws, and enforce them, and
break them, and think the whole performance is wonderful.
Most women would rather just ignore them.*

—Ursula K. Le Guin, *The New Atlantis*

There is a morbid thrill searching for the last of something. I considered this unsettling feeling while looking for the cactus *Uebelmannia buiningii* among the quartz hills of the Serra Negra in Minas
Gerais, Brazil. In this chapter, focusing primarily on experiences of
"cactoexploration," I turn from collecting practices to the illicit and
illegal and how matters of social and regulatory norms intersect
with, and at times amplify, collector desires to possess and seek out
rare, beautiful, and endangered plants. In developing an analysis of
collector desires where they encounter the illicit, we can begin to
see how desires to collect and possess, rather than standing wholly
in opposition to conservation, share strong affinities with conservationist urges to preserve and protect, even if their impacts on the
world and species may prove dramatically different. Detailing the
search for rare and beautiful cacti in Brazil with European collectors

is an opportunity to stay close to the colonial and imperial roots of plant collecting desires and taxonomic practices. At the same time, attention to what distinguishes the illegal and illicit instantiates the persistent role of the state in stories of illicit succulent life. For as much as these are stories of global trade and transit, it is the state that ultimately determines what is inside and outside the bounds of law, wedded to the spatially fixed contours of territory. And a seed, as we will see, is a surprisingly helpful guide to exploring these spatial and legal dimensions producing the illicit cactus.

Searching for the Last

Uebelmannia is a small genus of globular Brazilian cacti described by Dutch botanist Alfred Buining. The genus *Uebelmannia* is named for the Swiss cactus collector and former race car driver Werner J. Uebelmann, a lifelong collector, nurseryman, and devotee of Brazilian cacti.[1] These Eurocentric tendencies in species naming are common in botany, a field whose entwinement with settler colonialism and imperialism is deep and well researched in environmental history.[2] Thanks to our guide, an expert Brazilian botanist specializing in Brazilian cacti, we were equipped with the precise coordinates of one of the few known locations of the species, so our prospects for seeing *U. buiningii* were high.

But unlike other species I had encountered in both Brazil and Mexico, *U. buiningii* isn't threatened by farmland development or urbanization; according to species experts, including our guide that day, it is threatened above all by illegal collection for international trade. *U. buiningii* is restricted in habitat to an area of less than forty square kilometers, according to the IUCN Red List, with just a few small and isolated subpopulations remaining. The type locality for the species, or the location where a plant was first taken and used to formally describe the species on an archived herbarium sheet, is now absent any remaining plants. We had already driven well over a hundred miles down winding dirt roads, through a mountainous and forested landscape interspersed with eucalyptus plantations for charcoal production, small cattle ranches, and agricultural fields, on our way to see other *Uebelmannia* populations. For several hours, our group made intermittent stops to scan the slopes of hillsides that might be home to unrecorded populations of known *Uebelmannia* species, or perhaps even a new species or subspecies of the genus. As we scouted the landscape, we looked out for the presence of quartzite (the genus's preferred growing substrate), as well as known companion species, including *Pilosocereus aurisetus,* better known as the hairy torch cactus. After several hours of failing to identify anything resembling what might be a new kind of *Uebelmannia,* we drove on toward the known coordinates for *U. buiningii* held by our guide.

Along the way, I spoke with two members of the group about *U. buiningii,* extinction, and the ethics of collection. "I think these are going to be ex-populations in a few years," the Belgian collector said, his tone sad and earnest. Of my traveling companions, he was often the most comfortable talking about the emotions that could bubble to the surface in speaking about plants. I responded by delicately bringing up that our guide said illegal collection was *the* driving force behind their march toward extinction. "Well, that is what he says he *thinks* is the cause. But I think most people are aware now you shouldn't collect plants from the wild anymore," he replied. One of the British collectors chimed in, "Beginning in the 1980s, it was becoming frowned upon to collect from the wild." He recounted reading an article in the 1980s in a hobby journal with tips on taking plants from habitat and repotting them at home. "I read this, and I remember thinking, this is *wrong,* you shouldn't be publishing articles like this." I refrained from mentioning several recent incidents involving European and American collectors caught with hundreds of live plants in their luggage attempting to illegally transport CITES-listed plants across international borders.

We arrived at another slope covered in quartzite and inhabited by thousands of hairy torch cacti, their green skin shielded by an overcoat of cream-colored hair. Though cacti are often spiny, I was surprised to learn how many are also furry or hairy. The palette of the landscape was dusty greens and muted whites and gray; it mirrored the lichen coating the quartz surface of the hill, complementing the cacti with their understated blue-green hues. We searched for over an hour for *U. buiningii,* everyone weaving their own slow paths in and around the protrusions of quartz outcrops and clumps of cacti, the two indicators that *Uebelmannia* might be present.

Our group of six continued to search for *U. buiningii* in vain. The botanist and a Dutch collector talked while surveying the valley and hillside opposite us, the collector resting on a large boulder nearby (Figure 14). "I was here twenty years ago," the guide explained. "We came here with the farmer who lives over there [pointing to the slope opposite]. And back then we found some one hundred plants. And now there are none that we can see, with six of us looking for an hour." He shook his head, resigned. I asked him what he thought was the cause of their absence. "Overcollection," he said firmly. "There is a tipping point, where there are too few individuals left. Maybe there are still seeds in the seedbed, but maybe there weren't enough to maintain a population, and maybe it is just gone." The Belgian collector, who had walked over then, interjected, speaking to the Dutch collector. "That's the reason I didn't go to Madagascar with you [on another cactus trip]. Because I saw it when it was still beautiful, and I didn't want to go back and see how much worse it has gotten." "But it's all context," the Dutchman replied. "I hadn't been to Madagascar before and thought it was pretty great!" So many of our conversations on this trip returned to such sentiments, the pleasures the men described in seeing a landscape before it was "despoiled" by development or overcollection.

Figure 14. Looking for *Uebelmannia buiningii* amid a hillside of *Pilosocereus aurisetus* in Minas Gerais, Brazil. A collector rests after a long time of searching for the cactus without success. His face is blurred to preserve collector anonymity, in line with required research ethics protocols; it should not be misinterpreted to signal "wrongdoing" or that the collector was engaged in illicit activity.

The anticipated thrill of seeing something truly rare was soon replaced by the forlorn prospects that we were instead bearing witness to the extinction of a species, an entire genealogy of life millions of years in the making. I asked our guide if it was still worth looking for a bit longer, and he suggested I look below the walking path that cut across the hillside. "Well, there has got to at least be *one* plant here," the Dutch collector exclaimed with a sigh. Just as I headed toward the path below, a color caught my attention amid the washed-out landscape, a blotch of muted purple haloed in white. "Is that one?" I asked excitedly, pointing toward the ground a few meters past the boulder. Though I had not seen the species before, I was sure this was the genus; several days spent scouring the ground for other *Uebelmannia* attuned my eye to the look of the plant. The botanist and Dutch collector rushed over to confirm that I had found *U. buiningii*. My field notebook captures the experience's immediate effect on me:

> It felt *exactly* like the time I found my first morel mushroom alone in the woods.[3] This upwelling elation. A leap of the heart, a warming sensation around the stomach. I felt over-joyed. We had all just accepted that the plant was likely locally extinct here, one of just a couple of known populations of the entire species. And here it was. Honestly, I nearly started to cry. A life persisting against extraction at a pace that is at odds with its own sense of time in this world.

This moment of fleeting awe is important for understanding part of what drives many passionate collectors in their search for enjoyment, and I was grateful to experience such a moment myself as a pathway into understanding one dimension of the collector experience. If searching for "the last" can embody in Lacanian terms a kind of *jouissance,* an aching and excess of painful pleasure, as Stasja Koot has argued in the case of endangered rhino tourism, the awe I felt as I encountered this cactus also speaks to Walter Benjamin's sense of aura, which he approached in relation to "natural objects" as "the unique phenomenon of a distance, however close it may be."[4] There is a decidedly spatial dimension of proximity to encountering the aura for Benjamin. To encounter the cactus at a close distance was to feel the life of a very different other in sudden and immediate proximity. If, for Benjamin, we feel the aura of the mountain when its shadow passes over us, it was the sudden rupture of witnessing absence traded in for sudden, even shocking presence that cast the cactus's aura over me and my traveling companions.

What remained in the wake of this encounter was the "enjoyment" of *jouissance,* but looking back, I also wonder if this was also a brief encounter the Lacanian sublime. This is when an ordinary "object," here a cactus, is "elevated to the dignity of the Thing," when an object takes on the residues of the Thing (that imagined yet unattainable source of overwhelming pleasure we encircle through the drives), leaving an excess of *jouissance* in its wake.[5] To understand this better, we can turn to the only place (to my knowledge) where Lacan discusses collecting practices. In an all too brief anecdote, he details how everyday objects, such as those in collection, might be explained through this process of sublimation, in which the aura of the Thing gives real "objects" or "things" greater unconscious meaning. He writes about visiting a friend with a notable matchbox collection, in which each matchbox had its little drawer open just enough to connect one box to the other, linking them as a pleasing "object of objects" in a chain of connection and meaning:

> I believe that the shock of novelty of the effect realized by this collection of empty match boxes—and this is the essential point—was to reveal . . . that a box of matches is not simply an object, but that, in the form of an *Erscheinung* [apparition], as it appeared in its truly imposing multiplicity, it may be a Thing. In other words, this arrangement demonstrated that a match box isn't simply something that has a certain utility, that it isn't even a type in the Platonic sense, an abstract match box. . . . The wholly gratuitous, proliferating, superfluous, and quasi absurd character of this collection pointed to its thingness as match box. Thus the collector found his motive in this form of apprehension that concerns less the match box than the Thing that subsists in a match box.[6]

Perhaps the search for the cactus left it with an overdetermined status in my mind, as something imbued with multiple and contradictory kinds of signification: desire and lack, extinction and care, of wanting (to see) something *badly* and yet realizing the seeing was tied to collection, the cause of this plant's unmaking as a species in the world. In its overdetermination, it became touched by the Thing itself, a sublime object of greater unconscious import.

As my gaze found the cactus, this experience of shock or awe as a close encounter with the Thing collapsed great distances between me, the cactus, and the men with whom I was sharing time. Awe can translate into what geographer Jamie Lorimer, drawing on the work of Deleuze and Guattari, describes as interspecies epiphanies, or when a person is "affected or reterritorialized by a nonhuman organism."[7] Deleuze and Guattari write about becomings as a way to characterize how the boundaries of bodies and the individual break down and are reinscribed in relation to others. This sense of becoming is captured better in more contemporary work by Karen Barad, specifically Barad's notion of *intra*-action (as opposed to interaction). Intra-action describes how it is through encounters between beings that categories of knowing emerge and agencies are enacted, in contrast to supposing that discrete and fixed entities precede these formative relations.[8] How, for instance, would this moment of encounter have been experienced otherwise if different taxonomic histories splitting *Uebelmannia* occurred or if my knowledge of the species' diminishing abundance was unavailable to me? In homing in on the emergence of relations shaping individual agencies, the work of Simone Fullager helps make sense of the meaning of awe here as formative to becoming. She writes, "Is not awe an intense experience of reverberation felt as a movement of transformation, a becoming other?"[9] But returning to Lacan and the possibility that this encounter marked the sublimation of the cactus, it is also possible that alongside my own transformation, the encounter was marked by my reworking of the cactus into something exceeding the plant before me; it became something of an encounter with the sublime, which is to say, marked by the excessive residue of the Thing, the cactus as what Lacan calls *objet a*.

Figure 15. The author surrounded by *Pilosocereus aurisetus* in 2018 moments after encountering the singular *Uebelmannia buiningii*. The small cactus is seen toward the bottom, center right of the image, close to the author's hand. Photograph used with permission of an anonymous collector.

Encounters across species lines hold great affective potential, but at the same time, I cannot think of my encounter with this cactus without thinking of the men with whom I traveled and their own inscriptions of meaning and desire through seeking out this plant on a trajectory toward extinction. Although I witnessed a variety of ways cactus collectors seek enjoyment during "cactoexplorations," I had not, until this moment in Brazil, experienced in affective registers the kinds of emergent person–plant relationships structured through awe I had heard others relate and recount to me. Becomings can emerge through the way the gaze changes or how the ear tunes in to the calls of birds or the sound of trees; it is to have the sensibility to ask and practice what it means to know another being (Figure 15).[10]

As the intensity of experience subsided, I took photos of the cactus alongside everyone else. I received several friendly slaps on the back for finding the plant. The Dutch collector announced that at a minimum, it made the day, and maybe the whole trip. I posed with the cactus for a photo, and I later noticed that I wrote "my cactus" in my fieldnotes when describing it—an acknowledgment of my acculturation into the world of cactus "hunting." I made a joke of pretending to hold up the plant's invisible horns, mimicking people who pay large sums of money to shoot gazelle or lions and other animals on safaris in South Africa or Tanzania. After crowding around to take photos, we spread out to look for more plants, revitalized despite the heat. But after another thirty minutes, we still hadn't found another. It was difficult to contemplate that this one mature plant was not just alone on a hillside but quite possibly alone in the living world (except in collection, of course). Our guide noted no sign of reproduction around it, no small offspring nearby, no offsets, no flower, no fruit. He said that just three weeks prior, he had visited one of the only other, if not *the* only other, remaining subpopulation of *U. buiningii,* where he said he found just three living plants. The species was going extinct, he explained; functionally, it likely already was (Figure 16).

While others continued to look with declining interest, I sat with the Dutch collector and our guide by the newly found cactus. "The strange psychology of collectors in this hobby is that some people would say now, OK, this is the last one, and we should take it home, to protect it. Plenty of people would say that," the collector said. The Brazilian guide nodded in agreement. The Dutchman continued, "I think we should be proud of our strength and courage in not doing this. I mean, you can also just buy this plant in Holland if you really want it!" In the end, we found only the one cactus on the hill. Turning the phrase's original meaning around on its head, we might consider new wisdom in the writing of Walter Benjamin when he wrote, "Only in extinction is the collector comprehended."[11]

Figure 16. A close-up view of the only *Uebelmannia buiningii* found at the location. This view permits one to notice the signs of maturity and aging on the plant, including signs of corking, bleaching, and the scars resulting from attacks by insects.

A simple way to read this earnest acknowledgment by the collector is as a repressing of his desires. Instead, however, I see in this response a registration that even if "our" desires are not "ours" alone, shaped as they are by the Other, there are layers to these desires, informed by our place in history and the social structures that work to guide our desires (for instance, toward repetitive acts of consumption). Instead of recognizing the collector's desire as rooted only in possession, if we see the collector as desiring a more fundamental encounter with an Other, there is room for analyzing this moment not as the repression of desire but rather as its recognition and the layering of signification therein. Mari Ruti explains these tensions of the ethics of pursuing desire:

In other words, the point of analysis is not to obliterate our psychic destiny, but merely to elaborate it in more satisfying directions, away from the incapacitating effects of the repetition compulsion and toward the rewards of subjective autonomy. The point is to peel off some of the layers of social conditioning so as to allow us to access forms of desire that might evade the demands of both conventional morality and economic exigency, that might express something elemental about our singular way of taking up the challenge of living.[12]

The collector's recognition of the work of desire at play in relation to the cactus as an object of desire reflects that "challenge of the living." Rather than repression, I see in this collector's perspective a humble acknowledgment of the power of desire.

Learning with the Illicit Seed in the Pocket

One day in Brazil, I noticed one of the collectors with whom I was traveling holding a fallen fruit from a cactus. Pushing his finger into the fruit, he showed me how embedded inside its bright pink flesh were hundreds of tiny black seeds (Figure 17). I marveled at the contrasting colors between fruit and seed, the faint citric scent, and their quantity. He then put the fruit in a bag. Later that night, he would clean out the seeds in his hotel bathroom, lay them out to dry on tissue paper, and pack them away in a small, labeled paper envelope to be tucked into his luggage at the trip's end. This is not the work of a cactus profiteer; he would later distribute these seeds to anyone within his own cactus society in Europe who desired the opportunity to germinate and grow the species.

P. aurisetus is a species with a large distribution range and a stable population in Brazil. I weighed this information against the act of *illegal*—but to the collector and most of his acquaintances, not *illicit*—acquisition I had just witnessed.[13] Although these terms

Figure 17. *Pilosocereus aurisetus* fruit, opened by a collector to show me the quantity of tiny black seeds inside and the bright magenta color of the fruit's interior.

are often used interchangeably, even by academics, the (il)legal and the (il)licit point to different phenomena that regulate social life. While the boundaries of what determine legal versus illegal trade remain tied to the state, its laws, and both national and international legal frameworks governing such trade, matters of the (il)licit are about social norms of acceptability and do not necessarily follow such tidy political boundaries. The (il)licit molds to the contours of social life, which are themselves prone to change. What is deemed licit or illicit is contextual and ephemeral (consider marijuana smoking, or the medicinal or recreational use of psychedelic mushrooms, or even LSD); it is the outcome of ongoing contestations over social legitimacy in the public sphere and acceptable norms and conduct by parties—including sovereign

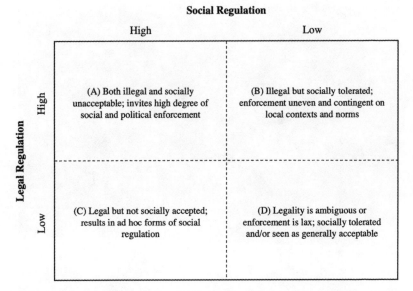

Figure 18. A typology of the illicit and legal drawing on the work of Van Schendel and Abraham (*Illicit Flows and Criminal Things: States, Borders, and the Other Side of Globalization* [Bloomington: Indiana University Press, 2005]) in relation to social and political regulations. As there are not strict boundaries between categories, interior lines are marked with dashed lines. Adapted from Nicholas Magliocca et al., "Comparative Analysis of Illicit Supply Network Structure and Operations: Cocaine, Wildlife, and Sand," *Journal of Illicit Economies and Development* 3, no. 1 (2021): 50–73.

states—invested or engaged in a particular trade, its taxation, and/ or its policing (Figure 18).[14]

What counts as illicit or illegal is not only nearly always a matter of contestation but is also better described as a spectrum negotiated through competing social and legal forces. The case of pocketing *P. aurisetus* seeds serves as a useful example for describing and differentiating between illegal and illicit succulent trades and the murkiness between them, as well as what these terms both represent as ideas and also actively do in the world. Most of the serious collectors I interviewed—and several conservationists as well—balked at the notion that cactus seeds, for instance, should be treated the same as plants in regulating international trade, yet currently cactus seeds from Mexico are listed in Appendix II of CITES (international trade requires country export permits), whereas those from other countries are not. Given the slow growth of many cactus species, as well as their global circulations, which predate many CITES appendix listings, it is easy to imagine how murky the regulatory waters can become.

"Because of my interest in conservation, I've had to break the law," a cactus collector who described himself to me as the "Indiana Jones of plants" declared as we discussed the fate of the cactus collecting hobby and its marginalization by mainstream conservation actors. How should we understand such a statement? Why, if as many collectors claim, they are passionately invested in cactus and succulent conservation, do many engage in activities that conservation and law enforcement actors declare as harmful to the species, to say nothing of their illegality? Answering these questions requires wading into the sometimes confusing and challenging world of international trade regulations. In chapter 1, I described an incident in which a Belgian collector explained he was in possession of perhaps the only legal *Aztekium ritteri* cactus in Europe but that he was unable to prove this *legally*. This was because the plant left Mexico prior to 1975, when CITES entered into force, but he technically had no way to prove this. *A. ritteri* is a CITES Appendix I listed species, meaning it is recognized by CITES Parties as threatened with extinction. As an Appendix I species, all international trade is banned, except under "exceptional circumstances," which would require both country import and export permits and likely apply only for scientific research purposes.[15] As he explained to me, "I could grow out its seeds, but how would you prove it was one of these original plants? I only knew it came from Ritter because my neighbor recognized Ritter's handwriting."

If the collector tried to sell or otherwise trade internationally in offsets or seeds from the original plant, he would have no formal recourse by which to prove to the appropriate CITES authorities that this was a legally acquired plant. The only thing keeping this plant from being "illegal" is its age—the plant traveled to Belgium prior to the species being listed in CITES Appendix I. It is possible the collector might be able to use a botanical expert's statement as evidence to the appropriate authorities that the plant was so old that it predated CITES based on its condition and size, but the collector would then still have to prove when he came into possession of it. Even decades-old *A. ritteri* plants are small, mere centimeters in width and proportionally fewer in height. Despite the maturity of a forty- or fifty-year-old plant, its roots remain shallow, adapted to growing in the crevices of steep limestone mountain slopes and canyons. It would be nearly just as easy for a collector to pry a decades-old *A. ritteri* out of the ground as a five-year-old individual—if they were even able to spot it. Evidence of its age would therefore be no justification to authorities that the plant had not been illegally pried from the ground from its small geographic range in the Rayones Valley of Nuevo León, Mexico. As this short anecdote reveals, it is not always easy to distinguish or evidence clear boundaries between the (il)legal and the (il)licit; this challenge matters in shaping species futures when they intersect with collector desires.

Returning to the stolen seeds in Brazil, these matters become ever more complex. Brazil has its own strong national legislation regulating the export of Brazilian species of plants, animals, and even microorganisms under a variety of interrelated genetic heritages, Indigenous knowledge, and biodiversity laws. Brazil is also a party to the Convention on Biological Diversity (CBD), an international treaty that, among many things, sets down protocols and rules regulating access and benefit sharing (ABS) between countries related to genetic resources.[16] Although the whole of the cactus family is registered as Appendix II by CITES, meaning that trade is permitted but requires a country export permit, there is no readily available legal method by which foreign cactus collectors can visit Brazil and acquire seeds from wild plants, even though the seeds themselves are not listed in any CITES appendix. Although it is unambiguous that if a collector wished to depart Brazil with a cactus seed harvested from a wild plant without a Brazilian permit, they would be doing so illegally, it is less clear where this person would stand upon declaring the seed at a destination outside the borders of Brazil; it would depend on the legislation of that country. Many countries, for instance, ban importing live seed without appropriate phytosanitary permits, whereas others do not. Some countries enforce CITES rules only for species native to them, whereas others fail to delineate penalties for CITES infractions at all.[17] One could argue that it doesn't matter what the importing country's rules are because it is an illegal action in Brazil. But in practice, it does matter, because customs and border enforcement agents are expected to make determinations of what can and cannot enter a country and the legality of those materials once they arrive. More practically, it is unlikely that a small packet of tiny black seeds would be remotely identifiable at a border crossing, to say nothing of their discoverability at all, concealed in a shirt pocket or shoe.

Geography and the reproductive capacities of plants further mediate their illicit and illegal trajectories. An international illicit trade in cactus seeds depends on the particularities of the countries between which trading takes place. Any international trade in Mexican cactus seeds without CITES paperwork *originating* from Mexico is unambiguously illegal, but the status of Mexican cactus seeds produced from plants grown in cultivation elsewhere is murkier. Even though seeds produced from artificially propagated Mexican cacti could be exempted from CITES trade restrictions, it would also be necessary to demonstrate to the relevant CITES authorities the legal provenance of the plant from which the seeds were derived. Despite the very global nature of illicit cactus trades, the territoriality of state borders continues to reassert a powerful, if oftentimes underacknowledged, presence in determining something as illicit or illegal. This ambiguity also facilitates the production of so-called gray markets, to which I return more closely in the next chapter.

The foregoing examples help add some clarity to an otherwise blurry sphere surrounding the legal and the illegal, but what separates the licit and the illicit is a matter of social concern. Broadly speaking, within the cactus and succulent collector community, a sizable portion of the hobby does not find it terribly objectionable (if at all) to collect and distribute seeds from wild plants, even when doing so is illegal. As my collaborative survey of cactus and succulent collectors I describe in chapter 1 showed, 42 percent of collectors found it either "very" or "somewhat" acceptable to collect wild cactus and succulent seed, while approximately the same percentage found it unacceptable. In fact, not only do many within the hobby not find this practice objectionable but many advocate for illegal seed collection as a social *good,* as important conservation work. As one survey respondent wrote,

> when a new species has been discovered, there will always be a demand for this species and it will find its illegal way into collections. The Czechs are very good in rapidly multiplying a new species, thereby strongly diminishing the pressure on that species in its natural habitat. *Somehow, there should be found a legal format for this, because, although illegal, it is for the benefit of the species in nature.*[18]

To paraphrase countless pithy quotes about the morality of breaking the law for just causes, many cactus collectors see a moral obligation to knowingly disobey CITES trade regulations. While our survey also suggested that many collectors might unknowingly be breaking international trade laws, many collectors do so quite intentionally.[19]

Other actors besides Customs and Border Patrol agents and collectors and plant poachers shape the contours of illicit plant trading. I encountered numerous examples of botanical researchers and conservationists complaining about the very same rules and international trade regulations as collectors, though their complaints and justifications may have differed. Then there is the frequent-enough case of countries confiscating illegally traded plants only to then destroy them or hold them in perpetuity in greenhouse facilities rather than rematriating them to their countries of origin or moving them into botanical gardens (i.e., the law is upheld, but to little or no benefit to the plant itself). I visited numerous such facilities in the United States, Europe, and Mexico during this research; how strange it is to see thousands of cacti and other plants living under perpetual lock and key in accordance with the law.

In a more obvious case of illicit crossover, a botanist, aware that they had discovered a new and rare species of cactus, ensured that viable seeds made their way to persons in the collecting hobby who could germinate the seeds abroad, providing new plants for the commercial market after the species was formally described in the botanical literature. This was an effort to theoretically curb demand for wild-collected plants, though there is a lack of data about the effectiveness of such market intervention approaches.[20] This was also an informal and, arguably, illicit act. Yet, from the perspective of the botanist, we might think of this as a case of ecological harm reduction. As the plant was not yet formally described, and therefore did not legally "exist" in national endangered species registries, the legality or illegality of the transit of the seeds outside the country was made all the more opaque.

But where botanists or conservationists might gripe about slow bureaucratic machinery or research delays caused by trade regulations and red tape, the threat of damage to their professional legitimacy is usually sufficient to keep them operating within the bounds of the law. This is not the case for many collectors, whose drive in the pursuit of plants may exceed their concern for possible prosecution under the law (which remains restricted typically to relatively minor fines) but who also frame their own practices as either ethically acceptable or even commendable. As criminologists Simon Mackenzie and Donna Yates describe, in collecting cultures in which collectors appear to answer to a "higher authority," collectors do not seek to "neutralize" their illicit activities through expressions like "yes, I know it is wrong, but . . ." and instead are more likely to frame their activities as "it is not wrong because. . . ."[21] It is therefore crucial to consider seriously the perspectives of collectors and the framing of illicitness. Doing so helps to clarify how and why such practices persist to the great consternation of actors external to them invested in cactus and succulent conservation.

What's the Harm in Taking a Few Seeds?

I return to the incident of seeds slipping into a bag to consider illicit succulent life more closely. Would it really matter to the long-term health of the local *P. aurisetus* population if a few dozen—or even a few hundred—seeds made their way to Europe, to be germinated and sold or exchanged with other enthusiastic cactus collectors? How outraged should we be by yet another example of natural resource exploitation operating in the direction of the Global South to the Global North? The seed that slips into the pocket opens the door to working through, in material terms, important distinctions differentiating the (il)legal and the (il)licit in wildlife trades, among these other important themes. In an interview I conducted some months later at the Huntington Botanic Gardens in Pasadena, California, home to one of the greatest living collections of cacti and succulents in the world, a curator summarized some of these tensions well:

I think the imperialistic exploration of the world and gathering of specimens was an ethic that was perfectly acceptable from a European perspective for a couple of centuries before the implementation of CITES, and biodiversity treaties and so on. . . . A lot of the grey areas . . . are still operating under that historical ethic, and in fact are in denial of more modern sensibilities. . . . So there's a tension there that hasn't been resolved. I think certain *pragmatic* conservation efforts are undeniably proving to be more effective than many of the *official* regulatory efforts of conservation, and that needs to be resolved by both parties, somehow.[22]

It is worth highlighting here the admission that current regulatory efforts to protect species may not necessarily be well designed for the task at hand compared to what they describe as more "pragmatic" efforts. But this statement also reflects a longer history of uneven relations in which species and resources have been exploited and stolen by centers of power and empire from places they have colonized or otherwise exploited. How the (il)licit and (il)legal are shaped and defined today should be read through these uneven and extractive histories of colonization, imperialism, and exploitation of the Global South by the Global North.[23] Furthermore, these seeds reveal a murkier entanglement that denies clean separation between the licit and the illicit, what best represents care for the species, and how these ambiguities and tensions are produced as an outcome of so-called gray markets of cactus and succulent trade. Like many revered institutions that hold popular collections developed through what often amounted to colonial-era theft rendered licit by way of formal institutionalization and the passage of time,[24] the Huntington's unsurpassed collections of rare and endangered succulents are wrapped up in these histories of "imperialistic exploration" that continue to persist through the lives of plants.[25] This blurring of how, when, and to whom illicitness is applied demonstrates the nature of illicitness as describing a set of tensions mediated by the ethical rules and norms of collector communities and their desire for plants, contrasted against the rules and regulations of the state.

During a conversation with a botanist in Brazil, he told me that he used to agree with other botanists that taking anything from habitat (inclusive of seeds) was wrong. But every year he went back to places where there used to be cacti, only to find them replaced by cattle pastures or mining quarries. As a result, he no longer thinks it is such a problem if hobbyists take some seeds, except for some truly rare populations, as his far greater concern remains the problem of both legal and illegal development sending species into extinction. "It means at least the plants exist somewhere," he said. "If you think about how many seeds [many of] these plants produce every year it is staggering, and most won't germinate and go anywhere, so I don't mind if they [collectors] take them, I really don't think it matters."

To many (if not most) conservationists, this perspective is flawed, even dangerous. In an interview I conducted earlier in the year, a Mexican cactus conservationist insisted that the ban on trade in Mexican seeds was genuinely meant to protect species and that it was working. While acknowledging that in theory, for a robust population of cacti, the occasional taking of cactus fruits and seeds would not impact their long-term conservation, that might not be the case if the collection pressure was persistent and intensive. The expert argued that, although there is a significant degree of variability across the cactus family, in general, the likelihood that a cactus seed will not only germinate but survive to become a reproducing adult plant is exceedingly low, with young cacti often experiencing high mortality rates. Many cacti fail to produce viable seedbanks (where seeds persist in the soil and may germinate at some point in the future under favorable conditions), while other cacti may produce relatively few seeds per year or simply have very poor germination rates. "Maybe taking a few seeds or a hundred seeds won't matter much to some populations, but how many collectors are doing it? If hundreds are doing it every year, that could really impact these populations," the expert argued. These two ardent conservationists with deep knowledge of cacti agreed that many species produce abundant seeds, but their interpretations of the significance of low germination rates led them to very different conclusions and ecological politics. While one advocated for widespread dissemination of seeds, even if outside the bounds of law, the other insisted on the need for a stricter, preservationist mind-set.

But other policy makers, conservationists, and botanists leverage another argument in framing the collection of seeds as illicit. This is based on the notion of ecological sovereignty, or that the seeds in question are the national patrimony or common heritage of a country. Proponents argue that it is ethically wrong for foreign tourists—and in the context of Latin America, especially U.S. or European tourists—to remove elements of Brazilian (or Peruvian, or Mexican) *heritage*. This perspective was best summarized by a Mexican bureaucrat within La Comisión Nacional para el Conocimiento y Uso de la Biodiversidad (National Commission for the Knowledge and Use of Biodiversity; CONABIO), Mexico's lead agency overseeing the use and knowledge of biodiversity. I asked him why he thought many European cactus collectors did not seem to find it troubling to take Mexican cacti and their seeds in contravention of CITES trade rules. He laughed, responding, "They've been stealing from us since 1492, why would now be any different?"

Captured in this statement is the shadow that colonialism and imperialism continue to cast over the cactus and succulent collecting hobby as a historically Euro-American tradition, one closely tied to notions of discovery, exploration, and the hunt in foreign lands for "exotic" plants.[26] Especially for conservationists across Latin

America, there is a feeling of emancipation in claiming species as one's "own" as a distinctly anticolonial position. But against ecological sovereignty as a rejection of colonial power dynamics, others, such as philosopher and environmental scholar Mick Smith, critique such moves as yet again reproducing harmful human–nature distinctions and normalizing the owning, possessing, and commodifying of—and therefore objectifying—nonhuman life.[27] Smith argues from a radical ecological perspective that claims of political sovereignty over nonhuman life reproduce the "natural" world as one to be territorialized, dominated, and commodified by humans, rather than recognizing humanity as part of, rather than apart from, a more-than-human world.

I am sympathetic to Smith's arguments against ecological sovereignty. At the same time, we must confront the colonial harms embedded within ongoing debates and challenges to species conservation as an effort to abate extinctions.[28] It is important to recognize that cactus and succulent collecting is no longer a hobby enjoyed only by Europeans and North Americans, of course. Still, the legacies of colonialism that haunt botanical "exploration" and description, just as they haunt the disciplines and institutions of botany and conservation writ large, remain largely intact in characterizing what constitutes illicit behavior and trade in plant life. These legacies are part of the "colonial present" within cactus and succulent collecting cultures, as well as of who feels entitled to possess plants from around the world and what the work of "saving" entails.[29] As Susan Pearce writes, "collecting is not only an inscription on the world; it is also an imposition on the world."[30] To fully conceptualize desire and the (il)licit in plant collecting worlds, we must therefore also attend to such impositions, especially those marked by the legacies of colonial violence and their contemporary forms. Why is it, for instance, that so many botanists of the Global South must still travel to institutions in the Global North to study plants from their own countries? The history of these dynamics is well known, but the work to decolonize the herbarium or botanical collections, for instance, to repair past harms and return what amounts to looted materials, has barely begun.[31]

Temptation Close at Hand

An incident midway through my time in Brazil brought many of these thematic threads on matters of illicitness, desire, and colonial relations into clear view. After another long day of taking photographs of cacti, the last stop of the day was to see a new species not yet formally described or even named in the scientific literature but that would be soon by a Brazilian botanist. It is a species that for now is known by the botanist to be living only on one hill, although the region has not yet been sufficiently surveyed to resolve this definitively, he explained. The plant—a species of the *Arrojadoa* genus, a group of thin and fragile-stalked Brazilian cacti restricted to the states of Bahia and Minas Gerais—was not particularly compelling to look at, which I remarked to one of the collectors on the way back to the car after seeing the plant. "Yes, but in flower they are *really* attractive," he insisted (Figure 19). As we got back in the car and were joined by another collector, our conversation turned to discussing the urge to "pinch" a plant. "I must say it is tempting to take one home. If it had been a *Ferocactus,* I wouldn't have been able to resist, but I don't like *Arrojadoa,*" the older of the two collectors said. "Well, it will be in collection soon enough," the younger collector replied. "But wouldn't that be illegal?" the older collector asked. "That hasn't stopped others, has it?" the other replied. I asked the younger collector, who liked *Arrojadoa,* why he didn't take a cutting of the plant. "Because that's just not what's done now," he replied firmly. The Brazilian botanist would later tell me that he was aware that seeds of this yet-to-be-described species were already in Europe, being grown and propagated as young plants by an enterprising and well-respected senior member of

Figure 19. An *Arrojadoa* species in flower. Despite their somewhat unremarkable features—"a spiky, sticklike cactus," as I first described them in my field notes—the flowers of the *Arrojadoa* genus are particularly striking in bloom, such as this one.

the cactus collecting community. "He's just waiting for me to describe it [in the literature] before he starts selling it," the botanist explained. I asked the botanist if this bothered him. "No, I don't mind that he took seeds, it's fine, we need plants in cultivation so there isn't a black market for wild plants, that's my thinking."

I asked one of the collectors whether, if this new plant showed up for sale at a cactus convention in Europe, it would be legal. The collector said no, "it would have to be sold under the table." "But who would control that?" the botanist replied. "Nobody," the collector said. What a black market in cacti signified to the botanist differed from what was nevertheless an illegal trade, as his greater concern was the potential growth of a market leading to removal of mature plants from habitat, in contrast to the illegal transport of seeds and subsequent growth of new plants elsewhere. One perspective points to a concern for the law, the other to the more practical consequences of collectors' desires and their impingement on succulent life. Attention to these differences enriches the detail and nuance of illicit trades, to better understand the illicit succulent trade as a broader category indexing a variety of kinds of activities, transactions, and transgressions. Whereas one collector might recognize their behavior of collection as both illegal and illicit, but collect anyway in the name of profit, for another, it is the very illicitness of the act that proves a source of enjoyment. "There is a thrill in knowing you've got something no one else does!" one collector said later during our trip in Brazil. Still another will insist that illegally taking a few wild-collected plants or a hundred seeds to propagate and sell to a larger body of collectors is the ethically correct thing to do in the name of conservation, to avert species extinction.

The incident with a yet-to-be-named *Arrojadoa* species shed light on the Dutch collector's comments that surprised me at the beginning of the chapter as we discussed the fate of *U. buiningii.* I was stunned by the admission of the Dutch collector that many collectors would feel compelled to take the last *U. buiningii* as an act of preservation. But staying close to the connections between collector desires and expressions of preservation helps to make sense of how thematic threads of desire, the illicit, and collection weave together through cactus life and what collectors seek in cacti as they are transformed into objects of desire with greater signification. I appreciated that the collector saw himself as upholding a higher moral code that exceeded this urge to take (the cactus was left in place). Still, he nevertheless indicated that it was an urge he understood and felt. MacKenzie and Yates offer valuable insight into this perspective on what "saving" means to collectors of rare things:

> On the surface the argument is that to acquire them saves
> them from destruction: antiquities and rare orchids will be

kept by the collectors in the best conditions to store or nurture them. . . . There is, however, another type of saving which is less obvious in the discourse but which is a fair interpretation of the sentiment connecting many collecting reports: the collector saves the objects from obscurity. This is therefore an argument in favour of display rather than preservation as such. Antiquities and orchids may in fact be perfectly well preserved in their original findspots around the world. . . . Yet even if they did not need the collector to save them from potential destruction, there is a strong sense in the collecting narrative that they deserve to be appreciated—they deserve to be loved—and in this sense the collector offers salvation.[32]

"Saving" collectible things may represent both a selfless act to preserve the treasured item and the possessive urge to contain and display. Or, in a more psychoanalytically minded reading, as objects of desire, they become endowed with the aura of the Thing, an object as source of jouissance. But in the case of *U. buiningii,* this urge also reveals how the drive to possess can easily double back on itself. *U. buiningii* was precisely in need of saving *because* of collector desires to possess or "save" the plant "from obscurity." The idea that this same mentality might also benefit the species reveals this urge as anything but selfless; instead, it is centered on the collector as the true subject in these stories of collection. "For what you really collect is always yourself," as Baudrillard writes.[33] Through the stories of an unnamed *Arrojadoa* and *U. buiningii,* a small purple cactus on the verge of extinction, the boundaries between desires to "save" species and collect species collapse through recognition of processes at work in the realm of the unconscious. Attention to the unconscious and the psychic work wrought through collections reveals deeper motivations of the collector to "discover" and seek out the absent term in a quest for satisfaction and enjoyment.

On Memory and Inscription through the Vegetal Other

The day before my encounter with *U. buiningii,* I stood with the Dutch member of the trip on an outcrop of rock overlooking a beautiful vista of flourishing cacti. He explained that one of the reasons these trips were so important was that other people would likely revisit our collective travelogues for years to come. This was not a wholly unreasonable comment, as he is well known in the collecting community for giving engaging talks about his travels abroad. But it was also clear that in his mind, the recording of our presence in these landscapes was part of an important effort to satisfy inscription of the self-in-landscape. In visiting and record-ing the stories of our travels and the plants we had seen (and not seen), it was as if we had signed a visitor's log of the who's who of cactus history. "We are literally following in the footsteps of Ritter," he explained, again referencing Friedrich Ritter, the same famous twentieth-century German cactus expert who extensively surveyed Brazil and other South American countries for cacti. "I think that is quite exciting. And it's exciting to think that in the fu-ture, next generations might say the same things about us." There was a silence between us for a minute as we both scanned the gor-geous scenery. "It really gives you the feeling of living on a planet where there are still things to discover—and you are empowered to discover them," he added.[34]

Back in the SUV, I struck up a conversation with our guide about the day's events. "I see these *Uebelmannia* on eBay, they are so old, so rare, and yet they sell for very little. Ten euros—that's nothing for these plants that are so old," he said, still frustrated by our impoverished encounter with this cactus endling.[35] The discussion of finding *U. buiningii,* its extinction, and the urge that the Dutch collector described to take this last of a species home to "protect" it continued on our drive to the next stop through conversation that wove together many of the contradictions and ambivalences embedded in what constitutes the work of species care. I was struck by the collector's response that so many other collectors might have felt the urge to take the last of the species to protect it. There was a deeply imperialist sentiment that clung to this description of powerful urges to possess, extract, and protect in geographies marked by settler colonialism. It also felt steeped in familiar contradictions about who does conservation work (i.e., white Anglo-Europeans with savior complexes), where it ought to be done (the Global South), and what remained unspoken about the forces driving species loss at the global scale. These are the uneven dynamics so often embedded and reproduced within protectionist conservation discourses. Yet they were also the same dynamics I repeatedly heard articulated by European collectors describing cacti as being "better off" in their greenhouses than left in countries "where conservation priorities are low and [the] Indigenous population is not interested [in conservation] when their livelihood is more important."[36] There is a remarkable symmetry in thought between old-guard conservation thinking and collector possessive desires, even if conservationists might balk at the suggestion. But as numerous studies of protected areas demonstrate, isn't exclusionary conservation management—which so often has involved the dispossession of traditional and Indigenous stewards of the land—also the expression of possessive desires to covet the Other, simply by another name and at a more ambitious scale?[37]

That some collectors believe they have a moral imperative to remove a plant from the wild to protect it when the very source of its decline is other collectors like them taking plants sets up an especially strange kind of paradox. And yet, as I describe in detail in chapter 4, only days later, I would enthusiastically bear witness to plants of another critically endangered species being removed from their habitat, but in an incident that felt dramatically different—at least in the intent to care—than what I had experienced and felt in relation to the little purple cactus as the last of a kind. These acts of illicit cactus acquisition, one hypothetical, the other not, cut across the grain of illicitness and illegality in ways that reiterate the inherent nature of the "illicit" as a malleable product of social and political construction. In the words of one of the trip's collectors, "it's very technical what is legal or illegal. It means nothing to the plants." But these acts also push past questions of illicitness and illegality toward urgent matters of more-than-human care and, ultimately, what is left unnamed in speaking of succulent desires.

Encircling the Production of Desire

Traveling with cacti and collectors not only highlights the production of the illicit as entwined with contests of sovereignty and criminality but also points us in the direction of desire. Visiting *U. buiningii,* I speculated on what might have occurred if it were known differently, perhaps not as a species but as a subspecies or varietal of another *Uebelmannia.* If *U. buiningii* was not categorized as its own species but merely as a variant of another, would this form of species "lumping" potentially offer it a greater degree of protection from those who seek complete collections of the genus and are incited by new or rare species? Or would this possibly only make it more vulnerable, as endangered species legislation might not apply to it if this larger species category were now of a sufficient size to no longer meet the requirements for holding an endangered status? These productions of botanical difference, the work of "splitting" or "lumping" by enthusiastic collectors, botanists, or cactoexplorers who desire to "discover" or name something new, have material consequences for the plants we come to know as species. This is especially true where it concerns how desire finds expression in the world.

Difference is linked to the production of desire. *Uebelmannia* is a genus that has undergone a variety of revisions in species names since it was first described as a genus in the 1960s by Alfred Buining, who was assisted in the field by Leopoldo Horst, the founder of a major cactus nursery in the Brazilian state of Rio Grande do Sul (still open today).[38] These trips to describe and collect new species in the mid-twentieth century were funded by Werner Uebelmann, as the intention was that newly described species could be sent to his Swiss nursery, which he operated until the 1980s, where he would for a time hold a veritable monopoly on the sale of these new cacti species. It is rumored that on these expeditions, Buining would pay Horst a bonus for newly described species. In time, several previously identified *Uebelmannia* "species" (among many other species in other genera they described) would later be recategorized as "subspecies" or "variations" within larger species "groups" or "complexes." These nonspecific terms nevertheless used in both professional and collector settings tilt at the messiness, hybridity, and porosity of vegetal life that make clear delineations of difference in the world of plants quite difficult in taxonomic terms. In this way, the three men all profited through producing difference. Buining's botanical reputation increased as he continued to describe new species, and Horst and Uebelmann both profited from these formal descriptions, which served as scientific support for new species they could then sell to collectors hungry for newly described species.

With the production of desire in mind, John Hartigan Jr.'s concept of species formations helps both to historicize and also to rearticulate species "as an active mode of 'species thinking.'"[39] Species are not atemporal static entities. The species is an epistemic category of knowing that conceptually maps better onto some living beings than others (tigers as opposed to many cacti, for instance, to say nothing of fungi or bacteria). Species thinking indexes efforts to know, order, and structure understandings of the world that might help scientists (among others) better navigate living within it and better care for other beings. But species thinking emerged alongside other taxonomic efforts of classification, racialization, possession, and imperial domination that continue to do great harm in the world in reasserting racialized and classed hierarchies that (re)produce geographical difference. Extending Hartigan's ideas of species thinking through the production of desire, we can now begin to imagine how species formations can also become powerful "objects" that incite collector desires and how, in turn, capitalism so brilliantly maps onto and takes hold of human desires through the commodification of vegetal life. As Todd McGowan writes, "capitalist accumulation envisions obtaining the object that would provide the ultimate satisfaction for the desiring subject, the object that would quench the subject's desire and allow it to put an end to the relentless yearning to accumulate."[40]

Because the subject discovers over and over again that no such commodity exists, capitalism itself is propelled ever forward. Whereas McGowan centers his discussion on the pernicious capacity of capitalism to tap into the psyche's desires, we can also observe these phenomena in how desirous collectors seek out new species for collections.

"It's quite interesting to look at the intentions of describing authorities in naming things," the Dutch collector tells me one day while out searching in the field for more *Uebelmannia* as we discussed the legacies of Buining, Horst, and Uebelmann. He continued:

Once a plant has a formal description, it stands that later on another scientist might come along and say it actually falls in another [species] complex. So it may be described then as a synonym. The pendulum swings back and forth between having very broad definitions of species to really narrow species concepts. . . . As there is no formally written down definition of a species, it comes down to the identifier's opinion. But then as more species are described, you start to notice commonalities between them.

Not one to shy away from provocation, he then added knowingly, "But you have to question the naming and motivation for
identifying *difference*." The collector was gesturing to these more
explicit practices of producing profit from naming novel species
by tapping into collector desires for the "missing object" in a collector's series of plants (e.g., an example of every species of a genus) that might provide the satisfaction I described earlier. As a
Czech botanist later explained to me, "there are some people who
put new names [on species]; if you have a new name in a catalog,
it's a best seller, and the personal motive to have your name on a
new species [is there]. So those are private interests, to be famous,
to be rich." Such stories of entrepreneurial cactus enthusiasts like
Buining, Uebelmann, and Horst profiting from the "discovery" of
new species that in time are discredited or reshuffled by botanists
are common.[41] But differences have also emerged between communities of scientists working on different taxonomic groups in
how species are understood, as an evolutionary ecologist with the
Smithsonian Natural History Museum explained to me: "So the
taxonomists working on orchids have completely different species
concepts than those working on cacti, and everybody knows orchid
taxonomists are the minute-est little splitters; that is why there
are twenty-five thousand species of orchids." Or as another botanist put it, "the species concept doesn't always work so well for
many plants in terms of what matters for conservation. As a botanist, the species concept doesn't work very well in general, and it
doesn't work well for many cacti." Such practices are also found in
communities not interested in profiting from succulent life or scientific reputation but that seek out their protection through law. A
botanist noted that plants are formally recognized and protected
by endangered species legislation only at the species level in Brazil
(like most countries), so identification of unique forms or subspecies means nothing in the context of enforcement and legal protections. "I would name a new species even if I really knew it was just

a subspecies or form," he explained. "I would do it if it meant a type of plant in need of protection would receive it."

Desire stitches together urges to know and possess and profit from vegetal life. But in all these instances, desires are articulated and manifested through species as knowable entities that take on greater meaning than the lives that preceded being named as such. The production of species through taxonomy not only maps so well onto capitalist orderings of life because Linnean taxonomy renders living organisms into hierarchically arranged, classifiable, and discrete categories but because it produces opportunities to render life-forms as novel commodities, a flourishing of objects onto which desires might "hook" wherever they can.[42]

A Dialectic of Preservationist Urges

After our group left the single *U. buiningii* where it belonged (as I describe at the beginning of the chapter), we piled into our two SUVs to hunt for other possible localities. Conversations about *U. buiningii* and the work of conservation turned to a discussion of the merit of ex situ conservation, what it would mean to "save" *U. buiningii* by taking it out of habitat, and the possible role of collectors as conservationists in this regard. Ex situ conservation is the idea that there is a role for conserving species not in their natural habitats (in situ) but elsewhere, such as in zoos, seedbanks, and botanical gardens. "Every now and then, I consider my greenhouse a zoo for plants," the Belgian collector said. He joked that I would want to write that down, which, of course, I did. "It is an interesting way to think about a collection," I clarified, gesturing to the idea that private collections might serve a conservation value. Ex situ conservationist-collectors are perhaps the newest breed of cactus and succulent collectors. In the first issue of an online hobby journal called the *Cactus Explorer,* this sect of the collector community is described as "those who look upon their collection not only as a scientific resource but also as a microcosm of nature that is under their personal protection . . . and look upon their collection as a remote extension of habitat."[43] I asked the Belgian collector if he had any *U. buiningii* specimens in collection, but he didn't. The younger British collector asked him if it was readily available to purchase in Europe. "It's not difficult at all to get for a collection," he replied, "but it's very difficult to keep alive!"

U. buiningii, like most of the species in the *Uebelmannia* genus, is notoriously hard to keep alive in greenhouses in northern Europe, and the notion that private collectors' greenhouses might serve a legitimate ex situ conservation value for cacti is contested.[44] Most botanists I interviewed were skeptical of the idea that hobbyists' collections could provide meaningful conservation value and said the effort it would take to maintain collections of sufficient quality for this purpose would be too great for most private collectors. As a world-leading cactus botanist, sitting in his office at the National Autonomous University of Mexico, explained to me about six months earlier, "I think a very important part [to these discussions] is the theoretical basis . . . [for] the word *conservation*. What do I understand by *conservation* as a biologist here in this country, sitting here? And what does a collector in some city in England understand by *conservation*? For me, conservation is not having a collection of ten plants; for me, conservation is an interaction between environment, plants, and animals. For me, that is conservation. For me, real, effective conservation takes place in the original environment, in the original site of the species, or else off-site in an academic and formal program of maintaining a collection of plants, with appropriate genetic diversity, because otherwise I don't conserve anything. For me, the person in England who has a collection of Cactaceae, all he is doing is keeping a clone, but he is not keeping the diversity of the species, and that is what I want."

The reason for putting in such effort to maintain ex situ collections, at least in theory, is based on the idea that if a species were eventually to go extinct or become endangered, it could later be repopulated. This presumes that whatever sort of pressure drove it to extinction in the first place has been stopped or reversed. Successful examples do exist but typically involve closely regulated and controlled propagation with botanical researchers and a dedicated commercial nursery operation.[45] Extending ex situ conservation efforts to become more inclusive of a distributed array of private collections would be a much more speculative effort. Ideas of ex situ private collections and preventing species extinctions are also not necessarily ideas that share similar temporalities. The maintenance of a personal collection against the long arc of extinction time is a study in contrasts. Regardless of the possibilities of enthusiastic cactus and succulent collectors to assist in the conservation of plants, it was clear that this was not going to be a long-term, viable option for a plant like *U. buiningii*.

More interesting, I think, is what motivates collectors to "grow plants at a rate that simulates that in nature, and look upon their collection as a remote extension of habitat," as Mottram describes of ex situ conservationist-collectors.[46] No longer desiring to grow plants that are perfectly shaped, watered, and nurtured in plastic pots, the "conservation grower" as a collector archetype often overlaps with growers who seek to simulate "natural" growth patterns, shapes, and qualities within the greenhouse. This can include, among other things, growing cacti on substrates that mimic the landscapes from which species originate, such as a pockmarked slab of limestone or gypsum sand. (These can turn into truly stunning displays of cascading, self-propagating plants; see Figure 28 in chapter 3.) As if possession of the species were not enough, we see in this interest in "hard growing" plants or replicating cactus landscapes in miniature a preservationist mind-set at work in the microcosm of the greenhouse. A desire to possess what the collector sees as already lost—flourishing ecologies in the world—is reproduced within the confines of the private space of the collector's

greenhouse. Cacti are imbued with greater meaning through significations of absence elsewhere.

Our last destination for the day was a location that our guide said,
based on satellite imagery, might represent a suitable habitat for
U. buiningii but was one he had never visited. After arriving at the
location, we searched for about an hour for signs of *U. buiningii* under an intense afternoon sun. Despite the presence of companion
plants and quartzite, it appeared we would turn up empty-handed.
It felt strange to think of the near-overwhelming elation I felt earlier in the day in finding the one lonely *U. buiningii* now standing
amid its absence in this new locality.

Then a member of the group gave a shout and said he spotted
one, a very small *U. buiningii* with a brilliant, deep reddish color. As
we gathered around to see it, our guide quickly spotted four nearby.
They were much smaller than the plant I had found earlier in the
day, but our guide said this was the size of cacti he expected to see
at the other location, indicating that the cactus I found earlier was
in the later stages of its life. He also said it might be a different
"form" of the species. He showed me how this location's population
had more pronounced ribs than the plant at the other site, something it took me some time to notice even after he pointed out the
differences. This was a new population that wasn't yet recorded by
collectors or scientists as far as our guide was aware. We eventually
found thirty to forty small plants, many almost completely embedded within the quartz sand. "They are a small and hidden plant,"
our guide mused to himself as we inspected the ground. That there
could be so many more just hiding beneath the surface was a wel-
come thought.

As we prepared to leave, I asked our guide if he was going to take
a specimen of this population to send to an herbarium, to formally
record the presence of the new locality. "I think it is best if we leave
it unknown for its conservation," he replied. In the complicated

business of saving species, that leaving these plants unregistered represented doing conservation work to the botanist was a matter of cold pragmatism. Avid collectors are also often dogged researchers; if the locality were registered in a database with geographic data, the locality could become vulnerable. But without being registered, the population will likely not be monitored (formally, at least), or considered in future species assessments, to say nothing of being excluded from scientific research. This liminal status, known yet unknown, presents an interesting case of an effort to care for a species. In displacing this local population of *U. buiningii* from the realm of scientific concern, the guide saw his intentional exclusion as an act of care.

Penetrating to the Depths of Desire

Cacti, as living beings, coproduce affective experiences with passionate collectors through moments of encounter as well as through the extended work of care. But the production of desire is restricted not only to matters of emergent relations between people and plants but also to epistemic ways of knowing species that are structured through processes of scientific knowledge creation. These processes are also not separated from capitalist practices of commodification and the territorial boundaries of the state. In the world of succulent collection, the production of desire emerges as a set of interrelated processes linking political economy, the unconscious, and knowledge production, drawing close relations between our unconscious and conscious selves and a wider ecological web of life.

Despite the many revelations to be found in seeking out a "small and hidden plant," my conceptualizing of the production of desire remains incomplete. Although existing literature on collecting cultures in the European tradition and psychological studies of collecting behavior have informed my analysis of cactus collecting cultures so far, neither literature speaks to the important ways the liveliness of plants incites collector desires and in turn mediates trajectories of cactus flourishing or diminution. This leads me to approach the cactus hunters (in their many forms on either side of the law) as the central subjects of this book, in concert with the succulents that send them "hunting" in the world on a path laid out by desire. As a tethering of human and vegetal life, this conjoined succulent subject speaks to the relations as well as the distances emergent between people and plants through the unconscious, connecting the interiorities and exteriorities of our entangled inner and outer worlds.[47] Through the lens of a political ecology of desire, the succulent subject comes into focus through attention to the entwinement of the psyche in the world or the extimacy of psychic relations. Desire is what brings these knotted connections into relation through expressions of the unconscious in the world, the emplacement of the void that constitutes our being as both within and alien to us, and what moves the collector to imagine how certain coveted plants might lead to a deeper kind of satisfaction. And, as we will see in the next chapter, history also has a part to play in shaping these succulent desires.

\\3//

Between the Iron Curtain and the Glass House

It's said these rogue cactus-fanciers are capable of anything.

—Karel Čapek, *The Stolen Cactus*

What enjoyment a man has in his lifetime! But most of them carry with them a pain, a bad memory, a bad consequence. Only nature can give man pure, unadulterated pleasure.

—Alberto Vojtěch Frič, *About Cacti and Their Narcotic Effects*

I woke up on one of the first frosty mornings of fall 2018 in an old farmhouse in rural Czechia, where I was greeted in the kitchen downstairs by an elderly woman plying me with a shot of slivovitz before breakfast. Fortification against the cold, she explained. I spent the night on a whirlwind tour of some of Central Europe's greatest private collections of cactus and succulent plants with one of the more highly regarded—and, depending on whom you ask, notorious—cactus and succulent growers and distributors anywhere. In the coming days, I would meet some of the most skilled cultivators of cacti in the world and their equally impressive

Figure 20. Cacti in collection embody lives past while continuing to grow into the present, forging new forms of human–plant bonds along the way. Seen here is a noteworthy collection of mature cacti in Czechia with a large grouping of Brazilian cacti in the *Uebelmannia* genus in the foreground.

collections of plants (Figure 20). I would also encounter many plants that—legally speaking—I should not have.

Where chapter 2 introduced how desire and the illicit entwine through collection and practices of categorizing plants, this chapter takes a historical turn to recognize that desire does not exist out of time and space. In short, as Joan Copjec summarizes, "psychoanalysis requires history; it can begin only by gathering the facts."[1] In this chapter, we turn to some historical "facts" to understand how history and place have shaped the contemporary political economy and geographical distribution of the illegal cactus and succulent trade. I begin by sketching out the history of Czech cactophilia through the pivotal figure of Alberto Vojtěch Frič, an iconic botanist working at the beginning of the twentieth century. I also place him within a wider view of Czech antiestablishment tendencies, colonial anxieties, and Western fantasies through the work of German cowboy western novelist Karl May, as well as Jaroslav Hašek's bumbling and chaotic character of the Good Soldier Švejk. Putting these diverse historical and literary sources into conversation with interviews and time spent with Czech collectors, on one hand—including a real-life succulent "Švejk"—and Mexican and Czech CITES bureaucrats, on the other, I develop an argument about what I call *Robin Hood conservation.* Robin Hood conservation, as a moral narrative and modus operandi for succulent smugglers, serves to justify illegal acquisition of cactus and succulent material as a practical response to the threat of extinction resulting from collector demand and collection as a pragmatic act of more-than-human care. Robin Hood, the legendary hero of English folklore who robs from the rich to give to the poor, is a helpful archetype for exploring how collectors and actors operating within illicit succulent economies and gray markets negotiate and justify their engagement with illicit and illegal behavior and what constitutes ethical collecting conduct. Robin Hood conservation is a helpful discourse for critiquing how collector desires can profoundly shape global ecologies and, at the same time, reassert uneven and exploitative relations that subvert the moral authority of the Robin Hood archetype. The chapter concludes with a discussion of the ambiguous but vital role of gray markets in enabling contemporary collector practices to persist while highlighting their unsteady ethical terrain. Ultimately, the story of Czech cactus and succulent collecting pushes us to probe more deeply into the ethics of desire.

The Cactus Hunter

In 1901, and at just eighteen years old, Vojtěch Frič set off for southern Brazil in search of cacti. Frič was the son of a respected Prague family whose extended relations included prominent Czech revolutionaries, politicians, and intellectuals. From a young age, Frič showed a penchant for botany and other natural history subjects. His first cactus was an *Echinopsis eyriesii,* a species from southern Brazil, Uruguay, and central Argentina, the region of South America where he would soon spend most of the next decade. The species is well loved by collectors for the enormous white blooms it produces, much larger than the cactus itself, which protrude from an unusually long flower stalk (peduncle). As Frič wrote of his first encounter with this cactus, after caring for it for some time, he noted his cactus was soon putting out buds. After watering the plant, a few days later, three "beautiful," "glossy white" flowers emerged. His description of this moment of cactus enchantment through the emergence of the flower closely mirrors that of the retired coal miner from chapter 1, who also has a penchant for *Echinopsis.* Frič was struck by how such a "shapeless, unsightly plant" could produce "a beauty I had not yet known in nature." He describes in his writing sitting with the cactus for several days, until the flowers finally withered. "I observed the stamens, watched the flies and bees transfer pollen from the pistil to the stigma, and observed a change in myself. I had become a cactus grower, although I did not realize it at the time" (Figure 21).[2]

Within a short time, Frič became well known for his collection of cacti, which grew rapidly. At age sixteen, he won the silver medal in a Prague horticultural exhibition for his display of three hundred cacti.[3] A year later, in winter 1900, when Frič was seventeen, and just before his high school graduation, his entire collection of cacti froze during a severe frost. This gave him the idea to mount a botanical expedition to search for cacti in Brazil.[4] That such a loss would precipitate his desire to travel far from his home speaks to the powerful fascination these plants held for the young Frič. And, as is so often the case, it was lack that set this desire in motion.

For a year, Frič traveled through difficult terrain, endured repeated fevers and bouts of tropical disease, and purportedly, armed

Figure 21. "The cactus hunter." Alberto Vojtěch Frič with a very old *Cephalocereus senilis* cactus at home in Prague in 1924. Photographer unknown. Photograph used with permission of the heirs of A. V. Frič, archive of A. V. Frič, Praha, CR.

with only a small hunting knife, fought off a jaguar.[5] Inspired by the likes of Alexander von Humboldt, his interests were initially focused on cacti, but once in Brazil, they shifted toward people and ethnography.[6] "I arrived to the conclusion that it is more important to study the life of free human tribes than plants and insects, as these peoples would soon die out, while the rest will remain," Frič wrote.[7] Much like his penchant for cacti, Frič's newly discovered passion for ethnography emerged out of a perceived threat of loss, the erasure of life occurring before his eyes through the ongoing genocide and violence committed by European settlers against the Indigenous peoples of southern Brazil and Paraguay.

Frič was pragmatic when it came to monetizing his exploits to continue his ethnographic research. The collection of plants supported Frič's expeditions as he sold them to dealers back in Europe, such as the famous Belgian de Laet commercial nursery, which hungrily bought up whatever plants and seeds he could send it. But back at home, Frič became most famous for his public lectures on the Indigenous tribes of Paraguay and Brazil he studied, presenting their cultural artifacts and ceremonial objects to rapt audiences while recounting tales of his adventures. Frič's reputation in the Czechoslovak Republic was much greater than in neighboring Germany, a country to which he had close ties on account of fulfilling orders for German museums anxious to amass ever-larger collections of cultural objects from tribes they expected would soon disappear. The irony of what this anxiety over Indigenous genocide incited—a desire to possess, covet, and collect material culture, a desire to further dismantle the very thing museums and ethnologists expressed anxiety over losing—should not be lost on us. Yet it still pales in comparison to the even greater, bitter irony that it was the German colonists of southern Brazil and Paraguay themselves, among other European colonists, who were responsible for this ongoing Indigenous genocide in the first place.[8] Materials collected by Frič are found to this day in some of the world's most prestigious museums, including the Smithsonian National Museum of the American Indian in Washington, D.C., and the Ethnological Museum in Berlin.

As an amateur, Frič was already an outsider in elite European academic circles, but he soon became a pariah on account of his politics. Frič was outspoken in condemning violence perpetrated by German colonists in southern Brazil, to the great rancor of German colonists, European institutions on whose behalf he collected, and the leading intellectual figures of German ethnology. In 1908, at the sixteenth International Congress of Americanists in Vienna, Frič was publicly criticized by German scholars and politicians alike for his condemnation of the lack of action to safeguard Brazil's Indigenous populations against what he described as the brutal and premeditated efforts of colonists to destroy Indigenous tribes entirely.[9]

Frič passionately described German settler colonists using all manner of tactics, ranging from biological warfare in the form of smallpox to the hiring of *bugreiros* (professional Indian hunters) to the murder, rape, and enslavement of Indigenous populations.[10] These atrocities were primarily motivated by settler colonists wishing to dispossess Indigenous peoples of their land to make way for farms, ranches, and other industries. Frič demanded that his colleagues formally and forcefully condemn these acts, but they did not. As a result of his formal rebukes, Frič was marked as a "Czech nationalist," a threat to German superiority and its power abroad.

Although Frič greatly sympathized with the plight of Indigenous peoples of South America, his activities still served to elevate Czech aspirations toward their own, "softer" colonial fantasies, enacted through less overt or physically violent means.[11] Frič, like other Czechs, sought to raise Czech standing in the world through exploration, scientific learning, and the collection of cultural artifacts. From a contemporary perspective, as historian H. Glenn Penny writes, Frič embodied the ethos of what is understood today as "salvage anthropology," what Samuel Redman calls the "desire to 'salvage' information about human societies that were thought to be disappearing from the earth." Salvage anthropology became a major project of ethnological museums and anthropology as a whole from the mid-nineteenth through the early twentieth centuries.[12] Anthropologists worked in a veritable frenzy on behalf of museums to collect and hoard as many cultural artifacts, songs, customs, photographs, and stories of these vanishing societies as they could, while rarely reflecting on their enrollment in the very project of colonialism as a cause of this incalculable loss of human life and culture. "The great irony in the case of Alberto Vojtěch Frič," Penny writes, "[is that this] controversial adventurer did more for the plight of Brazilian Indians than the combined efforts of all the professional ethnologists who frequented Brazil around the turn of the century."[13]

Figure 22. Alberto Vojtěch Frič, in 1942, two years prior to his death, with some of his cactus collection at his home in Prague. Photograph used with permission of the heirs of A. V. Frič, archive of A. V. Frič, Praha, CR.

Frič remains more widely known today in academic circles for his role as an amateur ethnographer than for his botany.[14] But beyond the academy, Frič is most revered and celebrated by today's Czech and Slovakian cactus and succulent collectors. "Frič was central to showing people it was possible to grow cacti here. He popularized cacti here in the Czech Republic. He connected plants with stories and nature," a leading figure in the Společnost Českých a Slovenských Pěstitelů Kaktusů a Sukulentů (Society of Czech and

Slovak Cactus and Succulent Growers; SČSPKS) would tell me. In his lifetime, Frič would describe more than two hundred species or varieties of cacti, but most of these species were later discredited due to his unscientific method of description. Frič also kept vague records of the exact locality of many of the species he would describe, afraid that other cactus collectors would find them and destroy their populations. Still, today, at least seven cacti species bear Frič's name (as species name *fricii*) in his honor. Throughout his various occupational turns, Frič maintained a cactus greenhouse in Prague at his family's home (Figure 22). This greenhouse full of cacti from Brazil, Argentina, Paraguay, and Mexico would perish only shortly before Frič. His collection of a reported forty thousand cacti in Prague—argued to be the largest in Europe—froze to death in September 1939, after the Nazi invasion of Czechoslovakia that year, when he was unable to procure enough fuel to heat his greenhouses. In November 1944, Frič scratched himself on a rusty nail while tending to his backyard rabbits. He contracted tetanus and died shortly thereafter on December 4, 1944, at the age of sixty-two.

Chasing Cowboy Fantasies and Western Desires

Frič remains just as admired today by cactus collectors as a daring Czech explorer as for his specific contributions to botany. It is impossible to conjure the character of the Czech cactus smuggler today without understanding the self-image of the collector mirrored through the legacy of Frič. Frič's legacy places demands on the collector to seek adventure, face danger, and endure hardships in search of "undiscovered" species and "seeing plants in habitat." The memory of Frič asserts the desire to imprint a Czech legacy within foreign landscapes, as much today marked by naming Mexican cactus species in Frič's honor as by engaging in activities that are seen to model those of his own life. The highest honor paid today

Figure 23. Inside a Czech greenhouse, featuring the flags of Mexico *(left)* and the United States *(right)*. In between these flags on the back wall is a plaque featuring the face of a young Alberto Vojtěch Frič *(middle right)* as well as a souvenir plaque from Jujuy, Argentina, featuring a dancer in ceremonial dress on top of a cactus.

to a member of the SČSPKS is the Golden Alberto, a gold-plated ceramic plaque of Frič. His profile also adorns the greenhouses of many of the most devoted growers (Figure 23).

Frič did not discover a passion for cacti outside his own social milieu. Undoubtedly, Frič's uncle, the curator of natural history collections of the Prague National Museum, left his own mark on Frič, just as stories of the "Wild West" during Frič's childhood became especially popular among Czech and German children at the turn of the century, especially through the adventure novels of the German writer Karl May. May's fictional characters of Old Shatterhand, a German immigrant of lowly upbringing turned western gunslinger, and his "blood brother" Winnetou, an Apache American

Indian chief, are prominent across his novels. Old Shatterhand was portrayed as a friend to American Indians and the heroic protagonist, while Winnetou was his constant companion and brother in arms, a trope reproduced repeatedly in the cowboy western genre. Despite hardly being known to the English-speaking world, May's cowboy western novels profoundly influenced generations of German, Czech, and other Central European children and adults. His writing has instilled long-held fantasies of the American West in May's readers, as well as fantasies about, and a sense of imagined allyship with, the Indigenous peoples of the Americas.[15] Despite building a legendary career in his own lifetime on the stories of Old Shatterhand and Winnetou in the fight of good versus evil, May never visited the American West—though he claimed otherwise—and only visited the United States four years prior to his death.[16]

During his traveling exhibitions, Frič drew indirectly on imagery from May's books and characters in his advertisements to draw in paying crowds, as Markéta Křížová argues.[17] This was most explicit in Frič's yearlong 1908 tour accompanied by Cherwish Mendoza, a member of the Chacamoco (Isher) tribe from what is today northern Paraguay. The justification for bringing Cherwish (referred to by his first name in Frič's writings) to Europe was to diagnose and treat him for what would eventually be identified and successfully treated as hookworm.[18] But Frič also took Cherwish on a national tour, where Cherwish would perform songs and dances to paying audiences for the material benefit of both Cherwish and Frič.[19] Frič leaves us with a complicated history in relation to his place within anthropology, especially in contemporary contexts—at once rebellious and outspoken against colonial violence and variously naive and possibly exploitative.[20] Yet his place within the history of Czech cactus collection remains unsurpassed, reproduced today as emblematic of the Czech spirit of "discovery" and adventure in the name of botanical acquisition and knowledge. Dreams of a Wild West and the competing fantasies of an

Figure 24. Studio portraits of Alberto Vojtěch Frič (*left*, 1901 or 1902 in Prague) and Karl May (*right*, 1896). The photo of Frič was taken either prior to or shortly after his first trip to Brazil. Although he never saw the lands where dozens of his novels were based, May was often seen dressing as his fictional character Old Shatterhand, complete with a fringed leather frock and bear-tooth necklace. Photograph of Frič used with permission of the heirs of A. V. Frič, archive of A. V. Frič, Praha, CR. Photograph of May courtesy of the Karl May Museum.

imagined allyship with oppressed Native Americans alongside assertions of cultural supremacy over others structured Czech ideas of the Americas and its botany, in no small way thanks to the likes of celebrities like Frič and May (Figure 24).[21] But alongside these fantasies of a wilder country across the Atlantic, another literary source has a role to play in telling us something about the nature of specifically *illicit* Czech cactus desires, and his name is Švejk.

The Genius of Idiocy

Jaroslav Hašek is one of the most famous Czech authors of the twentieth century. Friend to Frič, he is best known today for his book and titular character *The Good Soldier Švejk.*[22] *Švejk* is a riotous, vicious satire of World War I and power-hungry men, based on Hašek's own experiences in the war. Hašek was an anarchist, bohemian, mischief maker, and heavy drinker, the latter trait leading to his early death.[23] In the (now) great tradition of Czech satirists like his contemporary Karel Čapek and, in time, Bohumil Hrabal, Hašek helped to establish a Czech literary style whose skepticism and cynicism toward power, the state, and foreign aggressors were modeled as much in language as in content. Power and well-laid plans for conquest and domination are thwarted time and again by what appears as the blinding idiocy and bumbling chaos of Švejk.

Švejkism is nearly as instructive as Frič's legacy for understanding the culture of contemporary Czech cactus collecting. Josef Švejk, Benjamin Ziemann writes, "can be and has to be read as a synecdoche of Czech national identity and of the Czech's attempts to grapple with issues of foreign hegemony and national liberation in the twentieth century."[24] In *The Good Soldier Švejk,* one is never certain whether Švejk is in fact an idiot or a cunning trickster, a question that plagues the military authorities who continuously find themselves interrogating Švejk. Is he a spy? An antiwar activist? Or just wildly (and, for readers, hilariously) incompetent? Such is the brilliance of Švejk; he cheats and lies and steals, and one is always left wondering to what end or purpose. As the late anthropologist F. G. Bailey wrote, describing what has become known as *Švejkism,* "the Švejks, lying, cheating, stealing, sabotaging the collective interest and—even worse—doing it apparently for their own advantage, may nevertheless be admired and, like Švejk himself, may become minor folk heroes."[25]

Anthropologists, sociologists, and even psychiatrists have turned to Švejk as a source of insight on topics ranging from "weak" forms of organizational resistance to psychiatric malingering.[26] To this end, *Švejkism* is a recognized term across several academic fields. To sources of power, Švejk is a cheating scoundrel and menace to authority; to his adherents, Švejk turns incompetence into a debilitating force wielded against institutions of power. As an archetype, Švejks are often beloved, with an aura of Robin Hood morality about them.[27] Švejk finds purchase as a chaotic disruptor of social norms and expectations while upholding a determined, if complicated, set of ethical principles that disregard more publicly acceptable, liberal-democratic forms of challenging authority. As Bailey wrote, "Švejkism always involves a conflict of moralities, a potential argument about where duty lies."[28] Journeying into the fantasies of May's western landscapes, Frič and Švejk serve us well in weaving together the story of a modern-day Czech cactus smuggler who, depending on whom you ask, is either a real-life botanical Robin Hood, a clever thief and trickster, or a black market cactus kingpin.

Meeting "the Czechs"

I first met the man I would come to think of as "Švejk" at what might be the world's largest cactus and succulent expo. After an overnight ferry from the United Kingdom, I spent the next two days in an otherwise quiet Belgian seaside resort town marveling at tens if not hundreds of thousands of cactus and succulent plants for sale by specialist vendors. The exhibition is not only a massive plant sale but an important site for exchange and reunion and includes a full weekend of lectures by notable members of the hobbyist community, botanists, and botanical photographers.

"If you go, go to the parking lot. Most of the illegal transactions are made in the parking lot," a leading Mexican conservationist and former Mexican CITES representative instructed me about nine months earlier in Mexico City. This was made evident within moments of my arrival in Belgium. As I approached the expo with a few other members of the Sheffield branch of the BCCS, a grower I'd met earlier in the year in the United Kingdom came bounding toward us with a huge grin on his face, carrying a large cardboard box with a variety of mature cacti of suspicious origin he had just purchased from the back of a minivan in the car park. The show had just barely opened, but trading in the parking lot was well under way.

Czech collectors have achieved a notorious status among North and South American conservation agencies concerned with illegal trade in cactus and succulent plants. Within Mexico, Czech collectors are arguably the most infamous for engaging in illegal trade, followed by German, Dutch, Belgian, British, American, and Japanese collectors, the Mexican CITES expert who first suggested I attend the convention explained to me. When she was previously working with Mexico's environmental law enforcement agency, Procuraduría Federal de Protección al Ambiente (PROFEPA), she explained, "We detained several Czech citizens . . . oh *boy,* they are professional." She laughed as she said this, shaking her head. "It's not [organized crime] like rosewood . . . but let me tell you, if we are strict in the definition . . . they are organizing to come and knowledgeably perform an illegal activity—that, honey, is an *organized crime.*"[29]

In nearly every interview I conducted with representatives from environmental management, scientific, and enforcement agencies responsible for implementing CITES in Mexico, Czech collectors surfaced as a vexing source of consternation and frustration. "It passes from generation to generation. . . . A lot of Czechs keep coming," a representative of Mexico's scientific authority to CITES, CONABIO, explained to me in February 2018 at its offices in Mexico City. She continued, "A researcher at the University in Chapingo was telling me that for every Mexican researcher that is in field, there are twenty Czechs! It has been one of the toughest things that when a species has *just* been described, and soon after it is already being sold by the Czechs or the Germans."

To meet "the Czechs," once at the expo in Belgium, I turned to a trusted gatekeeper, a highly respected "bridge" figure in the international cactus and succulent community with feet firmly planted in both the formal conservation arena and legal commercial trade. Later that evening, I entered the bar at the expo to meet him. It was crowded, filled with cactophiles from across Europe and even farther afield, catching up with old friends and regaling each other with stories from expeditions past. Over the din of laughter and clinking glasses, we spoke about the problems and challenges of CITES and international trade. After an hour, and seemingly satisfied with the seriousness of my research, he told me who to ask for at the expo the next day.

The next morning, I approached the booth operated by "Švejk." I noticed a large quantity of very rare but seed-grown *Turbinicarpus nikolae,* a species described only in 2015, for sale for ten euros. They were about two centimeters in diameter and on their own roots in loose containers of potting mixture. I looked up at the big sign in the expo tent that proclaimed all sales at the expo must comply with CITES rules and regulations. All *Turbinocarpus* species are Appendix I plants. While it is true that CITES-registered nurseries are permitted to trade in artificially propagated CITES Appendix I–listed plants (there are only four such registered nurseries in the Czech Republic, and this was not one of them), Mexico has never given an export permit for the species, meaning in principle that there are no legally available *T. nikolae* plants in Europe. The plants before me were not the only plants for sale at the expo that seemed to fly in the face of the advertised prohibitions against breaking CITES regulations. But, as the vendors were selling plants to others within the European Union (EU)—and therefore not engaging in direct international trade (the EU is a Party to CITES, so trade between EU member countries does not require CITES permits)—a sufficient-enough gray area leaves wiggle room for organizers to ignore it. Even more suspicious to my eye were the assembly of mature cacti that a few vendors had sitting below their booths behind tablecloths. Signs of a life led outside, including insect and disease damage, bleaching from sun exposure, and corking—when the base of plants lignify, or turn "woody"—were indicators that these may not be exclusively cultivated specimens. At this expo, at least, selling "under the table" was taken literally.

About a month later, I was in a small car racing through the Czech countryside with Švejk and Jan, his occasional assistant and also friend.[30] Jan is a longtime cactus enthusiast and lecturer at a university in Prague. Crucially, Jan also agreed to serve as a professional translator during my time in Czechia. Over the course of a couple weeks and in between visits with expert cactus collectors in Czechia, we had long conversations in the car about the politics of cactus and succulent conservation, CITES, international trade, and what it meant to be an ethical collector. On our first leg of this marathon trip, I started my questions where I often did with collectors, by asking Švejk how he first became acquainted with cacti. "I was in kindergarten, six years old. It was an *Echinopsis* hybrid, it was on my mom's window," he said. I asked him if it was a gift from his mother, as this was a common enough origin story among male cactus collectors. "It was my mother's cactus, but I . . . confiscated it," he replied, laughing as he drove. I couldn't help but note the mischievous parallels to how Frič also obtained his first *Echinopsis* cactus in an illicitly tinged plot.[31]

Švejk's love for cacti was nearly immediate. "I was interested in the shapes, the beauty, but also I read the Karl May adventure books, and these adventures were connected with this place, the West." A stubborn trickster with a track record for performing hoaxes (*mystifikace*), Švejk was frequently reprimanded by authority figures and written off by his teachers. He became a member of the local cactus club at just eleven or twelve, which meant his father, who was not particularly interested in cacti, had to join the club on his behalf. "When I was ten or eleven, I got a small greenhouse on my balcony. It was four meters square, which is already big enough, but then when I was thirteen, I started to build a greenhouse with my father. It took about a year, and it was done when I was fourteen. This was the same time when I started to read the book by Frič about cacti, and I got the feeling I had to travel.

"Mexico was the dream, and then within two years, the revolution happened, but in the meantime, I had army service. One time a soldier screamed at me, 'Once you get to the army we will beat the Švejk out of you!' And I looked like Švejk too!" he laughed. But unlike the real Švejk, who failed to malinger his way out of army service in World War I, this Švejk was more successful. "I've always had problems with authority. I knew I couldn't go into the army. I got a doctor's help." A false medical evaluation and fictive spine condition ensured that Švejk dodged army service. During these years, Švejk's reputation in the cactus community grew. "I had a kind of graphic, or photographic memory, and I was enthusiastic, I became an encyclopedia of cacti. So people started to call me 'Little Frič,'" he said. Like Frič, Švejk's passion and talent for cactus collection emerged within the social context of his times: Czechoslovakia following the 1968 occupation by the Soviet Union. This period served as a crucible not only for the future emergence of an independent Czech Republic (now referred to as Czechia) but for the Czechoslovak cactus and succulent collecting community. This collectively traumatic period of isolation and repression would orient and amplify collecting desires and Švejk's own emergence as a world-class grower, propagator, and, eventually, succulent smuggler.

Encasing Desire

While Frič ensured that the cactus became a fixture of the Czech imagination, Soviet-era communism ensured that the desire for rare and newly described cactus and succulent plants only intensified behind the Iron Curtain. "The greenhouse was another world, a space from communism, an escape into private life," an older Czech collector explained over beers outside his backyard greenhouse. As Czechoslovak collectors struggled to obtain new plant material from abroad, the Iron Curtain had the surprising and unintended consequence of amplifying collector skills. Consequently, Czechoslovak collectors following World War II would ascend in a matter of decades to the pinnacle of cactus collecting lore (Figure 25).

"The effect of communism on the cactus community was [actually] positive," a leading Czech collector summarized with a chuckle. "People literally wanted to get away from the regime, people worked to internally escape the regime, so they dedicated time to their hobbies, not only cacti but other hobbies, private activities, to keep some . . . space." As another collector described, linking plants with the West more directly, "the cactus represented an exotic country, it was a substitute. People were bound to home and unable to travel. There was a very romantic imagination about these exotic countries."

There is an important legacy left by May among other cultural purveyors of the Wild West and the exotic Americas as a place of democratic freedom rendered in place which imprinted on the Czech imagination. "During communism, people romanticized the desert in the Southwest," another collector said. These imagined landscapes were imbued with new and varying significations during different periods of Czechoslovak history, including the Soviet occupation of Czechoslovakia.[32] Especially under Soviet occupation, Czech interest in (and imagined allyship with) the Indigenous peoples of the Americas, romanticized ideals of primitivism,

Figure 25. Various cacti in a cold frame for storage during the winter in the Czechia. These cacti will be moved outside (while kept sheltered) during the summer months.

and the freedom indexed by time spent outdoors (with their attendant ecologies) is best evidenced by the unique history of Czech "tramping" culture.[33] A subculture grew around tramping as a form of camping, including participants producing DIY "western wear."[34] Campsites were erected—sometimes featuring log cabins, other times teepees—with secret names, and affiliations to camps were designated in the use of covert flags and patches.

During more intense periods of Soviet repression, tramping also served as an important space of antiestablishment expression, particularly in the 1950s and then again following the invasion of the Soviet Union in 1968. Tramping affected both Czech place-making practices and articulations of an imagined American wilderness and Wild West, as well as deeply shaping Czech music and cultures of camping and how spending time outdoors is enjoyed.[35] Tramping culture did not have explicit affiliations with cactus and succulent collecting, but many of the older collectors I met during my time in Czechia recounted the importance of tramping for them as "a space away from communism" that mirrored how they spoke about the greenhouse and their collections of New World plants. Both tramping and the greenhouse also spoke to a desire for an imagined "private life" of the kind many living within Soviet-era communism imagined Americans to enjoy under Western capitalism. The fantasy of an enclosed private life (thus also demanding the need to purchase more things to fill one's "personal castle") under Western capitalism is one with great staying power, despite profound evidence that subjects in the capitalist state today have less privacy than ever before.[36]

The cactus and succulent collecting hobby blossomed within Czechoslovakia, though formal cactus clubs were disbanded and subsumed within the larger, state-sanctioned union of gardeners, adding an illicit edge to the hobby and the plants themselves. Acquiring new plant material became especially challenging for collectors, forcing them to increase knowledge and skill of seed germination and plant propagation techniques. "Eastern Germany was the good source," one collector explained. "Western German growers . . . could travel, so Czechs and East Germans got material from the West in late communism [after 1968]. My father was a diplomat, so he could go to West Germany, and that was how he was able to see many collections, and he could buy seeds in East Berlin."

Throughout the twentieth century, many new species of cacti were described. One of the challenges for Czech collectors was not just access to these new species but how to share and spread the material around. Perfecting the arts of grafting and seed germination became essential to successfully sharing new plant material among Czechoslovak collectors. "Under communism, you couldn't get seeds, and of the five seeds I finally got [of a particular species], only one seedling survived, but it got sick, it was infected, so I tried grafting it to save it," a collector explained about his early experiments with propagation. Grafting, the art of splicing two different species together, is a long-practiced horticultural technique, used worldwide in everything from fruit and nut cultivation to accelerating the growth of slow-growing and challenging cactus species. Today, many of the cacti sold worldwide are grafted. Not only does grafting accelerate the growth of species and increase disease resistance but propagating species can also have the effect of causing them to pup, producing many new clones out of a single plant.[37] Once excised and grafted again, this cycle can enable a skilled propagator to rapidly multiply a single plant into hundreds of new clones.

A Longing Amplified

The limitation on access to seeds—to say nothing of plants—only intensified desires for new species by Czechoslovak collectors. Not only did communism force growers to become some of the most skilled cultivators of cacti and succulents in the world but it mediated the emotional and psychic bonds between collectors and their plants. "The scarcity made things more emotional," one collector said. "So once you got it, you were really happy about that. You had to learn to be efficient with the material you had." We might imagine the intense lack embodied in the hard-to-obtain cactus material inscribing the species with the resonance of *objet a*: "Once you dream of a plant," the collector added, "but you just can't get it—it might be anything, a woman, a toy, a cactus—[and] you must put in the effort [to get it], and it's not for free, it keeps the thrill," he said. "And these were dreamt [of] lands," he added. Captured here are the links forged between the object of desire as the thing out of reach (that which is absent) sutured to cacti as "New World" species and the imagined western landscapes and economy so many

Czechs desired. Plants became emplaced within both "dreamt lands" and the psychotopology of collector desires.

"Under communism, people were always hungry to travel," Jan said one day while we were touring another private greenhouse collection. "I never had a place for a collection [of cacti] since childhood, so I was an observer, looking at habitat pictures, and I thought, 'This is beautiful,' but I didn't have it. . . . And definitely this thrill of waiting makes it special. It's about consumerism, yes . . . but the longing, under communism that was supported, it had this role. Communism was a long longing—longing amplified."[38]

Under communism, collector desires were amplified and pushed them to develop what are now widely recognized within the international hobby as some of the greatest grafting, propagating, and seed germinating skills in the world. During this period of time, some ardent collectors chose to specialize in a particular skill, and to this day, informal networks of collectors work together to disseminate new (often illegally obtained) plant material, with one collector working to coax cactus seeds to germinate before those seedlings are sent along to another grower who excels in grafting plants, which are then moved along to another expert in propagating cultivated material, before moving into a wider network of exchange relations.

"It's interesting, we are such a small country, and yet we have so many cacti," a Czech collector mused in one of my first interviews in Czechia. There was far more being said here than what was put into words. The activities of Czechoslovak collectors during this period link the physical barriers erected through geopolitical conflict with the material properties of plants and the structure of the unconscious. Desires are articulated in the world and find attachment with real "objects" in it. This is the extimacy of a more-than-human geography on full display.[39] Lack conjures desire. The politically forced absence of new plant material in Czechoslovakia set in motion a cascading series of multispecies reconfigurations in which

Figure 26. An impressive private collection of cacti and other succulents inside a greenhouse in Czechia.

exoticized plants from an exoticized landscape and economy took hold of collector imaginations through that which was lacking. These twists of desire had the effect of turning the greenhouse into a space where collectors might seek another satisfaction, where the desire of the Other was rerouted into desire for plants as literal "objects" of desire. That these objects were alive, with their own biogeographical relations, matters a great deal. Through cacti, collectors forged psychic connections between the literal ecologies of the Americas and the imagined ecologies they sought as a fantasy through cacti as covetable species. The production of desire for cacti under communism, to phrase these relations another way, reconfigured people, species, and places into new social relations with entwined psychic and ecological consequences (Figure 26).

It was within this wider social milieu of a post-1968 Czechoslovakia that Švejk was maturing into a leading and respected cactus expert. A few years after the Velvet Revolution in 1989, Švejk finally got his chance to visit Mexico. He trained prior to the trip by hiking up and down mountains and spent several months in Spain first to learn Spanish. In a matter of years, not only would Švejk come to describe several new species of Mexican cacti but he would become one of the most infamous smugglers of cactus plants and seeds in Europe.

The Good Smuggler Švejk

During my time in Czechia, I continued to wonder about the ethics of collection that seemed to guide Švejk. It became clear to me over the ensuing weeks that Švejk was trying to maintain a set of competing and complex responsibilities: responsibility to a community of collectors and their thirst for plants; to himself and his desire to seek out and describe new species while maintaining a "rogue" and antiestablishment image; and to the species of plants about which he was so passionate and that gave him pleasure. It also became clear to me in my time with Švejk that he was one of the most knowledgeable people with whom I had ever spoken about cacti. "A similarity between Švejk and Frič is how institutions hated them both. He [Švejk] cannot work with institutions, he is for revolution, like Frič. He had this opportunity to build Czech Republic's greatest nursery and greenhouse, but then the owner told Švejk what to do, and he wouldn't listen; he is too proud, his ego wouldn't allow him to be obedient. . . . Švejk is naive in some ways, too proud in another," a friend and collector said of him.

Švejk's passion for cacti was equally infectious and a wonder to behold. I have no doubt Švejk's passion for plant conservation was genuine, which is not to say he behaved in a way that was congruent with the actual conservation of wild-growing species. It became clear to me that at various times in his life, his competing passions may have led him not only to break the law but to un-ambiguously cause damage either directly or indirectly to cactus species in Mexico. By sharing locality information about species with collectors less immediately concerned with their impacts on species populations, he may have caused far more harm than he is willing to acknowledge or account for.

"Švejk always takes some seeds in his pockets. You can't get a permit [from authorities], the only way is to be a criminal," a senior collector, considered one of the greatest in the Czech Republic and even a father figure to Švejk, explained to me, sitting in his living room on a brisk fall morning, surrounded by an immense personal library dedicated to the study of cacti. "The demand is too high, the market will never be destroyed, so it will be a black market or another market, but there will always be a market," he explained as Švejk listened, nodding. He gave me the example of one spe-cies, *T. alonsoi,* which was first described in 1996 by Mexican scien-tists. "In 1996 five seeds came here [to Czechia], and today there are billions of seeds in Europe." This collector runs a well-regarded commercial cactus catalog, and he chose to offer seeds of the spe-cies to collectors for free through the catalog. Thousands of collec-tors took him up on the offer of the seeds. Soon thereafter, Czech CITES authorities came to his greenhouse for an inspection, seized plants, and filed a court case against him, but ultimately, it was not successful. "I paid a small fine, but generally I proved that the seeds I had came [here] before the law was implemented [referring to the 1997 amendment to CITES that upgraded Mexican cacti seeds to CITES Appendix II].

"We didn't import a plant, just five seeds. We brought the seeds [to Czechia], grew them, grafted them, it only took a year on graft to get new seeds. On their own roots, it might be at least three to four years, but on grafts, we could get them maybe within a year," the collector added. I asked why he listed them in the cat-alog for free. "The goal was to spread it, among the people." "Also,"

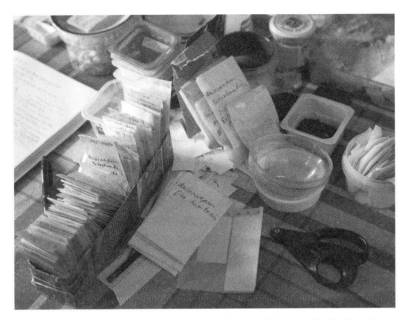

Figure 27. A collector's personal seed catalog, including individual packets of species and varietals with locality data, an accompanying ledger, and preparatory materials.

Švejk interrupted, "it was a protest, and for conservation. . . . The *Turbinocarpus* case is a good example of the case between common sense and paperwork. So this is like ten years ago, there are billions of seeds [now], they are everywhere" (Figure 27).

I asked him to clarify if all the plants I had seen across Europe of this species really came from just those five seeds. "Practically," he replied. "But still today, one of the only registered CITES nurseries [in Czechia] was bullied because of having these plants, and it's ridiculous because they are everywhere! It is common sense, and they [Czech CITES authorities] are still trying to stop it somehow, because it got here illegally," the collector added.

Švejk began to raise his voice. "The ratio of the number of plants in culture to nature is like a hundred to one already. . . . I cannot imagine a better way to protect this plant than what we did. But it was illegal. The country of origin [Mexico] knows [about] this. . . . It's like they know it, but they would like to do it [propagation and trade] without us. Maybe it is just nationalism. . . . There are other motivations, bad characteristics of people, envy. . . . [But] people in countries of origin, they just don't want Europeans to get profit from these plants, they would like to do it themselves, but they have not done it." Silence followed. I recognized, given Czechia's far more nuanced relationship to colonialism and power within Europe, that I had until then felt far more sympathetic toward Švejk's and other Czech collectors' descriptions of their urges to visit cacti "in habitat" and the lack produced by Soviet occupation that amplified these desires than I might have been when speaking to a Belgian or British collector. But hearing Švejk speak of Mexican nationalism and envy was an important reminder that colonial sentiments and Eurocentrism manifest in a multitude of forms.

An interview a few days later with an old friend of Švejk and a professional horticulturalist troubled some important details in this story of *T. alonsoi* and its arrival in Europe. "One of my first [significant] experiences was with Švejk in a bathroom," the horticulturalist recalled. "Švejk came back from Mexico, that bathroom was *full* of *Turbinocarpus alonsoi*, maybe thousands of plants." The horticulturalist explained that he now saw this behavior as unethical and believed Švejk did as well. "They were the first *T. alonsoi* in Europe. This was probably just after the discovery of the locality. The idea was probably to bring back seeds. . . . This was maybe in 1995. He produced millions of seeds," the horticulturalist added.

The truth about Švejk, his intentions, and the broader intentions and actions of members of the cactus community who admitted to certain illegal activities while perhaps concealing others is not something I aimed to settle definitively as part of my research, which differs from investigatory work in a number of crucial ways, especially in relation to how much emphasis is placed on collecting facts from what else is being said discursively. But being aware of people lying about illegal behavior during this fieldwork is import- ant. "Usually with people that steal, it's a condition," a U.S. Bureau of Land Management law enforcement officer with experience of sa- guaro poaching cautioned me in Arizona in March 2018. "You may see that profile with individuals you're dealing with," he advised me.

It is easy enough to understand why conservation and law en- forcement officials depict Švejk and others like him as thieves plun- dering Mexico's heritage and natural resources. But as a thief, Švejk nevertheless would still seem to have a code, even if it is one that has evolved over time. Following the Velvet Revolution, Švejk, like many other Czechs, seized on the opportunity to finally visit Mex- ico and other countries with cacti and succulents. In their lust and greed to possess long-sought species, they poached living plants from the ground. Nevertheless, I am willing to cautiously admit that I don't believe he does so anymore. This is no absolution from past crimes or those he may continue to commit through theft and illegal trade in seeds and their cultivated progeny. In "destroy- ing the market," as he so often put it, if Švejk is practicing a kind of Robin Hood conservation, it is a strange sort of conservation, one that isn't based on blue skies thinking but that he sees as ur- gent and terribly practical, even if it is thoroughly illegal. It is also steeped in, and reproducing, uneven Eurocentric power dynamics. I saw plants in culture across Europe—as well as the United States and elsewhere—whose genetic progeny are almost certainly trace- able to just a few seeds (or maybe plants) that Švejk had stolen. But to think of Mexico as rich while Europe is poor—even if it is true in terms of cactus species richness—becomes ridiculous when one considers the powers shaping the uneven economies of the global cactus trade and where it is centered and where it is not. Attention to these power-laden dynamics unmasks the archetype of Robin Hood as an instantiation of the settler colonial mind-set that re- produces the conditions in thought and action necessary for the objectification of nonhuman life.

Black Markets, Gray Markets, and the Murky Waters Stirred Up by Cactus Taxonomy

Time spent with Švejk, much like my time with other cactoexplorers in Brazil, further demonstrated the importance of taxonomy in structuring not only desire by presenting collectors with a new object of desire to collect but also the illicitness of species trades and affordances of protection granted to them based on how species are known. On another day with Švejk, we walked together through an exceptional set of greenhouses maintained by a revered collector, and the three of us stopped to admire a gorgeous display of *Ariocarpus* cacti. These were pebbled, almost warty-looking things; their flesh was an unusual deep green. "*Ariocarpus bravoanus*," Švejk began. "It has been destroyed in habitat. I feel bad, I was too generous in giving people location information, and at the time I didn't work to flood the market. I was probably the second European to find it."

"I think I probably produce more seed here than in the wild," the collector added, looking over his collection.

"Why did *A. bravoanus* fare so badly, just because it grows slowly?" I asked.

"*A. bravoanus* has been devastated," Švejk said. "*Ariocarpus* is generally attractive, it was new, it's quite small. It only grows in one spot—north of San Luis Potosi, near the main highway. Still, it wasn't easy to find," he added with a laugh. But that combination—attractive, new, small, and inherently rare—contained all the indicators for a species that would be in immediate high demand among collectors. But the IUCN Red List assessment for *A. bravoanus* paints a more complex picture of the threats the species faces. While the report describes this population as having been practically destroyed by collectors, it clarifies that *A. bravoanus* as a species has taxonomically changed and now incorporates what was previously known as a distinct species—*A. fissuratus* var. *hintonii*.

The consequence of this decision "greatly expanded the known range" of *A. bravoanus*.[40]

What the collectors were describing as *A. bravoanus* today is (mostly) agreed upon by scientists to be *A. bravoanus* subspecies *bravoanus*. This is because *A. fissuratus* var. *hintonii* was more recently reclassified as *A. bravoanus* subspecies *hintonii* (these are long, complicated names, but stick with me!). Although only a few thousand individuals of subspecies *A. bravoanus* subspecies *bravoanus* are left, and in only one location, *A. bravoanus* subspecies *hintonii* exists in at least three different populations and has an estimated total population of five thousand to ten thousand plants. While *A. bravoanus* subspecies *bravoanus* is classified as critically endangered by the IUCN, at the species level, thanks to its "lumping in" with *A. bravoanus* subspecies *hintonii*, *A. bravoanus*—as a species—is now "only" endangered. *A. bravoanus*—in all its guises—shows just how important species taxonomies are to conservation and the assessment of endangerment, as well as how vital basic population data are to assessing the conservation status of the species. Just like the British collector in the previous chapter who questioned the intent of some collectors and botanical experts in the naming of new species, it also tells us a great deal about the relations between desire and difference and how the desire for a new object is parasitized through the commodity form.

Švejk's concern for *A. bravoanus* stems from his long-standing concern with how approaching the "species" shapes matters of care or concern for cacti. He believes that the "species" as a taxonomic unit does not serve cacti and their conservation or trade regulation well. "The reality is some of the taxonomic units don't fit well into boxes," he said. "Realistically, we will need to prioritize conserving particular localities." What struck me most about Švejk's discussion was how concerned he was for smaller units of categorizing and knowing plants, alongside concerns about which I rarely heard other collectors speak, such as climate change and the maintenance of in situ genetic variability among smaller localities of plants. Yet it was only two days later, in another greenhouse, looking at another world-class collection of cacti, that Švejk would firmly declare, "If CITES didn't exist, the cacti would be more protected in nature. The people being harassed by CITES are the best growers who could be feeding the market. There are always articles in cactus magazines about new species—and they are already here and I'm going to propagate them."

One consequence of collector desire for new species is that there are fewer and fewer new species to taxonomize over time, especially for a taxonomic group as heavily studied as Cactaceae. For the die-hard community of growers interested only in collecting "true" species (as opposed to the large segment of the community who also collect and breed hybridized cultivars), the time between the description of new species grows longer. This means that when something new comes along, collector desire may latch on to it with abandon, even if it is later discredited as a species. New species, especially highly collectible ones, will often see the kind of market demand and associated prices you find in any novel, limited-supply, demand-driven market. Seeds can shoot up to fifty dollars *per seed,* and collectors will spend hundreds of dollars—if not thousands—on a single plant.[41] This demand in a supply-limited environment is how collectors like Švejk justify their illegal behavior as *licit* behavior. In the absence of supply, prices can shoot up alongside demand, and unscrupulous collectors can turn to harvesting mature wild plants as a lucrative source of profit. "It would be helpful if CITES would facilitate rather than hinder rapidly propagating and getting plants into the market to destroy the demand for wild plants," Švejk said to me during another long drive between collector greenhouses.

Shifts in how plants are known by scientists also further muddy the waters of the gray market. But what gray markets signify varies between actors.[42] Most in the cactus and succulent community characterize the gray market as the ambiguous space between what collectors imagine as the threat of a truly criminal black market operated by crime syndicates and the legal "white market."[43] The most common narrative about different shades of markets among European collectors is that while trading isn't necessarily always legal, it isn't a black market in the sense of involving organized crime syndicates trading in cacti. For collectors, a true black market would represent an underground market where expensive, hard-to-source cacti are sold by organized crime groups that simultaneously traffic in arms or drugs, perhaps using the dark web as a preferred marketplace. This contrasts with the scenario today, in which loose assemblages of collectors subvert authorities to illegally obtain new plants or seeds through what "green" or environmental criminologists would describe as *disorganized* networks," where, according to Tanya Wyatt and colleagues, "the smuggling apparatus are characterized by swift and sometimes temporary and fluid relationships between actors that react to socio-economic, political and ecological changes by looking for opportunities for illegal activities."[44]

According to Švejk, "right now it's a gray market, not a black market. Because there are so many enthusiasts that produce it or sell it for a price that doesn't make it such a good price for a real black market. But if it wasn't being done by enthusiasts, who do it for more than money . . . if the criminalization continues, it could push enthusiasts out, raise prices and demand, and a real black market with actual criminal networks could move in," he said. At the same time, it is hard not to see parallels in how actors behaving illegally are framed differently across axes of race and country of origin, with European cactus smugglers at times referred to as "gentlemen collectors" who "cheekily pinch a plant or two," whereas collectors from China, Japan, and South Korea (for example) are more likely to be referred to as "poachers."[45]

But gray markets, as Hannah Dickinson recently showed in

her work on the material politics of caviar trade in Europe, are not only about the sorts of actors involved in these trades (as Švejk and many collectors suggest) but about how actors exploit loopholes and complexities in regulatory frameworks and laws to launder illegal goods into legal trades. As Dickinson explains in relation to wildlife trades, "CITES place[s] prohibitions or extreme limits on international trade in wildlife species deemed at greatest extinction risk. Nonetheless, trade in these species may be permitted if the plants or animals are captive-bred. This legal technicality creates loopholes for wildlife laundering. For example, illegally harvested wildlife is sometimes fraudulently marketed as captive-bred by legitimate businesses."[46] Thus, for green criminologists and scholars of IWT and wildlife markets, "a 'grey market' describes a phenomenon whereby contraband commodities are disguised as legal goods on the marketplace."[47] With this understanding in mind, gray markets are unambiguously rife across the international trade in cactus and succulent plants.

Whether or not Švejk's vision of a cactus black market would come to pass (and see chapter 5), there is ample evidence from a range of illegal trades that harsher criminalization can lead to more serious criminal actors becoming engaged in the production, conveyance, and marketing of illicit goods.[48] "It could become a self-fulfilling prophecy," he said. "This criminalization could push out enthusiasts. What if the narcos really did take over the market because it becomes profitable enough?" Švejk asked. "Someone should be responsible to make the cycle, so that this plant can get to the market as quickly as possible so it doesn't just get dug all up." I agreed with him on this point, even if I didn't agree with him that he was the one to be doing it, and I wondered why a legal remedy remained largely unrealized.

The Robin Hood Conservationist Gets Away (with the Help of Some Vegetal Companions)

It is reasonable to wonder how it is that Švejk and others like him can continue to break CITES trade rules and legally operate commercial nurseries. It is also worth asking why a legal, sustainable alternative trade has not yet been developed to put illegal cactus traders out of business. To try to answer these questions, as well as better understand the perspectives of those who see Švejk as nothing but a criminal working against the interests of species conservation, I turned to the experiences of both Czech and Mexican conservation and wildlife law enforcement authorities. We discussed why it was that Czechs, compared to other collectors, seemed especially prone to engaging in illicit trade. "These people who are propagators and collectors, they are *fanatics*, they want to have big collections and different species and rare species, so of course we know there are such guys, and we have some knowledge about illegal trade," a staff member of the Agency for Nature and Landscape Conservation (Agentura Ochrany Přírody a Krajiny; AOPK), which serves as the Czech CITES scientific authority, explained to me one morning in an office park on the northern side of Prague. "They want the species so much they are going to do anything to get them. . . . They are very good at searching for localities in Mexico. I don't know how they are doing this, but you have like, endemic species which are only in a very small area in the Mexican mountains, and the place was never published, but in two years, the Czech guys will find them—I don't know how—but they always do," he said, shaking his head in a way that suggested being both impressed and exasperated.

Mexican and Czech authorities are both very aware of the "Czech problem," while Czech authorities even expressed a sense of embarrassment to me that they had not done more to address it. A major justification for why these illegal trades persisted from the perspectives of the authorities I interviewed in both countries was a lack of capacity and the lower priority and fewer resources plants receive compared to combating illegal trade in animals. "We don't have any expertise on plants, and we have too few people, we won't be able for a couple of years to cover this gap of cacti and succulents," an officer with the Czech Environmental Inspectorate (Česká Inspekce Životního Prostředí; ČIŽP) explained to me. "Usually the smugglers are a step or two ahead of us," she added. "I don't want to say plants are not our priority," the officer at AOPK said, "that's not true, but we are very busy with other topics . . . parrots, reptiles, and rhinos and tigers . . . and it's very difficult, the enforcement with plants; one problem of course is species identification. With cacti, it's very difficult, and the enforcement people, if they go there, they are not cacti specialists, so they need to have some help . . . but this is another problem, because these people know each other very well, and it's a small community," he said.

Czech agency officers tasked with enforcing CITES felt that in the war of public opinion, they were the ones being demonized, rather than the other way around. "Everyone in the cactus community knows each other. . . . If we asked a botanist to come with us from the botanical garden to identify plants in someone's greenhouse, he will refuse. He would be seen as a traitor. People doing the right thing are demonized here, and people doing the wrong thing are admired, because they escaped our iron claws," the officer laughed.[49] "The problem is most Czech cacti specialists are also the smugglers. . . . In the Czech Republic, the smugglers and the bad guys are put on a pedestal and even admired. It's not a question of only the cactus hobby, it's a general rule here in the Czech Republic. Not following the rules is our national hobby."

Another issue authorities expressed in regulating illegal cactus and succulent trade was more technical. In Czechia, all CITES-listed animals kept in the country must be individually registered and microchipped, with their information stored by authorities. To register all CITES plants in the country, the ČIŽP officer explained, "you would need individual IDs for every plant. Would you put a transponder in them? A microchip? Or [use] genetics? But genetics are much more difficult for plants. . . . With animals, we have a database with a single ID for every individual registered, with a photograph. You need to be able to distinguish each individual animal." This would be impossible for a collection of cacti measured in meters squared (this is how serious collectors talk about collection sizes, not by the number of plants), especially given the number of clones that circulate through the hobby, to say nothing of the ongoing absence of a technology that would enable rapid species identification.

Practical, technical, and even epistemological challenges facing cactus conservation and trade regulation are exemplified through the description of a species previously unrecorded in the botanical scientific literature. New species names set all kinds of desires in motion, inclusive of agencies, scientists, smugglers, and collectors. It takes time, for instance, for Mexican authorities to determine the conservation status of a species new to science and make formal assessments of its population, prior to which a species will have fewer protections under federal environmental law. This is even more complex if a species' existence as a kind is contested. Is it a new, incredibly rare species? Or is it a subpopulation of a larger, preexisting one? One way that CITES often handles such cases is to focus on listing plants by genera (such as *Ariocarpus*) as opposed to taking a species-by-species approach. But this is not always the case—while *Aztekium ritteri* is listed in CITES Appendix I, still other members of the *Aztekium* genus are not.

A case in point is the highly desirable species *A. valdezii,* first described by Mexican botanists in 2013.[50] This species caused a sensational amount of interest within the international collector community, but by 2016, it had been demoted to a synonym of *A. ritteri.*[51] While scientists may disagree about its taxonomic status, *A. valdezii* remains a highly coveted plant and generally accepted species among many collector communities. Within a year of *A. valdezii*'s description, the plant was for sale on the internet from Europe, with prices ranging from €180 to €1,200 per plant.[52] Undoubtedly, the plant was already being grown and propagated in Europe before its formal description by Mexican botanists. Certain Czechs may have even found the species before the botanists did and were simply waiting for the species to be described before releasing it on the market. *A. valdezii*'s shifting taxonomy intersected with its lootability as a very small cactus and may have muddled the capacity of enforcement agencies to respond swiftly to its international trade.

If sellers at a European cactus expo are selling a species that scientists don't agree on as a species, it becomes more challenging to say exactly what it is and therefore what precise laws are being broken. Any inspector would need to be well versed in the most up-to-date cactus taxonomy, to say the least, although they are aided by the entire Cactaceae family being listed in CITES Appendix II, save a few exceptions. The persistence of the gray market, I believe, also alleviates agencies tasked with enforcing CITES of some of the burden to do so. As much as the ČIŽP enforcement officer argued in favor of all Mexican seeds being listed in CITES for the sake of legal clarity, as long as there is ambiguity in the market, there are practical reasons why more stringent enforcement becomes challenging to pursue. The technical knowledge and skill that such enforcement requires were recognized as a burden by enforcement agencies I interviewed but, in practice, also created a technical-legal quagmire justifying a lack of action to adequately respond to illegal trade.

The Big Cactus Seed Debate

A major collector complaint expressed throughout my research—and justification for continuing to engage in illegal activity—was the decision proposed to CITES by Mexico in 1997 to include Mexican cactus seeds in the CITES appendices. Many collectors believe this has hurt rather than helped species conservation, although many conservationists disagree. This single decision has also played an outsized role in reshaping the contours of illicit succulent trade and collection. The previously legal and generally licit collector behavior of trading in cactus seeds from Mexico internationally without permits suddenly became illegal. Much of the illegal trade in which Švejk and others like him are accused of participating relates to taking Mexican cactus seeds out of the country, growing them into plants, and trading them without permits. Twenty-five years on, this change in CITES rules remains a controversial decision not only within collector communities but among CITES parties concerned about its enforceability and capacity for implementation. I asked the ČIŽP officer about this decision and whether this was ultimately the right call for protecting wild species. "The Mexican government did the right thing," the officer said, without hesitation. "The Mexican species are highly sought by collectors. . . . Every time you release more legal things, the more illegal things you'll find hidden among them. It's much better to protect the seeds. If everything was protected, it would be much easier to know that things were illegal."

From the ČIŽP officer's perspective, the primary value of including seeds in CITES Appendix II was to reduce the opportunities for introducing "gray" areas into enforcement. The practical challenges facing customs officials in learning to identify and distinguish the legal and illegal in wildlife trades are many; it is easier from the perspective of enforcement officers to categorize broadly and reduce the need to distinguish. But from a conservation standpoint, not all authorities agree with this perspective, even in Mexico. Some officials acknowledged that in principle, the best thing would be for CITES-registered Mexican nurseries to be selling cultivated seeds abroad. Although this could happen under current CITES rules (Mexican nurseries could be granted CITES export permits and aided in facilitating that process or waiving associated fees, for instance), in practice, this is not happening at any meaningful scale. Officials blamed a variety of capacity, bureaucratic, and institutional reasons, to say nothing of the distinct economic disadvantages any new commercial operation opening in Mexico would face while trying to compete in a mature global marketplace, where European nurseries have already been selling Mexican cacti for hundreds of years at scale. So long as there are cactus seeds for sale internationally for cheaper prices, it is hard to imagine that an emerging Mexican market would become competitive without a concerted effort of placing social pressure on collector communities to alter their purchasing habits. This has resulted in the scenario where, barring few exceptions, it is exceedingly difficult to legally obtain any cactus plants or seeds of species described after 1997 from Mexico, when the change to CITES rules for Mexican cacti seeds came into effect. "If no one saves the plant from the place, and the plants are lost, then smugglers will have been right, but it isn't their place to do it [get plants into propagation], it is the Mexican authorities' job to do that," the ČIŽP enforcement officer said.

The aim of including Mexico's seeds in CITES was to reduce unsustainable harvesting and better regulate the trade to ensure that profits from this market were principally derived in Mexico, as the main architect of Mexico's proposal explained to me at her home in Mexico City. "Think of a community, a very poor, rural community, in a desert-like area, all they have around them are some cacti," she said. "But they are completely . . . oblivious that those cacti have value in some other country. . . . How can we manage to talk about conservation without involving these local communities?"

This perspective, that the goal of regulating cactus trade should be to support local conservation alongside the livelihoods of people who live within the habitats of traded species, was shared by many and aligns with access and benefit-sharing requirements outlined in the CBD. I asked if she could expand on what this vision might look like in practice. "Why don't we work together [Mexicans and European collectors] and train these people who live in the natural distribution of the endemic or microendemic species . . . and show them how to artificially propagate . . . where you can have very robust plants, and you can create job opportunities," she said. "And this production can be exported to the EU, and certified as a product. . . . Then these people that are profiting from artificial propagation, they have the obligation to take care of the environment where the wild plants live. That is a win-win situation."

But when I asked why this had not been realized in Mexico given that twenty-five years had passed since the seed ruling was made, she clapped her hands together and said, "Because *nobody* cares about plants!" Other officials suggested various other reasons such projects have largely either failed to materialize in the past or failed to begin, including a lack of initial capital, lack of incentive within rural communities to engage in a new and uncertain economic endeavor, and in-country problems of bureaucratic red tape. But I kept returning to what the expert had said: did it amount only to a failure of the Mexican government, and perhaps international institutions that might provide financial backing for such endeavors, to demonstrate care for plants? Or did it also speak to the longer durée of colonial extractive relations? European collectors and commercial nurseries maintain thousands more cultivated individuals (and the capacity to reproduce them) of likely dozens of Mexican cacti species than currently exist today within their distribution ranges. As Švejk demonstrated through the example of *A. bravoanus,* in which one Czech collector was possibly producing more seeds in his single greenhouse than all the wild plants of that species in Mexico, it becomes harder to imagine European cactus smugglers as Robin Hood figures when we take the realities and challenges of practicing conservation in Mexico to heart. If Robin Hood steals from the rich and gives to the poor, the moral logic that would seem to justify a Robin Hood ethos among Czech collectors is unsteadied within the context of recent world history, in which places of rich biodiversity have had their botanical bounty looted for centuries by European nations, even if some of those nations were historically oppressed by others.

With these uneven economic and political dynamics and exertions of colonial desires in mind, I wonder about what Mexico is owed and who in Mexico is owed the most. And, just as pressingly, what would it mean to repay such a debt if, following the critique of Mick Smith against ecological sovereignty I described in the previous chapter, it is recognized that a state "owning" nonhuman life reproduces many of the same harmful binary nature–culture logics that are concomitant to such exploitative violence against nonhuman life in the first place?[53] More practically, would developing a commercial nursery program, such as the one envisioned by the conservation expert in Mexico, ultimately stop those collectors whose drive is pushed forward not only by desire for the species but seemingly also by the experience of "authentic" collection and "discovery," such as those experiences I related in chapters 1 and 2? Will commodification really beget flourishing? Are institutions willing to do the work to assess if rural communities across Mexico are even interested in growing plants for profit in the first place? These are crucially important questions cacti demand the international conservation apparatus to answer.

After several rounds of beers over plates of pickled vegetables and cheese and hours of animated conversation about cacti one night, around midnight, Švejk pulled me aside to tell me that he was considering a trip that upcoming January to Mexico and that I was

Figure 28. A sprawling display of *Strombocactus disciformis, Ariocarpus,* and *Lophophora* (peyote) cacti. Fantasizing about encounters with wild plants is closely mirrored within some collector greenhouses. A small but deeply skilled subcommunity of collectors aim to replicate species as growing in natural landscapes within the greenhouse. The cacti depicted here are grown by a Czech collector indoors to approximate how these species might appear in Mexico within their normal distribution range. Some collectors are so skilled in this art that their cacti are in fact capable of reproducing "on their own" within these constructed, indoor microhabitats.

invited. He told me that he wanted to show me where *A. valdezii* lives (the plant I described earlier as both existing and not existing as a species, depending on whom you ask). "I know a back way nobody else does to the plants!" Švejk exclaimed. His "shortcut," as he described it, involved several days of remote trekking, followed by descending through a steep canyon, crossing underneath a giant waterfall, and risking attack by swarms of colorful parrots that protect the entrance to *A. valdezii*'s habitat. It became hard in that moment to think that *A. valdezii* didn't taxonomically "exist" as a species as scientists now suggest. Whether or not it was its own species, the image Švejk conjured of this plant left me desperately wanting to see it and the ecology in which it evolved. I fantasized about this locale as he conjured it in my imagination (Figure 28).

This trip to Mexico with Švejk never manifested, but I admit that during my time in Czechia, I was dazzled by Švejk's charisma and the way he spoke so passionately about these plants and the great lengths he would go to find them. As both the "little Frič" and "Švejk" of the cactus collecting world, it was not hard for me to see how Švejk would likely remain the rebellious antihero of the Czech cactus community, always two steps ahead of the well-meaning, if misguided, authorities (as he saw them). What remains to be seen is how conservation and collector communities invested in succulent flourishing might find new and more productive opportunities to engage with one another, despite past failures to do so.

Between History and Desire

Although I offer a historical approach in this chapter to understanding how it is that Czech cactus collectors became some of the most revered and notorious in the world, above all, these stories assert the power of desire in transforming ecologies and human–plant relations. Historicizing succulent desires perhaps points us toward what geographer Milton Santos described as a "metadisciplinary" analysis of the conditions through which unconscious tendencies mobilized through desire find purchase in the world, adhere meaning to "objects," and, in the process, transform environments.[54] The psychoanalytic insights of Lacan about the structure of the unconscious, evidenced well by Czech cactus growers and smugglers, reveal how desire is above all structured by the absent Other and the lengths desiring subjects go to seek out a satisfaction made possible only by the lack left in the Other's wake. "'The Other' propels, where nature, instinct and nervous excitation do not," Lacanian scholar Malcolm Bowie writes. "It [the Other] is that which always insinuates itself between the individual and the object of 'his' desire; which traverses those objects and makes them unstable; and which makes desire satiable by continuously moving its target."[55] Drawing again on the work of McGowan, we can see how fantasies of a "private" space in the greenhouse away from Soviet-era occupation amplified the resonances of the Thing within exoticized cacti as overdetermined "objects" of "freedom," always just out of reach.

Bridging a history of Czech cactus collecting with a Lacanian theory of desire and the unconscious points toward *more-than-human* as a term that indexes not only the ecologies in which humans exist but how "to be" human is always composed through relations with nonhuman others. But this sense of being is a far cry from any notion that "I" might knowingly call "myself" into being through the act of thinking it. Crucially for Lacan, there is no me—no subject—that exists outside of "my" efforts to imagine it, no "I" separate from any attempt to conjure "myself" in words or thought. The subject of Lacan is fundamentally a split subject brought into being by an Other as "an alterity raised to the second power."[56] Contra Descartes, Lacan writes with typical wit and wordplay, "I am not, where I am the plaything of my thought; I think about what I am where I do not think I am thinking."[57] "I" am brought into existence as a split subject through the world of language the moment I aim to speak of this "I," impossibly knotted into being with the Other. When Lacan says over and over that desire is desire of the Other, he does not suggest any ability ever to know this "Other's" desire—it is unfathomable, it is lack itself. "And it is this very lack that causes our desire," Joan Copjec clarifies.[58] This is to say that the succulent subject demands attention to the structure of the unconscious; it is insufficient to turn to historical events alone to understand the work of desire.

In the next chapter, equipped with a deeper appreciation of how the nature of the unconscious and history can collide in producing new trajectories of succulent life, I return to Brazil to confront the ultimate lack found at the heart of any discussion or debate over species conservation: extinction itself.

\\4//

Confronting Extinction Anxiety in Cactus Country

A ring of park staff, cactus collectors, Brazilian botanists, and conservationists watched as a small columnar cactus was placed in the ground by the woman for whom the species was named (Figure 29). It was an attractive, if unremarkable, cactus—the kind of plant I could buy for five dollars at a hardware store. To my non-botanist eye, the cactus's spines were the only distinguishing feature. Unusually long and flexible, almost wispy, the bright golden needles looked more inviting than foreboding, though I confirmed that they were sharp. An older Dutch collector proudly tapped the soil around the newly planted cactus with the backside of a shovel. As he knelt next to the woman to pose for photographs, I turned to the botanist standing next to me, who was responsible for formally describing the species. "Do you think it will live?" I asked. He inhaled, pausing before responding. "Well, it was raised in an apartment, so it should be shaded until it can be hardened. Otherwise, no," he replied.

Although we were gathered to celebrate both the discovery and the protection of this species, the botanist's concerns for this plant were justified—the cactus was not shaded. The ceremony felt like a strange combination of a funeral, a bris, and a bar mitzvah. While

Figure 29. The cactus *Arrojadoa marylanae,* newly planted, held in place by stones.

these ceremonies all mark important—and distinct—life stages, this gathering around a young cactus blended aspects of all three: birth, mourning, and a celebration of becoming. In intent, we were meant to celebrate a cactus still relatively new to science, one worthy of our shared efforts and intention to conserve it. It might have been the heat and humidity, or the fact that people were hungry, but the mood felt decidedly more mournful than celebratory. The species, while only recently described in the scientific literature, is also on the brink of extinction.[1] The botanist sighed and walked away into the shade. The cactus now planted in the ground outside the visitor center at the Floresta Nacional Contendas do Sincorá in the state of Bahia is known to science as *Arrojadoa marylanae.*

It was carefully grown for the past seven years in a glass flower-pot in the nearby city of Vitória da Conquista. More than three years since that planting, the cactus is also very likely dead now, scorched by the tropical sun, unprepared to survive outdoors.

That this specific location was not known ever to have sup-ported a population of the cactus we planted seemed a notable omission, both glaring in its importance and at odds with the com-bined ecological knowledge of the group assembled to celebrate it. What were we doing planting an imminently endangered cactus in a place it had no place trying to grow? The Sincorá, a protected area of approximately 112 square kilometers, is a relatively new national forest in Brazil, obtaining legal designation in 1999. In its recent past, it had been used for intensive agriculture, timber, and char-coal production. The Brazilian Caatinga is a severely fragmented dryland landscape, making this an important site for the long-term conservation of the Caatinga ecosystem amid rangelands, agricul-tural fields, and urban settlements. On the ground, the landscape feels tangled and harsh, full of thick, dry brush and woody shrubs studded with imposing thorns. It is not a place that will permit *A. marylanae,* a species known to grow only on the peak of a small, nearby mountain, to flourish.

After planting the cactus, park staff gently laid rocks around its base, both to keep it in place and to mark its location in the ground to avoid trampling by future visitors. Now surrounded by stones, I could not help but see it also for a grave—less for the individual plant then for the species it represented. It reminded me of the Jewish practice of placing small stones on tombstones; some say this practice speaks to the permanence of memory, others to how the lives of the departed are bound up in the cycling of life.[2] But where human graves mark the presence and memory of individu-als, here we were marking the loss of an entire kind.

The ceremony, I came to see, had very little to do with this cactus as a celebration and much more to do with how to contend

with extinction as a traumatic experience of ruptured, intergenerational time. This was a ritualizing of extinction as a profound
moment in time, the becoming present to accelerated extinction as
a human-induced event. Despite this anticipated extinction resulting directly from human action (as we will see), extinction nevertheless pushes against—and, perhaps, exceeds—human capacities
to understand death in familiar or meaningful temporalities. The
small and solitary cactus centered between us and our waning collective attention represented far more than a single cactus, or even
a species; it seemed to focus our attention through a preemptive
ritual of grappling with loss. But beyond this loss remained an excess of emotional energy tied to something I was not yet prepared
to name—something about the whole production felt *off*. I couldn't
shake the feeling that I was missing some key analytical insight to
make sense of what I had just witnessed and participated in, and
what proceeded the day after. After some final words by the Dutch
member of our trip about the importance of saving *A. marylanae*
and what brought us all together on that day, our gathering dispersed, and we went to lunch.

Whither Extinction? Scratching a Psychoanalytic Itch

Ceremonies often mark the passage of time, just as others can sanc-
tify space. But unlike ceremonies that ritualize life or loss, this one,
I believe, was doing heavier lifting in psychic registers than it first
let on. If I have learned anything through engaging with psychoanalysis, it is that my first instincts of interpretation often prove
incorrect. Psychoanalysis irritates, and it is this irritation that often
points toward something revealing. Despite the organizers' insistence of this planting ceremony as a celebration, or even my own
sense amid it (and thereafter) of the ceremony as a ritual of grappling with loss, I now believe that the event is better understood

through an analysis of a ritual intended to mask what at least many of us gathered knew to be true but sought to evade—the anxiety thwarting efforts to care. This effort to conceal through ritual the sanctity of capitalism as of greater import than a spindly cactus on a lonely little mountain brings to the surface questions of anxiety and its role in shielding the desiring subject from uncomfortable, unconsciously held truths. Anxiety, as Lacan writes, is a "signal," but "of all signals, [it] is the one that does not deceive."[3]

Extinction maintained a lurking presence as the unnamed thing in delicate conversations about the consequences of (over) collection with cactus and succulent collectors. Conversely, extinction was at the fore of discussions about succulent collecting with concerned conservationists. Despite the distances between these communities (at times) in practice, there is more that binds them in what underpins the emergence of species as objects of desire. The story of *A. marylanae* is a story of anxiety with more-than-human consequences, a reading that proves essential to engaging with what lies behind extinction yet the unconscious works to protect from the conscious subject. In this way, a cactus leads me to confront another powerful example of how capitalism hijacks desire and what it takes to free desire from capitalism's tenacious grip. At the same time, the story of a cactus teetering on the edge of disappearance leads me to examine the psychic costs of extinction and what might instead lead toward species flourishing.

Extinction, as a permanent loss of a way of life, is an *ontological* loss, the loss of being itself. The loss of a way of life is a loss that forecloses any possibility for future life of a kind. The "presence" of extinction is only a shattering absence. Extinction breaks the knots that bind species in relation with the world, whether or not we are aware of those knots. Psychoanalysis has much to teach about how such a loss makes desiring possible. For Lacan, the capacity to become a desiring subject occurs through loss, a split in which the Other and the desiring subject together come into existence.[4] In the desire for the fantasy of the impossible (re)unification of the self with this preseparated state, it is the ontic split from the Other that makes the desiring subject come into being; imagining the Other's desires as one's own, but also to desire the Other's desire.[5]

In the final instance, it is therefore loss and lack that make desiring possible, but what keeps it going is something else. "In the desire of every demand," Lacan says, "there is but the request for object *a*, for the object that could satisfy jouissance [enjoyment]."[6] *Objet a* and *jouissance* are some of the most complex ideas in Lacanian thought and also evolved in their meaning over the course of Lacan's life. For Lacanian scholars, *jouissance* and *objet a* are forces that dramatically shape the psyche and are widely considered Lacan's most important contributions to psychoanalysis. *Jouissance* and *objet a* help to disentangle how *A. marylanae* became a signifier of profound loss and absence, not a materially "real" object imbued with specific meanings but something distorted until viewed "from the side," the perspective from which the unconscious meaning in the encounter with the cactus might be grasped.[7]

Throughout the first chapters of this book, I have shown how various cacti and succulent plants become objects of desire. These are "objects" that the desiring subject believes hold the potential to offer true satisfaction but of course never do, at least not in the way the collector might imagine. Objects of desire differ, then, from the important Lacanian insight of the object-cause of desire *(objet a)*, that which makes the object of desire desirable. The object of desire is the thing the subject supposes might yield satisfaction, when instead, as we have seen, it is the repetition of *failing* to achieve this satisfaction that ultimately brings the subject pleasure. The object-cause of desire, in contrast, is what makes desiring possible. Something that is not the object in front of us makes going to all the trouble of failing over and over again in seeking satisfaction in objects (be they material things, cacti, or other people) worth doing. This absent "object" is *objet a.*

Objet a is the leftover excess emergent in the formation of the subject recognized through the imagined lack of the Thing. *Objet a* is a tricky and paradoxical "object" because it "emerges" only as a "lost object," a symbolization of what is imagined to have been lost in the fantasy of lacking the total *jouissance* as imagined in the void that is the Thing. Slavoj Žižek works to clarify that "das Ding [the Thing] is the absolute void, the lethal abyss which swallows the subject; while objet petit a [*objet a*] designates that which remains of the Thing after it has undergone the process of symbolization." *Objet a,* he further explains, "gives body to a lack."[8] As Paul Kingsbury elucidates further, *objet a* is "both the object of the drives and an object that incites desire."[9] With these various definitions in mind, we can consider *objet a* as a "lure," a horizon or target to be pursued through the search for *jouissance* that wraps around the absence of the Thing.[10] *Objet a,* in other words, is an object that sets desire in motion, but *jouissance* fuels the search.[11]

We have already seen in previous chapters how *jouissance* is surplus enjoyment "beyond the pleasure principle,"[12] a yearning for "total satisfaction" that can only produce the "ache of desire."[13] As psychoanalyst Lewis Kirshner writes, "desire, if it operates within the pleasure principle of symbolic social reality, cannot attain *jouissance,* which lies beyond, unassimilable to any satisfaction that could be represented in the symbolic dimensions."[14] *Jouissance* sits at the core of Lacanian theory on desire; it is "the aim of the drives . . . and involves an ineluctable yet fleeting, alluring yet threatening painful pleasure."[15] The *pursuit* of *objet a* epitomizes the pleasure that is *jouissance*—a pleasure that is never wholly satisfied, a pleasure-pain that emerges through the pursuit of the drives but is ultimately unattainable. For desire to "work," however, *objet a* must remain in its proper place, on the side of desire. Sticking close to how loss, the repetition of failure to obtain satisfaction as the source of *jouissance,* and *objet a* structure desire reveals important insights into the troubling, challenging psychic confrontation extinction poses. In a desire to compose flourishing worlds, a proper orientation toward extinction and its place in psychic registers is essential. Reading anxiety in a Lacanian register, as a moment in which desire becomes impossible, is to read extinction anxiety as an important signal alerting us to unconscious trouble.

Ascending the Dark Mountain

The day after our planting ceremony, I observed a botanist plucking seeds off a tall, spindly cactus swaying in the wind on the edge of a doomed mountain (Figure 30). As a member of a group of European and Brazilian cactus enthusiasts and scientists, we arrived at this small, thirty-meter-high mountain turned quartz mine in the state of Bahia to informally assess the recently described yet imminently threatened cactus species *A. marylanae.* Like many species in the world of conservation biology, this plant's entrance into scientific knowledge was almost immediately marked with the threat of extinction. The botanist assured me that this species would be extinct in a matter of years, if not sooner, once the dynamite came, save perhaps for our collective efforts to assist in producing a different species trajectory. In a related vein, extinction studies scholar Thom van Dooren describes species themselves as "flightways," what he characterizes as "a 'line of movement' through evolutionary time."[16] Approaching species as movements through time, I was curious to observe on this mountain what other trajectories *A. marylanae* might follow in concert with those interested or invested in its care.

A. marylanae is known to grow only in this one location, the Serra Escura (Dark Mountain) in the municipality of Tanjaçú in southwestern Bahia. Despite what its name would suggest, the

Figure 30. A row of mature *Arrojadoa marylanae* on Serra Escura, fading out of view.

bright quartz surface of Serra Escura's peak gleams in the light of the sun, jutting out of an otherwise flat landscape. This region is a center of high cactus biodiversity and endemism within both Bahia and Brazil as a whole, making it one of the more species-rich regions in the world for cacti. The cactus was first identified as a new species in 2003 by the botanist Marlon Machado and named *A. marylanae* after a graduate student who organized a biodiversity survey to Serra Escura in 2001. The student and her colleagues found a cactus they couldn't identify and sent photos to Machado. Machado would eventually return to take samples himself and confirm its status as a new species to science based on his botanical expertise.

As for what makes *A. marylanae* what it is, I refer to a short excerpt from Machado's original description of the plant in the *Cactus and Succulent Journal*:

> *Arrojadoa marylanae* readily stands out from all other *Arrojadoa* species due to its bigger size, thicker and unbranched stems, greater number of ribs, flexible spines, woollier cephalic, flowers with thin, spreading perianth segments, fruits with watery pulp and flower remnant narrower at base and shallowly inserted in the fruit apex. The flowers of *A. marylanae* are unlike the flowers of any other species in the genus. . . . The cephalic seems particularly well-developed in this species when compared to other *Arrojadoa* species: it occupies the whole apex of the stem, and is much woollier.[17]

Machado's description is useful for thinking with the conventional plant species concept for what it reveals about its comparative nature: *A. marylanae is* because of what it qualitatively is *not*, compared against previously described members of the *Arrojadoa* genus. This morphological approach to knowing the species contrasts with less visible, more quantitative (but arguably still arbitrary) ways of distinguishing like from like through the more recent practice of molecular phylogenetics. These methodological approaches to knowing the species dictate the terms by which it becomes acceptable to say "yes, *this* is a new species." This is the formative *doing* of species work, a process of species coproduction, but one that nevertheless fails to adequately convey species as unfolding formations in time.[18]

I wonder by what unlikely event of seed dispersal *A. marylanae* arrived here on Serra Escura from some distant locale, or alternatively, if this population instead represents the last stronghold of a much older, diminishing kind of plant that once dotted the hilltops across the region. Was I bearing witness to the death knell of an already dying evolutionary line or watching something just setting out on a new pathway becoming cut short? Phylogenetic and ecological research could help answer these questions and explain the species' small habitat range, but that research has yet to be conducted and likely never will be. Yet this kind of basic knowledge can be an essential starting point for the enactment of species flourishing.[19] Truly little is known about the kinds of ecological company *A. marylanae* keeps.

I reviewed Machado's description of *A. marylanae* prior to visiting Serra Escura because its morphology and botany lay a path toward establishing a relationship. Understanding how a plant works to tempt a lizard (something Machado believes *A. marylanae* does through its watery fruit) is another means of both inciting wonder and "cultivating arts of attentiveness" or "arts of noticing."[20] I am struck by the cephalium rings punctuated by bursts of bright pink flowers at even intervals up the stems of larger plants. Like tree rings spaced vertically rather than horizontally, these rings, according to Machado, are useful in estimating the plant's age, as he believes the plant will produce one per year of growth after the juvenile stage. I observed some larger specimens of *A. marylanae* on Serra Escura with as many as fifteen or even twenty cephalium rings, suggesting that these cacti can live twenty years or more. I stood near an individual plant about four feet tall, observing the way the cephalium pushes the plants' fruit out, and noticed a small pile of pink, candy corn–shaped fruit scattered on the ground beneath, perhaps enticement for a thirsty lizard.

When Machado first published his formal description of *A. marylanae* in 2005, the plant faced few, if any, threats to its survival. Collectors did not want it because they did not know it existed. Even if they had, it is not the sort of cactus to cause a collecting frenzy—it can grow to more than two meters tall (making it difficult to keep in a greenhouse), and though it is certainly a beautiful cactus, especially when mature and studded with rings of flowers, it does not have any uniquely striking morphological features when young, when its charms are less apparent. Its location on top of a small mountain meant it was also relatively secure from the common problems of urbanization and agricultural development that often impact cactus conservation in the region. This all changed only a few years ago. A mining company, Minas Stones, acquired the land of Serra Escura with the plan to transform the mountain into a quartz mine for sixty years. Referred to as the Dark Mountain Project (Projeto Serra Escura), the company website explains that the mining site at Serra Escura will be used to extract quartz for the processing of silicon metal and ferrosilicon alloys, materials used for a variety of industrial manufacturing purposes, including steel production. That the mountain is home to a species that exists nowhere else in the world is merely an inconvenience on the road toward the mountain's excavation. This is not an exceptional case; rather, it is representative of the constant and mundane conflict embedded in choices about how life is prioritized, or not, in the face of capitalist economic development.

After a short jeep ride up the mountain on tracks made for excavation vehicles, we completed the climb to the top of Serra Escura on foot. The walk permitted a close-up view of piles of gleaming white quartz growing into small hills alongside the cavernous new opening into the mountain's core. The cacti we observed on one side of the mountain were mature adults, scattered among the craggy top and hugging the steep escarpment's edge. For several minutes, I stood and watched the plants sway in the strong wind whipping across the mountain's peak. On the other side of the summit, I encountered much younger individual transplants, individually staked in a gridded pattern. The cacti were recently relocated from one side of the mountain to the other, just a matter of a few dozen meters away, to save them when the mountaintop is blasted out for quartz. This side of the mountain, company representatives told us, would be spared, thus ensuring this species new to science, whose entire population of a few thousand individuals is known to grow only in this specific place, might survive in perpetuity (or until more natural forces result in its extinction). If not for this relocation, *A. marylanae* would soon be blown up into nothingness.

I asked a botanist in our company for his opinion on the prospects for *A. marylanae*. He gestured to the side of the mountain where the thin, young plants studded the ground, labeled with numbered wooden stakes. "It's too small, it's just that small hill over there, it isn't enough to sustain the population. There are already plants lying around, dead." I observed them as well, locations where wooden stakes marked cactus death, their desiccated bodies scattered across the rocky ground. I considered how, because of their succulent structure, it can take much longer to notice when cacti have crossed a threshold beyond the point of repair or resuscitation and wondered how many of the other small, relocated cacti were also already well on their way to an untimely end. "The plant will go extinct," the botanist said. I asked him about the greenhouse at the bottom of the mountain, where the company is working to propagate the plants that will be affected by its operations. "Ex situ conservation?" he replied, shrugging his shoulders, his palms open to the skies, a gesture that conveyed skepticism, cynicism, and resignment in equal measure.[21] So little is known about *A. mary-lanae* and its ecology that to the botanist, it was preposterous to think that this effort to move the plants off the mountain while the company destroyed the only place they are known to grow could be meaningfully considered conservation work.

Frustrated by the botanist's attitude about *A. marylanae*'s fate, I pressed him for more information. If the plant was formally described and is recognized as endangered, shouldn't it be protected under Brazilian law? "We put it in the Red List as critically endangered," he replied. "We proposed to list it in the Brazilian list of endangered species; it should be included in the national [Red] List as critically endangered, but because the process is so slow, the mining company already got their license. Now the plant is listed as critically endangered on the state of Bahia's list of endangered species, so it will likely be included in the national list, but it's too late, the company already has their license, and they are mining," he said.

I failed to formulate a response to his grim assessment. That the species registers as a matter of concern—it appears on the list of threatened Bahia flora—does not otherwise permit scientists to intervene in curbing profitable mining and do literal work of care for the species. Despite the comparatively charming nature of cacti within the botanical world, the plant does not compel people in power who might intervene on its behalf to greater action.[22] Ultimately, I could say little in reply to the botanist. In the case of *A. marylanae,* it seems the law will fail to provide recourse to stop the mining because of the order of events by which permits were obtained and species were described and registered on lists of endangered flora. This human-caused extinction will be to the letter of the law. This is the banality of biopolitical power at work par excellence: a power that fosters and cherishes some lives, while excluding others.[23] Given how little is known about *A. marylanae* and the relations it maintains in the world, however, I later wondered how this story might have unfolded differently if the plant were known better; what might have become possible if this isolated cactus were seen otherwise, as a dynamic, charming, unfolding formation of life?

I next walked with the botanist to the eight-hectare "reserve area" on one side of the mountain, where approximately sixty *A. marylanae* plants were moved and replanted a year prior (Figure 31). This area was originally covered in a shrubby mix of vegetation, cleared to make room for the relocated cacti. I noticed that the ground there had a distinct topsoil layer, unlike the rocky quartz where the cacti were once growing. The botanist noted that unless they kept clearing the scrub, the area would likely be taken over again by denser vegetation. Without consistent management, it seems the cacti will be outpaced by plants that grow more quickly. And what about sixty years from now, when they expect mining operations to cease: will *A. marylanae* recolonize the ruins of a mined mountain? It is certainly possible, and something that Minas Stones, at least in theory, is hoping to achieve as part of its project's formal sustainability plan. Later we saw this project's greenhouse, where the plants removed from the mountain (*A. marylanae* among them) are maintained and propagated for future planting. But I wondered, as the botanist did, where these relocated plants, many of which did not appear to be thriving in their new home, would grow. According to the botanist, there is no similar mountaintop nearby, to say nothing of the unknown ecological relations *A. marylanae* keeps on Serra Escura. The "sustainability plan" for *A. marylanae* felt tenuous, its capacity to conceal the lurking threat of extinction incomplete.

Before we left the mountaintop, the former graduate student who first suspected that *A. marylanae* might be a new species approached me with a few of the bright fuchsia fruits from the cactus named for her. She asked me if I'd ever eaten a cactus fruit or seeds, and I told her no, save for prickly pear fruit. "All cactus seeds are edible, did you know that? But some are better than others." She

Figure 31. Transplanted *Arrojadoa marylanae* on Serra Escura.

popped a few of the fruits into her mouth. "Try it," she encouraged me. I found it slightly uncomfortable to eat the fruits of an endangered plant in front of the person for whom it had been named. But they were also sweeter than I'd expected.

Between Extinction and Desire

This is not the end of the story. But first, I need to say more about anxiety and extinction and how anxiety relates to desire and the place of the unconscious in the world. Desire is not only expressed as an experience between our unconscious selves and the external world; as Paul Kingsbury explains, the mental and the social are enjoined: "the interior is present in the exterior and vice versa."[24] The unconscious, as Maurice Merleau-Ponty says, "is to be sought not at the bottom of ourselves, behind the back of our 'consciousness,' but in front us, as articulations of our field. It is 'unconscious' by the fact that it is not an *object,* but it is that through which objects are possible, it is the constellation wherein our future is read."[25] This raises our eyes to a more-than-human psychoanalytic possibility focused on the interactivity of unconscious desires operating in the world with profound reverberations for the living world and how we understand the world to be. Such an appreciation is vital to establishing how we might approach a living cactus on the road to extinction as a "lure" in the desire for *jouissance* yet also an "object" signaling the presence of anxiety.

In my research, extinction was the raison d'être left unsaid behind why desire matters in telling multispecies stories of variously rare and endangered plants. If flourishing is the aim of species care, extinction is its antithesis, not as a discrete category of difference but as a trajectory of being. Developing a conversation between desire and extinction is productive in at least two important ways. First, we can see how extinction serves as the ultimate absent term for both collectors and conservationists in inciting practices of acquisition and possession (the urge to take and possess in the private realm versus the urge to enclose [and, at times, dispossess]). Extinction as ultimate concern brought the practice of modern conservation into being. Similarly, as we have seen in collector desires to take the "last" of a species, extinction, as lack, is the absent term behind connotations of rarity and what lies just out of reach. In this way, extinction, as a profound loss of being, serves an important role in structuring how desires for flourishing life can, in a psychic twist, be transformed into acts of possession through the production of desire.

As we have seen in previous chapters, the desiring subject continuously seeks out the missing "thing" that might lead toward a satisfaction that can never be met by any sort of "real" object because the thing that ultimately sets this desire in motion is not a true object but *objet a* (as much as we might imagine otherwise in the purchase a new phone, car, or, for some, cactus). This essential Lacanian insight leads us, then, to see that it is the repetitive failure embedded in *jouissance* (always aiming but never obtaining), rather than true attainment of a specific thing, that is the source of the desiring subject's pleasure. However, it is only certain "objects" that will speak back to this desire; not just any object will do. This is what I mean when I link production with desire: desire emerges between the desiring subject and the object; desire is not a one-way street. We can understand desire to be *produced* in the sense that a subject must have an object that "grabs" her desire, and there is an economy of production that presents these objects to the desiring subject as just the thing. As Todd McGowan writes, specifically thinking through desire with the capitalist commodity form and Marx, "the commodity speaks to the possibility of a desire in the consumer, and if it speaks successfully, the desire will form."[26]

Reading extinction as the absent term through *objet a,* it becomes possible to see how certain "objects" might, in various moments of encounter, become imbued with significations of the ultimate absence or lack, permitting them, however ephemerally, to stand in for *objet a* itself. We could instead consider the cactus on the road to extinction—contra anxiety—through the Lacanian notion of the "sublime object," such as in my encounter with the singular cactus *Uebelmannia buiningii* in chapter 2 or Lacan's matchbox collector, where the object is raised "to the dignity of the Thing."[27] There is certainly merit to such a reading given extinction's presence as an ontological absence. But in what follows, and against this reading—as seductive as it may seem—I would argue that *A. marylanae* directs us to a second important opportunity that arises through a dialogue between desire and extinction. This is an encounter with anxiety as what occurs when desire is thwarted and when trouble brewing in the unconscious realm finds its way into (conscious) speech.

Through attention to an encounter with extinction's nearness, we also confront Lacan's theorizing of anxiety, which differs in marked ways from everyday conceptions of anxiety as a kind of generalizable hand-wringing and worry. Anxiety, for Lacan, marks when desire becomes impossible. Anxiety is a signal, a warning of the proximity of unsettling and harmful unconscious thoughts working to rupture into the realm of the conscious subject. The unconscious aims to "protect" the conscious self through the presentation of anxiety. But moving anxiety into the realm of the political—and, therefore, potentially transformative—anxiety also alerts us to important information that demands confrontation to enact meaningful change in ourselves and, consequently, for the world.[28] There is no universal or flat "we" to speak of in contending with planetary anxieties or the consequences of global environmental change. Still, the acceleration in diagnoses of climate change anxiety, for instance, suggests that while individual experiences of these global and catastrophic changes in the biosphere are experienced very unevenly across geographies and forms of racial, class, and social difference, these anxieties are currently experienced by many, even if the material impacts of these changes are dramatically and differently experienced in emotional, material, and economic terms.

Against ideas of anxiety as being without an object, for Lacan, anxiety has an "object," but it is a different sort of object: it is *objet a*.[29] When the position of *objet a* shifts away from its proper place (the side of the Other) in relation to the desiring subject, anxiety may arise, thwarting the capacity to desire. Anxiety is not—as Lacan importantly instructs—an emotion; anxiety is an affect, an irruption of bodily response. Anxiety emerges when *objet a* comes "too close," when the fantasy of the split subject begins to disintegrate. Consequently, anxiety's affective closeness signals desire falling away, when lack, what makes the desire to desire possible, *recedes*. The presence of anxiety occurs when "lack lacks."[30] As Derek Hook writes, "anxiety thus is not tantamount to desperation, but rather . . . a type of *expectant dread*."[31] It is the absence-presence of the thing being made extinct—the unnerving proximity of true absence close at hand—that causes extinction anxieties to arise. In the context of global species declines, this excavating work of the unconscious produces important opportunities for grappling with extinction anxieties to see what lies beyond.

I now return to *A. marylanae* to see what else was encountered on Serra Escura besides a "sustainability plan" and withering, relocated cacti. As method, I turn to psychoanalytic self-analysis in making sense of bearing witness to cactus extinction. This approach to ethnographic research, as Jesse Proudfoot writes, includes "the discovery that key elements of my research were inextricably connected to my own anxieties as a researcher."[32] Recognizing that psychoanalytic theories of the unconscious are inextricable from the European imagination through which they emerged, I approach my arguments against a backdrop of understanding the colonial psyche as one that represses the "violent acts and desires of colonization."[33] My presentation of psychoanalytic self-analysis in contending with extinction anxieties is thus inevitably also a reading and critique of Euro-American conservation desires expressed in-landscape in Bahia, Brazil.

Extinction Anxiety

Before we left the mountain, I stood with the botanist at the mountain's edge as he scanned the horizon. "It's a nice spot, it's so sad . . . it can be preserved in cultivation, but I don't see it being safe anywhere else. There must be a reason this plant only grows here. Maybe it just never dispersed to other hills that are like this, but none are near here." I suddenly heard myself saying out loud, "*If only we could ask what it needs . . .*" before trailing off, self-conscious that this was an embarrassing remark. The botanist smirked at this glib, Pollyanna response, not missing a beat: "The plant needs to be here. Now you see the real problem—it's not people taking a few seeds or cuttings of plants, it's development." I blushed.

Shortly after this conversation ended, I became aware of energetic activity nearby. The botanist and I quickly joined others in the group who were busying themselves some meters away. I wrote in my field notes on the mountain,

> [People] start digging out small plants and putting them in a bag with a penknife. I feel like I've been thrown into a strange version of the monkey wrench gang. I *want* them to have these plants . . . it feels sad but also victorious? Someone passes a penknife off in front of the company biologist. It's hard to imagine she isn't aware or didn't see what it was used for, it still has dirt on it. Maybe she is glad, or just doesn't care . . . or maybe she does care, maybe she understands what is going to ultimately happen to this species on this mountain.

These acts illustrate the at times complicated meanings of more-than-human care work. What are we to make of the quick and covert ripping of plants from the only place they are known to flourish as a purported act of care? Alongside questions of care, these acts point to anxiety as a vital inflection point, an impediment to desire.[34] How are we to understand the "object" of extinction anxieties in relation to the diminishing of *A. marylanae*?[35]

Given the fluidity of the species concept for plants, and the various ways that species difference is enacted in thought as well as scientific practice, I find it easy enough to speculate on the possibilities that other populations of the species might turn up elsewhere, as they did for the imminently threatened *U. buiningii* I describe in chapter 2. Or maybe the species will be recategorized or combined with another newly discovered *Arrojadoa* species that is less imperiled. It is possible to imagine how social and scientific practices that coproduce species might somehow redirect *A. marylanae* away from extinction even if the biopolitical forces shaping its extinction trajectory remain unchanged. Still, I see a discordance between discussing these possibilities for how *A. marylanae* might be known in the future in a way that saves it from extinction in contrast to how I actually felt watching these critically endangered cacti swaying in the wind, as if surveying their own impending demise.

There is a sense of deeply privileged intellectual curiosity in writing about species as coproduced categories amid watching a plant's extinction unfurl. Drawing on various ways of marking difference, collectors and botanists have named roughly twelve thousand different species of cacti over time, but only fifteen hundred to two thousand or so are formally accepted as species today by the scientific community. It is therefore easy enough to wonder about *A. marylanae* in this context—might another botanist come along and declare that, based on genetic analysis—as opposed to the morphological approach I described earlier—*A. marylanae* is not in fact a new species but merely a subspecies or local variation? How would this alter my relations to this plant I have now spent years thinking with? Revealing the critical workings of science as a social process can leave one feeling increasingly ambivalent about emotions attached to thinking of a species as teetering toward permanent absence. But as much as taxonomy and species epistemologies may change as scientific knowledge evolves, the living creatures that they are meant to represent do not diminish or become any less real or significant; they are real regardless of whether that "real" evolves as a process of knowing.

In stark contrast to this detached intellectual distance, on the mountain, I felt an urgency, a compulsion to care for this plant imbued with signifiers of rarity and imminent threat by the scientists and collectors I accompanied. I was moved *to care* (at least, this is how I understood it at the time), and in being moved, I recognized in the actions of others crossing thresholds of possible illicitness a last-ditch and likely futile enactment of what I believe they perceived as a labor of care. What moved us toward caring therefore matters a great deal for thinking about how extinction stories might be rewritten toward other trajectories and what *A. marylanae* represented as a species when we planted a small, house-grown plant in the Sincorá as part of what I see as a ritual meant to mask the psychic threat of extinction's cause.[36] I cannot speculate on how others unconsciously encountered *A. marylanae* on Serra Escura. Perhaps some were simply in the thrall of the experience of witnessing extinction itself as a fetishized experience of *jouissance*.[37] "Enjoying" extinction is a noteworthy application of Lacanian thought for political ecology, and it is very likely that some of the members of my group experienced an excess of aching pleasure as some of the few visitors permitted to watch a cactus in the process of being unmade by extractive capitalism. Or perhaps others were able to successfully shrug off the affects and emotional weight of encountering extinction, concerned more with the collection of seeds that might enable the species to persist, if not flourish, within the confines of their own collections. Maybe some of them didn't care at all and were only concerned with temporarily fulfilling that seductive urge to covet and possess yet another plant. But staying with the tension between thinking and feeling species is vital to the task of learning with nonhuman life while also revealing the import of the unconscious and psychoanalysis as method to bring the unconscious to the level of speech. For this, I must stay with my own encounter as a confrontation with the place of the unconscious in the making of the world.

I give attention now to when I heard myself say "*if only we could ask it what it needs*" while looking out over Serra Escura. Psychoanalysis tells us that such a blurting out of speech is often very meaningful, especially if the conscious self recognizes it, as I immediately did, as an embarrassing remark. Embarrassment, Lacan writes, is "when you don't know what to do with yourself any more,

[and] you look for something behind which to shield yourself."
Embarrassment is a "slight form of anxiety."[38] Anxiety becomes
present when "something that should not have been exposed, as
something meant to remain hidden, becomes present."[39] Through
the lens of psychoanalysis, I interpret this remark to mean that "I"
(the conscious self) heard "myself" (the unconscious self) speak.
Imagine inserting the word *but* into this expression—*"but* if only
we could ask what it needs." This *but* is an insertion of a kind of uncertainty into speech. In "[but] if only . . . ," we can say another discourse is present. As psychoanalyst Bruce Fink explains, this *but* is
"announcing the unconscious subject of enunciation, and thereby
showing that the subject is split—of two minds, so to speak . . .
conscious and unconscious."[40] For Lacan, it is in this brief temporal
moment, a flicker of what would seem to be someone else's speech
within our own, that we see the unconscious make itself known to
"us." The unconscious slipping into the conscious reveals how anxiety manifested through *A. marylanae* as "a signal," an interruption
alerting me to what was being exposed beyond the plant itself, yet
signified through it.

To understand the cactus in relation to desire, we must place
the cactus within a chain of signifiers.[41] *A. marylanae* was by no
means the only cactus I encountered during several weeks of participatory cactoexploration with my primary research subjects.
I saw other tall, columnar cacti on other mountains in Brazil,
some so exceptional in color and form that they felt ethereal and
otherworldly—the stunning blues and great wisps of golden hair
of cacti in the *Pilosocereus* genus, the enticingly smooth blue-gray
skin of *Cipocereus bradei*—but they did not affect me in the same
way *A. marylanae* did. It was not the cactus itself as a corporeal being that lured me to care, but neither does this negate the charms or
living wonder of these plants. We can see, then, that *A. marylanae*
became something else; it became inscribed with other meaning

through these topological twists affixing the unconscious in the world, the extimacy of succulent life.

The "signal" of the fading away of the cactus marks the fading away of desire through the imposition of anxiety. Anxiety, which as a "cut," in Lacan's words, works to safeguard the conscious self, also alerts us to what might emerge through the work of analysis rather than negation. I see a desire for flourishing becoming knotted through contending with the anxiety that extinction elicits when confronted by its nearness at hand. "It's upon the cutting edge of anxiety that we have to hold fast."[42] The cactus alerted me to the painful recognition of accelerating intergenerational unmaking of life, yet producing a sense of psychic immobility to enact a world otherwise.[43] The knotting of desire, to think knots further with Donna Haraway, speaks to how "actual encounters are what make beings" and how the unconscious becomes articulated through encounters in the world.[44] In this way, we can see desires as entangled in the creation of beings as knotted encounters, inside and out.

My embarrassing remark "*if only we could ask it what it needs*" was the bringing to the level of speech an unconscious desire of the Other's desire (was I asking, for instance, "what does this cactus desire from *me*?"), but one thwarted by the anxiety emergent from extinction close at hand. On the mountain, there was a buzz and excitement to rescue *A. marylanae* from the grips of impending doom. My field notes, photographs, and videos from this day resonate with a high-intensity energy to care, in which people removed plants from the only habitat in which they are known to survive, justified as work to maintain and continue the species "as well as possible" elsewhere in Brazil.[45] Two years later, this sentiment is more ambiguous. Perhaps a cutting of *A. marylanae* now grows in a greenhouse in Bahia or a seedling has emerged in Belgium. So what? Although care on the mountain might appear as an enactment of responsibility, such a reading is also a missed opportunity to understand this effort to care as anxiety in motion.[46] Approaching this desire to care instead as an affective engagement with anxiety, some clarity emerges: I now see in these activities the anxiety in extinction's nearness being "cut away," materialized through the literal cutting away of the plants themselves, to conceal what their diminishing presence painfully asserted.[47]

What occurred on the mountain with *A. marylanae* was a prompting to care, but care set in motion by anxiety's presence. Each fallen seed encased in bright pink fruit felt so important, at risk, precious. Why did the cactus not only move us but *lure* us to care?[48] A turn toward psychoanalysis to understand what motivates cactus collectors' desires (and anxieties, including my own) is not an effort to develop a generalizable understanding of what "the cactus" signifies to collectors writ large. The value of a psychoanalytic approach here to writing a political ecology of succulent life is its bringing of the unconscious to the level of speech to excavate how cacti function as signifiers in ways that mediate their relations with human practices. In turn, this shapes their trajectories as species toward flourishing or diminution.[49] This is a journey of psychogeographic excavation to reveal what might permit reorientations toward flourishing and the obstacles that trip up the desiring subject along the way.[50] To bring the unconscious to speech is the praxis of psychoanalysis, and in the context of thinking with extinction, it is a praxis of more-than-human consequence. Coming to grips with *A. marylanae*'s extinction, I would argue, speaks to the profound difficulties of engaging with extinction as a disorientating disruption in time, one in which the anxieties of accelerated extinction become fixated through the absence of species as movements of life in time lost. Extinction anxiety is therefore anxiety over the disruption of time itself made manifest through an expectant, dreadful, permanent absence.[51]

Confronting the Signal That Does Not Deceive

Something truly disturbing is embedded in the dislocated temporalities wrought by extinction. To speak of extinctions accelerated or brought about by human hands and economies is to speak of absence in an altogether different register than the absences we as individuals all navigate in the life course through love, kinship, and loss. In this vein, the late Deborah Bird Rose described extinction as a "double death," which gives attention to extinction not as death itself but as its profound *amplification* "so that the balance between life and death is overrun."[52] Bird Rose wrote powerfully about multispecies temporalities as "embodied knots of multispecies time" as a way into reconciling—and perhaps intervening in—the profound losses of species wrought through generational death. She refers to extinction elsewhere, drawing on the work of James Hatley, as *aeonicide.* In this way, aeonicide—intergenerational death—is an attack on time itself.[53]

Plants are wedded into place in a way that animals are not, literally connecting the earth and the sky through their very existence. Plants bridge worlds just as they bring others into being and sustain so many more.[54] To understand the destruction of a mountain in relation to the life of a plant species in formation is, in the words of Nan Shepherd, to contend with Serra Escura as a "living mountain."[55] Emergent in the story of *A. marylanae* is the incredible anxiety of the Anthropocene (or what I prefer to think of as the Capitalocene) as a psychogeologic moment, in which the causes of this great unmaking are named and yet (some) feel a compulsion turn away in horrific shame rather than contend with the weight of desire, the enactment of flourishing.[56]

My invocation of "we" here is not meant as an inclusive universal—a limitation of my analysis, of course, is that it is a *self*-analysis, though I hold the conviction that it has analytical power that extends beyond me (or I would not have put it in this book).

Scholars like Robin Wall Kimmerer, Marisol de la Cadena, and Sophie Chao, among many others, describe decidedly different kinds of human–plant relations across a number of Indigenous cultures immersed in reciprocal forms of human–plant care that also speak to understanding extinction as a matter of concern otherwise.[57] There have always been peoples who both recognize the varied intelligences and personhoods of plants that perhaps render these Anthropocenic anxieties illegible and in varied and distinctive ways maintain and seek out reciprocal relations of human–plant flourishing. This "we" is an exclusive "we," one that seeks to recognize the long-standing harms of human–nature dichotomies that Euro-American societies and psyches have wrought. It is also these societies that remain chiefly responsible for the interlinked and ongoing global crises of pollution, climate change, and biodiversity loss.[58] Exclusions also mark absences; I do not know more about people who currently or may have once held different relations with *A. marylanae* or Serra Escura prior to its enclosure. The time I was afforded in Bahia to learn with *A. marylanae* was altogether too brief and limited to interrogate how its history intersects with the profoundly violent past of Bahia's colonization and nearly wholesale extermination of Indigenous peoples, its brutal history of slavery, or Serra Escura's more immediate history of quarrying and mining over the past several centuries. By the time of my visit to Serra Escura, the mountain was held by a mining corporation, and my visit was restricted to a matter of hours under the watchful eye of corporate staff. But to return to my own experiences and those of the communities of conservationists and collectors that were the focus of my research, the story of *A. marylanae* demonstrates that much work remains to be done in grasping for routes out of dismal Anthropocenic thought.

As a signifier of extinction's nearness through *objet a,* the cactus in this story is not the object of desire; it is a signal of the misplaced object-cause of desire. To approach *A. marylanae* "directly" as

an object of desire would be to miss how it is inscribed with significations that elicited the attention and focus of both myself and the
collectors I was with that only become apparent when viewed from
the side.[59] The *jouissance* experienced in encountering *A. marylanae*
is thus also the pain of how the cactus operates as a signifier of
extinction as an "open wound," revealing the unmaking of planetary possibilities for flourishing. But thinking with others and the
politics this signal begets, we must move beyond fantasizing about
unmaking—we are compelled, in Natasha Myers's words, to "resist
the lure of apocalypse like your life depends on it. . . . The only way
to thwart the momentum of the Anthropocene is to break the spell
of capitalism and activate processes of decolonization. And while
it is clearly time to dismantle Anthropocene thinking, there is no
need to wait until the end of this world to begin to conjure livable
ones."[60] Thinking with Myers, it is important to recognize that for
many Indigenous peoples, this sense of a portending apocalypse is
not a lure set in the future but a tangible and horrific experience
of the past. As Diné geographers Andrew Curley and Majerle Lister
write, drawing on the work of Potawatomi scholar Kyle White, "Indigenous peoples have experienced world-changing catastrophes
before. Settler states such as Australia, Canada, New Zealand, and
the United States (US) are already existing Indigenous dystopias."[61]
For many, then, this "lure of the apocalypse" is not imagined as a
profound new rupture of life on earth itself but instead as a new
wave in ongoing colonial violence that continues to assault Indigenous life.

In moving to care for plants, then, as a movement of radical
thought to think beyond alluring dystopia, caring might entail in
part what Michael Marder names plant-thinking, the radical work
of nourishing the "proliferation of vegetal life," a praxis of care
in thought/action through becoming open to (in Myers's words)
the "vegetal sensorium."[62] This work of thinking and acting with
plants otherwise demands respecting the "dispersed" and unique

"botanical ontologies" of vegetal life that continue to be rendered otherwise through capitalist logics of acceleration, uniformity, and individuation.[63] Here we arrive back at the significance and stakes of the politics of caring for vegetal life when confronted by Capitalocene-induced extinction as a deep rupture in the flow of vegetal time that cannot be dislocated from space. The roots of plants ensure that such distinctions between time and space are not so clear; plants point us in the direction of geography as a way of seeing time enacted in place.[64] To care for plants is to confront and insist on possibilities for flourishing through enactments of response-ability, protecting the vegetal flow of time, whose roots run very deep. To foster flourishing geographies is therefore to enact collaborative efforts in opposition to Anthropocenic thinking as a vital (and, here, vegetal) politics of interdependent futures.

The production of desire is never a matter internal to the subject alone but always in relation with the external world and what grabs our desire.[65] Plants, as Sophie Chao writes, "are good to think as an embodiment of relational becoming."[66] Perhaps, just as plants often drift into the background in so many stories of multispecies life, they can also "grab" us in unique ways. Plants do not live and die as we do; they inhabit what Michael Marder refers to as heterotemporalities. For the plant, as he explains, "is a loose alliance of multiple temporalities of growth—some of its parts sprouting faster, others slower, still others decaying and rotting."[67] Maybe there is something about how many cacti *appear* more as individuals and less as heterotemporal collectives than other forms of plant life that so enraptures collectors and botanists. To the human eye, *A. marylanae* do appear as singular beings on Serra Escura—individual columnar cacti bodies studding craggy outcrops of quartz. It is unambiguously the case that some cactus collectors imagine closer affinities between people and cacti than other plants because they see something of themselves looking back when observing a tall, thin cactus like *A. marylanae* wavering in the wind on a mountain's peak. But we know so little about these plants and what binds them to Serra Escura as species formations within entangled ecologies.[68] Thus, when the botanist said that the plant "needs to be here," he was gesturing toward an unknown set of relations that connect the above- and belowground ecology, geography, and geology that permit *A. marylanae* to flourish.

The Warp and Weft of Extinction

What I find in analyzing my own anxieties in encountering this species perilously close to extinction is the challenge in coming to terms with loss, but also response-ability. Response to the species as a continuous flow of living time that deserves not only recognition and protection in a legal sense, as an expression of concern, but care as a more-than-human endeavor, a vital insistence for flourishing as a response to feeling arrested by Capitalocenic thinking and global biodiversity declines as an unraveling of time.

When I said *"if only we could ask it what it needs,"* I was not expressing an actual desire to ask this plant how to satiate its needs for it to flourish. I understood, before the botanist needed to remind me, that this species is part of a greater living mountain and that its demise as a flourishing being was always knotted within the ecologies of others that will also be unmade through this work of resource extraction, just as other ecologies on other mountains will also be unmade. This is not to deny the possibilities for renewal or unexpected futures or that *A. marylanae* still persists against the odds. Nor is this some circuitous route toward reasserting preservationist desires for "Edenic" natures absent human presence. Many species of cacti and other succulents quite happily move across great distances, ecosystems, and geographies either in association with other creatures or by human design. Perhaps, as the mining company suggests, in sixty years' time, these relocated plants will again find the means to persist or even flourish on a hollowed-out mountain. Or, perhaps not. But when my unconscious came to the level of speech, I do not think I had only this cactus in mind.

Extinction stories are more-than-human ventures. They thread the desire to know and the desire to care for nonhuman others through lifelines already transformed by human activity and the forces of global capitalism. Extinctions travel: even when their routes are not visibly linear, extinctions forge new connections, just as they mark the impossibility of return. But extinctions are also contextual and prone to conjecture; the lines of extinction are plagued by uncertainty as well as hopeful promise. As other stories of extinction in this book show, plants with remarkably limited habitat ranges can lead remarkably cosmopolitan lives, while others may be consigned to more provincial fates. Planting a small cactus in the Sincorá, protecting it with a ring of stones, was the marking of absence made present through the rupture of plant-time, but it also sought to conceal us from the painful present. Despite its prominence as a new species, it would be difficult to obtain *A. marylanae* elsewhere. But even if one could, what would it mean, dislocated from the lifeworld of Serra Escura as a living mountain? While other succulent species I encountered in researching this book are on trajectories toward "extinction in the wild" but persisting in the world in commodified form, *A. marylanae* is accelerating, it would seem, toward permanent absence, though you can already find its seeds for sale online from distant locales (mostly in Europe). This may seem a minor distinction in comparison to the weight of the species' functional disappearance from the wild as flourishing ecological beings, but it is a distinction that proves powerful in considering the possibilities for future trajectories of life.

Species trajectories are not only determined by evolutionary and biological constraints of vegetal being, nor economic or political forces variously transforming them into lively commodities, casting them out as life-forms beyond ethical concern, or aiding in their protection. All of these forces and constraints are further mediated by desire. Despite its prominence as a species new to science, *A. marylanae*'s future on the edge of a mountain remains exceedingly precarious; for better or worse, it fails to incite the kinds of interests that other cacti do. Death by development, however, seems far more certain, and as I found, the shadow of development can elicit deeply held anxieties about extinction as a "double death" at much grander scales.

Desire is both fickle and tenacious, and it forges new relations. For every cactus seeping with charismatic charms that so enrapture a botanist, another remains poorly described, with charms that remain unfamiliar or at a distance. For every cactus that compels collectors on multiday journeys across difficult terrain in the hope of finding viable seed from a plant teetering toward permanent disappearance, there are always more that face a quieter unmaking, not by the individual hands of desirous collectors, but by those who permit and profit from ecological destruction. Contending with desire in this light is more than the work of bringing the unconscious to speech; it is also to ask about the relations we desire to keep. What worlds are missed in failing to speak of desire?

\5/

A New Illicit Trade

*To kill a species is to shut down a unique story; and, although
all specific stories must eventually end, we seldom want
unnatural ends.*

—Holmes Rolston III, *Duties to Endangered Species*

Midway through my research on illegal trade in succulent plants, I
was led to Northern California by colleagues who told me about a
recent spate of large-scale succulent poaching incidents. "You have
to go see what's happening there!" a California botanist exclaimed
to me during a workshop in Querétaro, Mexico. News reports featured spectacular talk of plant heists involving rock climbing gear,
midnight raids, organized succulent gangs, stakeouts, and even
a helicopter-assisted succulent theft. I traveled to Northern California because I was interested to learn from those involved firsthand in these stories about an emergent illegal trade in the species
Dudleya farinosa, a coastal-dwelling succulent, and rising concerns
about species endangerment or even extinction as a result of the
plant's desirability (Figure 32).

What struck me as most perplexing about the *Dudleya* problem
was the lack of robust information on why these plants seemingly
became so desirous to succulent collectors so quickly. Dozens of articles in prominent international news outlets detailed profit-driven

Figure 32. Several *Dudleya farinosa* perched on cliffs overlooking the Pacific coast in Mendocino County, California.

narratives about why people stole thousands of plants for trans-continental trade. While it is likely that some people have made a lot of money selling species of *Dudleya*, deeper explanations for why a plant suddenly became so desirous as to make its illegal trade profitable and worth its notable risks remained thin. Given that *D. farinosa* was legally available for purchase from commercial growers, further explanatory details about drivers of their demand as well as the context for their widespread theft were sorely lacking.

In time, learning about the ecology of the *Dudleya* genus proved important to deciphering the emergence of this illicit trade. Water, too, plays a largely unacknowledged role in the stories of illegal trade that follow, but its presence (and absence) is essential to understanding the ecology of the *Dudleya* genus and what binds them together as "kin of a kind."[1] I was enraptured by the wetness of northern coastal California—an immersive ecology where water obliterates the boundaries between sea, land, and air. The air is thick with it, and the ground soaks it up like a sponge, where vegetation decomposes rapidly under the teeming weight of microbes and insects. *D. farinosa* is a species of succulent plant that thrives in this part of North America, equally famous for redwoods as for marijuana cultivation. It has learned to survive the strange seasonality of coastal California's precipitation patterns, where rain is withheld when many plants would need it most and comes in excess when they would not. In the coming days, I would take a series of long walks along the rocky coastal cliffs and beaches where *D. farinosa* lives in Humboldt and Mendocino Counties, between the turbulent Pacific and the spongy sedum-carpeted bluffs above. I have never found a place so immensely beautiful amid such relentless rain and cloud-covered skies.

Perhaps because I had another plant in mind, I'd forgotten that my drive north from Sacramento, where I'd conducted interviews at the headquarters of the California Department of Fish and Wildlife (CDFW), would take me straight into redwood country. Because of flooding on California's Highway 101 and my unwavering time optimism, the drive took longer than I expected, and it was late afternoon when I reached Mendocino County. Despite the fading light of mid-January, I abandoned my rental car for a walk in the forest. Gazing up until my neck ached, I was struck with awe by the giant redwoods above me, whose trunks and limbs seemed to stretch forever into a coastal fog and rain that came down in heavy drops within an even heavier mist, muffling the sounds of the forest like a blanket of snow. Water was everywhere and in everything—fat, slow drops fell from branches above, hitting my face with an audible thud; the air was soft and wet as it entered my lungs; currents of mist moved overhead as tree branches appeared and disappeared in and out of whorls of fog.

It was my first visit to these redwood forests, and I was unprepared for encountering this landscape and its sensuous, wet ecology. Before I departed and made my way farther north along the Pacific coast into Humboldt County, I pushed my hand against what looked like the solid mass of a fallen tree. I watched as my fingers, followed by my wrist and arm, passed through it with little effort into the newly forming soil. Watching my arm disappear within the matter of the decomposing tree later reminded me of a telling passage by Catriona Sandilands: "Tactile eroticism thus threatens atomism; the transgression of skin disrupts the certainty of self as it invites the possibility of experiencing a heated joining with another. More than that, eroticism creates a desire for the Other *as* Other, as a being whose very alterity marks the possibility of excitation; sensual desire is about courting difference itself."[2] There is much to be said about the desire for what appears as Other and the challenges this encounter presents as a moment of learning with radical difference. Still, this Other is not the Other the unconscious seeks through desire; it is a fantasy of encountering the Other. Recognizing what makes the otherworldly very much part of our worlding in seeking out the ineluctably Other of the Other is perhaps the greater challenge.

Succulent Crimes

I met the deputy district attorney of Humboldt County in the seaside town of Arcata, California, in early 2019. Over a round of dirty martinis seated at the otherwise empty bar of a dimly lit Italian restaurant, we discussed the particulars of why three foreign nationals would conspire to harvest and smuggle thousands of succulents from California to South Korea and how they were swiftly prosecuted by the DA's office. It was not that succulents were being illegally harvested and shipped from California to South Korea that interested me per se. Instead, it was how different these incidents appeared when compared to the other forms of illegal plant trade I had studied. *D. farinosa* is neither rare, new to science, endemic to a small geographic region, particularly unique in its appearance, nor listed as endangered on any state, federal, or international species lists. It is found on coastlines all the way from southern Oregon to Santa Barbara, California. For all these reasons, it also isn't regulated by CITES. Importantly, there is already a well-established and perfectly legal international and domestic trade in the species. Prior to several spectacular plant heists between 2017–2018 and the international attention that followed, *D. farinosa* was of little concern to the California conservation and law enforcement communities.

There are various reasons why parallel illicit economies exist alongside legal ones. Yet unlike other trades in which illicit markets come to be regulated as legal ones (such as the marijuana trade), the legal trade in *D. farinosa* predates the illicit one by decades. Sometimes an illegal trade emerges because of scarcity or access to licit goods (pharmaceuticals, for instance), but *D. farinosa* was readily available, and at competitive prices. What's more, prior to California law enforcement uncovering this new illegal trade, interest and demand for commercially available *D. farinosa* had declined in the United States. Many commercial succulent growers in California had even stopped including them in their annual plant catalogs. At a time of surging popularity and interest in succulent plants domestically, *D. farinosa* was falling by the wayside. As one California succulent grower commented, "at a time when they were stealing them out of the wild, we couldn't sell them at our plant stalls for five bucks."

In the case of *D. farinosa,* a focus on the production of an illegal trade requires attention to both the roots and routes of trade. To extend this vegetal metaphor, if excavating roots of trade leads to explicating consumer desires, then I needed to trace how those roots fuel the growth of new routes reaching into new locations and affecting diverse ecologies. I could do this only by following species in their global circulations. But the roots of trade can also be understood more literally. My understanding of the emergence and development of illicit economies in wild species is also aided through closer attention to the biology, natural history, and materiality of traded plants, which shape, enable, and disable species trajectories and their capacity to be transformed into lively commodities.[3]

Throughout this chapter and the two that follow, I develop an understanding of how an illegal trade in two *Dudleya* species developed. Furthering the overall aims of this book to theorize desire within a political ecology of plants, the story of *Dudleya* also reveals how species trajectories toward flourishing or extinction can unexpectedly become yoked to one another through processes of plant commodification, the psychologies of collecting consumer markets, and political and legal responses to IWT. Complex interactions between law, practices of commodification, and the unique capacities of plants can both transform and amplify succulent desires. And, as chapter 7 reveals, political agendas and harmful narratives rooted in stereotypes and racism can also affix themselves to plants in troubling ways. Whereas this chapter begins with a piecing together of a new illegal trade, it ends by reflecting on how discursive framings of conservation and IWT have changed in recent years through the deepening integration of security interests with conservation. These transformations in what the work of conservation entails, and how IWT is understood and responded to, hold serious consequences for people and plants alike.

To Catch a Succulent Thief

"Mendocino is a post office you can usually walk into and there's maybe one person in front of you. And [one day] there was an Asian gentleman who had sixty packages or thereabouts," a game warden of CDFW began to explain to me one late afternoon over coffee. In December 2017, a woman in line behind the man was irked by the long wait. She noted that dirt was falling out of the bottom of some of the boxes. When she inquired about what he was shipping, the man purportedly replied, holding a finger to his lips, "Shhh, something very valuable." When she asked him where the contents of the box came from, he pointed west, toward the ocean. Based on the man's responses, she worried he was shipping illegally harvested abalone, a prized food in many East Asian countries and a protected species along the California coastline after decades of overharvesting.

Armed with her concerns, the woman phoned the California Fish and Wildlife CalTip Hotline, alerting the agency to her suspicions. The tip made its way to the game warden, who connected to the post office and asked them to flag the packages for further scanning as he didn't have a warrant to search the boxes himself. When the warden received an email several weeks later that customs officials identified the contents as the succulent *D. farinosa*, he had to look them up on the internet, having never heard of the species before. "At this point, when I heard about the *Dudleyas*, I'm thinking, are they taking these things because they're medicinal, or do they have some other use? I have no idea. . . . I mean, you can buy succulents at Home Depot for five bucks," he says. That the man shipping the succulents was so cavalier about his activities suggested a lack of concern for a possible run-in with the law. It also signaled something about the status of concern afforded plants by law enforcement at this time: succulent theft was simply not on CDFW's radar as a matter of concern.

The game warden is an energetic and outgoing officer who agreed to meet with me to discuss the matter of *D. farinosa* thefts not only because he was the first officer in CDFW to become aware of the issue and bring greater attention to it but because he strongly felt that "the most important thing is to get this out to the public. All of our tips since that first case have come from people who read media articles. An informed public just expands our police." Others working on the side of the law disagree and have expressed concern that the attention this issue has received in national and international press might only drive others to steal more plants. The game warden acknowledged that the culture of law enforcement at CDFW is not to make a name for yourself in the public eye. His division does policework; and while I was given a warm reception on the phone by several members of the CDFW Special Operations Unit who worked undercover on several incidents of *D. farinosa* poaching, they declined to be formally interviewed, citing ongoing undercover investigations.

When I met the game warden in Point Arena, a picturesque coastal town full of stunning cliff walks and immense views of the Pacific, he arrived at our interview in a black CDFW truck with a drug- and abalone-sniffing German shepherd crated in the truck's kennel. Sporting black wraparound sunglasses, a bullet-proof vest, and enough conspicuous sidearms strapped to his legs and chest to intimidate a researcher, if not the public writ large, he painted a striking portrait as a lawman in the epicenter of California's infamous Emerald Triangle. Whereas Point Arena has developed into a popular tourist town, many small coastal towns in Northern California, especially farther north in Humboldt County, have not, as years of economic depression linked to a withering timber industry and other rural economies have been the cause of high unemployment, widespread drug use (mostly methamphetamines, but also opioids), and, as Lyndsie Bourgon recently described, valuable hardwood and redwood burl poaching.[4] For these reasons, strong antagonisms between rural communities in Northern California and CDFW, among other state conservation agencies, persist. Despite his imposing visage, the warden was excited to discuss the *Dudleya* subject as we made our way into a local coffee shop, where several wary customers glanced nervously in our direction.

Although the game warden was intrigued by the initial incident of *Dudleya* harvesting he encountered, he presumed it was an isolated matter. "A month later, I'm patrolling just south of Point Arena, and I get a phone call." The caller said, "Hey, I don't know if it's anything, but I was driving south and I saw this Asian guy with a backpack bail over the side of the cliff. There's another guy standing on the bluff. . . . He's looking around, he's obviously a lookout." I could feel my eyebrows raise during the warden's re-telling of this part of the story and what clearly sounded to me like racial profiling. "This is the MO [modus operandi] of abalone poachers. Every time," he says. "You go there during the low tide, there's three people on the bluff. There are guys down below rap-ing and pillaging, they've got radios, they've got cell phones. So I assume they're abalone poachers." They were not abalone poach-ers. The warden narrated the incident for me: "I scrambled down the cliff and see this guy taking plants. . . . He's got a backpack full of plants," the warden said. "He speaks a few words of English. He's a Chinese citizen. Lives in San Francisco. And I said, 'What are you doing?' He said, 'They're for my garden.' And I said, 'BS. I have you on video using a post office shipping plants out.' I just tried to guess it was him [from the previous incident] and he said, 'OK.' It was a lucky guess. I said, 'What are you getting for them?' He said, 'Twenty, twenty-five dollars a piece.' At this point, this is the first time anyone that we know of in California has contacted anybody for taking a succulent from the coast. . . . Really, I wasn't sure what to write him up for," the warden concluded.

Presuming that what the man was doing was illegal, but unsure exactly under what section of the California Penal Code, the war-den finally wrote the man a citation for violation of a niche section of the Penal Code he found specifically addressing the removal of plants from landscaped areas under management by the California Department of Transportation (CalTrans). Before letting the man go, the warden made him replant the *D. farinosa*. "The main thing I didn't do, that I would've done with pretty much any other spe-cies, abalone, deer, or bear—I didn't search his vehicle." He told me he regretted this, as future incidents would suggest he might have found many more *D. farinosa* inside the suspect's car.

More incidents soon followed. In March 2018, the same game warden apprehended two South Korean nationals in the United States on tourist visas, again near Point Arena. Like the incident before, he assumed the tipoff was for abalone poachers. Instead, he caught two young men stealing 850 *D. farinosa* on private property. The warden had the men spend four to five hours replanting the *D. farinosa* before releasing them. "What I found interesting here was their passports. They'd had a lot of entries into the States, but going through their passports and all of their paperwork, [they had] succulent vendors [names from] all over the world. They had succulent vendors in Europe, in Hong Kong, Korea. . . ." He was intent on the men receiving the harshest penalty the district attorney could manage. "This wasn't their first rodeo. These guys were global plant poachers. If you looked at their paperwork, it was all vendors, and vendors' purchase lists." The men eventually pled guilty to grand theft and were fined $10,000 each and ordered to leave the country in lieu of a prison sentence, a serious penalty in the context of California wildlife poaching sentencing, which usually results in a misdemeanor. Driving home the significance of their sentencing and its potential to serve as a strong deterrent, the warden explained, "A few years ago, we busted two guys for taking two deer out of season, no licenses, at night, spotlighting, trespassing on someone's property. You name it. Every code section is broken, and they confess to it and we caught them with the deer. They showed us where they did it, and they ended up paying $500." It was hard to imagine how the foreign status of the perpetrators in the *D. farinosa* case didn't play some role in these very different sentencing outcomes.

Successfully charging the men with a felony was a major win for CDFW and county prosecutors, the warden explained. "These are the precedent-setting cases. . . . [Now] we've got a felony on the books. That's huge." Here the fact that the plants were on private property made possible the charge of grand theft, resulting in harsher sentencing. At the time of the March 2018 incident, the warden still presumed the *D. farinosa* thefts were a problem isolated to their local area in Mendocino. But a few days after an article appeared in the *Mercury News* (a Silicon Valley newspaper) about the incident, he received a call from a post office in Humboldt County. "The woman at the post office said, 'I read the article [in the *Mercury News*]. I have a feeling the same thing is happening up here. This group of guys has been coming into the post office, shipping packages to Korea.' I said, 'How many packages are we talking? Ten? Twenty? A hundred?' She said, 'They easily shipped over two thousand packages over four years.' So at this point, I'm like, *whoa*. I thought it was [only] in Mendocino, or an isolated, one-time deal. So at this point, I immediately contacted our special ops team. I said, 'This is what they do, they do commercialization.'"

Following the tip provided by the post office worker in Humboldt, CDFW's undercover special ops team eventually caught up with a trio taking *D. farinosa* from multiple locations in Humboldt County. After tailing the group and capturing photographic and video evidence on stakeouts, the team was able to build a strong case. After apprehending them with a rental van containing more than one thousand plants, CDFW obtained a search warrant for a cabin the suspects had rented, where evidence of a larger, international network of *D. farinosa* clients was found. Ultimately, CDFW seized more than twenty-three hundred poached *D. farinosa,* not including those allowed to pass through customs while they were building the case as part of Operation Succulent Package.

There are a lot of things that made the *D. farinosa* case in Humboldt County unique—its brazenness, the scale of theft, and its international scope being a few—but perhaps most of all was the swift prosecution and severe sentencing of three foreign nationals who pled guilty to conspiracy, fraud, stealing plants, and intent to commercialize wildlife in one of the shortest cases in the state prosecutor's career. Whereas the previous incident occurred on private property, it is less common to receive a felony charge for taking plants from public lands, much less a sentence of nearly four years in prison and a $10,000 fine, which is what resulted in the Humboldt case. The swift prosecution and sentencing resulted from the organized casework of the CDFW Special Operations Unit, as the deputy district attorney who prosecuted the case explained: "I've seen murder cases that didn't have the [quality of] investigation that these folks did. It was really impressive," he said.

It was necessary to prove a degree of coordination and planning among parties to break California and federal law to charge the defendants with conspiracy, which raised the charges from a misdemeanor (the taking of plants from public lands) to a felony. "It's not a huge number of people. It's a small number of people taking a huge number of plants. That was the biggest surprise. What is disconcerting for us is, why *Dudleya*? You can go to . . . any yard garden store and find very nice succulent plants for $4.99," a captain of CDFW's Law Enforcement Division explained to me across his desk at their Sacramento headquarters. "It's just decorative. Yes, that's a little bit odd, but the fact of the matter is there is a demand, and it's high." In working with state prosecutors, CDFW wanted to set a strong precedent of supply-side deterrence to disincentivize would-be poachers from further illegal *Dudleya* harvesting. The DA explained:

> If a plant is in a public space, it is a misdemeanor to take the plant . . . and that doesn't necessarily really carry a heavy penalty. . . . In case law, there is a pretty good set of standards that the courts have laid out that says, "Hey, if you have a misdemeanor offense that is done in a manner that is conspired by other folks, you can charge a person with a felony, to try to commit a misdemeanor." And it should rarely be used,

but this was a situation that I felt very comfortable in doing it. We had three people, we had great evidence in terms of having them all on photograph, video. . . . They were all working together, they agreed to this crime of taking all of these plants . . . so I charged them with felony conspiracy.

The defendants were also charged with false filing with the state of California, essentially mail fraud, as the packages in which they were shipping out *D. farinosa* were variously labeled as bicycle spokes or clothing. "They ended up pleading to conspiracy, and each of them to one count of the false filing, and each of them to a count of removing plants, and a count of removing plants for the purpose of commercial sale," the DA explained. In addition to facing three-year, eight-month prison sentences, they were all required to pay $10,000 fines and forfeit $10,000 that was found in their rented cabin, to be used for putting up signs warning people not to take plants from public lands. The ultimate aim, according to the DA, was to put other would-be poachers "on notice." Instead of serving prison time, however, the judge permitted them to leave the United States within one week of their sentencing without the possibility to return.

The DA and I discussed at length the prosecution's strategy. It is remarkable to consider that stealing plants could result in such a severe sentencing until it becomes clear it was really mail fraud that enabled successfully charging the defendants with a felony. "One thing that sort of bothered me about this case," the DA explained, "[was] we got these people on postal [fraud], and agreeing to admit to this crime together [conspiracy], so I could see in a lot of places. . . . People taking all these plants, or one person taking these plants, and walking away with, maybe no jail time, and maybe a $500 fine. . . . So that was one thing that I wanted to start working on . . . some sort of legislative action that could be more responsive to situations like this. To try to deter behavior."

In addition to expressing his frustration that the law did not provide what he felt were stringent enough penalties for such large-scale theft, the DA reflected on his strong sense that the species in question also mattered:

> When it comes down to a practical reality . . . there is a better chance in prevailing in trial when you have a charismatic type animal like a bald eagle, like the symbol of our country, but even something cute, as opposed to something else. A lot of times you hear people that are skeptical, or adversarial, to the Endangered Species Act, they will bring up something like 'oh, it's some small, rare frog, who cares if it dies,' or if it is an insect. But when you talk about a charismatic animal like a bobcat, it changes the image. There was this . . . really brave advocate for the Endangered Species Act. Every time he'd go to trial, and he didn't have the [animal] victim with him—the victim couldn't be in court—he would put a stuffed animal of whatever the animal was at the end of the council bench and just have it sit there the whole time. And those things really matter.

The DA's perspective that legislative changes are required if plants are to be afforded the same kinds of protections as animals under the law resonates with the game warden's experience of encountering plant poachers for the first time and intuiting that it was wrong, but not knowing legally *why*. The DA went on to express that "there is more protection of the *habitat of creatures* than there is for plants."[5] Put another way, plants continue to be legally framed as the backdrop or the "habitat" for a livelier animal world.[6] Even within the U.S. Endangered Species Act (ESA), one of the most progressive and strong pieces of legislation ever written to protect endangered species, where the taking of any ESA-listed animal is strictly a violation of the act, ESA-listed plants are only explicitly protected on federal lands. This means that even for a critically endangered plant listed on the ESA, the law provides no protection for that species on private lands; this is especially concerning given that many ESA-listed plants are largely or even entirely found outside of federal or state protected areas. We might say that whereas the mobility of animals seems to afford them a sense of legal individuality (if not uniformly, legal personhood), plants are still largely seen as constitutive *of* place itself.[7] That the DA referenced the power of cuteness to make demands on people, courts, and institutions to care will resurface again in chapter 7, however.

A More Serious Crime

Based on prior intelligence work, in late 2018, CDFW was concerned about plans for a new large theft of *D. farinosa* plants and contacted a special agent with the U.S. Fish and Wildlife Service, who in turn requested a "lookout" with the U.S. Department of Homeland Security for a Korean man expected to be flying to the United States from South Korea. They suspected the man was involved in *D. farinosa* poaching. A few weeks later, CDFW was alerted to his arrival at Los Angeles International Airport by U.S. Customs and Border Patrol, and undercover officers quickly moved in to surveil him and his traveling companion.

About a week later, after picking up another man at the Los Angeles airport and renting a van and a car, the three men proceeded to Northern California and, over a series of separate trips, would remove more than three thousand *D. farinosa* and *D. caespitosa* (a closely related *Dudleya* species) from public lands and state parks. The man of primary concern to CDFW, Byungsu Kim, owned or had affiliations with commercial nurseries both outside San Diego and in South Korea. In a brazen move, Kim arranged for a visit from a county agriculture inspection officer for what he claimed were (a much smaller number of) cultivated *Dudleya* plants to acquire the necessary U.S. Department of Agriculture (USDA) phytosanitary paperwork for legal export of the plants to South Korea. In short, Kim's plan was to launder illegally taken wild plants into the legal market by attaching legal export paperwork to them, a not uncommon technique in a variety of wildlife trades but different from the previous *D. farinosa* poaching incidents described earlier. After receiving their paperwork, the men sought to transport these plants via a shipping exporter in Compton. CDFW was waiting for them. The plants were confiscated, and the three men were apprehended by CDFW agents.

In their mirandized interviews, Kim's accomplices admitted that it was not Kim's first time illegally collecting and exporting *Dudleya* plants from California. In fact, evidence presented in this case suggests that only the month prior, Kim had legally exported more than five thousand *Dudleya* plants via the very same mechanism, again listing the plants' place of origin as San Diego, with the same USDA inspection officer signing off on his export paperwork.[8] After meeting bail, Kim and one of the other men fled the United States to Mexico as fugitives, eventually making their way back to South Korea via China. Although they had their passports confiscated by authorities, they managed to obtain new passports from the Korean consulate in Los Angeles by falsely saying theirs were stolen. In February 2020, Kim was caught in South Africa in another plant poaching incident and convicted for stealing sixty thousand *Conophytum* succulent plants endemic to South Africa and Namibia. Some fifteen months later, on January 20, 2022, Byungsu Kim, now forty-six, was found guilty by U.S. District Court judge George H. Wu for his attempts to illegally export *Dudleya* species—mostly *D. farinosa*—to South Korea. One of Kim's original accomplices, Bong Jun Kim, pled guilty in 2019. Bong Jun Kim served four months in federal custody and was released in October 2019, after the judge imposed a sentence of time served. At the time of this writing, their third accomplice, Youngin Back, remains a fugitive.

As a result of the ongoing threat of *D. farinosa* poaching, on January 11, 2021, California State Assembly member Christopher Ward introduced legislation (AB 223) to specifically make the taking of any *Dudleya* species from state, local government, or private property without written permission of the landowner a misdemeanor in the state of California. For a first conviction, the penalty would be a fine of not less than $5,000 and up to $50,000, imprisonment for up to six months, or both the fine and imprisonment. For a subsequent conviction, the penalty would be a fine of at least $10,000 and up to $500,000, imprisonment for up to six months, or both. AB 223 was signed into law by California governor Gavin Newsom on September 28, 2021, and took immediate effect. It offers state prosecutors a new and more direct path for charging *Dudleya* poachers with a hefty penalty without requiring the proof of conspiracy. AB 223 makes *Dudleya* poaching one of the more severely punishable wildlife crimes (at least in financial terms) in the United States. Today, conservationists and law enforcement officials in California remain on high alert for *Dudleya* poachers.

Back in Point Arena, the game warden who first cracked the *Dudleya* case offered to show me another location at Point Arena's Coastal National Monument where CDFW recently apprehended several suspects rappelling off cliffs with rock climbing gear in the dead of night to illegally harvest *D. farinosa*. As we walked along the coastline, with the sound of crashing waves surrounding us, we caught sight of a man some fifteen or so meters ahead on the path bending down, as if to grab something. "Let's go see what he's taking," the warden said. I held back, allowing him to do his job while staying within earshot. As the warden approached, the man stood up, modestly alarmed, as an elderly couple looked on, curious about the unfolding drama and the heavily armed law enforcement officer. It turned out the man was picking up his dog's poop, which he hoisted into the air in a collecting bag. The warden explained to the man and the couple about the recent *D. farinosa* incidents, which they were surprised to learn about. "Never know nowadays, of course, he could have been stealing *Dudleyas!*" the warden chuckled as he rejoined me on the path.

But California, it turned out, was not alone in contending with the emergent threat of *Dudleya* desires. As serious as these cases of *Dudleya* theft had been, *D. farinosa* is not an endangered plant, and it remains unlikely that the species will be poached into extinction, though localized extinctions could certainly occur if illegal harvesting remains a sustained threat to the species. But as I would soon learn, another *Dudleya* shared an even more immediate threat to its survival.

A Very Rare Plant

Greek for "thick plant," *D. pachyphytum* is aptly named—its leaves are fleshy and blunt, ranging in color from a periwinkle blue to a bright yellowish green. Coated in a fine white powder, the leaves have a soft, matte sheen. Above all, what makes *D. pachyphytum* so striking is its overall appearance; despite its somewhat angular geometry and compact form, it has a soft, cute sensibility—it exudes charisma.[9] In my first interaction with *D. pachyphytum,* I was split between a heady sense of reverence for this extraordinary plant I had so anxiously anticipated encountering and a more immediate urge to pinch it. The story of *D. pachyphytum* converges with that of *D. farinosa* through entangled histories that exemplify the role of desire in shaping collecting practices. As species in the *Dudleya* genus became more popular in the last decade among succulent collectors, it only was a matter of time before the most ardent and passionate collectors would seek out *D. pachyphytum. D. pachyphytum* only grows on the north-facing cliffs of Isla de Cedros, off the coast of Baja California, Mexico, and nowhere else in the world.

Its habitat is difficult to access, requiring either harboring a boat and scrambling up steep cliffs pounded by forceful Pacific waves or taking an overland route, traversing twelve miles across the mountainous terrain of the island. You would then need a way to get the plants off the island—either by boat or by plane. The other option, if you were so bold, would be to charter a helicopter and fly directly to their location, steal what you could, and attempt to fly to mainland Mexico—which is exactly what several Korean collectors purportedly did in 2016.[10]

Isla de Cedros is a dry, mountainous island. Beyond the main town of Cedros, it remains largely uninhabited, save for a few tiny fishing villages (Figure 33). Cedros has a permanent population of approximately 1,350 individuals, and it has two main economies. The first is a local fishing cooperative that primarily traps lobster half the year and harvests abalone the other. Most of what the cooperative harvests is sent to China and other East Asian countries as high-value export goods. The second industry is a major salt export operation, a joint venture of the Mitsubishi Corporation and the Mexican government. Aside from these activities, Mexico's marines have a presence on the island, there is a drug and alcohol rehabilitation clinic, and there are a few sport fishing and commercial bluefin tuna outfits. Otherwise, it is a sleepy, quiet place, full of empty beaches, arid hills dotted with agaves and cacti, and, higher up in the mountains, beautiful Monterey pine forests at times shrouded in thick fog (the Spanish got it wrong in calling it the island of cedars). My first impression of Cedros was that it seemed an unlikely place to find *Dudleya*, much less the "crown jewel" of the genus. The Cedros landscape is primarily dry and rugged, yet the majority of *Dudleya* plants I had seen to date lived along the rain-drenched and sea-sprayed cliffs of California's coast or farther south along sunny coastal bluffs around San Francisco and Santa Cruz. On the drive from the airport to Cedros town, the agave, yucca, *Ferocactus*, and wild sage seemed right at home on the dusty

Figure 33. The harbor town of Cedros on Isla de Cedros, Mexico.

hills and ravines, and I remained curious about where *D. pachyphytum* fit in the landscape.

I did not travel to Cedros alone but with two of the foremost botanical experts of the Baja Pacific islands, who very generously agreed to let me join them on a trip from San Diego. While I was traveling to Cedros to find out more about *D. pachyphytum*, the botanists were heading to Cedros as a jumping-off point to visit the much smaller nearby island of Natividad, where they were planning to collect herbarium specimens of what they believed was either a new species or even an entirely new genus of plant. After arriving in the city of Ensenada from Tijuana, we were met by a lawyer with Mexico's Comisión Nacional de Áreas Naturales Protegidas (CONANP, the equivalent of the United States' National Park Service), who accompanied us on an overnight bus to the city of Guerrero Negro in Baja California Sur before taking a ten-seater prop plane to Cedros on one of the few commercial flights that come and go from the island. Cedros falls within the new Baja California Pacific Islands Biosphere Reserve, an effort to recognize and protect the Baja Peninsula's rich biodiversity and high species endemism through an 11,612 square kilometer multiuse reserve. The reserve includes areas of strict protection and areas meant for "sustainable use," such as fishing. Once in Cedros, we were also met by Cedros's two Biosphere Reserve staff members.

I was ultimately not permitted to see wild-growing *D. pachyphytum* on Cedros, however. I had wrongly assumed that permission to visit the plants in habitat would come from the Biosphere Reserve staff. In theory, this might be true, but the staff at the time informed me they still did not have their own boat. Instead, as was explained to me in an unexpected meeting with the fishing cooperative's president and several other cooperative members after first arriving on Cedros, it was the fishing cooperative that would grant or decline my request. After a brief discussion, my request was declined, as was my request to solicit interviews from cooperative fishermen who worked on the *vigilancia* (surveillance) boats to safeguard the cooperative's fishing waters. I was told that the cooperative's hesitancy was a matter of safety, though whose safety might be at risk was left ambiguous.[11] The cooperative may have been concerned about my request for a variety of reasons, but about a year after my visit in December 2019, two fishermen from a larger party of six heading toward Cedros—who were believed to have set out from the nearby peninsular town of Bahía Tortuga—were found dead, shot in the head, and their bodies dumped at sea.[12] Mexican authorities declared that their deaths were the result of an encounter between rival gangs, possibly between the Sinaloa and Tijuana cartels, over territorial access to Cedros, but possibly also over the extraction (or right of extraction) of *D. pachyphytum* plants. The first body was found alongside six containers filled with harvested *D. pachyphytum* from Cedros. The details and motivations behind the murders and who was responsible remain unclear,

Figure 34. Recovered *Dudleya pachyphytum* under shade netting on Isla de Cedros.

and possible witnesses (including the other four previously missing fisherman, since found) have not publicly disclosed more information. It is well known that the waters around Cedros are worked by boats that move a variety of illicit goods, from abalone to drugs (especially cocaine), along the Baja coast. Thus it is possible that persons normally engaged in trafficking other illicit products may have been hired to do a *D. pachyphytum* run that went awry. Other theories abound.[13] Cedros is considered a strategic fuel resupply and transport nexus for a variety of illicit supply routes, so it is difficult to completely disentangle the movement of *D. pachyphytum* from other illicit goods, as well as those involved in their transport, even if they represent decidedly different economies.

Although I was not permitted to interview fishermen, I was given the opportunity and permission to interview several local island public administrators and civic leaders, as well as Biosphere

Reserve and CONANP staff both on Cedros and on the Baja Peninsula. As for the plants, my consolation prize was a visit to see previously confiscated *D. pachyphytum* within the confines of the fishing cooperative's packing plant. The outdoor growing space was set up exclusively for the maintenance and care of *D. pachyphytum* seized by Mexican officials in 2017, when Korean plant poachers fled the country after a dramatic heist of more than five thousand *D. pachyphytum* rosettes (Figure 34).

Who Is a Plant Trafficker, Anyways?

According to locals on Cedros and regional CONANP authorities I interviewed, the first documented incident indicating that *D. pachyphytum* poaching might become a serious issue was in 2016, when a group of South Koreans was detained after using a helicopter hired from mainland Mexico to fly them directly to the plants' habitat on Cedros. According to involved officials, however, the suspects were detained at Cedros Airport before the helicopter could depart, but they were eventually released because of a "clumsy judicial process" in which the authorities were unable to read them their rights in Korean. The Biosphere Reserve staff I interviewed, both of whom were previous members of the fishing cooperative on Cedros, also started to notice problems with *D. pachyphytum* about this time. When visiting the plants in May 2016, they explained, it took about an hour's walk up the cliffs before they would encounter the plants, but when they returned six months later, it took about an hour and a half to reach them, suggesting that illegal extraction of plants was taking place, though likely in small quantities. This was before May 2017, when, according to authorities, a van with one Mexican and three South Korean passengers heading north was stopped at a military checkpoint near the border of Baja California and Baja California Sur. The group was traveling with a few *D. pachyphytum* plants but was allowed to pass through the checkpoint. Minutes later, an inspection of a fifty-five-foot tractor trailer uncovered sixty-four large boxes containing nearly five thousand *D. pachyphytum* plants, and the driver indicated that the plants belonged to the van's passengers up ahead. At this point, the authorities contacted PROFEPA, the environmental law enforcement agency of Mexico, which seized the truck's shipment before the plants could be exported from Mexico, but the men in the van were never apprehended.

Several things are remarkable about this heist. It is difficult to imagine that several individuals would be able to successfully arrive at Isla de Cedros, safely navigate to the plants, and have enough time to remove nearly five thousand individual plants from the extremely steep and challenging terrain where *D. pachyphytum* grows without being spotted or raising suspicion along the way. The theft would have undoubtedly required the assistance of people familiar with Cedros and its terrain, and potentially days of hard work. *D. pachyphytum* plants do not all grow in one section on the cliffs—they are clustered in patches, and several experts commented it would take time to work across them, moving from outcrop to outcrop. It is equally impressive that the men were then able to get so many plants from the island back to the mainland—again undetected—presumably in *pongas* (small fishing vessels). Last, it is astounding to consider that the total number of plants discovered in the truck exceeded what several experts believed at the time to be the *total* population of the species. Several experts I interviewed were surprised—and even skeptical—that there were any plants left on the cliffs at all. That more poaching incidents followed suggests there were, however.

A year later, in June 2018, at the airport in La Paz, the capital of the state of Baja California Sur, some 875 kilometers south of Bahía Tortugas, 496 multiheaded *D. pachyphytum* plants were discovered in a shipment of thirty plastic containers. They had been shipped to the airport via FedEx, where they were awaiting air transport to mainland Mexico. Unlike the incident the year prior, these were addressed to a commercial greenhouse south of Mexico City in Morelos, where it is presumed they would then be sold to domestic clients or other intermediaries abroad. Authorities believed the plants could have been separated out further through propagation into approximately three thousand individual rosettes to maximize profit from the hundreds of large, decades-old plants. The plants were shipped with false phytosanitary paperwork.[14] This incident, unlike the previous one directly involving foreign nationals working to obtain plants themselves, suggested the emergence of a domestic node in a larger international supply chain of *D. pachyphytum*. Further interviews with other CONANP officials detailed similar but smaller-scale incidents involving the transport of *D. pachyphytum* plants ultimately destined for East Asia via greenhouses in Mexico City and its outlying vicinity. Most experts agree that key transit actors are based in the fishing communities of Bahía Tortugas and Bahía Asunción, just to the south of Cedros on the Baja Peninsula, as well as the nearby larger city of Guerrero Negro. Here it is believed relatively impoverished fishermen could be easily persuaded into plant extraction and transport activities, which, according to some authorities, might garner as much payment as twenty to forty U.S. dollars per poached plant.

Organized Plant Crimes?

"It's easier to transport a plant than drugs," a staff member of the Biosphere Reserve told me over coffee at a small hotel catering to sport fishermen on Cedros. We were discussing with the CONANP lawyer why drug traffickers would enter the illicit plant economy on Cedros. "Why would anyone who professionally transports drugs bother with illegal plant trade?" I asked. Pound for pound, *D. pachyphytum,* even at its highest prices, bears no resemblance to the kind of value that flows through narcotrafficking networks. Although it is certainly less dangerous to transport plants than drugs, I have heard this narrative used elsewhere in relation to illegal cactus trade, but without any substantiating evidence. "Here is the biggest drug trafficking network for the United States, here there are *networks*," the lawyer for CONANP emphasized, to further contextualize this perspective.

I was puzzled at the thought that drugs and plants would overlap in forms of illicit transit, especially given that, like in California, it appeared the actors involved in stealing *D. pachyphytum* plants were predominately foreign nationals exclusively interested in succulents. It seemed hard to imagine that there would be strong integration between small groups of opportunistic South Korean succulent poachers and the Sinaloa or Tijuana cartel. But through this discussion and several that followed with other local civic leaders and authorities (alongside turning to the work of scholars in green criminology), I came to see the critical importance of distinguishing between discussions of individual actors, criminal organizations, and transport networks when analyzing this emergent trade.

There is a risky conflation in presuming people involved in the transport of illicit products on the ground are necessarily active members of cartels engaged in transnational illicit supply chains, rather than simply people with boats for hire. As wildlife criminologist Tanya Wyatt describes, "in the context of wildlife trafficking, the intermediary is the equivalent of a 'fence'—someone who moves stolen goods within networks. Presumably most of the time this is disorganized crime, where clearly there is some level of organization and structure to the offenders' actions, but it is not connected to an organized crime group."[15] Many people involved in trafficking illicit commodities around the Baja Peninsula, in which weapons and violence frequently make their presences known and felt, are not necessarily cartel "operatives" per se but fishermen (past or present) looking for work where they can find it, be it in the legal or illegal harvesting of abalone, transport of drugs, or poaching of plants, weighed against the costs of doing so. As Wyatt explained further, intermediaries "may then have some knowledge of wildlife, probably from experience of transporting them to be processed, stored, or sold elsewhere, but will also move any illicit product that can be sold. This means the intermediaries probably do not act out of ideology but purely from a profit motive weighed against the low risk of detection and/or minimal amount of punishment."[16]

"If I dedicate myself to the trafficking of prohibited substances, it has a risk, and the ultimate aim is to obtain money, and here [with plant poaching] the risk is very low, I obtain money easily, and the amount of money is very high," a high-level CONANP staff member explained to me over lunch in Guerrero Negro following my trip to Cedros. Unlike illegal abalone poaching from Cedros's waters, which must be conducted at night to avoid detection by the fishing cooperative's *vigilancia* crews, plant poaching on Cedros steers clear of territorial fights about fishing and therefore might be less likely to draw attention, especially if it requires only a small payment for someone to look the other way. It also sidesteps territorial fights between organized cartels over access to transit routes—or at least, it used to. The money might be proportionally less in poaching plants than moving drugs, but the risks would still be far less than those with more explicit consequences, from illegal fishing to drug trafficking. As Rosaleen Duffy summarizes, "the illegal wildlife trade is [potentially] attractive to organized crime groups because it can be low risk, high reward."[17]

Questions about the level of organization, and the presence—or not—of organized crime groups, were encircling the thefts not only of *D. pachyphytum* but of *D. farinosa* as well. Whereas the case of *D. pachyphytum* raised concerns about the kinds of criminal actors interfacing with or facilitating their extraction and trade, in California, the most pressing concerns that emerged in interviews with law enforcement were about how to equip prosecutors and law enforcement with sufficient tools to deter future supply-side crime. As the DA had expressed, it was hard to make people and courts care about the poaching of a plant they may have never heard of, in contrast with a charismatic animal. As Duffy explains in her work disentangling IWT from the broader category of "wild-life crime" and the dangers that arise in their conflation, "[illegal wildlife] trade covers a whole range of less well-known species and can in fact be very ordinary and mundane. Put simply, IWT can be *un*organized and *un*charismatic. When the focus is on larger and more charismatic species, other aspects of the trade can get little attention."[18] If the thefts of *D. pachyphytum* sustained the specter that more organized criminal groups were interested in trafficking plants, the emerging trade in *D. farinosa,* despite its magnitude, de-manded that prosecutors, conservationists, and law enforcement work hard to raise the profile of the species as part of their efforts to characterize these crimes as *serious wildlife crimes.*

Given that, in the United States, plants are afforded fewer pro-tections than animals in endangered species law, IWT policy, and crime prevention circles writ large, in the Humboldt *Dudleya* case, it became important from the prosecution's position to charge the defendants with mail fraud and conspiracy. This was necessary to reach the severe level of sentencing they sought as a deterrent to future incidents. Conspiracy requires proof of coordinated intent by multiple parties to defraud or commit an offense against the state. But the charge of conspiracy also had another effect: it raised the possibility that *Dudleya* incidents could be characterized and discursively understood as organized crime. In California, I asked the CDFW captain if the incidents of *D. farinosa* theft represented acts by organized crime groups:

> It's making people a lot of money and they are going to great extent and great risk to poach them and ship them back to

their own countries. . . . I don't have a legal definition of "organized crime" to reference my answer, but if you want to relate it to what I know to be either drug-trafficking organizations or criminal poaching operations, this is well within the definition of organized crime. There are people that are flying from another country, renting vans, driving to the coast. Everything is well planned out. They've got destinations for shipping the boxes back to. They've got funds to get the whole thing started. They've got considerable risk and they're taking considerable risk. They know they're violating the law. They are moving forward with very complex operations to make a profit selling something that is illegal. That's very well within the definition of organized crime, I figure.

Many people, including officers of the law, conservationists, and members of the media, agreed with the captain that these represented incidents of organized crime. This framing of *Dudleya* poaching is important: internationally, there have been sweeping efforts across high-level forums over the past decade to label IWT as a form of serious organized crime.[19] This designation serves a variety of important functions, including greater access to intergovernmental information and intelligence sharing, access to key United Nations institutional support and coordination, and elevation of these crimes as security issues by linking wildlife trade to other serious crimes, such as weapons and human trafficking. But in addition to the material and logistical benefits of labeling IWT as "serious," this discursive framing of conservation crimes serves to justify increased focus on law enforcement, intelligence, and even military responses to combat IWT. This transforms IWT from what was previously seen as a "boutique" conservation issue into a destabilizing and transnational security threat.[20]

As Duffy has shown, this shift represents a fundamental change in how IWT and wildlife crimes more generally are framed, discursively represented, responded to, and prioritized, affecting not only governmental approaches to combating IWT but also the funding landscape for conservation. Major conservation organizations both respond to and leverage this newer framing of IWT as serious organized crime to access new sources of money through unlikely channels, such as security and defense funding, with IWT intervention projects and programs justified as helping to combat transnational criminal networks.[21] Duffy's research demonstrates not only how conservation organizations are pitching grant and funding proposals to new donors but in turn how the security apparatus is turning conservation into a new site of promising entrepreneurism and financial opportunity.[22] Through their integration, conservation and security interests are strategically repackaging wildlife conservation interventions to align with broader geopolitical agendas. These include IWT's potential (if rarely proven) linkages to international threat finance and terrorism as articulated by high-level government officials and in national legislation and executive orders.[23]

It is therefore important not only to question and critique such moves to frame wildlife crime like *D. farinosa* poaching as serious organized crime without empirical evidence to back such claims but also to articulate alternative and more appropriate framings, as a number of scholars in the subfields of green criminology and wildlife criminology have worked to do.[24] In their research on the illegal trade in parrots, for instance, Pires and colleagues parse out key differences between "organized crime" and "crime that is organized," or how the presence of organized behaviors or coordinated efforts should not be conflated with the presence or activities of organized criminal networks.[25] In a similar vein, Tanya Wyatt and colleagues distinguish between "organized crime groups" and "disorganized criminal networks" involved in IWT.[26] They describe how the United Nations Convention against Transnational Organized Crime (UNTOC) offers an incredibly broad definition of organized crime that can include any crimes committed by a "structured group of three or more persons" so long as the committed offense is considered a "serious" crime, a definition that would enable its widespread application to any number of illicit activities. But "serious crimes" is further defined in the UNTOC as any "offence punishable by a maximum deprivation of liberty of at least four years."[27] This means that what defines serious organized crime in the UNTOC has more to do with the *severity of punishment*— something that varies widely by country and the nature of carceral and judicial systems—than with any specific kinds of activities we might conceptualize as "serious." This has major implications for thinking about the framing of wildlife crimes, IWT, and what justice looks like in the event of wildlife harms.

There are clear reasons to be both skeptical and concerned about such a country-specific and broad definition of serious organized crime. Such a definition theoretically lumps together human trafficking involving violent cartels into the same crime category as a few people who work together selling marijuana on a street corner or, perhaps, a small group of plant poachers. In contrast to this less-than-helpful definition of organized crime, Wyatt and colleagues offer a more specific definition of organized crime groups as groups existing for "a significant length of time" that are "highly-organized, disciplined, rational, and may use violence or corruption to control illegal goods and/or services for profit."[28] As they note, there are some examples of organized crime groups engaged in IWT, perhaps most notably in transnational rhino horn poaching economies, but even here, a variety of empirical case studies have shown the more common and widespread presence of *disorganized* criminal networks engaged in ivory and rhino horn poaching compared with formally "organized" crime.[29] Disorganized criminal networks can be understood as "more fleeting and less stable than a group" operating as "networks of opportunistic individuals . . . [who] establish temporary and fluid relationships to each other and sometimes to established organized and/or corporate crime groups to smuggle wildlife across the borders."[30] Disorganized criminal networks therefore represent much more opportunistic, fluid, and impermanent categories of illicit exchange networks than organized crime groups. Based on my research, this represents a far more accurate framing of the organizing patterns of those implicated in the *Dudleya* poaching incidents in both California and likely even Mexico, as well as across the many and varied illicit succulent trades that are the subject of this book.

In summary, the overlapping of actors engaged in the illicit plant trade and in narcotrafficking—as may have been the case on Isla de Cedros—should not necessarily be understood as the *integration* of these economic activities within organized criminal organizations. Instead, already existing transit routes were likely being exploited to facilitate an emergent and relatively lucrative yet low-risk form of illicit trade. As useful as these distinctions between disorganized and organized crime may be, the case of *D. pachyphytum* poaching adds further empirical evidence to the growing recognition of the fluid and blurry boundaries between them, the potentially lucrative world of succulent poaching, and the degrees to which disorganized crime networks, corporate and state crime actors, and organized crime groups may interface and rely on one another during various stages of IWT.[31]

As for why *D. pachyphytum* plants were being stolen from Cedros, most regional and local Mexican authorities I interviewed presumed it was desirable for similar reasons as other illegal trades destined for East Asia: a combination of natural rarity, "wild" properties, and even some form of medicinal value. As one authority explained in relation to *D. pachyphytum,* "the Asian culture wants natural things. . . . If we propose a program . . . we proposed selling [the plants], we must identify how to grow these plants but with a physical form that makes them look more natural, like in the environment, because when you buy a plant [from a greenhouse], the form of the plant is very different because they don't have the pressures of the environment." This perspective, that what makes the wild *D. pachyphytum* so desirable is its "wildness," mirrored similar perspectives of many California succulent experts concerned about the illicit *D. farinosa* trade. They expressed a concern that greenhouse-cultivated plants wouldn't meet consumer demand in East Asia either because the shape and form of the plants differ so greatly from those of wild-grown plants or because there was some innate value for consumers tied to their wild-origin status. But media outlets in Mexico as well as some Mexican authorities went even further, suggesting that the plants were desired as living plants not for succulent collectors but for purported medicinal or aphrodisiac properties, citing similarities with the rhino horn and totoaba swim bladder trades.[32] In chapter 7, I closely engage and critique these narratives in my efforts to understand *Dudleya* desires and what was driving consumer demand for these plants. Before doing so, however, in the next chapter, I turn to the importance of learning to know *Dudleya* better through situating them within their broader ecologies and socioecological relations. It was only through doing this that I came to better understand the dynamics of desires that drive demand for *Dudleya*.

Many studies of illicit trade divide analysis of consumer demand from studies of supply. But, as this chapter shows, a focus only on the illicit extraction of *D. farinosa* or *D. pachyphytum* fails to offer meaningful insight into the desires underpinning illicit activity or what fundamentally led to the emergence of a new illicit trade. Instead, by turning next to the literal roots of these trades— and the plants attached to them—a clearer sense of the importance of the biological capacities, adaptive qualities, and vegetal personalities of plants in shaping their trade and transit emerges.

6

Learning to Know a Plant

Each time a story helps me remember what I thought I knew,
or introduces me to new knowledge, a muscle critical for
caring about flourishing gets some aerobic exercise.

—Donna Haraway, "Awash in Urine: DES and Premarin®
in Multispecies Response-Ability"

Learning from plants as a means of social theorizing elicits other
kinds of knowledge compared to learning from people who share
relations with plants alone. While studying the emergent trade in
Dudleya farinosa, I spent several hours one day walking along a wide
stretch of exposed beach between the ocean and steep cliffs near the
town of Eureka, California (Figure 35). The cliffsides were blasted
by sea spray, rain, and wind and covered in sprawling masses of the
species. I crouched between great boulders dotted with them, mature plants with rosettes the width of my hand with fingers spread
wide, plants improbably clinging to near-vertical rockfaces with
stout, rose-colored inflorescences protruding two feet into the air.
I watched as clusters of multiheaded plants were pounded by inundations of heavy rain and wind, as water ran off their shallow roots
entangled in loose rock and thin soils into rapidly forming rivulets.
Looking out over a frothy, gray-green sea where the horizon line

Figure 35. *Dudleya farinosa* growing on the coast in Humboldt County, California.

was smudged out by distant sheets of rain, I felt at once lost and enmeshed in the infinite view where ocean meets sky.

It was through practices of attention with plants, modest attempts at trying to raise my own attunement to plant life, that I came to better understand the dynamic and relational being of *Dudleya*. Learning with *Dudleya* became a central task for understanding the production of *Dudleya* desires and how the physical and biological properties of plants mediate their movements in and out of illegal transit and illicit trades. This work involved, among other things, walking and sitting with *D. farinosa* on rocky coasts, writing botanical descriptions, making sketches, and creating films and field recordings of the plants in their environs. I visited *Dudleya* in botanical gardens, commercial greenhouses, and its natural habitats; I compared the shapes, colors, and more effervescent qualities of wild plants to their confined and cultivated relatives. At one point, I attached electromagnetic sensors to their fleshy leaves to see if they resonated as "alive" in that particular register (yes—but less well than thinner-leafed, broadleaf plants). My efforts extended to plants and their afterlives as well. I pored over the details of *D. farinosa* (the California species) and *D. pachyphytum* (the species from Isla de Cedros, Mexico) herbaria specimens in both physical and digital forms. I marveled at these desiccated plants tied, glued, and stitched to yellowing sheets of paper, marked with the particulars of who had collected them, where, and what they had looked like in another life (Figure 36). I once made the mistake of referring to these specimens in conversation with an herbarium curator as "dead plants." I was quickly corrected, as he explained that they were "preserved," not "dead." Read as biographies, herbaria sheets are phenomenal examples of nonhuman archival materials full of storied human–plant encounters and vegetal afterlives.

Through these diverse and experimental practices, informed and inspired by other researchers like Natasha Myers, John Hartigan Jr., and Craig Holdrege, I was able to forge my own deeper

Figure 36. Holotype herbarium sheet of *Dudleya pachyphytum* from Isla de Cedros, Mexico. The specimen was collected by Reid Moran and Michael Benedict on July 18, 1980. Location details are obscured for conservation purposes. From the San Diego Natural History Museum.

relations with these species.[1] I also developed a greater appreciation for how desire for particular species can emerge through relations with botanical histories and the humans engaged in efforts of thick botanical description and encounter. But this work to know plants better was more than merely interesting. Close attention to *D. farinosa* and *D. pachyphytum* as species in relation to one another, rather than as taxonomically distinct yet related entities with their own distinctive traits, reveals their deep entwinement. The production of succulent desires, at least in the case of *Dudleya*, bridges species divides. In what follows, we will see how these relations are not only found between species but affix in the minds of collectors and botanists alike, shaping the more-than-human psychotopologies of desire.

Introducing a Desirous Plant

To an inexpert eye like mine, *D. farinosa* was initially indistinguishable from the commonplace succulents that grace coffee shops and windowsills the world over, most typically from the *Echeveria* genus. This isn't terribly surprising—many species currently included in the *Dudleya* genus were formerly classified as *Echeveria*. *D. farinosa* features thick, fleshy green leaves covered in a powdery bloom (*farinosa* comes from the Latin *farina*, meaning "floury" or "powdery") and a roughly rosette shape; it occasionally exudes a long, flowering inflorescence (a stalklike thing with flowers on top). *D. farinosa* is more commonly known as bluff lettuce or powdery liveforever in English or as *siemprevivens* in Spanish, though these names are at times applied to other members of the *Dudleya* genus, which includes approximately forty-five species. This number is subject to change. Experts tell me that still more *Echeveria* species will in time likely be reclassified as *Dudleya*.

The basic work of doing good taxonomy—something that continues to evolve over time as botanical knowledge advances—holds great power in affecting how species incite desire. Although plants might not care about taxonomic changes as they are jettisoned from one genus to another, collectors do. There are several species of *Dudleya,* for instance, that experts now recognize as distinct species but that simply have yet to be formally described in the botanical literature because of limitations on the time and labor of botanists to do so. I was surprised to learn that publishing scientific papers formally naming and describing species is not given high regard in the biologically aligned sciences. I once heard a biogeographer refer to such work as "just stamp collecting." Many formal descriptions of new species end up published in hobbyist or amateur botanical journals (serious publications, but not necessarily with the same rigors of scientific peer review). But, assuming such descriptions of new *Dudleya* species are eventually written, it remains to be seen what doing so will mean for collectors, especially those who seek out the completion of a "series."[2]

Although even now I would be hard-pressed to identify many *Dudleya* species as belonging to the *Dudleya* genus compared against a variety of *Echeveria* species, at least several are now unambiguously *Dudleya* species to my eye. I am drawn to *Dudleya brittonii,* a large species with elegant, long leaves, covered in a powdery gray-white sheen. This powder comes off easily if you touch it, as I learned when I accidentally ruined an exceptionally lovely patina on one commercial grower's *D. brittonii* with my thumbprint, permanently marring it. On the overnight bus ride down the Baja California coast eventually to arrive at Isla de Cedros, as I describe in chapter 5, at dusk, I spent half an hour looking out the window at *D. brittonii* glowing in the fading light like iridescent orbs across the arid landscape. And then there is the adorably compact *Dudleya gnoma,* widely available in cultivation and a popular favorite among collectors, who often market it as "white sprite." You can't help but call it *cute.*[3] Despite its popularity in the marketplace, it is severely restricted in habitat to just one of California's Channel

Islands. This is a danger in studying passionate collectors fixated on objects of desire: desirous transference may occur. It suffices to say that I soon found myself in the thrall of *Dudleya*.

Lore holds that *Dudleya* species earned the moniker "liveforever" because an eighteenth-century Spanish botanist first collected herbarium samples of the genus and sent them to Europe by boat, where, despite their long journey, they successfully rerooted upon arrival. More likely, they may have earned their name from their slow life trajectory; they can live to be more than fifty years old. Another theory holds that their name stems from being incredibly drought resistant, capable of surviving long, dry California summers (*Dudleya* species go dormant in summer and grow in winter). The genus is named for William Russel Dudley, a preeminent expert of California flora and the first chair of Stanford University's Department of Botany.

As much as this chapter centers on how I learned from these charming plants, it would have been difficult to get to know the *Dudleya* genus were it not for the help of experts along the way. One such expert was a senior environmental scientist for CDFW. As he explained to me one day as we pored over maps of the Humboldt County coast at the Eureka offices of CDFW, "[*D. farinosa*] occurs in this narrow ecotone between essentially the bare rocks, the wave swept area, the rocky coast, and between that and this herbaceous zone, or ecotone, before it becomes shrubs and trees." The scientist showed me the locations where he was put in charge of replanting thousands of *D. farinosa* plants after they were recovered by CDFW officials following the series of successful poaching busts in Humboldt County I described in chapter 5. "So, successionally, [*D. farinosa*] would lose out in a shrub-dominated habitat because it would be shaded out; it would eventually go away. It's in this fairly narrow niche along the coast, and typically in a very erosive environment with a lot of salt spray and windswept bluffs," he said.

We looked at photographs together on his computer from the

replanting efforts, including images of the *D. farinosa* habitat: cliffs shooting up from a flat sand beach before flattening out into the coastal shrubby landscape. Waves crash along the rocks, sending sea spray into the air. "The place is dynamic, these *Dudleyas* are living in a *harsh spot!*" He pointed to the area of cliffs dotted with plants clinging to rocks. "Those are the *Dudleyas,* see that, that's where they are hanging out, past the wave-swept area and before the shrubs start. It's this little ecotone, that's it. They are not *here* because they would get blasted by waves, and they aren't *here* because that's where the shrubs start." Given the scientist's description of this very narrow niche where *D. farinosa* is found, it would be easy to presume that it is a rare or threatened plant. But while *D. farinosa* may exist only in this narrow ecological zone, at times just meters in width between the sea and the top of coastal bluffs, its habitat is a patchwork spanning nearly the entirety of the California coast, from its northernmost reaches and into Oregon all the way south to Santa Barbara. In short, although it is terribly restricted ecologically in relation to the ocean and land, it is still ubiquitous across the California coastal landscape.

The perspective that *D. farinosa* is not rare is mediated, of course, by how it is understood as a singular species. As the DA in Humboldt County—known for his work as a wildlife advocate—reiterated to me during our meeting in Arcata, "it's not listed as a rare plant, but . . . each little area has little subspecies that are different, and so even those little, small ones have slightly different characteristics, and each particular area could lose theirs very quickly, which is what we were facing here." With the stroke of a hypothetical pen, if *D. farinosa* conservation, rather than focusing on the plant at the species level, were instead to focus on the subspecies level, its conservation status could change. This could result in a demand for stronger protections or possibly produce a proliferation of new and desirous categories of plants for collectors. But legally speaking, this is not how plants are known and granted protection, be it under the ESA, the U.S. Lacey Act, or CITES. Nor is a "subspecies" approach how the threatened status of species is determined through programs like the IUCN Red List.

This duality of *D. farinosa* as both abundant and precarious is mirrored in tensions in how CDFW officials, conservationists, botanists, collectors, and commercial growers understand and speak of the species. It is both "a damn tough little plant" and yet in collection "can just be slowly going downhill"; it is both "really easy to propagate" and "very easy to kill"; it is "abundant," but "individual populations . . . can be wiped out really quickly" by overharvesting; it is "commonplace" and "not the prettiest *Dudleya* out there," yet also being stolen by the thousands as part of a "*Dudleya* mania." I was puzzled by what seemed at times like contradictory understandings of the species among my various interlocutors. This also speaks to the discursive construction of the species—how language sets the terms by which narratives about what *D. farinosa* is bring the species into being. These discursive as well as scientific maneuvers do important work, with material and even ecological effects. The work of coming to understand *D. farinosa* as more than a representation of the idea of a species, toward a more relational understanding of species as dynamic beings, is to move beyond what best or most "accurately" describes what is or is not *D. farinosa*. Instead, it engages in the more uncertain task of remaining open to a multitude of ways of understanding what *D. farinosa* is and what it can become.

I initially spent a great deal of time attempting to generate a sense of which of these perspectives was most accurate—is *D. farinosa* fussy and sensitive or a hardy, ocean spray–blasted survivor? This either/or perspective is a poor way to frame the question, and it limited the possibility for approaching the species on its own terms, rather than only through human modes of relating. I came to appreciate that the answers to my questions about the competing nature of *D. farinosa* were contextual and that these contexts were relational—between plants, people, place, and other kinds of environmental processes. By contextual, I mean it wasn't that the plants were *either* "finicky" or "tough"; *D. farinosa* can be both (and more), depending on place and time and the context of its access to its biological needs. By relational, I mean that the plants are always in the process of becoming with others, and in the case of *D. farinosa,* the act of knowing and regulating them as individualized or static "things" ignores how they ecologically exist in the world. A *D. farinosa* out on a coastal bluff, its roots entangling in the rocks, sand, and pockets of soil over decades, pollinated by particular insects and butterflies, and chewed on by aphids and mites, has different sets of ecological relations than a *D. farinosa* in a greenhouse in South Korea or Germany, and not just because one is in California and one is elsewhere. This doesn't mean a *D. farinosa* plant in California is more "real" or "authentic" than one in a ceramic pot in South Korea; instead, it is an acknowledgment of different trajectories and what they might become across the deep temporalities of plant-time. To understand the nature of plants is also to understand how they relate to others and in what time.

How *Dudleya* species have evolved to survive in an inhospitable climate shapes their capacities to incite collector desire, survive long periods of transit under stressful conditions, and potentially succeed as lively commodities. Walking along sea spray–blasted cliffs, these plants, it was apparent, evolved to persist through inundations of water, relying on the extreme verticality of cliffs to pull moisture off their roots to avoid waterlogging and rot. They have also evolved to tolerate the salinity of ocean salt spray. Some experts hypothesize that the exposure to salt may simultaneously reduce the risk of parasitism by certain mites and insects, while also exposing the plants to a degree of stress, which manifests in the reddening of their leaves. That the tips of *D. farinosa* leaves may turn red as a wounding response to the environment in which they live is a compelling moment to think with the temporality of plants. This colorful variation may be especially valued by some collectors, inciting their desire, in which the plant's greens and yellows bleed into a deep red. Yet within the confines of the nurturing, less stressful environment of a greenhouse, with regular fertilization and water, where their interactions with other life-forms and environmental stressors are diminished, this color can fade away, from red back to green, especially as the plants annually grow new leaves. Plants live within their own times, where growth and death occur simultaneously—what philosopher Michael Marder refers to as the heterotemporality of plant-time.[4] As an example, attention to the changing color of a plant's leaves due to possible salinity exposure over time helps locate the plant itself more centrally in stories of desire and explain how the time of plants; their growth; and their death, decay, and proliferation in bodily form profoundly mediate human–plant relations.

Consider a plant on a seaside cliff, its leaves tinged ruby red from exposure to the stressors of harsh sunlight and salty ocean spray. An enterprising plant collector spots the plant and is enticed, believing this color to be attractive and potentially of greater monetary value or desirable for their own collection. The plant is taken. Unmoored from the soil, its roots are damaged; the plant is further stressed by international transit in a shipping container or in the cargo hold of an airplane. The plant responds to these adverse conditions, even if not visually apparent to the human eye. The plant is weakened but survives, the water stored in its leaves helping to sustain it. Days or maybe weeks later, the plant arrives at a new location, a commercial greenhouse, where it is placed in a pot, and its pictures soon circulate in social media forums and online marketplaces. A would-be buyer is offered a real-time video viewing of the plant, whose damaged roots are now hidden beneath a layer of carefully selected growing substrate and contained within an attractive piece of earthenware pottery. The effects of its stressful transit have yet to fully materialize in its visual presentation. The plant is bought and shipped again, and an avid collector is temporarily elated by the emotional rush of the new acquisition, granting the new plant prime real estate on a collection bench.

Soon, the plant's declining health is apparent, the stress of transit and removal from the ground now causing leaves to wither. Perhaps if the buyer were inexperienced, this would be the end of the story. But the collector is knowledgeable, and the plant receives diligent care. They strip the plant of its now desiccated leaves to force new growth. The plant is repotted in a well-draining mix of grit and soil; the collector knows the plant will otherwise soon develop root rot and disease. The collector duly administers appropriate levels of nutrients and water, being careful not to inundate it; this collector knows that standing water on the plant's roots would spell a quick death. A year passes. The plant slowly recovers from the stress of its long and difficult trip, its roots begin to grow back, and new leaves emerge, adapted not to the harsh conditions of a windswept cliff but to the more muted sunlight of a shielded greenhouse with steady ventilation and air circulation. These new leaves do not turn red at the tips but remain a bright shade of green, adapted to the lighting of the greenhouse. The plant appears as something different than the wild plant someone took a year ago: its leaves are plump and smooth; it isn't pocked with the histories of mite bites or the damage of a fallen stone. And yet, of course, for all these changes, the plant has also remained very much the same, a remarkable display of resiliency and adaptation, the dynamism of the vegetal world at work in its own time.

Although hypothetical, attention to these vegetal capacities enables a more nuanced appreciation of plants in collection not simply as commodified and endlessly reproducible objects (even when cloned) but as dynamic beings adapting to changing environmental constraints. Referring to the plants themselves as subjects is not to suggest any form of evenness of power in their relations with the human subjects who upend and transform their lives. Instead, it recognizes what Rafi Youatt has described as the constitutional capacity of nonhuman life to "refuse to internalize the meanings of human language," which enables nonhumans "to resist becoming self-regulating subjects to a significant extent, relying instead on their own semiotic interpretations of the environment and acting accordingly." This means that nonhumans can exist as both "sites of resistance" and "active participants" within an enlarged biopolitical field.[5]

Biologically, a straightforward way of understanding these plant capacities is that *Dudleya* species exhibit physiological responses to environmental stressors, as a leading expert of the *Dudleya* genus described to me while we toured his impressive collection and working laboratory full of *Dudleya* specimens at the University of California, Santa Barbara Botanical Garden a few weeks after my visit to Northern California: "You won't get a certain look unless you get it from the wild, when it's been kind of harassed and tortured by the elements," he said. For the sake of argument, it is worth considering that from the perspective of care, *Dudleya* species can in fact do well enough in a greenhouse, at least when certain conditions are met. A plant under the close care and attention of a skilled hand will grow as a more aesthetically flawless plant than it ever could out on a wind-blasted bluff. Considered as individuals in need of care, rather than as a still-evolving species or members of a reproducing community, one might argue that *Dudleya* species would all be better off as greenhouse plants, like the plant in my imagined story. Nobody is advocating this position, of course—it would be akin to (but still not quite the same as) suggesting that all gorillas would be happier to live out their lives exclusively in zoos, well fed and tended to by professional veterinarians and caretakers. Noteworthy in this thought, however, is the potential relation between what some collectors purportedly desire—a particular form and color, a plant that has "lived a little"—and the dissipation of those very traits over plant-time and under conditions of cultivated possession.[6] As much as *Dudleya* species may be "readied as productive resources for capitalism and mined as repositories of genetic information," as Youatt describes, their capacity to resist their extraction as wild beings in a manner that perfectly transfers into the endlessly replicable commodity form is revealed through closer attention to the plants and their "dynamic charms."[7]

So when is *D. farinosa* a fussy, sensitive plant, as some experts described it to me, and when is it not? Several interviewees asserted that although with care, *D. farinosa* could be successfully raised as a garden plant in Northern California outdoors, raising it as a houseplant or in a very different climatic environment would be an altogether different matter. "I don't think they could ever be grown as a houseplant in an ongoing way and sustainably. I think in most situations, there would not be enough ventilation or light, enough airflow to really be able to grow them as a house plant. I find most plants are more susceptible to disease if they're not grown in the cultural niche that they grew up in. . . . They get stressed," a succulent expert and owner of a well-regarded specialist succulent commercial greenhouse explained to me on a cold and rainy afternoon in Fort Bragg, California. This question matters because one of the most common narratives—described both in media articles and by a number of interviewees—was that this sudden emergence of a market for stolen *Dudleya* plants was driven by their rapid ascendance in popularity among "Korean housewives" and Generation Z and "Millennial hipsters." The greenhouse operator explained further, "Even in the conditions of transport . . . [despite] their ability to withstand being wrapped, or being boxed, or being shipped, from the point of view of rot and root, I think that they would be highly stressed depending on the time it took them to get to whatever country. Then to act as a houseplant . . . to manage them, I think there would have to be a lot of use of pesticides, and then just absolutely the perfect growing conditions, which most households do not provide. It would have to be greenhouses and even at that, greenhouses with excellent ventilation," she explained.

This means that if the primary buyers of *D. farinosa* were amateur succulent lovers chasing the newest trend in succulent plants, but without the kind of slow-to-learn skill and craft of performing succulent care and appropriate growing infrastructure, most of the *D. farinosa* plants stolen from California were likely already dead. I return to this question of who was driving demand for *Dudleya* plants in the next chapter, but I raise this matter of *Dudleya* needs here to signal that the biological constraints of plants setting the limits of their environmental adaptability also constrain (or, we might say, resist) their possible trajectories as lively commodities and what kinds of commodities they might become.

Through the process of this research, I found learning to be affected by plants, to move into relation with them, a vital component of also coming to understand their trade. These efforts of grasping to know and feeling through new ways of relating are an extension of the work of theorizing species formations. As John Hartigan Jr. writes about his own efforts of learning with plants, "ethnographic detail is theorizing, and in theorizing a species in this setting I resort to botanists, the experts. . . . What I can imagine now is how I might be able to combine my expertise with that of my subjects in honing an analytic that would account for the role of sociality in species formation."[8] Through conversations with ecologists and botanists and my own observations and activities with plants (some more active than others), it became clear how *D. farinosa*'s capacity to survive the extremes of California's variable coastal climate is exceedingly particular, restricting it to erosive cliffsides where it cannot be overtaken by more robust vegetation but where it won't be overexposed to the physical force of waves and oversaturation with salt water. But what I also came to learn was that despite the incredibly narrow niche in which *D. farinosa* seems to flourish, under proper care and cultivation, it is nevertheless an adaptable plant that can persist along other trajectories, albeit ones that foreclose evolutionary plant-time. Theorizing with *Dudleya* brings together the lifeworlds of plants within an enlarged social field of more-than-human relations. Considering species as "species formations" brings together the perspectives and experiences of human subjects and their unique ways of relating to *Dudleya* plants with the botanizing efforts of learning to know plants in their own epistemological registers.

The Entwinement of Succulent Desires

While I was afforded the time and opportunity to get to know *D. farinosa* in a variety of contexts, my efforts to do so with *D. pachyphytum,* the "unique species" of the genus, were much more constrained, pushing me to dig deeper into archives detailing the engagements of others with the species. But in coming to know both species, it quickly became apparent how enmeshed their trajectories toward endangerment and extinction had become through the production of desire. It is therefore important to briefly revisit several key dimensions of collector psychologies for understanding the relationships forged between *D. pachyphytum* and *D. farinosa.*

Collecting behaviors, as I detail in chapter 1, can manifest as a means of systematically ordering the world in the form of a totality of objects, in which everything ultimately becomes a referent back to the (human) subject.[9] Collectors seek out series or sets of various kinds through which desires to control, constrain, accumulate, and even destroy are expressed. These series could be stamps from a particular country over a series of years or snow globes that are geographically representative of every city in a country or region. What constitutes a complete series is arbitrary, and for succulent collectors, what constitutes a "collection" might mean many things, botanically speaking. As its most casual expression, a collector's "collection" refers to all the succulents the collector possesses. However, most collectors have more specific groupings, or subcollections within their collection. At least in the Euro-American tradition, collections are commonly taxonomically arranged, such as when a collector desires one plant of each species of a genus. Regardless of thematic structure, however, a collection has at least a theoretical terminus, the point at which it might be considered complete.[10]

An important feature of what therefore drives many collectors to collect is the desire to complete a series even if it is not immediately recognized by collectors as such, and even if it is precisely this very act of completion that can deplete collecting of enjoyment. As Baudrillard wrote in *The System of Objects,* this sense of lack, or what remains missing from a collection, is experienced by the collector as a *positive* absence. As a positive absence, it amplifies desire and sets the drives in motion, aiming toward possession. Without this positive absence, the collection as a whole and the drive to complete the series would diminish in meaning. It is frequently reported in studies of collectors that, having achieved some finality to their collections, collectors quickly lose interest in them, neglect them, or even destroy them. "To collect up to a final limit," material culture scholars John Elsner and Roger Cardinal write, "is not simply to own or to control the items one finds; it is to exercise control over existence itself through possessing every sample, every specimen, every instance of an unrepeatable and nowhere duplicated series. It is to be unique. For the collector is then like God—not the God who created the world, but the God who chose to obliterate his own creation."[11] In conducting research for this book, I met a number of cactus and succulent collectors who reported that one day, they simply woke up and threw out all of their plants, or a particular subset of their larger collection, only to move on to something else, finding that what they had previously worked so hard to collect and painstakingly care for no longer brought them pleasure. This pattern was most evocatively illustrated by a Czech collector whose greenhouse during my visit was not filled with the cacti I was expecting to see but instead was teeming with Mexican chili pepper varieties. He told me he had gotten tired of all the cacti, that they had come to make him feel depressed, and he simply threw them away, including live plants that would have been coveted by others. He is not the only collector I interviewed who described throwing live plants in the trash despite months or years of previous care given to them. As Baudrillard notes, "madness begins once a collection is deemed complete and thus ceases to center around its absent term." This is the "pivotal point," according to Elsner and Cardinal, "where man finds himself rivaling God and teeters between mastery and madness."[12]

The profound lack of dialogue between studies of collecting culture and environmental change feels most pronounced in this moment between "mastery and madness," when either might hold profound implications for the species being collected. For example, a particularly rare or difficult-to-obtain object can remain out of reach to a collector for a variety of reasons, such as cost, scarcity, or illegality. It is often precisely such an object that becomes the most sought after as the object that might mark the completion of a series. For the avid succulent collector, *D. pachyphytum* is such a plant that remains out of reach. It incites desire precisely through appealing to a collector's sense of lack by "creating the illusion that it embodies a particular goal or end." *D. pachyphytum,* in this sense, is the "unique object."[13] In the original 1981 description of the species, botanists Reid Moran and Michael Benedict even went as far as to describe *D. pachyphytum* as "unique in the genus, in its blunt and very thick leaves. The rosettes thus recall those of some members of the Mexican genus *Pachyphytum,* for which we name it."[14] The name of both the species and the genus *pachyphytum* comes from the Latin for "thick" or "fat," thus "thick plant." The botanists found the plant's shape and form so unique among all other *Dudleya* species with which they were familiar—Moran being one of the world's foremost experts on *Dudleya* species—that they named it after a different genus altogether. Given that "succulent" as a category of plants is translated in a variety of languages as "fat plant" further instantiates *D. pachyphytum* as the most succulent of succulents.

Moving from the plant as botanically and symbolically unique to the collector, as Baudrillard writes, the unique object becomes "a symbolic distillation of that series without which it would not exist; consequently it acquires a strange quality, a quality which is the quintessence of the whole quantitative calibration of the series."[15] Susan Pearce summarizes this sentiment as when the sacred is made possible through the practice of sanctifying the otherwise mundane. "This is the central paradox of all collected pieces," Pearce writes. "They are wrenched out of their own true contexts and become dead to their living time and space in order that they may be given an immortality within the collection. . . . They are made to withdraw from daily life in order to enable another order of life to come about."[16] This extraction of objects from their "living time and space" takes on greater weight when the object in question is indeed not only a living object but a lively subject in its own right.

It is this seeking out of the unique object—in this case, the unique plant—and its extraction from one world into another that bind the fates of *D. farinosa* and *D. pachyphytum*. It wasn't that people were necessarily *so* desirous of *D. farinosa*; rather, they desired it as a more readily available substitute, a desire-adjacent object of what it most approximated. Collectors were truly desirous of something rarer, more precious, yet largely out of reach. In the words of an expert botanist, "*Dudleya farinosa* is the poor man's *D. pachyphytum*." If you couldn't get *D. pachyphytum,* at least you could get *D. farinosa*.

The Panda Bear of Plants

When I finally saw my first *D. pachyphytum* in a greenhouse on Isla de Cedros, I immediately understood what one Californian botanist meant when he called it the "panda bear of plants." It truly is "cute, charismatic, and rare" (Figure 37). This encounter with *D. pachyphytum* plants, even relocated ones—but nevertheless in their place of origin—was affecting. Walking along the rows of these stolen and recovered plants, different trajectories of diminution were readily expressed: extinction, on one hand, and the commodification of rarity, on the other. It was harder to see possibilities for plant flourishing in the greenhouse in the midday heat, however. Seeing what quite possibly amounted to most of the entire population of the species now sitting under shade nets awaiting an unknown future did not leave me with a sense that much had been accomplished in their seizure by authorities, at least from the plants' perspective. A year since the plant's seizure, no replanting efforts had taken place. At least a quarter of the plants showed visible signs of stress (confirmed by the botanists I accompanied to Cedros), either from overexposure to sun or simply from being removed from their cliff-side home and now finding themselves down along the hot and dry coast, where they would not grow of their own volition. The greenhouse where the *D. pachyphytum* plants were located is within the fenced compound of the Cedros fishing cooperative, where the cooperative sorts and packs lobster and abalone. There is an interest by the fishing cooperative and others on the island to monetize the protection of *D. pachyphytum,* potentially through ecotourism, but also through a legally regulated commercial greenhouse operation, through which domestic or international buyers could legally acquire the plants from the greenhouse, though neither venture has been realized.

Despite their less-than-ideal condition, grouped together on layers of grated trays, the plants resonated with significations far

Figure 37. A recovered *Dudleya pachyphytum* now in cultivation on Isla de Cedros, Mexico.

beyond the charismatic charms of the plants alone. So many of the stories surrounding those who were willing to go to great lengths to steal them—by land, sea, or even air—remain filled with speculation, rumor, possible exaggeration, the threat of violence, and, sadly, even murder. Over the duration of my stay on Cedros, I came to realize that I was less interested in the techniques of their illicit extraction than in what motivated the dedicated pursuit to obtain them. Did Korean succulent poachers really charter a helicopter in the style of a Hollywood crime caper to steal plants? Or did they simply pay off local fishermen to look the other way in a rented *ponga*? Instead of doggedly pursuing these mechanics of extraction in the style of investigative journalism, I remained fixated on what made them desirable, in-demand species, not only in terms of their inherent qualities but as the outcome of emergent multispecies relations. The importance of close attention to the plants at the heart of these stories as living beings becomes even more profound in turning to the production of *Dudleya* desires in South Korea (and elsewhere, as we will see) and those who so desired them.

Illegal trades do not spontaneously develop without cause. Unless there is someone who wants or needs something badly enough to make it worthwhile for that person or someone else to break the law to obtain it, such trades would never come into being. The research demanded, in other words, following desire as a mode of pursuing political economy.

D. pachyphytum demonstrates how desire for a species can mediate the trajectories of others. As Susan Pearce writes, "in the play of the imagination the objects themselves are powerful actors."[17] In the context of *Dudleya*, it is the unique object, and *D. farinosa* is its more readily accessible, more common sibling. It was possible, I realized, that this was the end of the story, that the charisma of *D. pachyphytum,* matched with its extreme rarity and the difficulty of the pursuit, was sufficient to explain the great lengths a plant poacher would go to obtain a wild, weather-beaten specimen. For many collectors (and not just of succulents), the most difficult-to-obtain object often becomes the most coveted. To make an effort to obtain the hard-earned object of desire, inclusive of the pain, costs, and sacrifices one must suffer in the name of its pursuit, is again to confront *jouissance.* One could easily argue that such a beautiful, rare, and difficult-to-obtain plant would naturally become subject to such attention. But was this desire also enough to explain the sudden surge in thefts of *D. farinosa,* the "poor man's *D. pachyphytum*"?

Fantasies and Enchanted Encounters with
Dudleya pachyphytum

As I was unable to visit *D. pachyphytum* in its habitat on the north side of Cedros, I became interested in stories of those earliest written encounters by botanists and passionate collectors with the species, to see if something might be revealed about the working of these plants in the imagination, as well as to learn something of their ecology (Figure 38). I was not disappointed when I read both the formal description of the species by Moran and Benedict from 1981 and a description of another encounter with *D. pachyphytum* published a year earlier by Alfred Lau, a famous (and, depending on whom you ask, infamous) German-born cactus and succulent enthusiast who died in 2007. While close engagement with decades-old descriptions may seem far afield from "learning to know a plant," I approach them as field guides to the encounters, fantasies, and engagements of others invested in the species and their desires routed through them.

Lau is responsible for naming a variety of cactus and succulent species and in turn has a number named after him. Lau and his family were longtime residents of the state of Veracruz, Mexico, where he was well known for financing in part his Christian missionary and education activities for Indigenous children by selling wild-collected Mexican cactus plants and seeds abroad. Eventually, he was deported from Mexico once these activities became illegal under CITES, especially when Mexican cactus seeds were added to the CITES Appendix II list in 1997. Whether it was ever sufficiently proven that he engaged in such activities in contravention of CITES rules and regulations remains contentious, however, and other nefarious rumors about Lau continue to circulate within the succulent community.[18] Lau had visited Cedros in 1970, but he did not encounter *D. pachyphytum* (a not-yet-named species) until a 1977 trip with one of the children from his school. Moran and

Figure 38. Michael Benedict *(left)* and Michael Astone *(right)* visiting the *Dudleya pachyphytum* habitat on Isla de Cedros, Mexico, in 1980. Photograph by Reid Moran. From the San Diego Natural History Museum.

Benedict would visit Cedros themselves in 1980 with Michael Astone to make a formal description of the species and its habitat, although this was not their first encounter with it either.

Who takes credit for "discovering," naming, and describing new species to science is perhaps unsurprisingly a point of frequent tension in the cactus and succulent community. For although Lau writes of discovering a new *Dudleya* species on his 1977 expedition to Cedros in his 1980 article for the *Cactus and Succulent Journal of America*,[19] in the 1981 issue of the same journal, Moran and Benedict wrote that Benedict encountered it as an unknown *Dudleya* species in 1971 and on a subsequent visit in 1975, further legitimating their claim to the right to formally describe and name the species.[20] Neither Lau nor Moran and Benedict appear to have made any effort to explore how the species was recognized and understood by Cedros residents. This seems especially strange, as Moran and Benedict go so far as to describe the species as "conspicuous and abundant, even predominant," where found.[21] Alternatively, perhaps they willfully chose not to consider how the species might already be known and understood in writing up their "discovery." Although it is not uncommon for species first to be "discovered" by someone and formally described by someone else (usually a professional botanist), one can't help but detect a tinge of one-upmanship when Moran and Benedict spend a paragraph detailing their many encounters with *D. pachyphytum* that preceded Lau's encounter by close to a decade.

Beyond providing a tantalizing window into some succulent drama, Moran and Benedict's description of *D. pachyphytum* is valuable for detailing a dynamic sense of the plant's ecology. In an extended passage, they describe how *D. pachyphytum* is "most abundant and best developed on exposed rocky cliffs and steep slopes outside the forest," where it "forms clumps of 10 to 20 or even 50 or more rosettes." They describe a plant with *movement*, explaining how like *"agave, ferocactus,* and *mammillaria* [kinds of cacti and succulents], it survives on talus partly because it is a successful roller: uprooted plants may roll with the rocks but re-establish themselves below."[22] And they describe it as a plant with associations, where "on recently exposed canyon walls, and on the upper faces of the highest sea cliffs, the *Dudleya* forms a unique association with *Viguiera lanata*," a flowering shrub. In addition to this thick botanical description, they give us an appreciation of their wonder seeing *D. pachyphytum* and *V. lanata* on the Cedros cliffs within a wider ecology where "the hundreds of scattered brilliant white dots of the two plants contrast strikingly with the dull gray and black walls of the huge cliffs and canyons. These and the stark white splotches of hundreds of pelican roosts, in the huge scale of the landscape, create an edge-of-the-world scene that is utterly awesome." Their depictions conjure enchanted images of these living plants rolling down scree from one place to another and huge *Dudleya* plants with as many as fifty connected rosettes interspersed by pelican roosts and barrel cacti. Moran and Benedict capture a sense of flow and movement in this steep and unlikely landscape on the far edge of the Cedros cliffs, a fog-shrouded habitat entirely different from the hot, dry landscape I saw in and around the town of Cedros on the other side of the island.

This imagery becomes even more potent when read alongside the near-biblical grandeur of wonder that Lau describes in his own depiction of first encountering *D. pachyphytum* in 1977. Lau's description provides insight into the affective dimensions of the moment of encounter between collector and plant but also the role of fantasy at work emplacing succulents within the psychotopologies of the unconscious. Lau describes the desire of the succulent "explorer" to enact Romantic fantasies of Edenic nature as embodying spiritual purity and divine inspiration, as well as an "authentic" experience of wilderness. In Lacanian terms, this is a fantasy of (re)unification of the biological and psychological, an impossible "mending" of the split that occurs through alienation of the subject, the split that brings the desiring subject into be-ing. This moment finds strong affinity with prior research about how tourists seek out "authentic" encounters with wilderness.[23] As Elizabeth Vidon describes in a study of visitors to Adirondack Park in upstate New York, "[tourists] are engaging bodily and psycho-logically with the fantasy of authenticity . . . as it is manifest in wilderness. The subject's (unconscious) desire to (re)connect to the biological child and to thus transcend alienation is one that finds a suitable stage in the fantasy of the authentic wilderness."[24] Fan-tasy, as Lacan writes, is "the support of desire."[25] To this end, it is worth quoting here a long passage from Lau's description of this moment of "discovery" to fully capture a sense of where desires meet the botanical (fantasy):

In November, 1977 I revisited the area with *Antonio Garcia,* one of our Mixteco Indian boys. A strong lad of 13 and an enthusiastic mountain climber, he stumbled on ahead of me toward the highest point of the area, wanting to find some shade under the pine trees at the top. Quiet, as Indian boys are, he made no significant effort to call me to the place where he was staring at the ground. . . . I looked down on a seedling which at first glance looked like an *argyoderma* or a low form of a *pachyphytum* with very succulent, rounded leaves. There was no doubt in my mind that *Antonio* had found a new spe-cies of Dudleya.

For hours we searched and searched but we could not find another plant. Either this was an extremely rare species or we were not at the right locality. The latter proved to be true. . . . From far away came an echo from another mountain and I heard *Antonio's* voice: *"Aqui hay muchos!"* Head over heels, I stumbled on ahead, heart pounding, toward where I expected to find him far ahead. Suddenly, I was with him—he was very close-by on that steep slope. His voice calling for me did not

reach me over the mountain top but had echoed from neighboring mountains.

I had to readjust my thinking as I could not have imagined
that the northwest slope bore a huge, white cover of our new
Dudleya. The covering of white powder protecting the leaves
looked like patches of snow. Some of the plants had as many
as 100 stems. There we stood, 2,100 feet above the blue ocean
where maybe no man's foot had ever trod before, with God allowing us to be the first to see this new marvel of His creation.
We were dazed and exhilarated—dreaming and wondering.
Could this be true? I do not believe I exaggerate my feelings;
as long as I live I shall never forget that moment of ecstasy.[26]

The language he uses to describe Antonio Garcia is paternalis-
tic and troubling. Focusing on his description of the species, there
is something truly remarkable in this narrative of *discovery* that
sounds like it was pulled from the journal of a Victorian botanist
rather than a 1980s hobby journal. Lau suggests that he and Antonio might be the first people to come across these plants, on an
island that has archaeological evidence of early fishing cultures
dating back as far as ten thousand years or more. This is to say
nothing of the much more recent gold and copper mining industry
on Cedros active during the early late 1800s and early 1900s or the
earlier Spanish colonization and logging of Cedros for shipbuild-
ing, a history of which Lau was certainly aware and that occurred
within one kilometer of *D. pachyphytum*'s habitat. But Lau is not
just weaving a tall tale for the sake of writing a juicy story for his
readers; Lau places these historical inconveniences aside to invoke
a greater meaning in the chance encounter with *D. pachyphytum* as
fantasy and his desire for an "authentic" encounter with wilderness
as he imagines it ought to be. Encounters, as Helen Wilson writes,
"are meetings where difference is somehow noteworthy," where
"encounters are not only about the coming together of different

bodies but are about meetings that also make (a) difference."[27] What Lau seems to be enacting in this encounter is a desire for the experience of the sublime through an imagined Edenic land-scape untrammeled by human presence. In doing so, he is willing to ignore his own awareness of Cedros as an island with a long his-tory of human inhabitation and environmental change, just as he is happy to ignore that other botanists had already frequented this same location numerous times in just the past decade. These men-tal gymnastics permit Lau to title his article "Discovery at a Virgin Outpost." For Lau, what was being collected above all on Cedros, more than the seeds of this new *Dudleya* species he gathered, was the memory of the encounter as sublime, the declaration of some-thing as new to existence in the world, his "moment of ecstasy" in a "virgin" landscape unsullied by human sin.

We can extend thinking biblically with *D. pachyphytum* and Lau even further, leading to a greater understanding of Lau's grandiose depiction of this encounter wrenched out of time and context as "making (a) difference." As Elsner and Cardinal describe, the sto-ries of Adam and Noah together tell us a great deal about Western desires to name and identify as entwined with desires to collect: "Adam classified the creatures that God had made; on the basis of his nomenclature, Noah could recollect those creatures in order to preserve them. Of course without the prior existence of the ani-mals, they could not have been named; equally, without their en-dowment with names they could not have been collected. In effect, the plentitude of taxonomy opens up the space for collectibles to be identified, but at the same time the plentitude of that which is to be collected hastens the need to classify."[28]

The desire to know and classify and the desire to possess and collect work hand in hand. Together, they make possible the world of collections, just as the act of collecting pushes "explorers" like Lau to seek out new organisms to "bring to life" through naming, enabling both possession and extending the horizon of desire. But these twinned descriptions of encountering *D. pachyphytum* are dramatically different in their focus, tone, and intent. Whereas botanists Moran and Benedict allow the plants as part of a wider ecology to enchant their description of a landscape that is "utterly awesome," Lau centers the affective encounter of discovery between himself and *D. pachyphytum* as the experience of the sublime worth collecting. In relating these experiences in print, Lau hopes to leave something of his own mark on history. Writing sixteen years later in the pages of the same journal, in his last installment of his long-running "South American Cactus Log" series, Lau makes this sentiment clear: "As I am getting older and have to accept the fact of life that not all is permanent . . . I trust that I have made many cactophiles happy with the numerous new discoveries that are now known around the globe. Many sacrifices were made to find these rare and unusual plants, but I would not have missed it for anything . . . I wonder whether there are cacti in heaven; it would surely enhance my expectations of eternity."[29] Lau is preoccupied with his mark on history through the discovery of new species, and like the plant passed from one collector to the next, many of these species will carry on his legacy past death with the species name *laui* (a *Mammillaria laui* sits on my kitchen windowsill as I type these words). Death and collecting practices are linked in many ways, of course—as Freud wrote in a letter to a friend on his own antiquities collecting habit just before his death a few months later, "a collection to which there are no new additions is really dead."[30]

As these guides to learning with *D. pachyphytum* reveal, learning with plants is a relational endeavor of also learning with many, and it is also an encounter with enchantment, which is to say, drawing on Wilson, enchantment as the "*experience* of encounter."[31] This is an engagement of more-than-human geography, centering plants within a wider field of relations inclusive of slippery rock slopes, agaves, cacti, wildflowers, people, and their memories, yearnings, and unconscious selves (Figure 39). As Jane Bennett recently

Figure 39. *Dudleya pachyphytum* peering over the northern cliffs of Isla de Cedros, Mexico, over a sea of clouds. Photograph by Reid Moran, taken on July 18, 1980, the same day as the herbarium specimen (Figure 36) was collected. From San Diego Natural History Museum.

wrote, enchantment "involves a force in excess of sentiments, emotions, or feelings. It is a prompt from outside . . . which strikes and impresses."[32] Like enchantment, the work of the unconscious, be it the repression of trauma or the presentation of anxiety, or to be awestruck and moved by desire, also prompts us from "outside" even when the "outside" is within us. It is in encounters with others (and other things) in a wider field of view that we see our desires expressed and the excess of *jouissance* "enjoyed" through the drives, or when we are confronted by the unsettling presence of *objet a* when anxiety rears its head. "What psychoanalysis presents," Kingsbury and Pile write, "is a dynamic landscape of the psyche, which can be appreciated in various ways, but not fully known."[33] Reading Lau's depiction of encountering *D. pachyphytum* resonates with the object as imbued with excessive pleasure, the object as sublime object, "elevated to the dignity of the Thing." We can aim to determine with some precision what moved Lau to be in the throes of *D. pachyphytum*'s enchantment, its aura, but the analysis does not depend on any certainty. "The certainties of interpretation may be a destination, but they are not the starting point, nor the journey," as Kingsbury and Pile write.[34] As different as Lau's story of his first encounter with *D. pachyphytum* is from Moran and Benedict's, there remains something wonderfully excessive in both that points us in the direction of the "enjoyment" encountered in suddenly finding oneself confronted with the radical difference of the indescribably sensuous in the imagined presence of the Other.

Staying with Desire, Following the Species

Leaving California and Mexico, as much as I learned about these species and their relations to one another through stories of succulent desires, I failed to answer why their value apparently skyrocketed in East Asia. What was conjured in the imagination through *Dudleya* species to produce such value, monetary or otherwise? I also remained fixated on the yet-to-be-resolved matter of time in this story: why was *Dudleya* poaching taking off *now*, and why, if these plants were not regulated by endangered species trade conventions, was there an illegal trade at all? Staying close to the plants would help me understand just how important plant-time is to the story of these *Dudleya* species and their illicit travels.

By this stage of my research, I understood that CDFW officers, Mexican conservation officials, conservation organizations, succulent enthusiasts, and, consequently, the media were promoting the narrative that demand for *Dudleya* plants was the result of succulents becoming a major new fad in mainstream Korean pop culture—a decidedly different consumer demographic than the mostly older, mostly white "cactus men" I describe in the first part of this book. I also understood that neither *D. farinosa* nor

D. pachyphytum was likely to survive in a very different climate as a traditional houseplant the way many other succulents, such as *Echeveria*, might. Still, it was presumed that it was the mass consumer succulent market that was driving the emergence of these illicit *Dudleya* trades. I also knew that at least a dozen or so people were implicated in illegally harvesting and selling *D. farinosa,* purportedly to East Asian clients for quite a lot of money. Estimates of their value ranged anywhere from $25 to $40 for a single rosette to $3,000 to $4,000 for a large, multiheaded plant. But nobody I interviewed had any firsthand knowledge of what the Korean or East Asian market for *D. farinosa* or *D. pachyphytum* was really like. This left two related questions unanswered: who actually desired these *Dudleya* plants, and why did this desire result in their large-scale theft?

There are rarer *Dudleya* species out in the world, but it was clear from my time on Cedros that *D. farinosa*'s place in this story was one of unfortunate kinship with *D. pachyphytum* as unique object-adjacent plant. Understanding these plants' respective futures, or ends, as entangled through desire was clear enough, but the production of desire as a more-than-human endeavor spanning species, the conscious, and the unconscious was another matter. Desire cannot be abstracted from the social worlds we inhabit. *D. pachyphytum* would have always appeared to me as a beautiful and charismatic plant when I first encountered it, but it was only through months of reading, discussion, and pursuit preceding my first encounter with it that the plant developed such intense resonances and layers of signification. The production of desire signals these relations as decidedly social practices as well, inseparable from the creation of exchange-value through the human work of plant commodification in capitalist economies. How were those engaged in the commodification and trade of *Dudleya* plants inciting desire through their social engagement with plants? What shaped the political economy, as well as the aesthetics, of this illicit global trade? How did actors in this trade work to produce *Dudleya* desires? I would not find those answers on Cedros. In the next chapter, I turn to those questions through following *Dudleya* to South Korea.

7

Disentangling Succulent Desires

Nine months after my first *Dudleya* encounter in California, I gazed on row upon row of impeccably presented *Dudleya* plants inside a greenhouse on the outskirts of Seoul, South Korea. It was a strange and uneasy feeling to see *D. pachyphytum* and *D. farinosa* again on the other side of the world. Perhaps even stranger, however, was seeing these species side by side on the display benches of a high-end commercial nursery.

In the course of the next month, I saw thousands of *Dudleya* plants across a variety of greenhouses, commercial nurseries, and plant warehouses in and around Seoul and farther afield in South Korea. But before encountering these cosmopolitan plants again, I spent my first few days in Seoul *not* seeing *Dudleya* plants. Based on the media accounts I had read prior to my trip, I expected to be inundated with the presence of *Dudleya* in the popular succulent markets and boutique plant shops I visited that dotted the cityscape, but they were nowhere to be found. My enquiries with local vendors provided little help. Most of the vendors had either never even heard of these species or told me they didn't sell them because they were not in high demand. While I was impressed with the diversity and kinds of succulents available to consumers, *Dudleya* was missing.

Despite its physical absence, *Dudleya* was nevertheless everywhere I looked *online*. There are several Korean-specific online plant retail and auction websites where individuals and nurseries can post plants for sale. In these online forums, there was no absence of *Dudleya*. It was as if there were entirely different succulent markets. Thanks to the assistance of colleagues in South Korea, I was soon connected with and accompanied by Dr. Jinah Kwon, at the time a recent PhD graduate in political science who is now working as a lecturer at Korea University and is a senior research fellow at Soongsil University for Peace and Unification, and Jaehyun Kim, a recent undergraduate preparing to apply for law school, in tracking down *Dudleya*. With their assistance (and within a matter of days, a shared succulent fervor), we were soon in touch with an entirely different tier of specialist nurseries.

In South Korea, I not only saw countless beautiful and well-cared-for *Dudleya* plants but some of the most exceptional, large, and diverse collections of succulents I have ever seen. In the coming weeks, I saw truly outstanding specimens of *D. pachyphytum* and *D. farinosa* presented in custom earthenware pottery with sticker prices in the thousands of U.S. dollars. I saw plants with thick, trunklike bodies and more than ten individual rosettes, presented in such a way as to resemble prized bonsai (or *bunjae,* in Korean). I marveled at row upon row of quite obviously wild-collected *D. farinosa* and *D. pachyphytum,* now cared for by skilled nursery owners and workers who closely monitored sunlight and water levels, delicately removing dead leaves from plants with sets of long tweezers. I was generously welcomed into nurseries by enthusiastic growers and hobbyists who greeted Jinah, Jaehyun, and me with coffee and snacks. These growers described an international marketplace for *Dudleya* in which discerning collectors—or even sometimes their personal plant-buying agents—were offered real-time video tours of individual plants over the phone. That among these were *Dudleya* plants illegally collected in Mexico and the United States was the elephant in the greenhouse.

I quickly confirmed that large quantities of stolen *Dudleya* plants had made their way to South Korea. But I also discovered that for many of these plants, Korea was not their final stop in their transformation from flourishing plants in the world into lively commodities, or what Rosemary-Claire Collard has also called lively capital.[1] Questions about the production of *Dudleya* desires remained unanswered. In following *Dudleya* plants to South Korea, I wanted not only to confirm what had happened to these harvested wild plants but also to understand why they had been stolen: what gap in the market did they fill, and why was it occurring now? I also faced new, more challenging questions about why media and enforcement agencies were wrong—or at least, seemingly misguided to different degrees—in speculating about the drivers of these new illicit trades. There was not, I came to find, a mass consumer "mania" for *Dudleya* driven by "housewives and hipsters," as reported in newspaper outlets.[2] Even if there was indeed a surging interest in succulents writ large across South Korea and East Asia, the same held true across much of the world at the same time.

Encounters with *Dudleya* in South Korea also opened other important avenues of more critical concern, leading me to consider ways this global illicit trade was mediated by matters of cultural stereotypes and powerful aesthetics. The plants became enrolled in the circulation and performance of narratives about wildlife trade and consumption across East Asia, in which blunt tropes about exoticized wildlife consumption were leveraged to explain the surge in illegal *Dudleya* poaching in North America that prove equally effective at deflecting the status of the United States among other Global North countries as some of the world's largest consumers of illegally traded wildlife.[3] The story of *Dudleya* thefts also pushed me toward new avenues for theorizing succulent desires in relation to the widespread and growing demand for all things "cute" around the world. Drawing on the work of cultural and aesthetic theorist Sianne Ngai, through cuteness, I came to understand a vitally important yet underexamined aspect of succulent commodification and its relationships to matters of possession, desire, and illicit trade.

Tracing Illicit Networks and Narratives

After several days of not finding *Dudleya* plants, Jaehyun Kim and I encountered our first *Dudleya* plant at a well-known street market for plants in Seoul. Eventually, we met a vendor with a more curated stall of succulents who, tucked away on an upper shelf, had one small, single-headed *D. pachyphytum,* the species of *Dudleya* from Isla de Cedros, Mexico, for sale for around $300 (Figure 40).

As our conversation turned to *Dudleya,* the vendor explained that different plants were always coming in and out of fashion. She showed us her colorful array of *Lithops* plants, a genus of species native to southern Africa and commonly known as living stones, explaining that the year before, they had been worth twenty thousand Korean won (approximately eighteen U.S. dollars) a piece, but now she was selling them for seven thousand won (approximately six dollars). She explained that this was no different for *Dudleya,* with the notable exception of *D. pachyphytum.* "Other succulents have fads, but *Dudleya pachyphytum* is always expensive, it's always rare . . . *D. pachyphytum* is always hard to get." She went on to explain how initially, she saw *D. farinosa* from California being sold for $600, but eventually more arrived, and the price fell to $200, and then to much less. She informed us, to my surprise, that the demand for *D. farinosa* was in decline: "one to two years ago, *D. farinosa* was a fad, but it's done now. . . . I don't bring it to the market, not that many people want it, the fad is already over."

The vendor was also aware of the stories of illegal collection of

Figure 40. A single-headed *Dudleya pachyphytum* in the hands of a succulent vendor at an outdoor street market in Seoul, South Korea. The thickness of the trunk and signs of scarring on some of the lower leaves strongly suggest that this was an illegally wild-harvested plant.

Dudleya specimens from the United States and Mexico. I asked her why she thought people would steal them from California: "[Because] it's just free!" she laughed. "If they grow [the plants] themselves, they need people and land to do it; if you steal [it] you only need labor, and it's a fad, and it fluctuates." She was also aware of a rumor about the popularity of *Dudleya* plants that I had yet to encounter in California: in the United States, media articles focused on a booming middle class in China and a succulent "fever" in South Korea leading to rampant desire for rare, wild-collected specimens.[4] But in the Korean media, additional narratives explaining this spate of poaching incidents included the belief that *Dudleya* species, like other succulents, were effective home air purifiers (they are not). Air quality, and in particular, problems of high concentrations of tiny air particles ($PM_{2.5}$) associated with a host of negative health effects, is a major concern in South Korea. It has been common for years for people in South Korea to wear the kinds of face masks that became ubiquitous around the world because of the Covid-19 pandemic, worn not to reduce viral transmission and exposure (though at times that as well) but to reduce inhalation of fine air particulate matter. That *Dudleya* poaching might be driven by atmospheric anxieties was a jarring notion, linking issues of environmental change, pollution, and environmental health on opposite sides of the Pacific.

Famous K-pop stars with their own TV shows have extolled the virtues of succulents as air purifiers to their throngs of adoring fans. As Jaeyhun speculated one day while we were discussing the potential merits of this theory, "California is known [in South Korea] for its pure air. Perhaps people thought that a Californian plant would be an even better plant to have as an air purifier." It was an interesting thought, if entirely speculative. We asked the vendor at the market what she made of this theory: "I have heard these rumors, but they aren't true. . . . The only people who collect *Dudleya* are specialist collectors—they are very hard to grow well. . . . Nobody is buying *Dudleya* as air purifiers."

This conversation highlighted some of the key challenges in disentangling "rumor" from "truth" in the study of illicit wildlife economies. First, it was becoming clear that just as English-language media reports were misinformed about the ultimate drivers of *Dudleya* demand, South Korean media outlets were equally guilty of spreading misinformation. To the credit of the reporters writing these varied stories, it was not so much that they were wrong about growing popularity and increasing demand for succulents both within South Korea and across East Asia as that they lacked specificity in understanding *Dudleya* as a taxonomic group of plants with unique traits. What also emerged was a need to consider more closely matters of supply and demand for groups of plants like *Dud-leya* and why it might be that a flurry of interest in certain species could emerge for a time, while others, like *D. pachyphytum,* had greater market durability.

Over the course of the next several weeks, Jinah, Jaehyun, and I would meet with a variety of dealers and growers with deep knowledge of and investment in *Dudleya.* The reasons why people familiar with the trade thought *D. farinosa* suddenly experienced intense pressure from wild collection were diverse and variable. Some reasons made more sense than others, while others were also clearly untrue (the vendor at the street market, for instance, incorrectly suggested that another reason for *D. farinosa* thefts was because the seed to grow them was not available in South Korea). Avoiding simplifying moves of attempting to separate fact from fiction, I focused instead on building up a redundancy of overlapping and complementary data, attentive to how particular understandings and narratives would make more or less sense as "true" to different kinds of actors. But this kind of work also demands integrating qualitative data with other kinds of evidence. This included placing requests for court documents in the United States, developing pricing spreadsheets for plants in online marketplaces, visiting markets to check prices and stock, and reviewing news reports, as well as reading individual collector blogs and even scrolling through Instagram. Teo Ballvé has called such a methodological approach "investigative ethnography." My research into the *Dudleya* trades was in alignment with this approach, which "combines ethnography's immersive fieldwork and its interpretive perspective with investigative journalism's emphasis on documentary evidence and public records research."[5] Although I was interested in the kinds of "fact-finding" questions journalists pursue when writing about illicit economies, I approached these questions through the lens of critical and qualitative research, seeking to understand a variety of nuanced and at times contradictory sets of perspectives and data from a range of interlocutors on the emergence of new *Dudleya* demands.

Dudleya Aesthetics

The collection of plants at Hollywood Succulents in Korea was unlike anything I had ever seen before (Figure 41).[6] Stately rows of diverse succulents in unique earthenware pottery lined wooden benches in a wide and airy greenhouse. The two owners, a husband-and-wife duo, greeted Jaehyun and me warmly as we sat down to discuss Korean and international succulent markets and their impressive inventory. Like many of the more specialist dealers I soon met, their business first started out as a serious hobby. In fact, despite a renowned reputation as one of the most high-end purveyors of succulents in South Korea, the owners had professionalized their business only about five years earlier, when, according to them, the commercial succulent trade really began to take off in South Korea.

Like the vendor at the succulent street market, the owners described the typical ebb and flow of interest in different species and how this correlated with matters of supply and demand. "When there's a lot of supply, the price goes down. [*Dudleya*] 'white greenei' [a cultivar of an attractive, smaller species, *D. greenei*] . . . it's easy to propagate, [so] because the number increased, the price went down," one of the owners explained. "[*D. farinosa*] used to be very popular before. . . . It was popular and expensive. One head was 100,000 or 150,000 won [approximately $75–$120]. Depending on the size, if the head is big, sometimes it could cost 200,000 or 250,000 [won] even [approximately $150–$200]." Unlike the more mainstream retail outlets and warehouses I visited earlier in my trip, where there was scarcely a *Dudleya* to be found, Hollywood Succulents was a highly specialized, upscale outlet. "We have the best [*D.*] *pachyphytum* in the country," one of the owners

Figure 41. A riot of color and shapes in succulent form. A scene from an exceptionally high-quality succulent commercial outfit in South Korea.

said. "*Pachyphytum* only comes from one place, Mexico," the other added. "They say there's a lot on an island in Mexico," she clarified.

As we looked together over some of their impressive array of *D. pachyphytum* plants for sale, the husband gestured to the plants. "These here were illegally collected. . . . They are not rare, but they say there's an island as big as Jeju [an island off the coast of mainland South Korea] in Mexico, it has a lot of these. They're collected there," the man said, flatly. "There are specific people who import *D. pachyphytum*," the woman later added. "When they import, they sell to the retailers [such as them]." Other dealers I visited were similar, often specializing in a specific group or even just a few species of plants, such as *D. greenei* or cultivars of *Echeveria agavoides*. One nursery I visited was nearly exclusively dedicated to just a few species of *Aeonium* (a genus of approximately thirty-five succulent species with very waxy, glossy leaves). One attentive owner with a specialization in *D. gnoma* was so passionate about his caretaking responsibilities that he played Simon and Garfunkel albums on a stereo in the greenhouse on repeat, explaining that the music was good for the plants' growth.

So what made *Dudleya* species so desirable, and what qualities mattered in capturing collector desires? One collector speculated that succulents had become so popular in general in South Korea, Japan, and China because few succulents naturally grow there and succulents were simply the latest trend in exotic plants. "I think it's a fad. Before, at a Korean home, you would see cacti. There were cacti, and for fathers, men grew orchids. And if you had space, you grew bonsai. People who were into that [bonsai] now are into succulents. The fad has changed. A lot of people who used to give orchids as gifts now gift succulent plants."

But beyond these shifting trends in consumer interest, it was important to understand if collectors in South Korea were purchasing these plants *because* they were wild-collected. If they were, this could have significant ramifications for the persistence of illegal trade that could not be tackled through cultivation and propagation alone. My conversation at Hollywood Succulents left me uncertain and concerned about this question. During our interview, they showed me pictures on their phone of *D. farinosa* growing on the coastline of Northern California. "You make it [to look like] wild [plants]," the man says. "[This is] wild bluff lettuce," the woman chimes in. "It has to be this pretty. Isn't it so pretty? . . . The sun is strong and it has good wind. It grows on dew drops," she says. "The California sun is the best," the man explains. "As much as we try to grow it well here, it won't look like this wild one." They clarified that although they might not be able to fully mimic the look of a wild plant, they worked hard to cultivate plants that achieved similar shapes as wild-grown plants.

But another high-end vendor explained to me a few days later,

"We [Koreans] don't care much about where it comes from. How pretty it is, and how pretty it can be made when it's mature, how pretty the shape can be, and how big it can grow [is what matters]. You can make [it] your own work [of art]. That's the charm." I noted that the *Dudleya* plants I saw for sale there, as elsewhere, including the ones at Hollywood Succulents that were undoubtedly of wild origin, were in impeccable condition. These did not look like the wave-blasted plants of the California coast, nor did the *D. pachyphytum* plants bear the signs of stress and sun I saw on Isla de Cedros. These plants had rich green hues, sometimes tinged with a subtle red (in *D. farinosa*); had plump leaves; and were absent of desiccated leaves from years past farther down their stems. These dead leaves were carefully removed by patient hands and tweezers. *Dudleya* species are somewhat unique among other succulents in that each year's leaves dry up and die but remain attached to the stem, a feature that is sometimes called a skirt. In South Korea, I noticed it was considered appropriate plant care to remove these dead leaves from the plants to expose their stems, while within collector circles in the United Kingdom and the United States, it was considered more appropriate to leave this material intact. It was impressive to see how much this aesthetic choice altered the look of the plants.[7]

The answer to the question about the value of the wild origin of the plants was complex. Although at Hollywood Succulents, the owners suggested that they admired and tried to replicate the wild qualities of the plants growing in California, this meant something different than the aesthetic of "hard-grown plants," such as those I saw in some U.S. and European collections. "Originally, wild ones were preferred [by some collectors], but they don't always adjust," one of the owners at Hollywood Succulents explained. He went on to clarify that *D. farinosa* was easy to cultivate under proper greenhouse conditions. He shows me photographs of battered-looking stumps of *D. farinosa* on a phone. "This is bluff lettuce [*D. farinosa*].

They come in bulk, like this," he shows me in the photographs. "Without roots. With nothing. They come like this and we grow them to look pretty, like this," he says as he shows me the beautiful *D. farinosa* before me, with unblemished leaves and plump rosettes. What was admired in the aesthetics of wild-grown plants and what commercial growers sought to cultivate in their greenhouses were not quite the same, in ways with important implications for wild-growing plants.

My questions about provenance—or the idea that people might desire wild-collected plants because they had a known geographic origin—also led to unexpected answers. As a government researcher at the Gyeonggido Cactus and Succulent Research Institute (one of the major sources of modern cultivars and hybrid succulents in South Korea) described, "it's nonsense to talk about 'wild' in the succulent market. . . . In succulents there is no market for wild things, so it was definitely size and color [that attracted buyers]; wild doesn't matter at all" (Figure 42). I pressed further on this question in the interview, clarifying that many news reports suggested there might be something about the plant's "wild" qualities that attracted buyers, as well as reflecting that many European and U.S. collectors were especially interested in plants with geographic provenance data. The two researchers I was interviewing together with Jaehyun laughed. "We don't care [in] which country the plants are produced," he said. "Where this plant is grown is not important for us, the flower is the flower. The plant is just a plant for the Korean [consumer]." Whereas more serious collectors and dealers in South Korea did know that *D. pachyphytum* came from Mexico, only some were aware that it came from an island. Others had a general sense that *D. farinosa* came from California or Mexico but were not always sure which, much less where specifically. These were markedly different orientations toward plant provenance to what I had encountered within European and U.S. cactus and

Figure 42. A private collection of succulents maintained within a professional growing facility, where they can receive adequate light, temperature regulation, and air circulation to maintain successful plant growth and color development.

succulent collecting communities, where many collectors would keep tags with precise latitudinal and longitudinal coordinates attached to their plants or in a separate database, indicating the plants' precise geographic origins, even several generations removed. The South Korean collectors and dealers I interviewed were not generally interested in such information. Instead, their interests were focused on plants with exceptional aesthetic qualities, especially relating to color, form, and age.

These qualities, however, *did* relate at times to plant origins, but not in the ways much of the reporting about these incidents presumed. As the owners of Hollywood Succulents clarified, while it was through their careful attention that imported *D. farinosa* could grow out beautiful, blemish-free new leaves, it took a long time to grow the stout, twisted stems older, wild-origin plants possessed. But the story of *D. pachyphytum* featured another twist. As a dealer (and collector) with a series of prized *D. pachyphytum* plants (including one they valued at $8,000) explained, whereas *D. pachyphytum* plants growing in Mexico had thick, compact leaves, under greenhouse conditions in South Korea or elsewhere, they could thin and lengthen under weaker sunlight. As another dealer explained, consumers in Korea and China didn't care about the geographic origins of the plants as a category, but *D. pachyphytum* plants taken from Cedros, as more mature plants, had rounder, thicker leaves. These rounder, thicker leaves were perceived as more attractive than the leaves of plants grown from seeds or cuttings in Korea. The ideal shape of *D. pachyphytum* leaves could be mediated by its time growing in habitat on Cedros, although even wild-harvested plants would slowly change in form over time as they acclimated to their new, more temperate and pampered environs. Still, this was a slow process, affecting plant pricing for *D. pachyphytum* specifically. "The ones produced from seeds [here in Korea]—their parent plants are wide and round shaped, but the ones you produce from spreading seeds, they're pointy. The leaves themselves are skinny. Those are not popular, not as much as the wild ones," the dealer explained. Key differences between the species were emerging.

Another dimension of succulent collecting that emerged in South Korea was a deep interest by collectors in plant color and color change. Many interviewees spoke at length about color changes of species or groups of plants based on the difference between nighttime and daytime temperatures, as well as sunlight intensity. This presented a variety of challenges for serious collectors who sought to develop plants with preferred color palettes, colors that can change dramatically at times with the seasons and temperature fluctuations. As an expert grower of *Echeveria agavoides* explained to me, "most succulents that you see people growing [in Korea], a lot of them are of the *Echeveria* variety. For the *Echeveria* variety to come out pretty, you need to grow them in a country like Korea, Europe, or America with four seasons. Gold varieties are popular everywhere, whether it's America or Europe. In Thailand, right now *Conophytum* is popular. *Echeveria* doesn't work [grow well] in Thailand because it's always summer there. You need different seasons for the colors to be pretty, but in Thailand it only gets big and doesn't become pretty. So the Thai people look for something small and easy to grow like *Conophytum* or *Lithops*." Many of these collected species originally derive from climates with dramatic temperature ranges, which meant that some of the colors and changes that incited collector desire (for instance, when viewing plants online) were difficult to replicate outside of their distribution ranges. I was curious to know if the same was true for *D. farinosa*. Did the deep red colors I sometimes saw fringing the leaves of plants in California make them more desirable, even if these hues might fade in different environmental conditions? I was surprised to discover, however, that these kinds of color shifts in *D. farinosa* were not always seen as desirable, contrasted with the deeper green hues the plants developed under less harsh

greenhouse conditions. Like any aesthetic, however, these preferences were also individualized; I saw some greenhouses where
D. farinosa plants were kept outside to encourage the reddening of
their leaves, whereas in other collections, they were kept sheltered
under partial shade to avoid this.

While the aesthetics of color preferences may be more individualized, more mature plants of greater size, especially with multiple heads, held greater value than younger plants. "After a few
years, the head [of *D. farinosa*] splits and one head becomes two.
And *D. pachyphytum* does that too . . . but it takes years. So that is
attractive. . . . All *Dudleya* are like this. And it's luxurious to look
at," one dealer explained. As another commented about *D. greenei*, "white greenei has its own charm. It's the smallest among the
Dudleya. It's the smallest size. As time goes by, they part, and one
head becomes two heads, two heads become four. . . . The price
goes up proportionately." But the same dealer also explained that
what made *D. farinosa* attractive was a different set of criteria from
D. pachyphytum. Although he believed collectors preferred the
rounder, fatter leaves of *D. pachyphytum* than what growers could
produce in cultivation, he said that there was really no point in trying to distinguish wild and cultivated *D. farinosa* in terms of their
market value. "At first, *D. farinosa* was rare, and therefore expensive, but these days it has popularized so much with its second and
third generations, and the price went down and therefore, there's
no point of comparing the prices. The price of *D. farinosa* has gone
down by two-thirds. What used to be thirty thousand won now
costs ten thousand won." It also appeared that Korean growers had
mastered the ability to grow cultivated *D. farinosa* in a manner that
produced a more desirable aesthetic. "When you cultivate them,
they come out almost the same [as wild plants]," another grower
said. "The size is the same too. It depends on the nutrition, but
they come out the same. . . . That's why they're strong and pretty
when they come out cultivated."

~

Two major conclusions emerged across these interviews. The first was that the traits of specific species mattered a great deal in understanding consumer aesthetic preferences and desires that were erased in talking about a rising "succulent fever." Color changes were especially important in *Echeveria,* whereas splitting heads and thick leaves were important for *D. pachyphytum.* Collectors particularly appreciated *D. farinosa* plants with thick stems supporting big bouquets of well-pruned and blemish-free rosettes with a rich, floury patina. Second, it became clear that the embodiment of time in plants is valued by collectors, but this value in cultivated plants is also inextricable from labor time. Bigger plants take more time and thus expenditures of resources and human labor to grow, and this is reflected in selling prices. In addition to the sunk costs of human labor and time, larger plants were seen as more desirable. I quickly learned, however, that much of the value in the *D. pachyphytum* and *D. farinosa* plants I saw online going for hundreds to thousands of dollars had less to do with their *total* size (for instance, measured in the number of rosettes or heads) than with the size and maturity of their stems. During one interview, a vendor showed me two plants that at first glance looked the same to me; both featured the same number of rosettes and leaves of uniform color. But, as the vendor pointed out, the stems were significantly different, as were their prices. The *Dudleya* plants with the greatest value, it seemed, were stout plants with thick, mature stems capable of holding up a significant amount of foliage and multiple rosettes (Figure 43). These plants can be nurtured into this appearance over time, but in the professional market and trade of succulents, time, as always, is money, but is also marked by care and the capacity to care well.

Wild-collected plants, if of a sufficient quality, enable vendors to avoid sunk costs of labor time and to sell plants with a greater profit margin than if they grew them from seed, waiting as they

Figure 43. A prized *Dudleya pachyphytum* surrounded by other high-value succulents in custom earthenware pottery. The sign with the plant reads "Only look with your eyes" (translated from Korean).

developed to a more mature size over five to ten years or more, soaking up water, electricity, and labor costs. Many of the professional dealers I interviewed had only moved into the professional market within the past five to ten years. Although many of them were now growing *D. farinosa* and other desirable plants from seed or through propagation, it would be several years before these plants would possess the kinds of qualities exhibited by wild-collected plants. This patience is further mediated by changes in fashion and taste and concerns about losing out on selling high-value plants during the peak of their popularity, as one grower who had disappointingly "missed out" on the *Dudleya* trend, as he described it, grumbled to me. As another grower explained, "recently [a] *Haworthia* variety [a large succulent genus with plants that look like tiny aloe plants] was a fad and made a sensation. And now, these days,

Conophytum and *Lithops* are quite popular." There were significant risks, therefore, for vendors who invested only in growing seedlings, as high-value plants today might become less valuable in a year or two, such as in the case of *D. farinosa*.

Plants on the Move

Succulents have moved back and forth between the United States and South Korea for long periods of time. What was made abundantly clear during interviews was that this market for *Dudleya* species in South Korea was distinctly international as opposed to domestic. Today some of the most popular varietals of cultivated succulents in the world are grown and bred in South Korea and are readily and legally available to U.S. and other international consumers. Vendors in South Korea explained that much of their stock material used to come from U.S. or European commercial sources, but this importation has waned over time with the growth of a robust domestic succulent production economy. Korean vendors today see especially strong buying clout from Chinese collectors and consumers in Japan, Hong Kong, Taiwan, and Europe—and even the United States. It is entirely likely that some number of illegally collected *D. farinosa* from California ended up back in the United States after being purchased online. As one U.K. collector related to me, "[a fellow collector] ordered a *Dudleya farinosa* online from Korea and was embarrassed to discover it came wrapped in California newsprint."

Why, then, were Koreans poaching *D. farinosa* if the bulk of the market wasn't even in South Korea? The answer seems to have more to do with skill and reputation than domestic demand, as well as a developed capacity to profit from a larger regional marketplace. "Korean ones [succulents] are the prettiest. We also grow them the best. . . . Whether it's from California or not, Korea has the best climate, the best conditions to grow it pretty," an expert grower said. Another commercial dealer explained some of these dynamics, saying that the turning point was when Chinese consumers became interested in succulents around ten years ago. "Since then, special consumption has been generated in China. . . . Korea's climate has spring, summer, fall, and winter and we have the skills to grow [succulents] prettily, so Chinese people looked for products that were grown in a pretty way in Korea that they could bring back and sell right away." As a result of Chinese clients buying plants in bulk, he explained, "the price went up by a lot. . . . Because the wholesale price went up, the retail price also went up by a lot. . . . China takes it as it is, they take it when it's cheap and they take it when it's expensive."

This same grower explained that the emergence of a Chinese base of consumer demand had a destabilizing effect on the succulent market in Korea for a time, causing rapid price fluctuations. "It was quite bad back when China made mass purchases before. But nowadays it's stabilized. . . . Back then, [with] new products, for example, we imported *Echeveria* products from the Netherlands, and grew them here, and when they were released, the price was set quite high. But now . . . people have learned that the price will adjust soon. If you do a mass production and release them at a high price, they won't sell now. So it's under control and customers know that too. So, for example, let's say a new product came out at fifty thousand won, then people won't buy it. Why? Because it'll become ten thousand won in a year and three thousand won in two years. People have learned this, so they won't buy it. So it's all organized [a more stable market] now."

I required little convincing to imagine that Chinese and other international customers valued Korean skill and capability in growing excellent plants. "*Manias,*" as Korean succulent collectors and vendors playfully refer to themselves and this passionate community, are skilled and take great pains to maintain and encourage their plants in collection to thrive. Passionate members of these communities actively engage with one another via Instagram and through group messaging apps and the popular media platform Naver, where they share photos with one another, provide growing suggestions and tips, and share word of newly available varieties and cultivars.

A key insight from my research in South Korea was that as the succulent growing and collecting hobby blossomed across East Asia, wild-collected *Dudleya* plants were transformed over time into desirable *Korean* succulents.[8] Dealers said it could take anywhere from one to three years for plants to be ready for sale at good prices after they were imported into the country. For the higher-end market, which most of these plants were destined to enter, the true value of the plants was in their potential to become high-quality, aesthetically picturesque plants. Although certain traits of wild *D. pachyphytum* were valued, the majority of the "wild" qualities of the plants on their arrival in Korea needed time to be grown out. This included time for old, insect-bitten leaves further stressed by international transport to wither away and be replaced by new ones and for plants to regain a richer green color and develop a soft, matte finish. In other words, the plants needed to become domesticated, nurtured, and coddled. They needed to become *cute*. I was struck by how soft, uniform, and pinchable these *Dudleya* leaves could become under cultivation; at the same time, they retained a sense of elegance and age as neat rosettes atop thick, dark stems. Seeing how perfected their aesthetic qualities could become under the coaxing and care of skillful hands, for a moment, I could almost forget that many of these plants belonged someplace else.

In summary, the principal thrust of what drove people to illegally harvest *D. farinosa* plants related to a disjuncture between the temporality of plants and the capacity to meet demand. *D. farinosa* grows slowly, and although desired by a specialist market, there was sufficient global demand well beyond the borders of South Korea to quickly deplete in-country cultivated supply. There was, several years ago, an unambiguous surge in interest in *D. farinosa* in South Korea, China, and Japan. But there was also demand in European countries and elsewhere, facilitated by social media platforms and rising fashion for these plants among specialist collectors worldwide.

So why weren't *D. farinosa* plants legally imported from the United States? From the perspective of succulent dealers, although *D. farinosa* is not listed in the appendices of CITES, phytosanitary certificates and plant export and import permits were described as cost prohibitive and simply "too expensive." "When you legally import them," one commercial dealer explained, "the procedure is complicated and time consuming, so they [those who illegally imported the plants] tried to smuggle and sell [them off]. . . . [It was a] cheap sales gimmick. Because, then, their margin goes up. . . . It's sort of bad businessman-ship." Within South Korea, there was a demand by retailers for larger *D. farinosa* plants and only a limited legal supply, and the cost of importation was seen as cutting too deeply into profit margins. "At the time, the price of *D. farinosa* was high. We didn't really have much supply. So, there was a big difference in the global prices."

Acknowledging the complaints of commercial dealers about the price of doing business legally is not meant as any kind of justification for engaging in illegal trade. Ironically, one of the reasons there was a limited supply of commercially (and legally) available *D. farinosa* plants within the United States (though they were nevertheless relatively affordable) was that there had been a declining interest in the species among U.S. succulent consumers. This created a profitable opportunity for the rise of an illegal market for imported *D. farinosa* plants. The fact that in 2019 *D. farinosa* plants were being sold by South Korean growers to Chinese and other international customers relates to the reputation of South Korean growers for producing high-quality plants. But further still, following the dynamics of labor costs in a globalized market, by 2021,

Korean succulent dealers were complaining that they were getting outcompeted in the *Dudleya* market by Chinese greenhouses with lower operating and labor costs.

The Narrative Politics of a New Illegal Trade

Understandings of *Dudleya* demand as they were characterized in news media articles contrasted in important ways with what I learned speaking with collectors and dealers in South Korea. A primary reason for this mismatch was the inappropriate conflating of mass consumer trends in succulents compared to what was driving these specific illegal trades. But more was at work: the critique I present of prevalent narratives circulating in the media serves to highlight the persistence of harmful stereotypes about IWT. During the Covid-19 pandemic and rising violence against people of Asian descent across many parts of the world, narratives about the illicit trade in *Dudleya* species revealed how IWT narratives are frequently underpinned by deeply held anxieties about the growing economic and geopolitical power of Asian countries within Europe and North America. These anxieties also become articulated through expressions of white supremacy and racism.

Worry about a variety of kinds of legal and illegal wildlife trades in East Asia became even more acute during the Covid-19 pandemic. Major conservation organizations, especially those located in the Global North, leaped at the opportunity to leverage Covid-19 to call for a global ban on *all* wildlife trades—legal or otherwise—regardless of their role in sustaining livelihoods or their sustainability.[9] But even before the Covid-19 pandemic began, the conservation community had been placing increasing blame for a variety of population declines of wild species around the world at the feet of East Asian consumers and governments over the use of animal products in traditional Chinese medicine, as part of luxury goods, and as ingredients in food. As Eskew and Carlson write, "these calls to action, and their disproportionate focus on Africa and Asia, often ring hollow given that many high-income countries routinely outsource their biodiversity threats to other nations."[10] Yet despite these uneven dynamics in where biodiversity threats emanate from and are felt, the dominant focus of IWT research and policy discussions related to demand increasingly center on Asian wildlife consumption.

Concerns about IWT and Asian consumer demand for wild-life have mounted steadily over the past decade, with IWT transforming from a "boutique issue" to an "international crisis" in the international policy sphere.[11] IWT now animates high-level international policy on geopolitical security interests and concerns over threat finance.[12] In the context of IWT in East Asia, many conservation organizations and actors see a momentous (or, alternatively, monstrous) challenge, pitting what they see as urgent questions about the survival of endangered species against the sensitive subject of cultural practices and traditions that appear at odds with Western ideals of wildlife protection. It is against this backdrop that the incidents of *Dudleya* poaching by South Korean and, to a lesser extent, Chinese foreign nationals occurred and were featured prominently in international media outlets ranging from the *Guardian* to the *New York Times*.

It is important to note that although China is the largest consumer of internationally traded endangered species and derived products, some of world's biggest markets for IWT products are still found in the United States and Europe. This reality is frequently left off the agenda of international policy meetings and campaigns to combat IWT, though, which remain focused on African and Asian countries.[13] Rarely, especially in high-level international forums, is equal (if any) attention given to IWT in the same countries that steer international agendas for combating IWT.[14] For the United States, the United Kingdom, and other leading European nations, questions of IWT are overwhelmingly framed as foreign rather than domestic policy matters. The world of illegally traded plant species is not immune to these biases.

Wildlife consumption practices in East Asia have served as fuel for rising anti-Asian sentiments, especially in Europe and North America. These sentiments also took hold in public expressions of outrage over the thefts of *Dudleya* plants and are symptomatic of a much broader problem of stereotypes circulating about the poorly understood motivations and demographic traits of Asian wildlife consumers. These are not just bigoted and harmful expressions found in the rants of online media forums alone (which I have chosen not to reproduce here) but perspectives that are given great latitude for expression at the highest levels of international conservation and policy debate. This is to say nothing of the speech acts of high-level politicians like former U.S. president Donald Trump, who used his public platform to incite anger and anti-Chinese sentiments among his political base during the rise of the Covid-19 pandemic.[15]

Beware the Narrative of the Asian Superconsumer

In 2019, I wrote a short critique with my colleagues Rosaleen Duffy and Rebecca Wong about our concerns over the prevalence of harmful stereotypes in wildlife demand reduction campaigns.[16] Demand reduction campaigns focus on altering consumer behavior through targeted messaging and information sharing, often relying on celebrities to communicate these ideas through advertisements to reach large audiences perceived as would-be consumers of illegal wildlife products. Blanketed campaigns that fail to target specific consumer demographic groups not only fail to connect with specific and more appropriate audiences but can harmfully reproduce notions of a catch-all Asian consumer who indiscriminately uses IWT products.[17] Duffy, Wong, and I called this the harmful myth of the "Asian super consumer." Interventions that rely on blanketed tropes and imagery are likely to be not only ineffective but harmful and counterproductive. Wildlife trade researchers Hoai Nam Dang Vu and Martin Reinhardt Nielsen argue, for instance, that while the uses of rhino horn significantly vary between Chinese and Vietnamese consumers, demand reduction campaigns rarely acknowledge these differences or appropriately target user groups. Furthermore, they suggest that many demand reduction campaigns that center on demonstrating the inefficacy of rhino horn as medicine fail to understand Asian medicine traditions and the intelligence of rhino horn consumers.[18]

In a similar vein, Claire Jean Kim critically assesses how anti-Asian sentiments in the United States trouble, coalesce through, and find purchase in the messy interface of animal ethics, wildlife consumption, and cultural relativism.[19] In her important study of wildlife markets in San Francisco in the 1990s, she describes revealing double standards and uncomfortable silences around how predominantly white animal rights activists in San Francisco worked to shut down Chinese live animal markets, while other live animal markets, such as the famous and upscale Fisherman's Wharf, remained beyond concern or critique, protected as an important tourist destination (and economic boon) to the city. Kim's work is important not only for the tensions she draws out in these debates over the "proper" treatment of animals but because she does not steer away from difficult questions embedded in discussions about animal welfare and rights in the name of cultural plurality.[20]

Concern about reducing Asian demand for endangered species is not confined only to animals either. Annah Lake Zhu has examined how and why "[Western] conservation campaigns aiming to reduce Chinese demand for endangered species are bound to fail" when they do not consider the importance of cultural values as well as Chinese history. As she examines through conflicts over the illegal trade in rosewood from Madagascar to China, Zhu finds not only that Western conservation demand reduction campaigns are often at odds with Chinese cultural (and, consequently, economic) value systems but that they reproduce two-dimensional and harmful tropes of "crazy rich Asians" that aggravate and offend—rather than appeal to—their intended audiences. "Too often, these demand reduction campaigns fail because their creators do not realize that in attempting to stigmatize wildlife consumption, they appear as though they are stigmatizing traditional Chinese culture more broadly."[21]

Dudleya species reveal similar reproductions of these problems and stereotypes in the global movement of plant life. The growing interest in succulents across mainstream culture in China and Korea was linked in news articles to a "massive dose of *Dudleya* fever,"[22] a sentiment that is repeated across a variety of news articles, such as this one from the *Guardian*: "In China, they [succulents] are prized for their chubby limbs and cute shapes. In Korea, they are a treasured hobby for housewives. But on the coastal cliffs of California, the *Dudleya* succulent plants are vanishing, snatched up by international smugglers and shipped to an Asian middle-class market hungry for California native flora."[23] There is an evocative discursive power in the threat of "international smugglers" "hungry" for California's "native flora" rising in a middle-class Asian market. This sentiment of a native species being threatened by an overwhelming foreign threat is similarly expressed elsewhere: "The current craze for hardy succulents, which started in South Korea and spread to China, has resulted in organized gangs stripping the US state of a plant crucial to its fragile coastal ecosystem."[24] Put even more evocatively, one interviewee in law enforcement in California described to me, "What I truly believe they were doing was working their way down the coast taking different species and then mailing them out at points . . . and just raping and pillaging all the way down the coast."

These are just a few examples of not-so-subtle language that reproduces troubling discourses of the "rape and pillage" of "fragile" ecosystems and "native flora" of the United States that are under threat from a growing "fever" rising in Asia. This is not to deny that Korean and Chinese nationals were illegally taking plants from California and shipping them abroad. What is revealing, however, is how naturally this rhetoric reproduces long-standing fears of an imagined white society being overrun by a menacing Asian threat. It also genders this threat as rapacious and male, whereas what is to be protected is fragile and female. Yet these rhetorical moves fail to explain or describe key dimensions of *Dudleya* demands. The imagery evoked in these stories resonates with common racist depictions from the late nineteenth and early twentieth centuries of California as a virginal feminine landscape under threat by a feverish and hungry "Far East."[25] As research in South Korea revealed, the species were not valued for any purported medicinal properties (as several interviewees speculated and especially as Mexican newspapers latched on to as an explanation for *D. pachyphytum* poaching), nor because of value ascribed to their innate "wildness." What lay at the heart of this new illegal trade was a combination of economic logics (however illegal) and the desire for specific aesthetic qualities, rather than any properties intrinsic to a "wild" plant.

While *D. farinosa* seedlings were slowly growing into attractive and blemish-free cultivated plants in greenhouses across South Korea and (increasingly) China, it is lamentable that wild *Dudleya* plants were removed from their ecological webs of relations to meet an international consumer demand. Developing an understanding of *Dudleya* desires reveals the theoretical and methodological power of thinking more carefully with plants as beings with the capacity to exert themselves and mediate outcomes of illicit trades as active subjects through their constitutional capacities and needs. As much as my interviews with vendors and collectors proved an insightful pathway to understanding this illicit trade, it was through these discussions with close attention to *Dudleya* plants as *Dudleya,* as opposed to just "succulents," that I was able to understand *Dudleya* desires as nuanced, selective, and truly global in scope. Whereas law enforcement or policy makers are unlikely to conflate tiger bone, rhino horn, and pangolin scale trades as one and the same simply because they are derived from animals, succulents (and even just "plants") by and large remain collapsed as a singular entity in discussions of IWT.[26] That so many of the *Dudleya* plants stolen from the United States and Mexico have not ended up withering away on the windowsills of the "housewives" and "hipsters" caught up in a mass-market succulent craze, as media reports suggested, will do little to assuage the concerns and fears of conservation officials and authorities. That these wild-collected plants were moved around the world was neither inevitable nor desirable from the perspective of the plants themselves, just as they continue to assert the importance of desire in understanding environmental change.

In the remainder of the chapter, I turn to more mass-market succulent consumer cultures in conversation with *Dudleya* desires and what it means to consider demand for *cute* plants. Although I have so far shown how media articles about "succulent fever" confused understandings of actual *Dudleya* demands, these articles were not incorrect in tracking the meteoric rise in popularity of cultivated succulents across mainstream South Korean society. In bringing attention to succulents as cute plants, we can come to see that theorizing cuteness is important for understanding succulent demands and their commodification writ large.

Theory of a Cute Plant

I used to think *cute* was just a diminutive adjective for describing little, adorable, and, at times, cloyingly endearing things. But in the hands of aesthetics scholar Sianne Ngai, *cute* is revealed as an active and dominant force of commodification in contemporary life. The cute object is the most "thinglike of things, the most objectified of objects."[27] Cuteness simultaneously hyperinfantilizes and sexualizes (e.g., baby talk) alongside rendering things as adorably vulnerable, yet in a manner that incites desires to dominate and control. Drawing on the works of a wide range of critics and theorists of aesthetics and the commodity form, Ngai presents an extended analysis of the contemporary pervasiveness of cuteness as both symptom and force producing a hypercommoditized culture of consumption.

Cuteness holds strong parallels with the production of desire as a dialectical relation between subject and object, through which fantasies of the desiring Other are twisted through "objects" that possess the aura of the Thing. Ngai shows not only how cuteness describes things from the infantilization of women by the fashion industry to children's toys to avant-garde poetry but how it holds immense power over the objectification of things themselves. Cuteness is the affective residue from the process of rendering cute, while also indexing the subject's desire to exert themselves over the cute object. As Ngai explains, "cuteness is not just an aestheticization but an eroticization of powerlessness, evoking tenderness for 'small things' but also, sometimes, a desire to belittle or diminish them further."[28] Cuteness cannot exist without a relationship between subject and object, in which the cute object would appear to call upon the subject to recognize it as such and through which the subject performs the fantasy of having little capacity to deny the cute object what the subject supposes it wishes.

In the world of commodities, cuteness is an entire genre of global consumer culture. In Japan, the word *cute,* or *kawaii,* has become a consumer aesthetic phenomenon now popularized around the world, although, as Ngai explains, the origins of *cute* are decidedly nineteenth- and twentieth-century American.[29] In South Korea, cuteness manifests through *aegyo,* a word recently added to the *Oxford English Dictionary.* Anthropologists Aljosa Puzar and

Yewon Hong define *aegyo* as "performed winsomeness" or "a layered articulation of behaviors, gestures, vocal and linguistic adjustments, narratives and fashions that serve to enact child-like charm and infantilized cuteness."[30] Articulations of *aegyo* include coquettish and flirtatiously childish behavior and use of a higher-pitched and whiny voice by women and girls, as well as "cute" gestures, such as producing the shape of a tiny heart through the pairing of the thumb and index finger. Cuteness—unlike beauty—exists above all in the realm of mass consumer culture. Cuteness is also not fleeting, and as Ngai notes, drawing on Stephen Jay Gould's arguments about the juvenilization of Mickey Mouse "from spiky rodent into a rounder, softer, more wide-eyed character," Mickey Mouse "testifies to the power of biological cuteness as *an evolutionary strategy.*"[31]

Cuteness reveals a great deal about the power of aesthetics and, with regard to cuteness, "an aestheticization of powerlessness."[32] Cute is a force that would seem to work in two directions: both in the extreme objectification of things as "cute" while also, in a doubling back on the subject, producing the affect of a vulnerable, "helpless" thing that seems to call on and make demands of the cute object's subject.[33] "*I just could not resist pinching his cheeks!*" As Ngai describes, drawing on the work of Lori Merish, "the cute commodity flatteringly seems to want us and only us as its mommy. . . . In a perfect mirroring of its desire, as if we had already put ourselves in its shoes, we as adoptive 'guardians' seem to 'choose' it. The cute commodity, for all its pathos of powerlessness, is thus capable of making surprisingly powerful demands."[34]

Cute things are pliant, shapeless, and wide-eyed and most commonly feature diminished mouths, which are often absent altogether. In general, the closer an object approximates reality, the less cute it is, a phenomenon I enjoyed practicing through drawing cute and not-so-cute cacti, depending on their approximation of the "real" thing (Figure 44). For Ngai, then, "the epitome of the

Figure 44. *(left)* My first attempt at digitally drawing a cactus (species unknown) in a pot. The drawing amusingly evokes stronger sentiments of distastefulness or aversion than anything approximating a cute plant. I suspect this is because the long and wispy spines of the juvenile cactus are too suggestive of human hair, giving the overall form the appearance of a hairy human leg or scrotum, or maybe a pineapple. *(right)* In contrast, diminishing the spines and subsequently adding large, forward-facing eyes to the plant, while reducing its likeness, lowers its distastefulness and conveys a mixture of cute vulnerability and helplessness.

cute would be an undifferentiated blob of soft doughy matter," though I would add a pair of big eyes and a tiny smile, or perhaps pudgy, three-fingered hands on feeble little arms.[35] It is no coincidence that the familiar expression "you're so cute I could eat you up" centers on consumption. As Ngai notes, "the ultimate index of an object's cuteness may be its edibility."[36]

Returning to *Dudleya* species, there is a powerful adaptive strategy at work in cuteness in how the cute object seemingly "grips" the emotions of the subject. Through their vulnerability, the cute object seems to beckon us as their subject. It is a "doubling back" of an Althusserian hailing: here the subject hails the cute object—"Hey, you!"—but in an interesting twist, removed of a mouth from which to speak, the fantasy of the cute object's power over us is revealed.[37] The object cannot respond to our hails, the hail thus circling back upon the original subject. The lack of a voice, as Ngai explains, leaves the fantasy of the power of the cute object confined solely to its gaze. Cuteness reveals the fantasy of the power these "hyper-objectified objects" hold over the desiring subject through vulnerable or helpless affectations. Yet embedded in this compulsion to care for, squish, pinch, or squeeze cute objects is the powerful force of maintaining the capacity (and desire) to kill, maim, or destroy them.[38] As a strategy, *Dudleya* species reveal how, as living subjects and not just objects, plants (like all lively commodities) disrupt neat delineation between the subject–object binary that remains unambiguously distinct in Ngai's work. More remains to be said about the work of cuteness in more-than-human, multispecies registers.[39]

Between the Succulent Subject and Object

When I first encountered *D. farinosa* in California, *cute* was not the word that came to mind—instead, there was something of beauty in these plants, but a beauty composed within a wider ecological frame. Ngai notes that beauty and cuteness are not separated by matters of qualitative degree—they signify categorically different aesthetic judgments:

> Cuteness contains none of beauty's oft-noted references to novelty, singularity, or what Adorno calls a "sphere of untouchability." Nor does the judgement of cute have any of the links to morality—indirect or direct—repeatedly ascribed to the judgement of the beautiful. Indeed, in vivid contrast to beauty's continuing associations with fairness, symmetry, or

proportion, the experience of cute depends entirely on the subject's affective response to an imbalance of power between herself and the object.[40]

The first *Dudleya* plants I encountered amid crashing waves and swirls of rain and wind, despite their abundance where found, nevertheless possessed a beautiful quality within a greater, powerful landscape—they exuded the beauty of *being in place*.[41] But there are easy slippages between an awareness and acknowledgment of being as emergent in place and something more dangerously universal and abstracted in what this sense of "intact" beauty can conjure in the mind. *D. farinosa* within-landscape could easily evoke something of a Kantian or Romantic reading of the sublime, that ideal of overpowering awe in the presence of a boundless greatness with its attendant invocations of morality and theology—at times uplifting and exhilarating, at others invoking sentiments of fear or submission.[42] I recall feeling entirely self-aware of *myself,* alone amid the dramatic and windswept coastal landscape where I first encountered *D. farinosa*, the only immediate mark of humanity being the imprints of my own footsteps in the sand. It was as if I were desiring to recreate my own Humboldtian journey (in Humboldt County, no less) despite "myself" or my better reason. Despite every inclination to avoid performing such a cliché encounter in a place transformed through the great horrors of Indigenous genocide and erasure that mark this landscape today, as well as the widespread destruction of its great redwood forests, I could feel myself desiring to experience this landscape as fantasy, cut off from the histories that reveal the falsehoods of those desires. Such are the powers of stories that worm their way through unconscious thought as the desire of an impossible fantasy, at times even more powerful than the living beauty and wonder of the actual world close at hand.

My first encounter with *D. pachyphytum*, despite its uncontested position as the "unique" *Dudleya* among all other *Dudleya* species, did not conjure such emotions, even if I was filled with a sense of thrill when I saw them under lock and key on Isla de Cedros. It was, sadly, an old photograph of them on Cedros (Figure 39 in chapter 6) that conveyed to me the real beauty of these plants as flourishing beings. To compare the plants in the Cedros greenhouse with the images of *D. pachyphytum* on Cedros's cliffs is a study in profound contrasts. But incorporating an image of these plants in a healthier, more cared-for condition, yet confined to pots in South Korea, presents another axis of contrasts. As a triptych, they reveal the work of "cute" as an active process of aestheticization *as* powerful objectification. Put another way, and thinking with the work of Nicole Shukin, alongside Rosemary Collard and Jessica Dempsey (as well as Ngai), through cuteness, we can come to better understand and see the processes of rendering *Dudleya* species into living capital at work:[43] the commodification of a beautiful plant into an objectified yet still living being of the world transformed into a cute "little thing."

Dudleya plants are instructive of the aesthetic power of cuteness and how cuteness shapes succulent life writ large, inclusive of how cuteness indexes the fantasy of the power of the plant as "object" over the human subject. Here, then, is a lesson in complex power relations for more-than-human political ecologies, in which we can recognize the intense powers of human hands at work in transforming vegetal worlds through commodification, while also permitting the succulent subject to persist through its varied acts of what Rafi Youatt considers "constitutional" acts of resistance or refusal.[44] We do not need a "flattened" ontological playing field (of the kind actor-network theory ascribes) to acknowledge and embrace the vital qualities of plant life while recognizing the very powerful role of humans in transforming them through capitalist consumer logics.[45] The living succulent does not simply become the perfectly cute succulent "object" just because the human subject wills it to be so. Succulents' colors change in response to temperatures and light exposure; they grow slower than markets demand of them. Some, like *Dudleya* species, refuse leaf propagation (unlike other succulents); they insist upon the labor of those exerting power over them lest they wither and die as their potential exchange-value is secreted like the commodities' ghost. Their *beauty*, tied up with the ecological relations they keep that sustain flourishing, is withheld, even as new desires are enacted upon them through the work of commodification.

As much as succulents might disrupt or variously insert "surprise" into efforts of homogenous plant commodification, humans have nevertheless become very adept at this work of objectification and domination.[46] At the Gyeonggido Cactus and Succulent Research Institute (GARES) outside of Seoul, I toured a series of massive greenhouses where thousands of cacti and succulents in a multitude of variations and forms were being carefully inspected and attended to by government staff. From the epiphytic *Schlumbergera* (Christmas cactus) variations I describe in the introduction of this book to grafted *Astrophytum* plants that looked like polka dotted cactus lollypops on their tall and narrow grafted rootstocks of another cactus species, cute plants filled this governmental facility. The purpose of the center is to develop, breed, and propagate new varietals of cactus and succulent plants to support the commercial wholesale growers of succulents in South Korea for both domestic and international markets. According to GARES, the facility encompasses 62 percent of all succulent, 69 percent of all cactus, and 53 percent of all grafted cactus cultivation in South Korea by area. During most of my visits to major wholesale and retail outlets for cacti and succulents while in South Korea, I spotted stacked cardboard shipping boxes bearing the center's logo within these private facilities. The South Korean government, I was surprised to discover, is very invested in succulent life. At the GARES facility, the names of succulents scream cute (if only they had mouths with

Figure 45. Designer *Echeveria* 'Cream Tea' *(left)* and being shown grafted *Astrophytum* cacti *(right)* on display at the GARES facility in South Korea. By growing *Astrophytum* grafted onto the rootstock of another, faster-growing cactus, the facility can accelerate growth rates before removing plants from the rootstock and potting them to sell on to wholesalers and subsequent consumers.

which to do so!). *Echeveria* hybrids developed at GARES in the past decade include 'Cream Tea,' 'Pink Tips,' 'Peach Girl,' and 'Minuet,' proprietary cultivars in rows of nearly identical plants in pastel shades of pink, red, green, and blue (Figure 45). Capitalism prefers uniformity, and here the researchers and technicians of GARES excel at reproducing cute plants with as much sameness as possible, leveraging the clonal capacities of plants to do so.

Cuteness even structures plant conservation efforts. In 2021, the California Native Plant Society (CNPS), to raise awareness about *Dudleya* poaching, released a series of free, online, animated "stickers," one for each California *Dudleya* species. These little, mouthless plant characters with big round eyes and colorful inflorescences dance, wiggle, and jiggle back and forth and up and down across electronic devices on an infinite loop (Figure 46). They are

Figure 46. "Cute" *Dudleya* stickers, including *Dudleya brittonii (left)* and *Dudleya farinosa (right)*. Created by David Bryant. Reprinted with permission of the California Native Plant Society.

both completely adorable and, after a few moments, like a repetitive mechanical toy, utterly annoying. I praise the ability of the designer, a former CNPS staff member, for producing these *Dudleya* caricatures that, with remarkable clarity, both convey key features of each species and simultaneously create little characters that seem to have unique *personalities*. The designer explained to me:

> I created the Dudleya mascots to endear audiences to the succulents and create information ambassadors, characters that could "speak" to the poaching issue and other complex topics in an approachable format. I was inspired by *yuru-kyara*, mascots in Japan that are used to promote organizations, clubs, cities, social movements and other entities.[47]

The *Dudleya* stickers are, of course, very *cute*. But there is something about the representation of these plants as dancing, mouthless characters that isn't purely innocent of the work of cuteness in conservation nor of desire upon the subject. It is noteworthy that the designer references his desire to give the succulents the power to "speak" while refusing them mouths with which to do so. But beyond this inability to speak as wide-eyed victims of succulent crimes is a more interesting and probing question about the power of the gaze that remains upon us, activating us seemingly as the subject of *their* desire. Absent any mouth with which to speak, their purported power over us, to make demands on the public to care, is found instead in their ability to "gaze back" and yet not return our hail. They return our gaze without a word and, in so doing, thwart total satisfaction. This is precisely where the fantasy of the cute succulent's power rests. But the gaze, as theorized by Lacan, reveals more than the power dynamics between subject and cute object. The gaze is a crucial moment for recognizing the power (and horror) of desire in twisting what otherwise we imagine as the true nature of things, especially in the visual field. In describing the gaze, Lacan wrote, "In this matter of the visible, everything is a trap."[48] The gaze reveals the distortions of the visual field caused by desire. As Todd McGowan explains, "the gaze exposes the tendentious nature of the apparently neutral visual field; what seems to be simply there to be seen becomes evident as a structure created around the subject's desire."[49] The gaze is found in the briefest moment in which we suddenly recognize the distortion caused by desire. To be caught in the gaze is to recognize the Other as making desire possible. The gaze is an occurrence that can be shocking or terrifying.[50]

The addition of big, forward-looking eyes to *Dudleya* plants as "faces" speaks to one of the most important strategies of cuteness via personification, what Paul de Man describes as "giving face" and Ngai describes as "cuteness's master trope."[51] "Giving face" is a powerful move in the work of conservation, one that intersects with debates over the value and power of anthropomorphizing species of conservation concern. Such practices mediate which species become flagships of major conservation campaigns, which species tour the world as goodwill ambassadors, and which species garner the most funds for conservation work.[52] As Robert Smith and colleagues determined in an analysis of international conservation organizations' use of flagship mammal species, these animals "are generally large and have forward-facing eyes," as such interventions aim to elicit "an emotional response from the target audience in developed countries."[53] Not only are there significant affective stakes in choices about the anthropomorphizing of species but there are also economic and political ones as well.

In the case of constructing "nonhuman charisma" through "giving face" to *Dudleya* plants—what Jaime Lorimer describes as a form of anthropomorphic charisma—the outcome is both affecting and also disconcerting. In attempting to draw out meaningful sentiments of care, empathy, and affective relations with *Dudleya,* it is through its rendering vis-à-vis cute objectification that *Dudleya* is imbued with face.[54] Although Meredith Root-Bernstein and colleagues argue that anthropomorphism should be seen "as a strategic tool within conservation's toolkit that can be used to improve the way human groups engage with efforts to conserve threatened biodiversity," they also recognize that species anthropomorphizing activities can cause harm just as they can instill desires to care.[55] Anthropomorphizing activities are therefore not innocent of the broader aesthetic categories structured through global capitalism that mediate their activities and outcomes. Thus, as Ngai argues, "giving face" shows "how easily the act of endowing a dumb object with expressive capabilities can become a dominating gesture."[56]

Dudleya plants aren't dumb, but neither have they appeared to gain much intelligence through the addition of big round eyes to their "faces." What attention to the *Dudleya* stickers demonstrates is that the same aesthetic categories at work in efforts to make people care for *Dudleya* as species of concern align with the same structure that manifests the fantasy of the cute *Dudleya* in more objectified form. The "face" beckons the human collector to care for the plant at the same time as the cute object would seem to beckon the subject to possess it. Highlighting these relations is not to collapse them as the same but to reveal the greater powers of an aesthetic category at work in unconscious registers. Contemporary cultures of commodity fetishism unconsciously structure not only consumer desires but what it means to care for nonhuman others through the work of conservation.

Dudleya species highlight the process of objectification through cuteness as an aesthetic category in two seemingly antithetical ways: one that centers on the work of conservation by attempting to instill in citizens of California a sense that they should care for these cute-ified plants, the other taking place across the Pacific, where wild-collected *D. farinosa* and *D. pachyphytum* are literally broken down into smaller, pruned and potted versions of their formerly flourishing, beautiful forms. This is not to deny that some of the larger specimens of plants I saw in South Korea still maintained a sense of beauty. Instead, these mirrored efforts highlight how the cute aesthetic plays a powerful role in the creation of lively commodities as a process of rendering the living commodity itself.

Drawing attention to activities of rendering cute the digital lives of dancing *Dudleya* plants as ambassadors or mascots for the species, we can see these processes of commodification are made to work both for conservation and for the trade in wild species.[57] In both cases, it is the unconscious and the structuring of desire that enable the cute object to hold a powerful position in the eyes of the desiring subject. In an era of hypercommodification, through this cute dialectic, we can see how pervasively commodity fetishism not only mediates human encounter and experience with other species and movements toward caring for them but also fundamentally transforms individual organisms and species themselves. In both instances, it is capitalism itself that latches on to the unconscious, leveraging our "desire to desire" through the displacement of *objet a* by the commodity as the object-cause of desire. Cuteness reveals powerful forces at work between the unconscious and the rendering of flourishing species into commodified forms; "14 Cute Succulents That Are Basically Impossible to Kill" reads the title of one popular online media article on succulents, with the tagline "Calling All Plant Moms."[58] And hail us as mommies they do. That succulents have emerged as exceedingly popular plants to care for because they "are basically impossible to kill" (even if this statement isn't very accurate!) speaks to the relationships connecting the desire to care and the desire to neglect, the desire to possess and the desire to exert power over another through its "thingification." "Aestheticization is always, at the bottom line, objectification," Ngai writes.[59] In Lacanian terms, the plant that seems to gaze back is a powerful moment for confronting how our desires ensure that these more-than-human relations are always more twisted than they seem, distorted by succulent fantasies leading us to care for charismatic plants or to seek them out as coveted commodities for personal satisfaction.

Dudleya desires entwine journeys of theft and international illegal trade with the reproduction of harmful cultural stereotypes with the powers of commodity fetishism through cuteness. These stories reveal how global geographies of illicit trade are mediated by more than matters of supply and demand, just as they are not reducible to blanket tropes regarding "cultural differences" or simple distinctions between heroes and villains. Staying with these plants as active participants in an illicit trade highlights the profound importance of plant temporalities in shaping forms of human–plant relating. It also demonstrates again the place of desire in shaping human–plant relations. For even if we must understand *Dudleya* "participation" in radically different ways than the human actors making conscious choices to illegally remove the plants from their habitat, the biological capacities and adaptive traits of the plants remain central to how these trades developed and evolved. Illicit

Dudleya trade certainly reveals the importance of banal machina-
tions of political economy and international trade regulations in
what motivated a few actors to profit by entering the realm of the illicit. Yet these stories also beg us see how what on the face of it may
look like simple matters of economy are questions about desire.

Coda: Unexpected Entanglements with the Succulent Kingpin

Having largely drafted the chapters of this book detailing the emergence of the new illegal trade in *Dudleya,* in June 2021, I was contacted by U.S. state attorneys asking if I would be willing to serve as
an expert witness in the case of *United States v. Byungsu Kim.* Kim,
as I describe in chapter 5, was the principal actor behind one of the
largest bouts of *Dudleya* poaching in California in 2018.

Kim was now awaiting trial—having been extradited from
South Africa to face charges in California (if you recall, he had fled
the United States as a fugitive following his arrest)—after being
indicted for one count of conspiracy and one count of knowingly
attempting to export plants taken in violation of California law. My
first instinct was to decline the prosecutor's request. In addition to
my wariness of cooperating with the criminal justice system, I was
asked if I could serve as an expert witness by writing a statement
estimating the monetary value of the plants Kim and his accomplices took in California. I thought someone in the commercial
nursery business might be more suitable. The attorneys expressed
a concern, however, that an expert witness from the commercial
sector might be seen as biased compared to an academic. It was
also conveyed to me that the severity of Kim's sentencing—how
long he would remain in prison if convicted—would depend in part
on the monetary value applied to the stolen plants. I was struck by
this approach to justice, in which the unit for measuring the severity of crime was seen as best determined by the monetary value

some people placed upon the stolen plants, especially given the va-
garies of succulent worth. Of course, this was not a court case on
behalf of *Dudleya* species as living plants with any sense of rights in
a court of law. Instead, it was the U.S. federal government seeking
retribution for the theft of U.S. property.

While conducting research in California that underpins chapters 5 and 6, I was unaware that just three months earlier, Byungsu
Kim, the South Korean man the *Guardian* described in 2022 as
"the world's most notorious succulent thief," had followed a path
up and down the California coast very similar to my own.[60] Publicly available court records chart in detail the route Kim and his
two accomplices took across California before they were arrested
by CDFW's Special Operations Unit on October 29, 2018, outside
a cargo export facility in Compton, California.[61] For two weeks,
CDFW's undercover agents surveilled Kim and his accomplices
from the moment they arrived in Los Angeles. Unbeknownst to
Kim, the agents trailed them as they prepped and then drove some
750 miles north from Los Angeles, arriving in Crescent City, at the
northern tip of California, on October 13. To build their case, the
agents would have to watch as the men harvested the plants rather
than stopping this harm from being done. For the next several days,
CDFW agents surveilled and photographed the three men as they
removed thousands of *Dudleya* plants along the coast. On October
22, the three departed back to the commercial greenhouse in Vista,
California, that Kim used as his base of operations to offload their
haul. The next day, the men set off for Mendocino County, where
they spent the next two days harvesting more *Dudleya* plants. The
men then returned to the greenhouse with crates of plants, and
the next day, Kim made an appointment for a USDA phytosanitary inspection. After receiving his signed paperwork on October
29, which listed only around one-third of the number of individual
plants Kim prepared for shipping (described as cultivated *Dudleya*

cuttings from San Diego on the paperwork), Kim and his accomplices drove the plants to a cargo exporter in Compton. After the men had dropped off the boxes of plants, CDFW agents intercepted them to arrest them.

Other important details emerge in these investigative materials.[62] The reports suggest that not only had Kim likely conducted similar *Dudleya* thefts for *years* in the United States without notice but USDA inspection officers had been providing him the necessary paperwork for export. Unlike the cases of *Dudleya* theft in Humboldt County, Kim never attempted to ship out plants (as far as we know) through false labeling. His crime (if only barely concealed) was presented, over and over, to the U.S. agency responsible for inspecting the plants and ensuring that they matched Kim's paperwork. Kim, or an associate, had previously received at least twenty-three separate USDA phytosanitary certificates for the legal export of live plants since 2013 to send plants from California to Seoul.[63] The number of individual *Dudleya* plants on these phytosanitary forms totals more than 122,000, not including thousands of other succulents, including Mexican species like *E. agavoides* and *Pachyphytum bracteosum*. The number of *Dudleya* plants Kim exported rose dramatically beginning in 2016.

It is not terribly hard to distinguish wild-sourced *Dudleya* plants from greenhouse-cultivated species. I wonder how it was that Kim was able to obtain USDA phytosanitary paperwork from authorities for tens of thousands of pounds of live plants that were clearly wild-harvested. It becomes very clear from these reports that multiple USDA inspection officers either simply took Kim at his word, lacked a basic familiarity with the species, or something worse. Especially worrying in these materials is the disclosure that a USDA inspection officer visited Kim's greenhouse and approved the paperwork, while the next day, armed with a search warrant, CDFW special operations agents found a greenhouse absent of almost any cultivated plants, yet littered with the removed dead leaves of *Dudleya* plants carpeting the floor, alongside hiking backpacks and boots, radios, and camping supplies.

It is impossible to know with certainty if the thousands of plants Kim sent from the United States to South Korea were exclusively wild-harvested. But, if the bust in Compton is any indication, it is plausible that he had removed more than a hundred thousand *Dudleya* plants from the California coastline over a period of years.[64] Kim's paperwork also suggests that over several years, he may have been exporting wild-harvested Mexican plants through California, to say nothing of his activities in South Africa. There authorities in a separate trial presented evidence that Kim, along with another accomplice, illegally harvested more than two thousand plants from South Africa—mostly the species *Conophytum pagea,* an increasingly popular succulent that has become heavily targeted in recent years. *C. pagea* grows in clumps and can have the appearance of a mouth wearing lipstick; it's an especially trendy plant in the world of succulent social media. A botanist with Kirstenbosch Botanical Garden in South Africa estimated the combined lifespan of the more than two thousand plants Kim stole as representing roughly 44,000 years of life, with the individual plants' ages ranging from anywhere between 10 and 250 years old. And much like Kim's activities in California, South African authorities disclosed that Kim had received legal CITES export paperwork for a variety of succulents over the past several years in South Africa for sending plants to the same facility in Seoul listed on his USDA paperwork.[65]

In researching these cases of succulent theft, the most shocking moment of all came while scrolling through reports I obtained from attorneys. There, suddenly staring back at me through my computer screen, was an image of Byungsu Kim holding a beautiful, wild-collected *D. pachyphytum* from Isla de Cedros. While it is unclear from the images where Kim is located in the photograph, I scrolled further to see an image of another man I have since identified as the owner of a Mexican nursery in Morelos eventually tied by Mexican authorities to at least one of the major *D. pachyphytum* thefts I describe in chapter 6. There are a series of selfies of the man posing with *D. pachyphytum* on the cliffs of Cedros, alongside images of various succulents and cacti being packed into boxes. There are images of wire transfers for tens of thousands of U.S. dollars between South Korean and Mexican recipients; at least one lists Kim's greenhouse in Seoul as the sender's address. And there are more images of Kim and others with *D. pachyphytum*. That such a small number of people could have such an outsized impact on the trajectories that succulent species take through the world is astounding, to say nothing of the jarring reality that, as I followed these species from California and Mexico to South Korea and elsewhere, I was, unbeknownst to me, also following Kim.

CDFW agents involved in the case estimated that the total value of the plants Kim intended to export from California was just over $600,000. As part of my own research, I had already attempted a similar valuation, which was lower than this estimate. I knew from my research in South Korea that the prices CDFW agents used often represented premium retail values and that it was unlikely Kim was selling individual plants but instead was selling boxes of plants on to retail succulent nurseries like the ones where I conducted interviews. I also was aware that plants advertised online were often offered for higher prices than they ultimately sold for, representing at times "aspirational" prices, as one nursery owner put it, intended to draw the attention of customers in the high-end succulent marketplace. Aware of these and other factors affecting price, I believed the monetary value of these plants was likely less than the original estimation by CDFW agents. I decided to offer an expert witness statement to the prosecutor's office and valued the plants' worth between $113,000 and $255,000.

It is important to disclose this unexpected turn of events by which my life and Kim's intersected through stolen *Dudleya* plants. Ultimately, I chose to make the formal valuation because I was confident in my estimate and confident it could only serve to reduce Kim's sentencing rather than extend it. I don't say this because I hold sympathies for Kim or take his crime lightly; rather, I do not believe imprisonment serves to better society. I offer this as a reminder and caution to others whose research now or in the future may intersect with matters of illegality.[66] Research will be read and used by authorities and others alike. While my own research ethics and approvals prepared me for thinking about the usual matters of research subject anonymity, safety, and data security, I could not have imagined at the start of my research that I would be asked to serve as an expert witness by federal prosecutors in a case of IWT. It is important always to remember that social research can profoundly alter the courses of others' lives.

On January 20, 2022, Kim was sentenced to twenty-four months in prison and given a $3,985 fine in restitution to the state of California. During the sentencing hearing, Kim's jaw was wired shut—the result of an altercation with another inmate while in U.S. custody. In a sentencing memorandum, Kim's lawyer argued that he had already suffered tremendously and should not face further prison time.[67] According to the memorandum, although he was given time served after three months in a Cape Town jail, he spent another nine months there waiting extradition to the United States in "filthy and unsafe" conditions, where "lice infestations were common" and inmates were fed only once per day. Kim will spend another nine months in jail after being credited with time served.[68] But this is not the end of Kim's ordeal in California. According to reporting by the *Guardian,* Kim was transferred in late January 2022 to the small town of Crescent City in Northern California to face two additional state court cases related to his original case of succulent theft and for fleeing the country during that prosecution. Kim's actions and his fate are not evidence of the work of desire; instead, they express the determined need to attend to how desires are embedded within matters of political economy and how the desires of others shape (illicit) economies and species alike.

❨ 8 ❩

For a Flourishing Geography of Succulent Life

Knowing another is endless. . . . The thing to be known grows with the knowing.

—Nan Shepherd, *The Living Mountain*

This final chapter is devoted to considering what enacting succulent relations that beget species flourishing could look like. To do so, I first turn back to matters of extinction and care. Extinction, in more-than-human registers, might be thought of as a cause of desire. Desire to care, desire to conserve (or possess), desire for satisfaction through knowing one has aided another—these are all impulses impelled forward by the possibility and threat of a permanent lack and the imagination of a future otherwise. In this light, I wonder if there is something of desire within the term *more-than-human* itself, the ache of desire in a request for relation building through that which is lacking—to recognize oneself through what ties us into knots and unto others. Extinction threatens these bonds. I cannot imagine it is any sort of coincidence that the project of more-than-human geography (now more than twenty years in the making) has occurred during an epoch of increasing awareness of fraying ecological relations.

One reason the extinction of a species is a kind of loss difficult to grasp is because this permanence of absence so greatly exceeds human temporalities. It stretches backward, connecting millions of years of history and accident. And it looks forward, the branches and nodes of evolution splaying out in a wider array of possibility at the same time we might speculate on what is absent from futures missed. Species are an entire world in the making, and extinction is a loss that reminds those taking notice that the moment of extinction is the death, not of a being, but of a kind. Yet, extinction is also bound up in the making of new life.[1] This begs the question, when does the threat of extinction, such as that of *Dudleya pachyphytum* or *Arrojadoa marylanae,* or any of the other species I describe at extinction's edge, become a matter of concern, and what impedes that vital gap between concern and care? As extinction studies scholar Thom van Dooren asks, "an estimated 99.9 percent of all species that have ever existed are now gone, why should we exert great effort, or indeed any effort at all, in holding onto [*sic*] the ones that happen to share our period of tenure on this revolving planetary tomb?"[2] His question is a facetious one, because now does not approximate 99.9 percent of planetary history, nor even 99.9 percent of human history—we live in truly unprecedented times of environmental change and ecological destruction.

As we saw in the story of *A. marylanae* in chapter 4, the recognition of a species as a matter of concern, typified by its listing as formally imperiled via scientific assessment, does not necessarily lead to the active work of species care. There is an important distance between the politics and ethics of demonstrating concern and the "hands-on" practices of care for nonhuman life.[3] Where concern holds more passive connotations of "worry and thoughtfulness," in the words of María Puig de la Bellacasa, care invokes more active practices, with a "strong sense of attachment and commitment to something."[4] This speaks to what Donna Haraway describes as response-ability, "a praxis of care and response . . . in ongoing multispecies worlding on a wounded terra."[5] But who is responsible? And responsible to whom, or what? Faced with accelerating species extinctions, what does response-ability entail for a cactus at extinction's edge, and who or what is involved in its enactment?

Perhaps the rupture in accelerated extinctions is too great, the loss too vast to be understood for so many because it is an unthinkable kind of time.[6] The weight of extinction is often presented as a problem of scale. "The sixth extinction," as some scientists have named it, signals doom in the volume of extinctions under way.[7] But the ability to respond, to enact response-ability, is also hampered by limitations in fully becoming present to extinction's shocking temporalities. Although the extinction of a cactus is linear in one sense (the end of something that started in another time), extinctions are also stories full of frayed ends and interwoven worlds. Nor are the endings of species always as definitive or as certain as extinction, conventionally understood, might suggest. Within the field of conservation biology, a self-described "crisis discipline," the extinction concept is understood as signaling varied degrees of permanent loss.[8] Every year, species thought to be extinct are also "rediscovered," rising like the phoenix, while likely many more extinctions are under way, unnoticed and unmonitored.[9] Often, witnessing extinction is a retrospective effort of noting sustained absence that, with rare exception, cannot be unmade.[10] Unfortunately, far too many of the plants detailed in this book—*D. pachyphytum, Uebelmannia buiningii, A. marylanae,* a number of *Ariocarpus* and *Aztekium* species—and so many more on which I could have chosen to focus instead teeter perilously close to this precipice.

Species in Formation

I have said relatively little about the species concept in this book, even as I evidenced how the notion of a "species" often does not seem to work very well as a category of knowing for the plants I write about. But briefly reckoning with what a species indexes is important in the context of any discussion of extinction and the work of care. This is especially true when we consider how the Linnean species, at least in the world of cactus and succulent plants, is not the most stable of epistemological categories. This is not to suggest that there is no means of ordering and identifying difference in the world through attention to discerning orders *of* the natural world; cultures the world over have developed means of categorizing, naming, and ordering nonhuman organisms, a major topic of academic inquiry across anthropology and ethnobiology.[11] But this instability of knowing how to know through the dominant Linnean taxonomic system does reorient how extinction takes on meaning, which in turn affects thinking about species flourishing. My questioning of species as wholly meaningful representations of the plants in this book matters for my analysis of failures to respond to extinction. Within the world of plants, the species concept fails to capture vegetal life in all its promiscuous and hybridizing forms, life as a process *in* time connected within a greater meshwork of deep time materialized in space.[12] Yet it is precisely how the sciences understand animals as species that structures so many of the efforts to know, as well as regulating vegetal life and moving to care on their behalf.

When pressed on the matter, many of the botanists, taxonomists, and ecologists I interviewed acknowledged to greater or lesser degrees the limited or hampered functionality of the species concept when describing the many beings that make up the vegetal kingdom. There is a reason why, in school, we typically learn about the species concept through examples from the animal world, where sexual reproduction more greatly limits the porosity of genetic flows between beings with greater or lesser degrees of likeness.[13] Plants are not so enclosed. Most of the scientists I interviewed encouraged me not to throw away the concept altogether but to interpret it with varying degrees of flexibility and generosity. Some used metaphoric examples to convey their approach to species, such as ephemeral tide pools, connecting then separating with the rising and lowering of the sea, with each tide pool representing a species with intermittent genetic access and relation to others over time. Others who pursue identification of species through attention to degrees of genetic difference admitted that this might not be the best approach, noting the somewhat arbitrary percentages used to determine when one species definitively "became" another. Still others simply said it was the best system we still had to make sense of classifying the world, even if it wasn't always a very good one. And finally, others pointed out that, for better or worse, the logistical and financial challenges that would come with revising the current taxonomic system, still fundamentally based on Carl Linnaeus's *Systema Naturae* (1735), pose too great a barrier.[14]

And so, species remain the primary unit in the study of plant life and its evolution.[15] Within the much broader scope of living creatures inclusive of plants, fungi, or even bacteria, the idea of the species as a fundamentally "natural unit" is far less convincing. Consider Darwin, the figure most commonly associated with species thinking today, who wrote, in *On the Origin of Species,* "I look at the term species, as one arbitrarily given for the sake of convenience to a set of individuals closely resembling each other."[16] But if there is not agreement on what it is that is going or has gone extinct, how does extinction retain meaning, especially when this meaning is so vital to enacting a politics of species flourishing and care?

In psychoanalytic terms, if *objet a* is the "missing" object of desire in the symbolic order, extinction may do work in similar psychic registers as marking a profound kind of lack. Extinction concretizes the species as a lost object of concern, its existence as a knowable kind fixed in time through marking its absence. And yet, as I described through a variety of examples in both chapters 2 and 3, the activities of both scientists and collectors are crucial in the production of species and their extinctions through how species are constructed as more-than-human endeavors. This is a process of "doing" species, or encountering species as a *verb*.[17] The possibilities for exploring the full range of expressions of extinction as a phenomenon are limited without acknowledging how coming to know (and identify) species is itself a process of meaning making. Just as extinction carries with it a variety of social and cultural meanings that exceed extinction's biological significance, so, too, does the species, a perspective that is furthered through attention to species as life's movement in time.

The case of agaves in Mexico helps to ground some of these ideas. Some agaves in Mexico are so imbricated within human activities that it is impossible to say from a botanical perspective whether they are "cultivated" crops or "wild" species. This can create problems for practices of registering species as matters of concern. For instance, during an *Agave* IUCN Red Listing workshop I attended in 2018 in Querétaro, Mexico, the gathered group of experts repeatedly faced the challenge in assessing species' threat statuses because the IUCN Red List assessment conducts assessments of the endangerment only of *wild* species, not agricultural landraces. This proved challenging at times for determining whether certain agaves could be assessed or their "native habitat range" established. Certain agaves both grow and reproduce of their own volition alongside being cultivated by people across regions of Mexico. When the group came to assess the status of the wild species *A. angustifolia,* the most commonly cultivated varietal of agave used in mezcal production (where it is called *maguey espadín*), one of the assessors held up a map with all of the known data points of the species and said, "OK, which ones are cultivated and which ones are not?" The botanists at the table burst out laughing; the dots were so densely packed that they rendered the map illegible. After much discussion and debate, they decided to include a taxonomic note with their assessment, describing the species as a "complex" of taxa. "It is a species complex or a very complex species!" one of the botanists joked at the conclusion of the assessment. The "species" asserted its presence as a meaningful, if at times confounding, category of knowledge politics with consequences for efforts of care set against the threat of extinction.

Species are always in a process of becoming.[18] Yet highlighting how a species may or may not exist as an irrefutably knowable thing does not foreclose the potential of naming species as relational entities. I think this turn toward relations can help to revitalize the species concept as a pathway toward responding to extinction. Here I am drawing on thinking with species through John Hartigan Jr.'s idea of "species formation." Hartigan describes how the "species is not a universal . . . but is historically articulated and sustained by a range of interspecies relations."[19] As a "range of interspecies relations," thinking with species formations is to think with species as processual events of relation with others. Taxonomy becomes a specific mode of species thinking that attempts to represent these events as a moment in time.[20] This sense of species was described decades earlier by Holmes Rolston III, who wrote that "a species is a living historical form (Latin *species*), propagated in individual organisms, that flows dynamically over generations."[21] We might consider, then, as a way of knowing, how encountering species means encountering a kind of life as a coherent moment of time as a measure of relating within shared temporalities.

Approached in this way, I see the "species" as retaining value for thinking politically with plants and their futures through enactments of care for species *as* relation building. Species formations may represent a possibility for making good relations with those others with which we share space-time. I can acknowledge the messiness of species as flows and relations just as I can recognize that holding on to the species categorically enables working to care politically on its behalf. Approaching species as formations adopts a more temporally centered and adaptive understanding of species, while the species formation also does work in granting attention to the pursuit of "grasping to know" other beings through the desire to do so. Species formations become an acknowledgment, even an appreciation, of species as an interdependent and active endeavor of becoming, always with others.

In "complicating" species and extinctions, I do not mean to naturalize very unnatural extinctions. As an approaching horizon, extinction demands response. But this horizon is not one of "our" collective making, and it is essential to recognize the profoundly unequal and unjust social relations that continue to reproduce the unearthly conditions for accelerated extinctions. Extinction is a process shot through with powerful asymmetries, the makings of a capitalist world ecology enabled through the immense violence of slavery and settler colonialism.[22] I name slavery, settler colonialism, and capitalism explicitly to clarify the terrain on which response-ability must be pursued in the name of multispecies justice. The extinction crisis is not a collectively caused human crisis but is nevertheless a crisis to which only humans can respond, whose effects will be unevenly but collectively shared.[23]

The Stakes of Caring about Extinction and Desire

In *Imagining Extinction,* Ursula Heise asks a vital question: "is it possible to acknowledge the realities of large-scale species extinction and yet to move beyond mourning, melancholia, and nostalgia to a more affirmative vision of our biological future?"[24] As much as extinction may signal the biological reality of a kind of life made permanently absent, it is also a culturally and economically inflected phenomenon, one that is inextricable today from the story of capitalism. How we think extinction mediates our understanding of it as a cultural experience, be it through elegiac tales of a species' swan song or the performance of heroic efforts to bring species back from the brink, while others quietly languish, awaiting their unmonitored demise.[25] Yet, Heise's question is not an easy one to answer when the fundamental economic drivers of species loss remain unabated. I do not see room for affirmation of a biological future so long as the basic drivers of extinction remain largely outside of critique in mainstream conservation discourse.[26]

The persistence of capitalism as the dominant economic system structuring world ecologies today does not mean it will or can last forever, and of course, if it is possible to imagine a noncapitalist world, there must be a (here biological) hopeful horizon of pursuit. Within this context, I consider the "affirmative vision of our biological future" for which Heise is searching as the horizon of flourishing geographies. My invocation of flourishing is inspired in part by feminist philosopher Chris Cuomo's theorizing of flourishing as an ecological feminist ethic for interspecies well-being as a requirement for advancing human well-being.[27] As Robin Wall Kimmerer, a member of the Citizen Potawatomi Nation, more recently wrote, "all flourishing is mutual."[28] For both Cuomo and Kimmerer, flourishing is an ecological engagement of interdependence. Flourishing acknowledges that fostering human and nonhuman life is an entwined endeavor without suggesting evenness or necessary mutuality. Flourishing, as Franklin Ginn and colleagues note, "always involves a constitutive violence."[29] Flourishing is a recognition of the articulation of time with space; the capacity to flourish is a geographical enactment. Cuomo uses the idea of "dynamic charm" to set the terms for appraising if a community's, organism's, or species' capacity to flourish is being met.[30] In charm, I see an acknowledgment of the participatory role of wonder and mystery in fostering encounters that beget flourishing.[31]

Flourishing geographies are spaces where life is afforded the possibility for becoming in an ever-changing and dynamic world, where an individual, a community, or a species can thrive across the distinctive (and, for plants, multiple) temporalities of life they inhabit. Extending this thinking here to matters of species care, I believe that caring demands contending just as much with what impedes the mental (and unconscious) capacity to enact flourishing geographies as with any material or biophysical capacities. To insist on flourishing geographies as a horizon is to resist the conscious, unconscious, and external efforts constraining life's potential for adaptation and change, where life, understood as a processual enactment, is not only accommodated but encouraged to thrive.

If flourishing composes a horizon, a fixed point of emergence, it also connotes what is lacking in the present. Flourishing, then, operates within the structure of desire and what keeps us searching as desiring subjects. If flourishing is an ethic, it should affirm the place of desire in its pursuit. In *The Ethics of Psychoanalysis,* Lacan says, "From an analytical point of view, the only thing of which one can be guilty is of having given ground relative to one's desire."[32] There are some clear reasons to find trepidation in this statement or to read it too literally—what if one's desires are harmful to oneself, to others, or to other species? But this is not Lacan's intent. Mari Ruti clarifies the stakes of Lacan's position:

> Lacan understood that there is no such thing as desire wholly divorced from its social environment . . . and that some of our desires are more primary (fundamental to our basic constitution) than the desires driven by the master's morality and the service of goods [the Other's desire]. Such primary desires reach toward the rebellious drive energies (jouissance) of the real rather than the conformist symbolic, which is why our capacity to animate them is essential to our ability to defy the hegemonic decrees of the latter.[33]

What this means is that as much as one's desires are the Other's desires, in the sense that one seeks out the Other's desires as one's own (under capitalism, one is compelled—*consume!*), there always also remains something of one's desires in excess of the symbolic order of the Other, grounded in the real. This helps to clarify how and why, in part, seemingly random objects of otherwise little import can take on such profound significance for a certain individual, while they mean nothing to another. The ethics of refusing ground relative to one's desires speak to this aspect of desire— those desires that stubbornly refuse or perhaps betray the moral and normative order of the Other.

In a world in which capitalism operates in the realm of the symbolic order as the Other, to insist on flourishing is to rejoice in being as a desiring subject and what is therefore always lacking and cannot be fully answered by heeding the call of the Other's desires. This is to say that there are layers to these desires; some are more "ours" than others, and we should hold fast to their political and ethical potential as steering toward a more hopeful horizon. As Lucas Pohl and Erik Swyngedouw recently wrote, "Lacanian psychoanalytic perspectives might also help to articulate the current deadlock that locks the Left in a state of melancholy, anxiety, depression, and/or impotent acting out. . . . Traversing the fantasy that circulates around 'the Thing' as a process of embracing the Real of the present condition could open a wedge to cut through the present deadlock."[34] Enacting flourishing as a destination is not a disavowal of desire but a reckoning with what sets desire in motion.

Caring in Collection

Many of the stories I share in this book are suggestive of or include harmful acts toward plants that occur as a result of the drives set into motion. How, then, can we imagine that a Lacanian ethics of desire might beget species flourishing? What Lacan is directing us toward here is an ethics in which lack is embraced as constitutive of our being as split subjects and the capacity to enjoy through the pursuit of the drives. I believe that the practice of ethical cactus and succulent cultivation is not only possible but can lead toward developing capacities for a caring toward other species that can do real good in the world. Although much work must be done to center a politics of multispecies justice within mainstream collector communities, my experiences and research over the past five years within these communities unwaveringly tilt me toward a hopeful attitude that meaningful change is not only possible but on the horizon, not through the repression of desire but through its celebration. The cactus may compel you to "enjoy," but this should be recognized as a fierce obligation to defend the capacity of cacti as species in formation to thrive, lest they wither as objects of desire. Enjoy, but enjoy as a commitment toward others' capacities to flourish as one's own desire.[35]

At the outset of this book, I made the claim that it is important to theorize collecting practices and dominant conservation activities as stemming from a shared psychic orientation, grounded in shared desires and anxieties about the living world. These desires, anxieties, and yearnings for satisfaction are expressed through diverse activities. They range from care-full enactments of cultivation and protection to harmful activities of dispossessing traditional and Indigenous stewards of land and species alike in the name of conservation, and they involve illicit thefts of plants in the drive for possession justified as the work of care. Because dominant conservation (and here I mean within the Western tradition of conservation as it is still largely practiced today) and collection are both responses of a kind to the threat of extinction and desires routed through possession and capitalist commodification, I hope this book can help convince those working within the field of conservation that they might have more in common with the collector communities they often vilify than they might wish to acknowledge. This will be a discomforting or irritating thought to many, but it is precisely that discomfort or "itch" that I would encourage actors invested in the care of the species to sit with, rather than dismissing it outright.

"Against this vortex [of extinction]," the late scholar of extinction Deborah Bird Rose asked, "what does one have to offer?"[36] As an offering, my experiences learning with plants tell me that there is so much more to learn from vegetal life in mounting collective responses necessary to reroute current extinction trajectories. As beings that connect above- and belowground worlds, plants suture time and space together in useful ways for thinking with species as intergenerational formations of time bound up with place that hold important lessons about care for the species. Plants demonstrate and demand caring with others; that "all flourishing is mutual"; that cultivations of care entail small, everyday acts as well as collective action. Thinking about a horizon of care composed against extinction as a source of overwhelming dread, I take shelter in the words of Jodi Dean, who writes that the horizon marks "a fundamental division that we experience as impossible to reach, and that we can neither escape nor cross."[37] This is a horizon composed through being as a desiring subject. With desire as a compass, perhaps plants are especially helpful guides for navigating toward a flourishing horizon, while the drives in pursuit of *jouissance* fill the sails. As transgressive beings, plants entwine the earth and sky (the spatial horizon) while further blurring the temporal horizon demarcating the past from what lies ahead.[38] Against the powerful vortex of extinctions under way, to assert flourishing as a horizon of pursuit is to commit to an orientation recognizing the importance of desire for remaking the world otherwise, even if a commitment to desire through what is lacking may feel profoundly disorientating in other registers.[39]

Writing a Political Ecology of Desire

When I began this book project, I had only a passing familiarity with cactus and succulent plants. Given my novice status in approaching this subject at the outset, it should by now be clear that the passions of cactus and succulent collectors rubbed off on me in no small way. This is to say that I am not a dispassionate narrator of the succulent stories that fill the pages of this book. In the process of my research, you could say that I, too, became the succulent subject, I responded to its "hail," and this book is a result of staying with that desire.[40] At times the cactus became something of a sublime object of my unconscious, or source of *jouissance,* or even an "object" imbued with the "non-object" presence of *objet a.* And I confronted my own anxieties about extinction as an unconscious effort to protect "myself" from the overwhelming recognition of capitalist development as cause of extinction. My own desires became directed through succulents, and in turn, these plants exerted their "plantiness" on me. Through the topological twists of the unconscious and its expression in the world through the extimacy of space, I mentally forged important and affecting new relations with plants just as their presence "inside" me felt bewildering or alienating.[41] There are plants that in turn moved me to care through the ways they engage and live in the world. "The goal of human-plant ethnography," writes Hannah Pitt, "is not to represent nonhumans by speaking for them, but to tell stories of them to enable others to discover plantiness directly."[42] Since I began this project six years ago, it is a marvel to consider the ways these plants have transformed my life.

As a result of conducting this research, I am now a member of the Cactus and Succulent Specialist Group of the Species Survival Commission of the IUCN, the group that, among other things, periodically assesses the Red List status of all known cactus and succulent species worldwide. I talk regularly to media outlets about plant poaching, and I give presentations to cactus and succulent societies about plant conservation efforts and illegal trade. In turn, I receive important feedback from these communities about my research findings. I have developed a sense of responsibility to care for the plants I write and think about. If anything, this book is evidence that encounters with others hold the potential to forge new emotional pathways and possibilities for modes of relating, that encounters "make (a) difference."[43] Encounters can instill a sense of obligation for more care-full forms of engagement with others, and the unconscious has an active role to play in shaping the meaning of those encounters.

In addition to detailing the nature of illicit trades in succulent plants, I hope this book goes some way toward demonstrating the analytical power of writing a political ecology of desire. A political ecology of desire is an encounter with the unconscious that not only occurs within a raucous and lively world but finds its expression through the world and the many lives of others with whom we share relations, obligations, caretaking responsibilities, and complicity in neglect or harm. To speak of a political ecology of desire is to insist on the need to bring the unconscious to the level of speech as a road toward personal change and, consequently, environmental change. Attention to the work of the unconscious is in no way a disavowal of the urgent need for coalitional, collective work, of the need for organized political action on behalf of other species with which humans cohabitate in the face of the interlinked crises of biodiversity loss, pollution, and climate change, among others. An insistence on a politics rooted in desire is antithetical to a neoliberal turn toward individual action or consumer purchasing power. Instead, a collective politics of action that insists on the rights for species to flourish must attend to desire and what happens when desire is interrupted by anxiety or when desire is abused by capitalist consumerist logics that present us with fantasies of satisfaction through the world of objects we can buy with the swipe of a credit card.

Such a perspective requires a stubborn attachment to desire. This is a desire that makes demands on us to seek out a greater satisfaction through seeing desires as rooted only in a recognition that something is missing, but it is a missing that will always be missed. True satisfaction arises from this lack rather than from attempting (and always failing) to find something to fill the void that makes desiring possible.[44] Confronting desire leads to the recognition that only in accepting that nothing can replace the absent Other of the unconscious can one truly begin to enjoy the pleasure of what is lacking.

Desires move us; they reshape and transform environments; they upend lives just as they forge incredible bonds. In previous eras, to desire was to conjure an ontological Other that might offer salvation. In the past, as McGowan writes, this "Other" was most often something divine, with God or gods only more recently replaced by capitalism.[45] A proper orientation toward desire insists that one must contend with the unconscious that makes this request for an Other appear legible in the first place. This is both a personal and a collective demand to desire otherwise as a hopeful political reorientation. The stories of succulent life woven through this book suggest how desires might be reoriented otherwise, away from practices of commodification and extinction and toward an insistence on flourishing, a celebration of the possible as cause of desire.

Keep Learning from Plants!

Learning with plants in researching this book as a multispecies ethnography has demanded a certain engagement with botany, of course. But I also found myself during this research drawn toward more speculative realms of vegetal thinking across other genres. Works of fiction, for instance, were not only sources of inspiration but creative prompts to think otherwise. As just one example, one of my favorite childhood stories was "The Sound Machine" by Roald Dahl, first published in 1949. In the story, a man invents a machine that can hear the otherwise inaudible frequencies (to human ears) of nonhuman sounds. Listening to plants through the device, the man is terrified to hear a shrieking sound of pain every time his neighbor cuts a rose or plucks a daisy: "He had been wrong in calling it a cry of pain," Dahl writes, "a flower probably didn't feel pain. It felt something else which we didn't know about—something called toin or spurl or plinuckment, or anything you like."[46] The story's climax is later reached when the man listens to the axing of a tree.

What I "enjoy" most about this story today is how Dahl points to the radical otherness of vegetal life; while we might recognize the differences between animal and vegetal worlds, it can become challenging even to possess language for describing them. There is something perturbing in this little tale of plants screaming and a man fretting over what he will eat now that he knows a potato might elicit a yelp when pulled from the ground. In 2019, researchers reported that by placing ultrasonic frequency microphones close to tomato plants and recording what happened when plants were withheld water for long periods of time, or had their stems cut, they discovered that plants emit sounds (imperceptible to human ears) in response.[47] Maybe plants scream after all. Or is greater harm done in overlaying ideas of animal being on plants, whose physiology is so radically different from the physiologies of the animal kingdom?[48] But how else to become more familiar with vegetal life than to do our best to relate to plants through ways of knowing to which we have access?

Dahl would not have known (and yet anticipated) that a veritable revolution in plant-thinking would soon be under way, questioning long-held assumptions across biology and botany, involving cutting-edge research illuminating the complex intelligences of trees and other plants and the rise of "plant neurobiology" as a legitimate field of inquiry.[49] This flurry of interest and attention to the communicative capacities of plants has also coincided with another sort of "vegetal turn" in the social sciences and humanities, with scholars now turning to plants as subjects as well as sources of knowledge for philosophy and political theory. Critical plant studies has emerged as a diverse space of academic inquiry across "the arts, humanities, and social sciences looking at questions of vegetal agency and at the ways plants are involved in constituting complex, multispecies worlds."[50] In many ways, the overarching project of critical plant studies shares strong affinities with speculative fiction, because the plant world can appear so different from human and animal worlds. Indigenous scholarship and ecological knowledge of the vegetal world, though long neglected by the dominant academy, are equally in bloom and in conversation with scholars whose work aligns with critical plant studies.[51] To invoke yet another vegetal metaphor, my learning process with plants continues to be pollinated by a variety of scholars, knowledge systems, and even fictive thought that help me to think carefully about vegetal life and how plants make their presences known and felt in coconstituting relationships with humans. This process of learning and unlearning with plants does not stop here.

There will undoubtedly continue to be people in the world who illicitly harvest plants because they see an opportunity for quick profit or because they allow their desires to run away with them at the expense of impacted species. But in concluding this book, I am left with a strong conviction that more and more people are becoming attuned to the wondrous lives of plants, what it means to care in multispecies registers, and see plants as more than mere aesthetic objects that look nice on a shelf. I believe such attention and attunement hold great promise for species futures. I am also left with the sense that much work remains to be done in the realm of conservation policy and international trade regulations to ensure vegetal flourishing. Against renewed and globally scaled efforts of expanding conservation's footprint via exclusionary forms of protectionism, my research tilts me toward the belief that cultivation with care within a framework of multispecies justice holds far more hope for ensuring succulent species survival than efforts dominated by reasserting human–nature dichotomies, territorial dispossession, or, in its most extreme forms, overt militarization of conservation law enforcement.[52] This work, across the realms of research, policy, and conservation practice, is urgent and vital. Luckily, some efforts in this vein of thinking—though not nearly enough—are already under way.

In writing this book, I stayed close to encounters between people and plants to understand the production of desire. The encounters I relate—and the desires they disclose—reveal the importance of the unconscious in shaping human–plant relations. Yet despite my insistence on attention to the unconscious, I find that the desire moving people to care for plants still conjures something of wonder, awe, and enchantment that exceeds my ability to understand such desire in its entirety. I was gripped by the succulent subject as much as I became one. As Nan Shepherd wrote, "the more one learns of this intricate interplay of soil, altitude, weather, and the living tissues of plant and insect (an intricacy that has its astonishing moments, as when sundew and butterwort eat the insects), the more the mystery deepens. Knowledge does not dispel mystery."[53] Learning from succulents and the company they keep leaves me more enchanted than ever by the living world, and more desiring to embrace that mystery.

Acknowledgments

I used to be surprised by the length of book acknowledgments—no longer! It was only through an abundance of generosity—from fellow academics, conservation practitioners, my family and friends, patient botanists, editors, and caring collectors, among many others—that I was able to research and write the book you hold. Much of this was written during the Covid-19 pandemic, amid physical isolation made tolerable only by the care, support, and love of family, friends, and colleagues near and far.

This book simply would not exist without the trusting mentorship and wise counsel of Professor Rosaleen Duffy at the University of Sheffield and her willingness to take a chance on me as an applicant for a postdoctoral research fellowship as part of the BIOSEC project. Her generously funded European Research Council project (under the European Union's Horizon 2020 research and innovation program grant agreement 694995-BIOSEC: Biodiversity and Security, Understanding Environmental Crime, Illegal Wildlife Trade and Threat Finance) made this work and the travel it entailed financially possible, but it was her willingness to trust in my decisions about the nature of my research and her encouragement to pursue it in the form of a book that gave me courage to do so. For that I am deeply grateful. Rosaleen also offered critical and important feedback on an earlier draft of the book, which helped improve it immensely, I assure you.

Acknowledgments

As part of BIOSEC, I came to know some of the most caring, critical, and thoughtful researchers, and now some of my dearest friends and closest collaborators. BIOSEC and its wider orbit of coconspirators included Francis Massé, Hannah Dickinson, Laure Joanny, Ruth Wilson, Lucy Dunning, George Iordăchescu, Teresa Lappe-Osthege, Anh Vu, Adeniyi (Niyi) Asiyanbi, Elaine (Lan Yin) Hsaio, Brock Bersaglio, Charis Enns, and Esther Marijnen. In ways large and small, through conversation and discussion and feedback on drafts and the earliest ideas for this project, this book benefited immeasurably from my engagements with this wonderful community. BIOSEC was a unicorn of a research project, and I have never had so much fun working in my life: thanks to you all. The external advisory board of the BIOSEC project comprised Dan Brockington, Libby Lunstrum, Dilys Roe, Tor Benjaminsen, EJ Milner-Gulland, Sabri Zain, Bram Büscher, and Maano Ramutsindela. They offered early feedback and suggestions about this project, and to them I am thankful. Within this group, I am especially grateful to Dan Brockington, whose work I have admired for so long and who welcomed me and the rest of the BIOSEC team into the unique orbit of the SIID intellectual community that he worked to cultivate as a space of creativity, critical debate, and excellent hijinks.

An extra round of thanks is due to Francis, Hannah, Laure, Niyi, Charis, and Brock for encouraging me to pursue this research to the full extent that I did, reading drafts of chapters (especially Francis) and tolerating (or, more likely, quietly suffering through) my inability to stop talking about all things succulent over the years we shared in Sheffield. Additional thanks are due to Brock, Charis, Francis, and Angela Holtzer for both adopting many a plant and tending to them (and my increasingly long instruction list!) during my absences from Sheffield as part of this research. Angela's memory is present in more ways than one in this book and through many of the plants Francis continues to care for and cultivate. Her memory is a blessing, and she is so dearly missed.

The wisdom, humor, and critical insights and suggestions big and small of my longtime friend Rob St. John have improved this book in countless ways. Rob endured more bad drafts and consequent hand-wringing angst than anyone else, and for that I am forever in his debt. Short weekends away into the Forest of Bowland with Rob and Eily were essential to my ability to see this work through. You both have my deepest appreciation and love.

Many other people helped support this book in ways large and small and contributed different kinds of important feedback and support over the years. Their encouragement and commiseration were essential. This is an incomplete list, but in no specific order, thank you, JH Pitas, Mariya Shcheglovitova, Erle Ellis, Dave Lansing, Maggie Buck Holland, Adrienne Adar, Sera Boeno, Ezgi Ince, Eli Breitburg-Smith, Aran Keating, Chuck Green, Joe Martin, Liz Vayda, Boris Volfson, Danielle Foley, Lara Hueston, Ben Nic mark, Shannon O'Lear, Krithika Srinivasan, Megan Betz, Sophie Sapp Moore, Burak Tansel, Alasdair Cochrane, Lucas Pohl, Bárbara Goettsch, Kendra McSweeney, Anwesha Dutta, Annette Hübschle, David Williams, Tarsh Thekaekara, BR Rajeev, the Oxford BCM WhatsApp group, and many more.

I am grateful to Paul Robbins, Sarah Moore, and Karen Bakker for including me in their session on psychoanalytic and posthumanist political ecology at the annual meeting of the American Association of Geographers in 2019, where Paul Kingsbury served as a brilliant discussant. At this meeting I finally committed to the idea of "staying with desire" as a key analytic for this book; even if it had been there all along, the feedback I received in the session gave me the confidence to embrace desire with abandon. I subsequently owe tremendous thanks to Paul Kingsbury for agreeing to read an earlier version of the book and providing important and critical feedback on its psychoanalytic dimensions, even if much more remains to be said in these registers than is present here. I hope subsequent articles and future writing can further these threads of thought and forge deeper connections with the enthusiastic community that exists around psychoanalytic geographies.

At the University of Alabama (UA), I have been very lucky to find community and some truly wonderful colleagues and friends. My deepest thanks for their intellectual insights, care, and friendship go to (Michael) Seth Stewart, Sara-Maria Sorentino, Gina Stamm, Misha Hadar, Elif Kalaycioglu, Megan Gallagher, Julia Brock, Brittany VandeBerg, A.J. Bauer, Garrett Bridger Gilmore, Sarah Cheshire, Nicholas Magliocca, Utkarsh Roy Choudhury, Matthew Therrell, and all my colleagues in the Department of Geography. I also want to thank Katherine Chiou, Michael McCain, and Michael Federoff for championing my efforts in the final stretch. I am deeply grateful to Elif and Misha, as well, for sharing their home with Heeyoung and me in the summer and fall of 2021. Additional thanks go to the Collaborative Arts Research Initiative at UA where I am a Faculty Fellow. At CARI, special thanks to Michelle Bordner, Rebecca Salzer, and Sarah Marshall. I also learned so much from students in a spring 2021 course on conservation politics and the kinds of prose and material they found engaging and instructive. Special thanks go to former students Trinity Donnellan and Owen Emerson for offering candid advice on an early draft of the Introduction.

I received early publishing advice from George F. Thompson through the UA Publisher-in-Residence Program and from James Brooks, who patiently walked me through ins and outs of the academic book publishing world. Chapters of this book benefited from feedback I received from colleagues and audiences, including those at presentations at University College Dublin's Environmental Humanities seminar series (thank you, Hannah Boast); the State of Biodiversity Symposium at the San Diego Natural History Museum; the Reilly Center for Science, Technology, and Values at the University of Notre Dame; the University of Sheffield Political Ecology Reading Group; the Succulent Plant Symposium at the

Huntington Botanical Gardens; the Rachel Carson Center for Society and Environment (RCC) in Munich, Germany; and a generous and enthusiastic group of participants in a book-writing workshop co-organized with Sophie Sapp Moore at the Dimensions of Political Ecology Conference (DOPE) in Lexington, Kentucky, in 2020. Several colleagues at UA, as part of the Gender and Race Studies Writing Group, provided invaluable feedback on an early draft of chapter 4. I am grateful to Utz McKnight and the entire GRS department at UA for welcoming a new geographer to campus through the many invitations to commiserate and join in their vibrant community.

I was very fortunate to benefit from UA's College of Arts and Sciences ASPIRE program, which gave me a one-semester teaching release in spring 2022 that I used to complete this book. This permitted me to take up a three-month writing residency fellowship at the RCC through its Landhaus Fellows Program. I am grateful to Christof Mauch and Arielle Helmick of the RCC, as well as the entire Herrmannsdorf community (thank you, Karl, Sophie, and Mathias!), for providing me with this wonderful opportunity to expand my community in the environmental humanities, for the time and space and community in which to write, and for the realization that this was a community I very much wished to call my own.

As part of the RCC fellowship, I lived at Landhaus, a house turned scholar-in-residence retreat on the Herrmannsdorf Landwerkstätten farm located in Glonn, outside Munich. For three months, I had the pleasure of living, writing, discussing, walking, commiserating, dancing, and staring at pigs with (in alphabetical order) Flora Mary Bartlett, Subarna De, Thibault Fontanari, Péter Makai, Diego Molina, Bright Nrkumah, Céline Pessis, Samantha Walton, and Moremi Zeil. What a time it was! Within a few weeks, Covid-19 came to Landhaus, and while many were spared, I was not, and the communal spirit and ethos of collective care and support that were shared will not be forgotten anytime soon. For the flowers, vegan gummies, soup, and moral and physical support, you have my eternal thanks. Additional thanks are due to Moremi for being a hero to us all; we did not deserve you. I am also grateful to the RCC for permitting me to stay on as a visiting scholar for an additional month in Munich in April, which provided me more time and space to write but also to get to know better many of the students (Sevgi Mutlu Sirakova deserves special mention here) and other visiting scholars at the RCC. I received incredibly smart and helpful feedback from several RCC community members on a draft of my book's Introduction during the weekly Works-in-Progress series, for which I am thankful.

This project would have never taken the shape it did had it not been for the generosity of members of the Sheffield Branch of the British Cactus and Succulent Society and other cactus and succulent society members in both the United Kingdom and elsewhere. I very much miss those Friday evenings spent above the scouting shop learning about plants. My deepest thanks go to Simon Snowden, Peter Cowdell, Greg Bulmer, Paul K., and Alain Buffel.

For the purposes of maintaining anonymity in line with my research ethics approvals, there are others I would like to list here by name but I cannot. Still, my heartfelt thanks go to "Svejk" and "Jan" in Czechia and to the dozens and dozens of passionate cactus and succulent hobbyists, collectors, and botanists with whom I had the privilege of speaking and spending time, and similarly to many generous research participants in South Korea and elsewhere. For assistance with facilitating and conducting research in Korea, I am grateful to Byungchun So, Sook Oh, Jinah Kwon, and Jaehyun Kim. My deepest thanks go to Jinah and Jaehyun for their research assistance as part of the nascent Seoul Succulent Detective Agency.

I also owe tremendous thanks to many professionals working in the arena of plant conservation for their time and expertise in the United States, Europe, Brazil, Mexico, and South Korea. My heartfelt thanks go to Jon Rebman and Sula Vanderplank from the

San Diego Natural History Museum; to the staff of the Botanical Department at the Huntington Library, Art Museum, and Botanical Gardens, especially Sean Lahmeyer and John Trager; and to Abby Meyer at Botanical Gardens Conservation International–US. Andrew Salywon, Kimberlie McCue, and other staff at the Desert Botanical Garden in Phoenix, Arizona, were gracious with their time and the attention they gave me in introducing me to issues of succulent conservation and poaching in Arizona. Jan Schipper of the Phoenix Zoo permitted me the wonderful opportunity to spend a weekend in the Arizona rangelands with him and his students. Gary Krupnick in the Botany Department at the Smithsonian National Museum of Natural History assisted my visit to explore their herbarium collections and provided key insights into the role of herbariums in knowing plants and attending to their conservation, for which I am most grateful. Further thanks go to staff and officials within Mexico's CONABIO, CONANP, SEMARNAT, and PROFEPA agencies for sharing their time and expertise with me, as well as to the many attendees at IUCN's Agave Red List workshop held in Querétaro, Mexico, in 2018. At UNAM, I am deeply grateful to Dr. Salvador Arias Montes, Dr. Abisaí Josué García-Mendoza, and Daniel Sandoval Gutiérrez—your collective expertise on Mexico's cacti, agave, and other succulents is astounding. I am also grateful for the time offered me by officials and staff in Korea's Ministry of Environment as well as by the Cactus Succulent Research Institute within the GyeongGi-Do Agricultural Research and Extension Services (GARES) in South Korea. I thank the officials and staff of the Czech Environmental Inspectorate and Nature Conservation Agency of the Czech Republic for their expertise and time.

At the University of Minnesota Press, I am very thankful for the patience, support, skill, and enthusiasm of my editor, Jason Weidemann, and consider myself lucky to have worked with such a thoughtful editor on this project. Jason saw value in my project early on and continued to support me in cultivating it while the project was still in its infancy. I am thankful for his keen editorial eye, encouragement, and patience responding to my many (often anxious) questions about the process. Thanks are due as well to Zenyse Miller for bringing this book into its final form and to Holly Monteith for the careful and impeccable copy editing. Thank you to two anonymous peer reviewers for their helpful suggestions, comments, and support of this manuscript. One of those reviewers I now know to be John Hartigan, who offered tremendous support and advice on how to improve this book: thank you so much.

My final thanks, love, and immense gratitude are saved for my immediate and growing family (by both blood and marriage), including my parents, Mary and Greg; brothers Ross Margulies, Charles Shimooka, and Trevor Wilhelms; sisters Abby, Molly, and Leah Margulies; and beautiful nephews and niece Cole, Quinn, Robin, and Aviva. My father became an unexpected reader and champion of this work in its later stages, and there are many simpler sentences in this book because of his helpful, direct feedback. It was a pleasure to be able to share this process with him and discuss the meanings of collecting and academic writing. My biggest thanks are saved for last: above all, I am grateful to have the support, love, critical feedback, and companionship of my wife, Heeyoung Kang, with whom I am lucky to share in life's mystery. Her enthusiasm and confidence in my capacity to complete this project were essential to my ability to do so. Thank you for everything, Heeyoung.

Additional Resources

For helpful guides to growing cacti and succulents, raising seeds, and propagating plants, I recommend readers visit the websites of the British Cactus and Succulent Society and the Henry Shaw Cactus and Succulent Society (an affiliate branch of the Cactus and Succulent Society of America). The Missouri Botanical Garden also has a useful grower's guide, and the Cactus and Succulent Plant Specialist Group of the International Union for Conservation of Nature has further information about the conservation of cactus and succulent plants and how to get involved in supporting its efforts.

Countless books, podcasts, and online guides to growing and learning more about these incredible species and other plants are available. Following are recommended titles.

Books

The Complete Book of Cacti and Succulents by Terry Hewitt (DK, 1993)

Kew Gardener's Guide to Growing Cacti and Succulents by Paul Rees (Quarto, 2023)

Cactus by Dan Torre (Reaktion Books, 2017)

Podcasts and Other Media

On the Ledge

In Defense of Plants

Crime Pays but Botany Doesn't

On Collecting Carefully

Avoid purchasing plants, especially mature plants and/or plants of dubious origin, over the internet, especially from unknown sellers. Ask local, reputable nurseries about where they source their plants to encourage more transparent succulent cultivation and trade. Swap and share plant material freely with others to cultivate caring for plants while respecting trade regulations. Above all, leave wild cactus and succulent plants where they are!

Notes

Preface

1. Jacques Lacan famously said, "The best image to sum up the unconscious is Baltimore in the early morning." In the predawn light of Baltimore, he saw expressed in spaces of shadow and light cast by neon signs and moving headlights his "thoughts, actively thinking thoughts" before him—thoughts and ideas expressed yet always only partially illuminated through encountering something of the sublime as a flicker, a flash, a momentary approach and receding of what is not quite within reach. Maybe I also saw something of my unconscious as expressed before me just beyond a cactus sitting on a windowsill on a muggy afternoon in a rowhouse in Baltimore.

Introduction

1. For a recent and important intervention to the illegal rosewood trade, see Annah Lake Zhu, *Rosewood: Endangered Species Conservation and the Rise of Global China* (Cambridge, Mass.: Harvard University Press, 2022). See also Lyndsie Bourgon, *Tree Thieves: Crime and Survival in North America's Woods* (New York: Little, Brown Spark, 2022).
2. Reteo Nyffeler and Urs Eggli, "An Up-to-Date Familial and Suprafamilial Classification of Succulent Plants," *Bradleya* 2010, no. 28 (2010): 125–44.
3. I am grateful to Olwen Grace, head of accelerated taxonomy at Royal Botanic Gardens, Kew, for reminding me via a presentation at the Huntington Botanical Gardens in August 2022 of the importance of defining succulents in a book about succulents!
4. Dieter J. von Willert, Benno M. Eller, Marinus J. A. Werger, Enno Brinckmann, and Hans-Dieter Ihlenfeldt, *Life Strategies of Succulents in Deserts: With Special Reference to the Namib Desert* (Cambridge: Cambridge University Press, 1992), 6.
5. A very enjoyable primer to cacti with color photographs is Dan Torre, *Cactus* (London: Reaktion Books, 2017), 15–45.
6. This book does not engage with illegal trade in animals, though of course there are opportunities for shared learning between kinds of wildlife trafficking.

Rosemary-Claire Collard, *Animal Traffic: Lively Capital in the Global Exotic Pet Trade* (Durham, N.C.: Duke University Press, 2020).

7. Virginia Blum and Anna Secor, "Psychotopologies: Closing the Circuit between Psychic and Material Space," *Environment and Planning D: Society and Space* 29, no. 6 (2011): 1031; see also Stephen Healy, "Traversing Fantasies, Activating Desires: Economic Geography, Activist Research, and Psychoanalytic Methodology," *Professional Geographer* 62, no. 4 (2010): 496–506.

8. Paul Kingsbury, "The Extimacy of Space," *Social and Cultural Geography* 8, no. 2 (2007): 235–58; Jacques Lacan, *The Ethics of Psychoanalysis, 1959–1960,* book VII of *The Seminars of Jacques Lacan,* ed. Jacques-Alain Miller, trans. Dennis Porter (New York: W. W. Norton, 1992), 139.

9. Bárbara Goettsch, Craig Hilton-Taylor, Gabriela Cruz-Piñón, James P. Duffy, Anne Frances, Héctor M. Hernández, Richard Inger et al., "High Proportion of Cactus Species Threatened with Extinction," *Nature Plants* 1, no. 10 (2015): 1–7; Kevin R. Hultine, Lucas C. Majure, Veronica S. Nixon, Salvador Arias, Alberto Búrquez, Bárbara Goettsch, Raul Puente-Martinez, and J. Alejandro Zavala-Hurtado, "The Role of Botanical Gardens in the Conservation of Cactaceae," *BioScience* 66, no. 12 (2016): 1057–65.

10. Olwen Grace, "Succulent Plant Diversity as Natural Capital," *Plants, People, Planet* 1, no. 4 (2019): 336–45.

11. Joan Copjec, *Read My Desire: Lacan against the Historicists* (1994; repr., London: Verso, 2015), 13–14.

12. This is not a swipe at Pollan; I enjoyed this book. Michael Pollan, *The Botany of Desire: A Plant's-Eye View of the World* (New York: Random House, 2002). See John Hartigan Jr., *Care of the Species: Races of Corn and the Science of Plant Biodiversity* (Minneapolis: University of Minnesota Press, 2017), xxi, for a critique of how Pollan ascribes agency to desirable plant species.

13. This move to decenter humans as the only actors capable of enacting meaningful change in the world is one shared by scholars of various kinds of "posthumanism" across a diversity of fields. Posthumanist perspectives are not without their critiques. Among critical scholars whose work centers matters of social justice, critiques include concern over the very real and material hierarchies of social difference that can be obfuscated in turning to posthumanist concerns. Another concerns the ongoing deprivileging of non-Western or nondominant knowledge systems, including Indigenous knowledge and belief systems that never presupposed a separation of human and nonhuman worlds in the first place. I share these concerns. Juanita Sundberg, "Decolonizing Posthumanist Geographies," *Cultural Geographies* 21, no. 1 (2014): 33–47.

14. The works of María Puig de la Bellacasa, Anna Krzywoszynska, and John Hartigan Jr. have been especially informative in this regard, among others, including Michelle Murphy and Natasha Meyers. See, in particular, María Puig de la Bellacasa, *Matters of Care: Speculative Ethics in More than Human Worlds*

(Minneapolis: University of Minnesota Press, 2017); Anna Krzywoszynska, "Caring for Soil Life in the Anthropocene: The Role of Attentiveness in More-than-Human Ethics," *Transactions of the Institute of British Geographers* 44, no. 4 (2019): 661–75; Hartigan, *Care of the Species*.

15. On desire in the research creation process, see Natalie Loveless, *How to Make Art at the End of the World* (Durham, N.C.: Duke University Press, 2019).

16. Paul Robbins, *Political Ecology: A Critical Introduction* (Hoboken, N.J.: John Wiley, 2019).

17. Jason Moore, *Capitalism in the Web of Life: Ecology and the Accumulation of Capital* (London: Verso, 2015); Todd McGowan, *Capitalism and Desire: The Psychic Cost of Free Markets* (New York: Columbia University Press, 2016); McGowan, *Enjoying What We Don't Have: The Political Project of Psychoanalysis* (Lincoln: University of Nebraska Press, 2013).

18. My use of lively capital comes from Collard, *Animal Traffic*.

19. There is an ever-growing body of scholarship within more-than-human geographies to which my research is indebted. The origins of this body of work are found primarily in Sarah Whatmore, *Hybrid Geographies: Natures Cultures Spaces* (London: Sage, 2002). This important vein of scholarship has spawned, inspired, and developed alongside dozens of related concepts, methods, and theories, including multinatural geographies, multispecies ethnography, and the broader field of posthumanist political philosophy. See also Ruth Panelli, "More-than-Human Social Geographies: Posthuman and Other Possibilities," *Progress in Human Geography* 34, no. 1 (2010): 79–87.

20. I borrow *arts of noticing* from Anna L. Tsing and the Matsutake Worlds Research Group. It connotes a method of ethnographic attention to nonhuman lifeworlds and how they shape and are shaped in return by human ones. Tsing, *The Mushroom at the End of the World: On the Possibility of Life in Capitalist Ruins* (Princeton, N.J.: Princeton University Press, 2017), 37.

21. There is much more to say on this impasse, which I intend to take up in future writing. But there are some important examples of work that do take up these concerns: Lucas Pohl, "Object-Disoriented Geographies: The Ghost Tower of Bangkok and the Topology of Anxiety," *Cultural Geographies* 27, no. 1 (2020): 71–84; Steve Pile, "Beastly Minds: A Topological Twist in the Rethinking of the Human in Nonhuman Geographies Using Two of Freud's Case Studies, Emmy von N. and the Wolfman," *Transactions of the Institute of British Geographers* 39, no. 2 (2014): 224–36.

22. Anna Tsing, "Unruly Edges: Mushrooms as Companion Species: For Donna Haraway," *Environmental Humanities* 1, no. 1 (2012): 144.

23. Donna Haraway, *When Species Meet* (Minneapolis: University of Minnesota Press, 2008), 42.

24. See, in particular, Paul Robbins and Sarah A. Moore, "Ecological Anxiety Disorder: Diagnosing the Politics of the Anthropocene," *cultural geographies* 20, no. 1 (2013): 3–19; Sarah A. Moore, Mohammed Rafi Arefin, and Heather

Rosenfeld, "Generating Anxiety, Short-Circuiting Desire: Battery Waste and the Capitalist Phantasy," *Environment and Planning D: Society and Space* 36, no. 6 (2018): 1081–1100; Robert Fletcher, *Failing Forward: The Rise and Fall of Neoliberal Conservation* (Berkeley: University of California Press, 2023).

25. The place of psychoanalytic geographies is well evidenced through several recent edited collections and the many important contributions included there: Clint Burnham and Paul Kingsbury, eds., *Lacan and the Environment* (London: Palgrave Macmillan, 2021); Paul Kingsbury and Anna J. Secor, eds., *A Place More Void* (Lincoln: University of Nebraska Press, 2021); and Paul Kingsbury and Steve Pile, eds., *Psychoanalytic Geographies* (New York: Routledge, 2014).
26. Lacan, *Ethics of Psychoanalysis,* 113.
27. Jacques Lacan, *Four Fundamental Concepts of Psychoanalysis,* book XI of *The Seminars of Jacques Lacan,* ed. Jacques-Alain Miller, trans. Alan Sheridan (New York: W. W. Norton, 1998), 185–86.
28. Lacan describes the absent Thing as the mother we will always miss, where the child recognizes its separation from the mother figure as embodying the possibility of total satisfaction, yet one that can never be obtained as it is foundational to the structure of the unconscious. Lacan, *Ethics of Psychoanalysis,* 67–68.
29. Mari Ruti, "Why Some Things Matter More than Others: A Lacanian Explanation," *Constellations* 23, no. 2 (2016): 207.
30. It is a challenge to summarize these key Lacanian concepts concisely and clearly, especially as they emerge across many of Lacan's key works and seminars over a number of years and develop sophistication or shift in meaning over time. Helpful texts for those interested in delving deeper into Lacanian thought include Lacan, *Four Fundamental Concepts,* and, more practically, Bruce Fink, *The Lacanian Subject: Between Language and Jouissance* (Princeton, N.J.: Princeton University Press, 1997), as well as Slavoj Žižek, *Looking Awry: An Introduction to Jacques Lacan through Popular Culture* (Cambridge, Mass.: MIT Press, 1992). Within geography, Paul Kingsbury's many articles drawing on Lacan are not only essential reading but helpfully bring many of Lacan's more abstract ideas "down to earth."
31. Lacan, *Four Fundamental Concepts,* 20.
32. McGowan, *Capitalism and Desire,* 23–24.
33. Though this does not mean "our" only desires are only those of the Other, even if the Other presents us with the dominant discourse of what those desires "ought" to be. On this point, see Ruti, "Why Some Things Matter."
34. Lacan, *Four Fundamental Concepts,* 235.
35. McGowan, *Capitalism and Desire,* 35.
36. "Drive is the other side of desire, the name for what moves us forward in our always failing attempt to become 'One' again." Lucas Pohl and Erik Swyngedouw, "'What Does Not Work in the World': The Specter of Lacan in Critical Political Thought," *Distinktion: Journal of Social Theory,* February 25, 2021, 5–6.

37. Ruti, "Why Some Things Matter," 207.
38. Paul Kingsbury and Steve Pile, "Introduction: The Unconscious, Transference, Drives, Repetition and Other Things Tied to Geography," in *Psychoanalytic Geographies,* ed. Paul Kingsbury and Steve Pile (Farnham, U.K.: Ashgate, 2014), 24.
39. Kingsbury and Pile, 20.
40. Paul Kingsbury, "Did Somebody Say Jouissance? On Slavoj Žižek, Consumption, and Nationalism," *Emotion, Space, and Society* 1, no. 1 (2008): 49.
41. Copjec, *Read My Desire,* 46.
42. Paul Kingsbury, "Locating the Melody of the Drives," *Professional Geographer* 62, no. 4 (2010): 521.
43. See McGowan, *Capitalism and Desire*; McGowan, *Enjoying What We Don't Have.*
44. Jacques Lacan, "Of Structure as an Inmixing of an Otherness Prerequisite to Any Subject Whatever," in *The Structuralist Controversy: The Languages of Criticism and the Sciences of Man,* ed. Richard Macksey and Eugenio Donato (Baltimore: Johns Hopkins University Press, 1970), 189; Kingsbury and Pile, "Introduction," 16.
45. Kingsbury and Pile, "Introduction," 5.
46. On what a Lacanian politics and ethics of desire might entail, see Pohl and Swyngedouw, "What Does Not Work in the World," and Ruti, "Why Some Things Matter."
47. It's important here to recognize the dangerous collapsing of "Indigenous knowledge" as its own form of violent erasure reproducing colonial harms that so often happens when diverse Indigenous onto-epistemologies are discussed as generically "Indigenous." Cash Ahenakew, "Grafting Indigenous Ways of Knowing onto Non-Indigenous Ways of Being: The (Underestimated) Challenges of a Decolonial Imagination," *International Review of Qualitative Research* 9, no. 3 (2016): 323–40.
48. Farhana Sultana, "Political Ecology 1: From Margins to Center," *Progress in Human Geography* 45, no. 1 (2021): 156–65.
49. During the sunbelt housing boom in the 1990s and early 2000s, TRAFFIC North America estimated that from just 1998 to June 2001, roughly one hundred thousand succulent plants, including saguaros and golden barrel cacti and others, with an estimated value of US$3 million, were wild-harvested from Texas and Mexico to supply the landscape garden market in Phoenix and Tucson alone. Christopher S. Robbins, ed., *Prickly Trade: Trade and Conservation of Chihuahuan Desert Cacti* (Washington, D.C.: TRAFFIC North America, 2003).
50. Ian Cook, "Follow the Thing: Papaya," *Antipode* 36, no. 4 (2004): 642–64; Eben Kirksey, *Emergent Ecologies* (Durham, N.C.: Duke University Press, 2015); Hartigan, *Care of the Species,* 97–98.
51. Collard, *Animal Traffic,* 142–43. See also Rosemary-Claire Collard and Jessica Dempsey, "Life for Sale? The Politics of Lively Commodities," *Environment and Planning A: Economy and Space* 45, no. 11 (2013): 2682–99.

1. On Collecting and Caring for Cacti

1. Berenice Fisher and Joan Tronto, "Toward a Feminist Theory of Caring," in *Circles of Care: Work and Identity in Women's Lives*, ed. E. Abel and M. Nelson (Albany: SUNY Press, 1990), 40.
2. Puig de la Bellacasa, *Matters of Care*, 4.
3. For important reviews of vegetal geographies, see Lesley Head and Jennifer Atchison, "Cultural Ecology: Emerging Human-Plant Geographies," *Progress in Human Geography* 33, no. 2 (2009): 236–45; Lesley Head, Jennifer Atchison, Catherine Phillips, and Kathleen Buckingham, "Vegetal Politics: Belonging, Practices and Places," *Social and Cultural Geography* 15, no. 8 (2014): 861–70.
4. Hartigan, *Care of the Species*, 98, emphasis original.
5. According to Rigby and Rigby, the first evidence of collecting as it is understood today began in the fourth century B.C.E. in Greece. Douglas Rigby and Elizabeth Rigby, *Lock, Stock and Barrel: The Story of Collecting* (Philadelphia: J. B. Lippincott, 1944), 118. However, Belk, drawing on a variety of sources, traces out a variety of lineages of collecting's earliest instances, including in Greece as well as later in Edo Japan and Ming China. Russel W. Belk, *Collecting in a Consumer Society* (1995; repr., New York: Routledge, 2001), 22–64.
6. On the percentage of North Americans who collect, see Susan Pearce, *On Collecting: An Investigation into Collecting in the European Tradition* (Oxford: Routledge, 1995), vii. Other key works on collecting include Russell Belk, ed., *Highways and Buyways: Naturalistic Research from the Consumer Behavior Odyssey* (Provo, Utah: Association for Consumer Research, 1991); Werner Muensterberger, *Collecting: An Unruly Passion* (Princeton, N.J.: Princeton University Press, 2014); and Susan Pearce, ed., *Interpreting Objects and Collections* (Oxford: Routledge, 1994).
7. Barbara A. Lafferty, Erika Matulich, and Monica Xiao Liu, "Exploring Worldwide Collecting Consumption Behaviors," *Journal of International Business and Cultural Studies* 8, no. 1 (2014): 2–3; Belk, *Collecting in a Consumer Society*, 66.
8. William D. McIntosh and Brandon Schmeichel, "Collectors and Collecting: A Social Psychological Perspective," *Leisure Sciences* 26, no. 1 (2004): 86.
9. American Psychiatric Association, *Diagnostic and Statistical Manual of Mental Disorders*, 5th ed. (Washington, D.C.: American Psychiatric Publishing, 2013). And see Ashley E. Nordsletten, Lorena Fernández de la Cruz, Danielle Billotti, and David Mataix-Cols, "Finders Keepers: The Features Differentiating Hoarding Disorder from Normative Collecting," *Comprehensive Psychiatry* 54, no. 3 (2013): 229–37.
10. Pearce, *On Collecting*, 27.
11. Donald O. Case, "Serial Collecting as Leisure, and Coin Collecting in Particular," *Library Trends* 57, no. 4 (2009): 731; Russell W. Belk, "The Ineluctable Mysteries of Possessions," *Journal of Social Behavior and Personality* 6, no. 6 (1991): 17–55.
12. As Pearce amusingly quips, "in only one aspect of developing cultural analysis

was collecting viewed as a process of significance in its own right. This occurred among the classic psychologists, who tended to concentrate on the first two syllables of the word 'analysis' rather than on its whole import." Pearce, *On Collecting*, 6–7.

13. Ruth Formanek, "Why They Collect: Collectors Reveal Their Motivations," in Pearce, *Interpreting Objects and Collections*, 334.

14. Susan Pearce, *Museums, Objects, and Collections: A Cultural Study* (Leicester, U.K.: Leicester University Press, 1992).

15. Jeff Greenberg and Jamie Arndt, "Terror Management Theory," *Handbook of Theories of Social Psychology* 1 (2012): 398.

16. McIntosh and Schmeichel, *Collectors and Collecting*, 86.

17. McIntosh and Schmeichel, 25.

18. Jared D. Margulies, Francesca R. Moorman, Bárbara Goettsch, Jan C. Axmacher, and Amy Hinsley, "Prevalence and Perspectives of Illegal Trade in Cacti and Succulent Plants in the Collector Community," *Conservation Biology* (2023): Article e14030, https://doi.org/10.1111/cobi.14030. Similar dynamics have been noted in other forms of wildlife crimes; see Ragnhild Sollund, "Wildlife Crime: A Crime of Hegemonic Masculinity?," *Social Sciences* 9, no. 93 (2020): 1–16.

19. Pearce, *On Collecting*, 199. Pearce shows how these ideas of acceptable social behaviors have unambiguous ties to collecting urges and desires of men who also seek to possess women through the bonds of marriage and male property ownership.

20. As an 1894 article titled "Cactus Becoming Popular," from one of the first print publications dedicated to the hobby in the United States, describes, "within the last few years, and especially since the existence of the Baltimore Cactus Society, the collecting and cultivating of the cactus seems to have gained so rapidly, that it has developed into a perfect craze, and *it is astonishing to find that the majority of the admirers of this particular genus of plant are ladies.* Now, why is it that they should become so fascinated with the cactus, the majority of them being so difficult to handle on account of their long and dangerous-looking spines? This question may be very easily answered in this way: Ladies are always the best judges of good things. They admire them on account of their beauty, grotesque growth, beautiful flowers, and more particularly their oddity." *Baltimore Cactus Journal* 1, no. 2 (1894): 12–13, emphasis added.

21. On women, botany, and the separation of women from the professionalizing of botany in the Victorian era, see Cheryl McEwan, *Gender, Geography and Empire: Victorian Women Travellers in Africa* (London: Routledge, 2000); Ann B. Shteir, *Cultivating Women, Cultivating Science: Flora's Daughters and Botany in England, 1760–1860* (Baltimore: Johns Hopkins University Press, 1996); Jeanne Kay Guelke and Karen Morin, "Gender, Nature, Empire: Women Naturalists in Nineteenth Century British Travel Literature," *Transactions of the Institute of British Geographers* 26, no. 3 (2001): 306–26.

22. I do not mean to discount the outrightly phallic morphology of many cacti,

nor the possibility that many men may very well find enjoyment in developing an ever-growing collection of phallic plants.

23. My identity as a white, cis-male researcher mediated my access to male collecting spaces as well. Whether it was in sharing hotel rooms in Brazil or overnight ferry bunks across the English Channel to attend a cactus convention, gender played a role in where and how I interacted with the collectors who are centered in this chapter and throughout much of this book.

24. Other options to this question on gender self-identification in the survey included nonbinary/third gender, prefer not to say, prefer to self-describe, and other. Margulies et al., "Prevalence and Perspectives of Illegal Trade."

25. On cuteness, see chapter 7.

26. Karel Čapek, *The Gardener's Year* (New York: Bloomsbury, 2005), 74.

27. There is much more to be said about what queer theory brings to understanding, unsettling, and imagining ecologies beyond the environmental destruction and destructive thought wrought by heteropatriarchies. Rather than trying to say here too little about a subject that demands much more, I direct readers to others, such as the scholarship of Catriona Sandilands, Nicole Seymour, Greta Gaard, and Stacy Alaimo, among their many interlocutors. As Sandilands writes, "queer ecology, then, is not just about representing g/l/b/t/q/t issues in ecological politics and analysis but is also about drawing insight from queer cultures to form alternative, even transformative, cultures of nature." Sandilands, "Lesbian Separatist Communities and the Experience of Nature: Toward a Queer Ecology," *Organization and Environment* 15, no. 2 (2002): 151. And see Alaimo, *Exposed: Environmental Politics and Pleasures in Posthuman Times* (Minneapolis: University of Minnesota Press, 2016); Seymour, *Strange Natures: Futurity, Empathy, and the Queer Ecological Imagination* (Champaign: University of Illinois Press, 2013).

28. Reinforcing this experience, Pearce notes that "seldom, it seems, do people collect outside the gender roles on offer to them." Pearce, *On Collecting*, 219.

29. "The desire of the mother is the origin of everything. The desire of the mother is the founding desire of the whole structure." Lacan, *Ethics of Psychoanalysis*, 283.

30. Russell W. Belk, "Possessions and the Extended Self," *Journal of Consumer Research* 15, no. 2 (1988): 139–68.

31. In the survey of collectors, 20 percent of self-identifying men said that their first plant came from a mother or grandmother, in contrast to female collectors, where 11 percent reported receiving their first plant from a mother or grandmother and only 6 percent from a father or grandfather (similarly, 8 percent of men reported that their first plant came from a paternal figure).

32. Donald W. Winnicott, *Playing and Reality* (1971; repr., New York: Routledge Classics, 2005), 1–7.

33. Winnicott, 7.

34. Jean LaPlanche and Jean-Bertrand Pontalis, *The Language of Psychoanalysis*, trans. Donald Nicholson-Smith (London: Karnac Books, 1973), 187–88.

35. LaPlanche and Pontalis, 63–64.
36. Lacan is also heavily indebted to Melanie Klein in developing his theory of sublimation and the notion of the Thing. Lacan, *Ethics of Psychoanalysis,* 112–15.
37. John Elsner and Roger Cardinal, *Cultures of Collecting* (London: Reaktion Books, 1994), 1.
38. John Forrester, "'Mille e Tre': Freud and Collecting," in Elsner and Cardinal, *Cultures of Collecting,* 232.
39. Even if collected objects become receptacles for the memory of others, in the end, objects are ultimately tied to the self. As Walter Benjamin famously wrote, "for a collector—and I mean a real collector, a collector as he ought to be—ownership is the most intimate relationship that one can have to objects. Not that they come alive in him; it is he who lives in them." Benjamin, "Unpacking My Library: A Talk about Book Collecting," in *Illuminations,* ed. Hannah Arendt, trans. Harry Zohn (New York: Schocken Books, 1969), 67.
40. Baudrillard offers probably the clearest instance of this line of argumentation: "The phallus, to put it in a nutshell, is not something one loans out." Jean Baudrillard, *The System of Objects,* trans. James Benedict (1968; repr., London: Verso, 2006), 105.
41. I am indebted here to discussions with my colleague Gina Stamm, who understands all sorts of psychoanalytic objects far better than I do.
42. Sigmund Freud, "Fetishism," in *Standard Edition of the Complete Psychological Works of Sigmund Freud: Vol. XXI (1927–1931). The Future of an Illusion, Civilization and Its Discontents, and Other Works,* 149–57 (London: Hogarth Press, 1961).
43. There is much more to be said and explored in terms of the fetishistic tendencies of cactus collectors that reaches beyond my analysis here. In the meantime, I would point readers to the fascinating analysis of fetishism in "The Sartorial Superego" in Copjec, *Read My Desire.*
44. Baudrillard, *System of Objects,* 104.
45. Michael Marder, *Plant-Thinking: A Philosophy of Vegetal Life* (New York: Columbia University Press, 2013), 95–112.
46. Friedrich Ritter (1898–1989) was born in Germany but moved to Mexico with his family in his twenties to work in ore mining. He became a devoted cactus collector and describer of new species at a time when cactus plants were wildly popular in Germany. In 1937, he chose to return to Germany to join Hitler's army, where he was strongly influenced by Nazi ideology as well as Nietzschean philosophy through personal study. He subsequently self-published three massive books in a series called *Das offenbarte Leben* (The revealed life). His later self-published memoir is replete with his racist worldviews, which he seemed to have maintained throughout his life. See Beat Ernst Leuenberger, "Biographical Notes on Friedrich Ritter (1898–1989)," *Englera* 16 (1995): 36.
47. This addition of value to objects via ownership is described in the collecting studies literature as contagion: "for example, a book by J. Krishnamurti that

is normally worth about $25 was recently offered for sale at a price of $400 solely because the book was once owned by actor Marlon Brando." McIntosh and Schmeichel, *Collectors and Collecting*, 92.

48. "The collections thus may become, with different degrees of intimacy, parts of our empirical selves. . . . There are few men who would not feel personally annihilated if a life-long construction of their hands or brains—say an entomological collection or an extensive work in manuscript—were suddenly swept away. . . . In every case there remains, over and above this, a sense of the shrinkage of our personality, a partial conversion of ourselves to nothingness, which is a psychological phenomenon by itself." William James, "Psychology, Briefer Courses," in *Writings 1878–1899* (New York: Library of America, 1992), 176.

49. Thom van Dooren, "Care," *Environmental Humanities* 5, no. 1 (2014): 293.

50. Hannah Pitt, "On Showing and Being Shown Plants—a Guide to Methods for More-than-Human Geography," *Area* 47, no. 1 (2015): 48–55. Pitt also draws extensively from work by Tim Ingold on "showing." See Ingold, *The Perception of the Environment: Essays on Livelihood, Dwelling and Skill* (London: Routledge, 2021).

51. Hannah Pitt, "Questioning Care Cultivated through Connecting with More-than-Human Communities," *Social and Cultural Geography* 19, no. 2 (2017): 1–22; Franklin Ginn, "Sticky Lives: Slugs, Detachment and More-than-Human Ethics in the Garden," *Transactions of the Institute of British Geographers* 39, no. 4 (2014): 532–44.

52. South African National Biodiversity Institute, "National Response Strategy and Action Plant to Address the Illegal Trade in South African Succulent Flora," Department of Forest Fisheries and Environment, February 2022, 1–25.

53. Pitt, "On Showing and Being Shown Plants," 50.

54. Susan Sontag, *On Photography* (New York: Farrar, Straus, and Giroux, 1977), 15. On mediatic representations of animals and safari tourism and its attendant politics, see Jim Igoe, *The Nature of the Spectacle: On Images, Money, and Conserving Capitalism* (Tuscon: University of Arizona Press, 2017).

55. Kingsbury, "Did Somebody Say Jouissance?"

56. As quoted in Paul Taylor, "Fetish/Fetishistic Disavowal," in *The Žižek Dictionary*, ed. Rex Butler (New York: Routledge, 2014), 93.

57. Lacan, *Four Fundamental Concepts of Psychoanalysis*, 186. And against reading these images as the fetish, see Copjec, *Read My Desire*, 98–116: "The whole point of the construction of the fetish is to satisfy the Other, not oneself. The fetish, then, must be 'rigorously of no use' to the pervert, who makes no claims on any rights to enjoyment and who busies himself with them only for the sake of the Other" (115).

58. Lacan, *Ethics of Psychoanalysis*, 125.

59. Joan Copjec, *Imagine There's No Woman: Ethics and Sublimation* (Boston, Mass.: MIT Press, 2002), 38.

60. Kingsbury, "Did Somebody Say Jouissance?," 50.

61. Sarah Elton, "Growing Methods: Developing a Methodology for Identifying

Plant Agency and Vegetal Politics in the City," *Environmental Humanities* 13, no. 1 (2021): 93–112; see also Jennifer Atchison and Lesley Head, "Eradicating Bodies in Invasive Plant Management," *Environment and Planning D: Society and Space* 31, no. 6 (2013): 955; Jake Fleming, "Toward Vegetal Political Ecology: Kyrgyzstan's Walnut–Fruit Forest and the Politics of Graftability," *Geoforum* 79 (2017): 27.

62. Michael Marder, "Resist Like a Plant! On the Vegetal Life of Political Movements," *Peace Studies Journal* 5, no. 1 (2012): 29.
63. "Care as a practice demands that care-givers attend to care networks: the webs of interrelations, connections, and dependencies that affect the life and well-being of the primary object/subject of care." Anna Krzywoszynska, "Caring for soil life in the Anthropocene: the role of attentiveness in more-than-human ethics," *Transactions of the Institute of British Geographers* 44 (2019): 664.
64. Aryn Martin, Natasha Myers, and Ana Viseu, "The Politics of Care in Technoscience," *Social Studies of Science* 45, no. 5 (2015): 625–41.
65. Fisher and Tronto, "Toward a Feminist Theory of Caring," 40.
66. For María Puig de la Bellacasa, "care is a force distributed across a multiplicity of agencies and materials and supports our worlds as a thick mesh of relational obligation." Puig de la Bellacasa, *Matters of Care,* 20.
67. Here Elton's urging to give attention to plant time to bring out more of the "plantiness" in human–plant geographies is most obvious. Elton, "Growing Methods." On recent intervention in thinking with plant time, see Sarah Besky and Jonathan Padwe, "Placing Plants in Territory," *Environment and Society* 7, no. 1 (2016): 9–28; Jeremy Brice, "Attending to Grape Vines: Perceptual Practices, Planty Agencies and Multiple Temporalities in Australian Viticulture," *Social and Cultural Geography* 15, no. 8 (2014): 942–65.
68. As Marder describes, plants inhabit their own "hetero-temporalities," living and dying simultaneously in ways distinct from the animal world. Marder, *Plant-Thinking,* 107–9.

2. Illicit Encounters with Succulent Collectors

1. That we were a group of (mostly) European men tracking down a Brazilian cactus named for two European men is of course revealing of the very long history between botany, empire, colonialism, and cultures of collecting in the Anglo-European domain.
2. Alfred W. Crosby, *The Columbian Exchange* (1972; repr., Westport, Conn.: Praeger, 2003); Londa Schiebinger and Claudia Swan, eds., *Colonial Botany: Science, Commerce, and Politics in the Early Modern World* (Philadelphia: University of Pennsylvania Press, 2007).
3. This moment of epiphany remains a delightfully precious and enchanting memory; in terms of the illustrative power of this event, it suffices to say I have been a mushroom forager ever since.
4. Stasja Koot, "Enjoying Extinction: Philanthrocapitalism, Jouissance and Excessive 'Environmentourism' in the South African Rhino Poaching Crisis,"

Journal of Political Ecology 28, no. 1 (2021): 804–22; Walter Benjamin, "The Work of Art in the Age of Mechanical Reproduction," in *Illuminations*, 222. There is a valuable analysis of Benjamin's use of the aura in explicitly psychoanalytic terms in Copjec, *Read My Desire*, 99–103. I am grateful to Judith Krauss for seeing these connections to Benjamin.

5. I return to sublimation again in chapter 4. Lacan, *Ethics of Psychoanalysis,* 112.
6. Lacan, 114.
7. Jamie Lorimer, "Nonhuman Charisma," *Environment and Planning D: Society and Space* 25, no. 5 (2007): 921.
8. Karen Barad, *Meeting the Universe Halfway: Quantum Physics and the Entanglement of Matter and Meaning* (Durham, N.C.: Duke University Press, 2007), 33.
9. Simone Fullager, "Desiring Nature: Identity and Becoming in Narratives of Travel," *Journal for Cultural Research* 4, no. 1 (2000): 60.
10. I consider how I have come to admire other organisms by learning through their particularities, to listen to rather than only look at trees, for instance. The sound of wind moving through paper birch is immediately knowable to me as an unmistakable shimmer distinct from other species I grew up knowing. While listening to birches might seem to suggest becoming is only about practicing sensorial attunement, in the words of Deleuze and Guattari, it is (also) about the forging of alliances. Gilles Deleuze and Félix Guattari, *A Thousand Plateaus: Capitalism and Schizophrenia* (Minneapolis: University of Minnesota Press, 1987), 238.
11. Benjamin, "Work of Art," 67.
12. Ruti, "Why Some Things Matter More than Others," 207.
13. In framing this project as a multispecies ethnography, I take seriously the question of the well-being of the plants in more-than-human research ethics. It is encouraging to see recent interventions about ethics in more-than-human research, but they tend to focus mostly on animals, such as Catherine Oliver, "Beyond-Human Ethics: The Animal Question in Institutional Ethical Reviews," *Area* 53, no. 4 (2021): 619–26. And see, for instance, the special issue on multispecies ethics edited by Heather Rosenfeld and Lauren Van Patter, "Ethics in Multispecies Research," *ACME: An International Journal for Critical Geographies* 21, no. 2 (2022).
14. A critical intervention on the cultural relativism of the illicit–licit boundaries is provided in Zhu, *Rosewood*. With important ethnographic detail, Zhu demonstrates how and why the illegal boom in rosewood trade looks so different through the lens of Chinese consumers and Western conservation organizations. On the disambiguation of (il)legal and (il)licit, see Willem Van Schendel and Itty Abraham, *Illicit Flows and Criminal Things: States, Borders, and the Other Side of Globalization* (Bloomington: Indiana University Press, 2005), 3–12.
15. See http://www.cites.org/.
16. On Brazilian biodiversity rules and regulations as well as Brazil's unique approach to environmental law, see José Drummond and Ana Flávia Barros-

Platiau, "Brazilian Environmental Laws and Policies, 1934–2002: A Critical Overview," *Law and Policy* 28, no. 1 (2006): 83–108; Elisa Morgera, Elsa Tsioumani, and Matthias Buck, *Unraveling the Nagoya Protocol: A Commentary on the Nagoya Protocol on Access and Benefit-Sharing to the Convention on Biological Diversity* (Leiden, Netherlands: Brill, 2014); Lesley McAllister, *Making Law Matter: Environmental Protection and Legal Institutions in Brazil* (Stanford, Calif.: Stanford University Press, 2008).

17. Understanding the rules and regulations of CITES is challenging work. See Tanya Wyatt, *Is CITES Protecting Wildlife? Assessing Implementation and Compliance* (New York: Routledge, 2021).

18. Emphasis added.

19. Margulies et al., "Prevalence and Perspectives of Illegal Trade."

20. Few studies have sought to study the effectiveness of supplying horticultural markets with desired species as a means to conserve. But an important example with cycads is Judy Kay, Arantza A. Strader, Vickie Murphy, Lan Nghiem-Phu, Michael Calonje, and M. Patrick Griffith, "Palma Corcho: A Case Study in Botanic Garden Conservation Horticulture and Economics," *HortTechnology* 21, no. 4 (2011): 474–81.

21. Simon Mackenzie and Donna Yates, "Collectors on Illicit Collecting: Higher Loyalties and Other Techniques of Neutralization in the Unlawful Collecting of Rare and Precious Orchids and Antiquities," *Theoretical Criminology* 20, no. 3 (2016): 352.

22. Emphasis added.

23. This is the work of the emerging discipline of southern green criminology. David Rodríguez Goyes, *Southern Green Criminology: A Science to End Ecological Discrimination* (Bingley, U.K.: Emerald Group, 2019).

24. Eugenia W. Herbert, *Flora's Empire* (Philadelphia: University of Pennsylvania Press, 2012); Richard Drayton, *Nature's Government: Science, Imperial Britain and the "Improvement" of the World* (New Haven, Conn.: Yale University Press, 2000). Within the world of botanical gardens, Royal Botanic Gardens, Kew probably has the most infamous history.

25. The Huntington supports some of its contemporary conservation work, for instance, through the annual sale of plants, including species whose original material was obtained by the same Friedrich Ritter who sold and distributed cactus material around the world prior to the development of CITES. But where the Belgian collector was left to wonder how he could legally ever sell materials from his pre-CITES *A. ritteri,* the Huntington, as a respected and trusted institution, is unlikely to face the same kind of scrutiny.

26. As Pearce writes, "'hunting for material' legitimises a great deal of brooding and wandering activity, sealed by the capture of finds to add to those already secured. . . . Hunting is very close to quest, an image which, with its stress on individual prowess and the overcoming of ordeals, runs particularly deep in the European psyche, and for many collectors a successful acquisition is indeed the Grail Achieved." Pearce, *On Collecting,* 184.

27. Mick Smith, *Against Ecological Sovereignty: Ethics, Biopolitics, and Saving the Natural World* (Minneapolis: University of Minnesota Press, 2011).
28. Today this is recognized, for instance, via requirements of the CBD for ABS of genetic resources through the Nagoya Protocol, which entered into force in 2014, even if implementation of ABS agreements in the exchange of biological diversity resources lags. Secretariat of the Convention on Biological Diversity, "Nagoya Protocol on Access to Genetic Resources and the Fair and Equitable Sharing of Benefits Arising from Their Utilization to the Convention on Biological Diversity," Convention on Biological Diversity, United Nations, 2011.
29. Derek Gregory, *The Colonial Present: Afghanistan, Palestine, Iraq* (Malden, Mass.: Blackwell, 2004).
30. Pearce, *On Collecting*, 184.
31. There was both great fanfare and backlash, for instance, when the director of science at the Royal Botanic Gardens, Kew called to decolonize its botanical collections. Alexandre Antonelli, "Director of Science at Kew: It's Time to Decolonise Botanical Collections," *The Conversation*, June 19, 2020, https://the conversation.com/director-of-science-at-kew-its-time-to-decolonise-botan ical-collections-141070. Yet within two years, those plans have already been scrapped under mounting public pressure: "Kew Gardens Boss Changes 'Decolonisation' Language after Backlash," *Express*, January 22, 2022, https://www .express.co.uk/news/uk/1550487/Kew-Gardens-decolonise-displays-botan ical-gardens.
32. Mackenzie and Yates, "Collectors on Illicit Collecting," 347–48.
33. Baudrillard, *System of Objects*, 97. As Pearce writes, "objects are our other selves; the better we understand them, the closer we come to self-knowledge." Pearce, *On Collecting*, vii.
34. I do not enjoy the repeated presence of Friedrich Ritter in the pages of this chapter (especially as a Jew), but his legacy remains unavoidable in a book about cacti. Incredibly (to me), Ritter's racist views and participation as a solider of the Third Reich went unremarked by cactus collectors with whom I spent time and whom I interviewed.
35. Simone Fullagar, "Desiring Nature: Identity and Becoming in Narratives of Travel," *Journal for Cultural Research* 4, no. 1 (2000): 58–76; Simone Fullagar, Wendy O'Brien, and Adele Pavlidis, "Creative Enactments in More-than-Human Worlds," in *Feminism and a Vital Politics of Depression and Recovery*, 171–200 (New York: Springer, 2019).
36. Survey response, February 28, 2021.
37. Consider here works like Prakash Kashwan, Rosaleen V. Duffy, Francis Massé, Adeniyi P. Asiyanbi, and Esther Marijnen, "From Racialized Neocolonial Global Conservation to an Inclusive and Regenerative Conservation," *Environment: Science and Policy for Sustainable Development* 63, no. 4 (2021): 4–19, and John Mbaria and Mordecai Ogada, *The Big Conservation Lie* (Auburn, Wash.: Lens and Pens, 2017).
38. This nursery is now operated by Leopoldo Horst's son.

39. Hartigan, *Care of the Species,* xxiii.
40. McGowan, *Capitalism and Desire,* 21.
41. Arthur C. Gibson, Kevin C. Spencer, Renu Bajaj, and Jerry L. McLaughlin, "The Ever-Changing Landscape of Cactus Systematics," *Annals of the Missouri Botanical Garden* (1986): 532–55. On the sedimentation of botanical practices of species naming in the age of empire (and for empire's benefit), see Christophe Bonneuil, "The Manufacture of Species: Kew Gardens, the Empire, and the Standardisation of Taxonomic Practices in Late Nineteenth-Century Botany," in *Instruments, Travel and Science,* 201–27 (New York: Routledge, 2003).
42. Jacques Lacan, *Anxiety,* book X of *The Seminars of Jacques Lacan,* ed. Jacques-Alain Miller, trans. A. R. Price (Cambridge: Polity, 2016), 101–3.
43. Roy Mottram, "The Grower Conservationist," *Cactus Explorer* 1, no. 1 (2011): 15.
44. Anna-Katharina Laboissiere, "Collect, Save, Adapt: Making and Unmaking Ex Situ Worlds," *Cultural Studies Review* 25, no. 1 (2019): 65–84; also see Irus Braverman, "Conservation without Nature: The Trouble with In Situ versus Ex Situ Conservation," *Geoforum* 51 (2014): 47–57.
45. Kirsty Shaw, "Reintroduction of *Echeveria laui* in the Biosphere Reserve of Tehuacán-Cuicatlan," in *Conserving North America's Threatened Plants: Progress Report on Target 8 of the Global Strategy for Plant Conservation,* ed. Andrea Kramer, Abby Hird, Kirsty Shaw, Michael Dosmann, and Ray Mims, appendix 2 (Glencoe, Ill.: Botanic Gardens Conservation International US, 2011).
46. Mottram, "Grower Conservationist," 15.
47. Blum and Secor, "Psychotopologies."

3. Between the Iron Curtain and the Glass House

1. Copjec, *Read My Desire,* 68.
2. Karel Crkal, *Lovec Kaktusů* (Prague: Academia, 1983), 19. This is most authoritative biography of Frič in relation to cacti, unfortunately available only in Czech.
3. I am grateful to Yvonna Fričová, the wife of Frič's grandson, for providing me with this anecdote and copy of the exhibition award. She also is responsible for providing me with the images of Frič in this chapter, and I am grateful for our productive email exchanges about the life of A. V. Frič, while recognizing that much more research is needed to place and contextualize him within a broader history of Czech botany.
4. Josef Kandert, "Alberto Vojtech Frič. On the Centenary of His Birth," *Annals of the Náprstek Museum* 11 (1983): 123.
5. Frič later Hispanicized his name to Alberto Vojtěch Frič. Markéta Křížová, "'The History of Human Stupidity': Vojtěch Frič and His Program of a Comparative Study of Religions," *Ethnologia Actualis* 18, no. 1 (2018): 46. The tale of the fight with a jaguar (and, later, a crocodile) is recounted by Yvonna Fričová. See Jan Velinger, "Alberto Vojtěch Frič—Part I—The Story of a Czech Adventurer and Ethnologist Who Brought a South American Indian to Prague," Radio Prague International, May 26, 2010, https://english.radio.cz/.

6. During his expeditions, he also established himself as a budding geographer and explorer working at the behest of the Paraguayan government. Kandert, "Alberto Vojtech Fríc," 112.
7. Quoted in Markéta Křížová, "'Wild Chamacoco' and the Czechs: The Double-Edged Ethnographic Show of Vojtěch Frič, 1908–91," in *Staged Otherness: Ethnic Shows in Central and Eastern Europe, 1850–1939,* ed. Dagnosław Demski and Dominika Czarnecka (Budapest: Central European University, 2021), 115. Between 1901 and 1913, Frič took four trips across various regions of southern Brazil, Uruguay, Argentina, and Paraguay. Kandert, "Alberto Vojtech Fríc," 112–17.
8. H. Glenn Penny, "The Politics of Anthropology in the Age of Empire: German Colonists, Brazilian Indians, and the Case of Alberto Vojtěch Frič," *Comparative Studies in Society and History* 45, no. 2 (2003): 249–80.
9. David Hall Stauffer, "The Origin and Establishment of Brazil's Indian Service: 1889–1910" (PhD thesis, University of Texas at Austin, 1955), 50–69.
10. The term *bugreiros* is etymologically derived from the Portuguese *bugre,* which was a pejorative and vulgar term used to describe Indigenous peoples in southern Brazil. The term shares its origins in the French *bourge,* as well as in the English *bugger.* Stauffer, 55.
11. Křížová, "Wild Chamacoco," 102–3.
12. Samuel J. Redman, *Prophets and Ghosts: The Story of Salvage Anthropology* (Cambridge, Mass.: Harvard University Press, 2021), 9.
13. Penny, "Politics of Anthropology," 277.
14. It is now known, for instance, that Frič fathered a child with a woman during his time living with the Chamacoco tribe. Frič's daughter, Hermína Frič Ferreira, was located by Frič's descendants around the year 2000. She died in 2009. Frič's descendants in Paraguay now number approximately two hundred. See Křížová, "Wild Chamacoco."
15. Rivka Galchen, "Wild West Germany," *New Yorker,* April 2, 2012, https://www.newyorker.com/magazine/2012/04/09/wild-west-germany.
16. Julian Crandall Hollick, "The American West in the European Imagination," *Montana: The Magazine of Western History* (1992): 18; Roger L. Nichols, "Western Attractions," *Pacific Historical Review* 74, no. 1 (2005): 8–9.
17. Křížová, "Wild Chamacoco," 116–17.
18. Křížová, 109.
19. Frič's relationship to Cherwish seems to have mirrored in many ways the (in)famous relationship between Berkeley anthropologist Alfred Kroeber and Ishi, a Yahi Native American.
20. A deeper and more comprehensive accounting of Frič's legacy, in particular drawing on primary archival sources and his extensive diaries, is lacking and remains to be completed, especially outside of the Czech language. I signal this as a limitation of my own engagement with Frič, as I relied primarily on secondary sources and interviews in discussing his legacy and activities.
21. See Jennifer Michaels, "Fantasies of Native Americans: Karl May's Continu-

ing Impact on the German Imagination," *European Journal of American Culture* 31, no. 3 (2012): 205–18, https://doi.org/10.1386/ejac.31.3.205_1; Křížová, "Wild Chamacoco."

22. Jaroslav Hašek, *The Good Soldier Svejk: And His Fortunes in the World War*, trans. Cecil Parrott, illus. Josef Lada (New York: Penguin, 1990). Notably, Jaroslav Hašek would come to write about Cherwish in his satirical story "The Indian and the Prague Police," recounting a series of misunderstandings in which Cherwish was arrested by Prague police for attacking a police officer during a tollbooth encounter gone awry. See Křížová, "Wild Chamacoco," 113–14.

23. Andrew Roberts, *From Good King Wenceslas to the Good Soldier Švejk: A Dictionary of Czech Popular Culture* (Budapest: Central European University Press, 2005).

24. Benjamin Ziemann, "Resistance to War in Germany, 1914–1918: The Traces of the German 'Schwejkiade,'" *Cesky Casopis Historicky* 114, no. 3 (2016): 721.

25. Frederick George Bailey, *The Kingdom of Individuals* (Ithaca, N.Y.: Cornell University Press, 1993), 15.

26. Peter Tyrer, N. Babidge, J. Emmanuel, N. Yarger, and M. Ranger, "Instrumental Psychosis: The Good Soldier Švejk Syndrome," *Journal of the Royal Society of Medicine* 94, no. 1 (2001): 22–25; Peter Fleming and Graham Sewell, "Looking for the Good Soldier, Švejk: Alternative Modalities of Resistance in the Contemporary Workplace," *Sociology* 36, no. 4 (2002): 857–73; Victor Kuperman, "Narratives of Psychiatric Malingering in Works of Fiction," *Medical Humanities* 32, no. 2 (2006): 67–72.

27. Bailey, *Kingdom of Individuals*, 15.

28. Bailey, 10.

29. I return to this question of what constitutes organized crime (or not), and the consequences of characterizing illegal wildlife trades as organized crime, in chapter 5.

30. Švejk and Jan are both pseudonyms, in accordance with my research ethics approvals, which required research subject anonymity.

31. Crkal, *Lovec Kactusů*, 18–19.

32. Michal Peprník, "The Affinity with the North American Indian in Czech Literary Discourse on the Democratic Roots of Czech National Culture," *Journal of Transatlantic Studies* 6, no. 2 (2008): 155.

33. Jan Pohunek, "A Century of Czech Tramping," *FOLKLORICA: Journal of the Slavic, East European, and Eurasian Folklore Association* 16 (2011): 19. The term *tramping* is borrowed from the writings of Jack London and his use of the word to connote his life as a transient "hobo."

34. Pohunek, 20–21.

35. Lee Bidgood, "The Americanist Imagination and Real Imaginary Place in Czech Bluegrass Songs," *Popular Music and Society* 41, no. 4 (2018): 393.

36. McGowan offers an important analysis of the "public" and "private" threats posed by totalitarian Stalinism and capitalism across chapter 2 of *Capitalism*

and Desire: "if capitalism ushers subjects into a private world, it is also developing a system of surveillance that appears to eliminate the possibility of privacy" (67).

37. Grafting can also be political. See Fleming, "Toward Vegetal Political Ecology."

38. It is precisely the repetition of chasing desire in the next object that capitalist consumerism latches on to, preying on the structure of the desiring subject through substituting the absent "Other" with the commodity form.

39. Paul Kingsbury, "The Extimacy of Space," *Social and Cultural Geography* 8, no. 2 (2007): 235–58.

40. H. M. Hernández et al., "*Ariocarpus bravoanus* subsp. *Bravoanus*," IUCN Red List of Threatened Species, e.T40958A2947203, https://www.iucnredlist .org/.

41. This dynamic, of course, is not limited to cactus collectors. Today there is an absurd market in variegated monstera and other tropical aroid plants, where fanatical plant collectors spend thousands of dollars for a single cutting of any number of especially precious white or speckled *Monstera deliciosa* varietals.

42. Simon Mackenzie and Donna Yates, "What Is Grey about the 'Grey Market' in Antiquities?," in *The Architecture of Illegal Markets: Towards an Economic Sociology of Illegality in the Economy*, ed. Jens Beckert and Matías Dewey, 70–86 (Oxford: Oxford University Press, 2017).

43. Hannah Dickinson has recently done important work to theorize "gray" markets in more-than-human terms within the IWT in caviar. See Dickinson, "Caviar Matter(s): The Material Politics of the European Caviar Grey Market," *Political Geography* 99 (2022): 102737.

44. Tanya Wyatt, Daan van Uhm, and Angus Nurse, "Differentiating Criminal Networks in the Illegal Wildlife Trade: Organized, Corporate and Disorganized Crime," *Trends in Organized Crime* 23, no. 4 (2020): 357.

45. I return to these racialized dynamics of IWT in chapter 7.

46. Dickinson, "Caviar Matters," 3.

47. Dickinson, 3.

48. The disastrous U.S. "War on Drugs" is just one of many examples. See Dawn Paley, *Drug War Capitalism* (Chico, Calif.: AK Press, 2014).

49. "Švejks may be admired because they can outthink the organization and its masters." Bailey, *Kingdom of Individuals*, 16.

50. Carlos Gerardo Velazco Macías, Marco Antonio Alvarado Vázquez, and Salvador Arias Montes, "A new species of Aztekium (Cactaceae) from Nuevo León, Mexico," *Xerophilia* 2 (August 2013).

51. *A. valdezii* is not accepted by David Hunt, *CITES Cactaceae Checklist* (London: Royal Botanic Gardens, Kew, 2016), 23.

52. Laura Hernández Rosas, "Comercio Internacional de Cactáceas Mexicanas: Estudio de Caso de las Especies Descritas Recientemente" (master's thesis, Universidad Internacional de Andalucía, 2017), 33.

53. Smith, *Against Ecological Sovereignty*.

54. "That is, constructing the object of a discipline and constructing that disci-

pline's metadiscipline are simultaneous, linked processes. There is only one world. It is seen through a given prism, through a given discipline, although, for a set of disciplines, the constitutive materials are the same." Milton Santos, *The Nature of Space,* trans. Brenda C. Baletti (Durham, N.C.: Duke University Press, 2021), 4.

55. Malcolm Bowie, *Lacan* (Cambridge, Mass.: Harvard University Press, 1991), 83.

56. Jacques Lacan, "The Instance of the Letter in the Unconscious," in *Écrits: The First Complete Edition in English,* trans. Bruce Fink (New York: W. W. Norton, 2006), 436.

57. Lacan, 430.

58. "It is first of all an *unsatisfied* desire that initiates our own, one that is not filled up with meaning, or has no signified. That that desire is *unsatisfiable* is a secondary truth resulting from this primary condition." Copjec, *Read My Desire,* 55.

4. Confronting Extinction Anxiety in Cactus Country

1. Compared to many more poorly described plant families, cacti are incredibly well studied; thus the "discovery" of a new species is increasingly uncommon, making fifteen years still relatively recent for a new species description.

2. As Abraham Joshua Heschel describes, Judaism is a religion of time, not space. Perhaps my identity, then, as a researcher—steeped in both Jewish and geographical thought—biases me toward registering geographic matters in temporal terms. Heschel, *The Sabbath* (London: Macmillan, 1995).

3. Lacan, *Anxiety,* 160.

4. Lacan, *Écrits,* 366.

5. Lacan, *Four Fundamental Concepts,* 131; Kingsbury, "Extimacy of Space."

6. Jacques Lacan, *On Feminine Sexuality: The Limits of Love and Knowledge,* book XX of *The Seminars of Jacques Lacan,* ed. Jacques-Alain Miller, trans. Bruce Fink (New York: W. W. Norton, 1998), 126.

7. "Desire comes from the Other, and jouissance is located on the side of the Thing." Jacques Lacan, "On Freud's 'Trieb' and the Psychoanalysts' Desire," in Lacan, *Écrits,* 724.

8. Slavoj Žižek, *The Plague of Fantasies* (London: Verso, 1997), 81.

9. Kingsbury, "Locating the Melody of the Drives," 521.

10. Natalie Loveless, *How to Make Art at the End of the World* (Durham, N.C.: Duke University Press, 2019), 80. I am grateful to artist Sera Boeno for directing me to this work during a discussion of what moves us into research-creation practices.

11. Kingsbury, "Locating the Melody of the Drives."

12. Lacan, *Four Fundamental Concepts,* 184.

13. Louis Kirshner, "Rethinking Desire: The Objet Petit A in Lacanian Theory," *Journal of the American Psychoanalytic Association* 53, no. 1 (2005): 84.

14. Kirshner, 91.

15. Kingsbury, "Did Somebody Say Jouissance?," 50.

16. Thom van Dooren, *Flight Ways* (New York: Columbia University Press, 2014), 27.

17. Marlon Machado, "The Discovery of *Arrojadoa marylanae*," *Cactus and Succulent Journal* 77, no. 2 (2005): 66.

18. Eben Kirksey, "Species: A Praxiographic Study," *Journal of the Royal Anthropological Institute* 21, no. 4 (2015): 758–80.

19. I return to flourishing in greater detail in chapter 8.

20. Thom van Dooren, Eben Kirksey, and Ursula Münster, "Multispecies Studies: Cultivating Arts of Attentiveness," *Environmental Humanities* 8, no. 1 (2016): 1–23; on "arts of noticing," see Anna Lowenhaupt Tsing, "Arts of Inclusion; or, How to Love a Mushroom," *Australian Humanities Review*, no. 50 (2011): 19.

21. On *ex situ* conservation, see chapter 2.

22. Lorimer, "Nonhuman Charisma."

23. Krithika Srinivasan, "The Biopolitics of Animal Being and Welfare: Dog Control and Care in the UK and India," *Transactions of the Institute of British Geographers* 38, no. 1 (2013): 106–19.

24. Kingsbury, "Extimacy of Space," 246.

25. Maurice Merleau-Ponty, *The Visible and the Invisible: Followed by Working Notes* (Evanston, Ill.: Northwestern University Press, 1968), 180. I first encountered this wonderful description of the unconscious in Loveless, *How to Make Art.*

26. McGowan, *Capitalism and Desire,* 108. McGowan shows how these crucial insights come back to Marx: "Production not only supplies a material for the need, but it also supplies a need for the material. . . . The need which consumption feels for the object is created by the perception of it. . . . Production thus not only creates an object for the subject, but also a subject for the object." Karl Marx, *Gundrisse,* trans. Martin Nicolaus (New York: Penguin, 1993), 92.

27. Lucas Pohl, "The Sublime Object of Detroit," *Social and Cultural Geography* 22, no. 8 (2021): 1063–79; Paul Kingsbury, "Sociospatial Sublimation: The Human Resources of Love in Sandals Resorts International, Jamaica," *Annals of the Association of American Geographers* 101, no. 3 (2011): 650–69; Jacques Lacan, *Ethics of Psychoanalysis,* 112.

28. Moore et al., "Generating Anxiety, Short-Circuiting Desire."

29. Lacan repeatedly states that "anxiety is not without object." Lacan, *Anxiety,* 159. As Roberto Harari explains, this wording of "not without" is exacting: "these two particles . . . structure the aphorism in a way that accounts for *the obscure, imprecise condition of the object at hand.*" Harari, *Lacan's Seminar on "Anxiety": An Introduction,* The Lacanian Clinical Field (New York: Other, 2001), 34.

30. Lacan, *Anxiety,* 54; Harari, *Lacan's Seminar on "Anxiety,"* 56.

31. Derek Hook, "Mapping Anxiety," *Psychology in Society* 48 (2015): 117.

32. Jesse Proudfoot, "Anxiety and Phantasy in the Field: The Position of the Unconscious in Ethnographic Research," *Environment and Planning D: Society and Space* 33, no. 6 (2015): 1135.

33. Heidi J. Nast, "Mapping the 'Unconscious': Racism and the Oedipal Family," *Annals of the Association of American Geographers* 90, no. 2 (2000): 215.

34. Lacan, *Anxiety*, 175.

35. Lacan, *Four Fundamental Concepts*, ix. On absence/presence, see Avril Maddrell, "Living with the Deceased: Absence, Presence, and Absence-Presence," *Cultural Geographies* 20, no. 4 (2013): 501–22.

36. I am grateful to Sophie Sapp Moore's attention to highlighting the ceremonial aspects of this chapter in early drafts.

37. Koot, "Enjoying Extinction."

38. Lacan, *Anxiety*, 11.

39. Harari, *Lacan's Seminar on "Anxiety,"* 56.

40. Fink, *Lacanian Subject*, 40.

41. Lacan, *Four Fundamental Concepts*, 79–90.

42. Lacan, *Anxiety*, 15.

43. Deborah Bird Rose, "Multispecies Knots of Ethical Time," *Environmental Philosophy* 9, no. 1 (2012): 127–40.

44. Haraway, *When Species Meet*, 67.

45. Fisher and Tronto, "Toward a Feminist Theory of Caring," 40.

46. Harari, *Lacan's Seminar on "Anxiety,"* 1–27.

47. There is a meaningful linguistic relation between care, concern, and the work of psychoanalysis as cure. See Harari, 5–8.

48. Lacan, *Écrits*, 724.

49. On the function of psychoanalysis as a method of change rather than understanding, see Bruce Fink, "Against Understanding: Why Understanding Should Not Be Viewed as an Essential Aim of Psychoanalytic Treatment," *Journal of the American Psychoanalytic Association* 58, no. 2 (2010): 260. And note the productive vegetal metaphor at work! "The goal is to get at its root by uncovering all the early childhood material holding it in place and everything that has since been grafted onto it—which involves dredging all this material up and *bringing it to speech.*"

50. Guy Debord defined *psychogeography* as "the study of the precise laws and specific effects of the geographical environment, consciously organized or not, on the emotions and behavior of individuals." This is not, however, my intended usage here. Debord, *Introduction to a Critique of Urban Geography* (1955; repr., Dublin: Praxis Press, 2008), 23.

51. Geographers Paul F. Robbins and Sarah A. Moore have similarly worked to understand Anthropocenic anxieties through *objet a* through naming what they call "ecological anxiety disorder." Whereas they are concerned with how those invested in the "Edenic Sciences" can overcome fear of novel natures to move toward a politics of action in the conservation of nonhuman life, here I am concerned with extinction as a particularly disturbing form of temporal absence that can bring *objet a* too close. Robbins and Moore, "Ecological Anxiety Disorder."

52. Deborah Bird Rose, "What If the Angel of History Were a Dog?," *Cultural Studies Review* 12, no. 1 (2006): 75.

53. Aeonicide thus "constitutes a sustained attack on the future of the group, and thus an attack on ethical time." Rose, "Multispecies Knots of Ethical Time," 127. See James Hatley, *Suffering Witness: The Quandary of Responsibility after the Irreparable* (Albany: SUNY Press, 2000).

54. Tim Ingold gestures toward plants as their own lines connecting worlds in his writing against hylomorphic creation and the advocacy of creation as process. Ingold, "The Textility of Making," *Cambridge Journal of Economics* 34, no. 1 (2010): 96. I thank Rob St. John for making this valuable connection (which is not a line!) for me.

55. Nan Shepherd, *The Living Mountain: A Celebration of the Cairngorm Mountains of Scotland* (Edinburgh: Canongate Books, 2008).

56. "Too often, the obstacle to confronting knowledge comes from within and is anchored in the very ontology of the subject itself. Lacan spelled this notion of shameful ontology 'hontology,' where French *honte* stands for 'shame.' Apparently, it is less painful for the subject to turn away from a deadly disaster, even at the cost of death, than to survive the disgrace of admitting that we knew what we were doing, that we knew about the potential consequences of our actions, and that we were both passively and actively complicit in the wrongdoings of others. . . . Humans are now bound in death with all other species on the planet, creating a novel sense of commonality on what might be the threshold of extinction." Svitlana Matviyenko and Judith Roof, eds., introduction to *Lacan and the Posthuman* (London: Palgrave Macmillan, 2018), 6. See also Jason W. Moore, *Capitalism in the Web of Life: Ecology and the Accumulation of Capital* (New York: Verso, 2015).

57. Robin Wall Kimmerer, *Braiding Sweetgrass: Indigenous Wisdom, Scientific Knowledge and the Teachings of Plants* (Minneapolis, Minn.: Milkweed, 2013); Marisol de la Cadena, "Indigenous Cosmopolitics in the Andes: Conceptual Reflections beyond 'Politics,'" *Cultural Anthropology* 25, no. 2 (2010): 334–70; de la Cadena, *Earth Beings: Ecologies of Practice across Andean Worlds* (Durham, N.C.: Duke University Press, 2015); Sophie Chao, "In the Shadow of the Palm: Dispersed Ontologies among Marind, West Papua," *Cultural Anthropology* 33, no. 4 (2018): 621–49.

58. Max Liboiron, *Pollution Is Colonialism* (Durham, N.C.: Duke University Press, 2021).

59. As Paul Kingsbury says, "the *objet petit a* only takes shape from the distorted point of view of the subject's desires and fears." Kingsbury, "Locating the Melody of the Drives," 522.

60. Natasha Myers, "How to Grow Livable Worlds: Ten Not-So-Easy Steps," in *The World to Come* (Gainsville, Fla.: Harn Museum of Art, 2018), 52.

61. Andrew Curley and Majerle Lister, "Already Existing Dystopias: Tribal Sovereignty, Extraction, and Decolonizing the Anthropocene," in *Handbook on the Changing Geographies of the State: New Spaces of Geopolitics,* ed. Sami Moisio, Natalie Koch, Andrew E. G. Jonas, Christopher Lizotte, and Juho Luukkonen (Northampton, Mass.: Edward Elgar, 2020), 252. See also Kyle P. Whyte, "In-

digenous Science (Fiction) for the Anthropocene: Ancestral Dystopias and Fantasies of Climate Change Crises," *Environment and Planning E: Nature and Space* 1, no. 1–2 (2018): 224–42.

62. Marder, *Plant-Thinking*, 181; Natasha Myers, "Conversations on Plant Sensing: Notes from the Field," *Nature Culture* 3 (2015): 43.

63. On botanical ontologies, see Lewis Daly, Katherine French, Theresa L. Miller, and Luíseach Nic Eoin, "Integrating Ontology into Ethnobotanical Research," *Journal of Ethnobiology* 36, no. 1 (2016): 1–9. On dispersed ontologies and vegetal life, see Chao, "In the Shadow of the Palm."

64. Santos, *Nature of Space,* 30–31.

65. Here I am referring to the Lacanian idea of the unconscious as outside, not an enclosed and noncommunicative interiority but something that dynamically engages with the world. See Kingsbury and Pile, "Introduction," 5.

66. Chao, "In the Shadow of the Palm," 637.

67. Marder, *Plant-Thinking,* 104.

68. The microbiological worlds of cacti, for instance, remain poorly understood. This is an important step toward fostering flourishing. See Christine Cuomo, *Feminism and Ecological Communities* (London: Routledge, 1998), 73.

5. A New Illicit Trade

1. Radhika Govindrajan, *Animal Intimacies* (Chicago: University of Chicago Press, 2018), 49.

2. Catriona Sandilands, "Desiring Nature, Queering Ethics," *Environmental Ethics* 23, no. 2 (2001): 186.

3. See chapter 1 for a deeper engagement with producing succulent commodities, and see Collard and Dempsey, "Life for Sale?"

4. Lyndsie Bourgon, *Tree Thieves: Crime and Survival in North America's Woods* (New York: Little, Brown Spark, 2022).

5. Emphasis added.

6. Jared Margulies, Leigh-Anne Bullough, Amy Hinsley, Daniel J. Ingram, Carly Cowell, Bárbara Goettsch, Bente B. Klitgård, Anita Lavorgna, Pablo Sinovas, and Jacob Phelps, "Illegal Wildlife Trade and the Persistence of 'Plant Blindness,'" *Plants, People, Planet* 1, no. 3 (2019): 173–82.

7. See U.S. Endangered Species Act, § 9(a)(2) (1973). For a legal review of persistent issues with protecting plants in the United States, see Katrina Outland, "Trapped in the Goddess's Mousetrap: Equitable Solutions for Poverty Poaching of Venus Flytraps," *Washington Journal of Environmental Law and Policy* 8 (2018): 362–91.

8. Much of the information in this chapter comes from publicly available documents, memoranda, search warrants, and indictments related to U.S. District Court for the Central District of California case *United States of America v. Byungsu Kim, Youngin Back, and Bong Jun Kim,* case CR 19-329-GW.

9. My understanding of nonhuman charisma as a "relational variable that emerges from the material and ecological properties of interacting, sensory

bodies" is informed by Jamie Lorimer, "On Auks and Awkwardness," *Environmental Humanities* 4, no. 1 (2014): 196. Nonhuman charisma is a relational process shaped by political-affective logics by which humans characterize and come to know species. Although Lorimer limits his analysis to the charisma of nonhuman animals, I find it analytically useful as a concept to extend it into the vegetal word, where certain plants do certainly exude charismatic charms. Lorimer, "Nonhuman Charisma."

10. That a helicopter was employed in one, or potentially multiple, *Dudleya* heists remains difficult to substantiate. Several Mexican government officials I interviewed in 2018 attested to at least one attempt being made by helicopter to steal *D. pachyphytum,* though I have not seen physical evidence to further substantiate the incidents. I left Cedros with competing stories from both official and unofficial sources about several certain and less certain *D. pachyphytum* heists. In the end, I find it less important to focus on the elements of the story that remain clouded in obscurity than to focus on *why* those particular elements remain stubbornly obscured.

11. An important critique of "follow the thing"—and what I've subsequently considered a "follow the species" methodology (such as what I employed in researching this book)—relates to how it intersects with issues of power, trust, and relationship building in social research. Although I still believe the methodology of "follow the species" to which I turned especially in the second part of this book has great merit, on Cedros I encountered this important and critical limitation that could have easily steered away from ethical research practice if I had attempted to continue my research as planned. I signal these shortcomings because it is worth paying attention to where research fails or goes awry, where particular methods can take you (or not), and the shortcomings of my own research efforts.

12. "Tráfico de codiciada planta, habría sido la causa de la agresión a pescadores del norte de BCS," *BCS Noticias,* December 15, 2019, https://www.bcsnoticias.mx/.

13. This is a plausible scenario based on secondhand information from interviews with Biosphere Reserve and CONANP staff as well as on media reports, but it nevertheless leaves more questions unanswered than addressed.

14. Investigaciones Zeta, "Crece mercado negro de la 'siempreviva,'" *ZETA,* July 17, 2018, https://zetatijuana.com/.

15. Tanya Wyatt, *Wildlife Trafficking: A Deconstruction of the Crime, Victims and Offenders* (New York: Springer Nature, 2021), 132. In the context of a different kind of wildlife trade, see Kristof Titeca, "Illegal Ivory Trade as Transnational Organized Crime? An Empirical Study into Ivory Traders in Uganda," *British Journal of Criminology* 59, no. 1 (2019): 40.

16. Wyatt, *Wildlife Trafficking,* 133.

17. Rosaleen Duffy, *Security and Conservation: The Politics of the Illegal Wildlife Trade* (New Haven, Conn.: Yale University Press, 2022), 49.

18. Duffy, 35.

19. Francis Massé, Hannah Dickinson, Jared Margulies, Laure Joanny, Teresa

Lappe-Osthege, and Rosaleen Duffy, "Conservation and Crime Convergence? Situating the 2018 London Illegal Wildlife Trade Conference," *Journal of Political Ecology* 27, no. 1 (2020): 23–42.

20. I return to these matters of deeper integration of conservation and security in chapter 7.
21. Duffy, *Security and Conservation*.
22. Duffy, 2.
23. This was further evidenced in my own research interviews with nonprofit conservation organization staff, who echoed these sentiments that there was "pressure" to "make links" between IWT, organized crime groups, and international security concerns. And see Francis Massé and Jared D. Margulies, "The Geopolitical Ecology of Conservation: The Emergence of Illegal Wildlife Trade as National Security Interest and the Re-shaping of US Foreign Conservation Assistance," *World Development* 132 (2020): 104958.
24. Angus Nurse and Tanya Wyatt, *Wildlife Criminology* (Bristol, U.K.: Bristol University Press, 2020); Michael J. Lynch and Paul B. Stretesky, *Exploring Green Criminology: Toward a Green Criminological Revolution* (New York: Routledge, 2016).
25. Stephen F. Pires, Jacqueline L. Schneider, and Mauricio Herrera, "Organized Crime or Crime That Is Organized? The Parrot Trade in the Neotropics," *Trends in Organized Crime* 19, no. 1 (2016): 4–20.
26. Wyatt et al., "Differentiating Criminal Networks."
27. United Nations Office on Drugs and Crime, *United Nations Convention against Transnational Organized Crime and the Protocols Thereto* (New York: United Nations, 2004), 5.
28. United Nations Office on Drugs and Crime, 353.
29. On the disorganized nature of rhino and ivory poaching in sub-Saharan Africa, see Titeca, "Illegal Ivory Trade"; Annette M. Hübschle, "The Social Economy of Rhino Poaching: Of Economic Freedom Fighters, Professional Hunters and Marginalized Local People," *Current Sociology* 65, no. 3 (2017): 427–47.
30. Wyatt et al., "Differentiating Criminal Networks," 357.
31. As Wyatt et al. note in their analysis of these different organizational forms and actors, "our three proposed categories of groups and networks have varying levels of involvement. Importantly, they also have varying levels of interaction with one another" (359).
32. On the theory of the plants' purported medicinal value, see Investigaciones Zeta, "Crece mercado negro de la 'siempreviva.'"

6. Learning to Know a Plant

1. These practices were especially informed by the work of Myers, "Conversations on Plant Sensing"; Hartigan, *Care of the Species*; and Craig Holdrege, *Thinking Like a Plant: A Living Science for Life* (Great Barrington, Mass.: Lindisfarne Books, 2014).
2. On the series in collecting, see Baudrillard, *System of Objects,* 96–97.

3. There is, according to Sianne Ngai, a relation here between cuteness and the desire to possess, dominate, and destroy, a topic I take up in depth in chapter 7.

4. On plant-time, see Marder, *Plant-Thinking*, 93–117. See also John Charles Ryan, "That Seed Sets Time Ablaze: Vegetal Temporality in Judith Wright's Botanical Poetics," *Environmental Philosophy* 14, no. 2 (2017): 163–89, and Catherine Phillips, "Telling Times: More-than-Human Temporalities in Bee-keeping," *Geoforum* 108 (2020): 315–24. I return to discussion of the time of plants in greater length in chapter 8.

5. Rafi Youatt, "Counting Species: Biopower and the Global Biodiversity Census," *Environmental Values* 17, no. 3 (2008): 394.

6. I return to the question of whether desire for *Dudleya* was actually driven by this "wild" look in chapter 7.

7. Youatt, "Counting Species," 394. I write more about these dynamics of "refusal" in plant commodities in Jared Margulies, "Care for the Commodity? The Work of Saving Succulents in the Laboratory," in *The Work That Plants Do*, ed. Marion Ernwein, Franklin Ginn, and James Palmer, 53–70 (Berlin: transcript, 2021). On dynamic charms, see chapter 8 and Cuomo, *Feminism and Ecological Communities*.

8. Hartigan, *Care of the Species*, 281.

9. See chapter 1 for deeper engagements with the psychology of collecting, in particular its gendered dynamics.

10. Many cactus and succulent collectors would not suggest this is necessarily the case—most of their collections grow and shrink over time—but on reflection, many acknowledged that those contractions and expansions related to shifts in particular interests changing over time, and there was always something *lacking*—a particular plant that was missing. This point is further complicated by the limits to understanding lively succulent subjects as objects, as detailed in greater depth in chapter 1.

11. Elsner and Cardinal, *Cultures of Collecting*, 3–4.

12. Baudrillard, *System of Objects*, 99; Elsner and Cardinal, *Cultures of Collecting*, 9.

13. Baudrillard, *System of Objects*, 98.

14. Reid Moran and Michael Benedict, "*Dudleya pachyphytum* (Crassulaceae), a New Species from Isla Cedros, Mexico," *Phytologia* 47, no. 2 (1980): 87.

15. Baudrillard, *System of Objects*, 98.

16. Pearce, *On Collecting*, 24–25.

17. Pearce, 27.

18. Lau's legacy, as well as his standing within the international cactus and succulent collecting community, remains mixed, but it is uncontested that his impact on the field was immense and lasting. At least eighteen cactus species are named in his honor with the species name *laui*. But in addition to aspersions related to his commercial trade in species, in contravention of CITES rules and regulations, there are persistent rumors within the collecting community that Lau used his position of running a school for Indigenous children in Mexico to commit acts of sexual abuse. As far as I have been able to ascertain, these

accusations have never been substantiated or formally described, nor were they ever evidenced in any court of law.

19. Alfred Lau, "Discovery at a Virgin Outpost," *Cactus and Succulent Journal* 52, no. 5 (1980): 238–40.

20. Reid Moran and Michael Benedict, "*Dudleya pachyphytum,* of Isla Cedros, Mexico," *Cactus and Succulent Journal* 53, no. 3 (1981): 132–36.

21. Moran and Benedict, 134.

22. Moran and Benedict, 135.

23. Daniel C. Knudsen, Jillian M. Rickly, and Elizabeth S. Vidon, "The Fantasy of Authenticity: Touring with Lacan," *Annals of Tourism Research* 58 (2016): 33–45.

24. Elizabeth S. Vidon, "Why Wilderness? Alienation, Authenticity, and Nature," *Tourist Studies* 19, no. 1 (2019): 4.

25. Lacan, *Four Fundamental Concepts,* 185–86.

26. Lau, "Discovery at a Virgin Outpost," 240.

27. Helen F. Wilson, "On Geography and Encounter: Bodies, Borders, and Difference," *Progress in Human Geography* 41, no. 4 (2017): 464.

28. Elsner and Cardinal, *Cultures of Collecting,* 3–4.

29. Alfred Lau, "South American Cactus Log," *Cactus and Succulent Journal* 68, no. 6 (1996): 295–97.

30. Freud wrote this in a letter to ex-analysand and friend Jeanne Lampl de Groot in 1939, a few months before his death. Quoted in J. Forrester, "'Mille e Tre': Freud and Collecting," in Elsner and Cardinal, *Cultures of Collecting,* 227.

31. Wilson, "On Geography and Encounter," 458.

32. Jane Bennett, "Afterword: Look Here," *Environmental Humanities* 14, no. 2 (2022): 496.

33. Kingsbury and Pile, "Introduction," 19.

34. Kingsbury and Pile, 19.

7. Disentangling Succulent Desires

1. Rosemary-Claire Collard, *Animal Traffic,* 5–6.

2. Charley Lanyon, "California's Succulent Smugglers: Plant Poachers Seed Asia's Desire for Dudleya," *South China Morning Post,* September 9, 2018, https://www.scmp.com/magazines/post-magazine/long-reads/article/2163157/californias-succulent-smugglers-plant-poachers.

3. K. M. Smith, C. Zambrana-Torrelio, A. White, M. Asmussen, C. Machalaba, S. Kennedy, K. Lopez et al., "Summarizing US Wildlife Trade with an Eye toward Assessing the Risk of Infectious Disease Introduction," *EcoHealth* 14, no. 1 (2017): 29–39.

4. Erin McCormick, "Stolen Succulents: California Hipster Plants at Center of Smuggling Crisis," *Guardian,* April 27, 2018, https://www.theguardian.com/environment/2018/apr/27/stolen-succulents-california-hipster-plants-at-center-of-smuggling-crisis.

5. Teo Ballvé, "Investigative Ethnography: A Spatial Approach to Economies of Violence," *Geographical Review* 110, no. 1–2 (2020): 238.

6. Names of nurseries have been changed to protect interviewee identities.
7. Simon Snowden, "Dudleya, a New Love," *Cactus and Succulent Review* 43, no. 26 (2020): 37–43.
8. The ways this chapter discloses the "remaking" of Californian and Mexican succulents into "Korean" succulents leading to increased value find strong parallels with the insights and research of Annah Zhu's work on the illegal rosewood trade. Zhu shows how rosewood is understood to be "improved" through its interactions with people through carving by skilled artisans in Chinese contexts, in which "the material convergence of human intention and the cosmic order immortalized in the form of furnishings or implements that would survive for generations to come." Zhu, *Rosewood*, 45.
9. Dilys Roe and Tien Ming Lee, "Possible Negative Consequences of a Wildlife Trade Ban," *Nature Sustainability* 4, no. 1 (2021): 5–6.
10. Evan A. Eskew and Colin J. Carlson, "Overselling Wildlife Trade Bans Will Not Bolster Conservation or Pandemic Preparedness," *Lancet Planetary Health* 4, no. 6 (2020): e215.
11. Massé and Margulies, "Geopolitical Ecology of Conservation."
12. On unsubstantiated linkages between threat finance and wildlife trade, see Duffy, *Security and Conservation*.
13. Collard, *Animal Traffic*; Zhu, *Rosewood*, 38.
14. Massé et al., "Conservation and Crime Convergence?"
15. Jared D. Margulies, Rebecca WY Wong, and Rosaleen Duffy, "Understanding Drivers of Demand, Researching Consumption of Illegal Wildlife Products: A Reply to Bergin et al.," *Geoforum* 117 (2020): 279.
16. Jared D. Margulies, Rebecca WY Wong, and Rosaleen Duffy, "The Imaginary 'Asian Super Consumer': A Critique of Demand Reduction Campaigns for Illegal Wildlife Trade," *Geoforum* 107 (2019): 216–19.
17. See Laura Thomas-Walters, Hubert Cheung, Tien Ming Lee, Anita Kar Yan Wan, and Yifu Wang, "Targeted Values: The Relevance of Classical Chinese Philosophy for Illegal Wildlife Demand Reduction Campaigns," *People and Nature* 2, no. 4 (2020): 964–71, and Laura Thomas-Walters, Diogo Veríssimo, Erica Gadsby, David Roberts, and Robert J. Smith, "Taking a More Nuanced Look at Behavior Change for Demand Reduction in the Illegal Wildlife Trade," *Conservation Science and Practice* 2, no. 9 (2020): e248.
18. Hoai Nam Dang Vu and Martin Reinhardt Nielsen, "Evidence or Delusion: A Critique of Contemporary Rhino Horn Demand Reduction Strategies," *Human Dimensions of Wildlife* 26, no. 4 (2021): 390–400; see also Rebecca WY Wong, *The Illegal Wildlife Trade in China* (New York: Springer, 2019).
19. Claire Jean Kim, *Dangerous Crossings: Race, Species, and Nature in a Multicultural Age* (Cambridge: Cambridge University Press, 2015).
20. In a related thematic vein, see Claire Jean Kim, "Murder and Mattering in Harambe's House," *Politics and Animals* 3 (2017): 1–15.
21. Zhu, *Rosewood*, 44–45.
22. Lanyon, "How Californian Plant Lovers Are Stalking Asian Smuggling Rings."

23. McCormick, "Stolen Succulents."
24. Lanyon, "How Californian Plant Lovers Are Stalking Asian Smuggling Rings."
25. Erika Lee, "The 'Yellow Peril' and Asian Exclusion in the Americas," *Pacific Historical Review* 76, no. 4 (2007): 537–62.
26. Margulies et al., "Illegal Wildlife Trade."
27. Sianne Ngai, *Our Aesthetic Categories: Zany, Cute, Interesting* (Cambridge, Mass.: Harvard University Press, 2015), 93.
28. Ngai, 3.
29. Ngai, 59.
30. Aljosa Puzar and Yewon Hong, "Korean Cuties: Understanding Performed Winsomeness (Aegyo) in South Korea," *Asia Pacific Journal of Anthropology* 19, no. 4 (2018): 333; see also Puzar, "Asian Dolls and the Westernized Gaze: Notes on the Female Dollification in South Korea," *Asian Women* 27, no. 2 (2011): 81–111.
31. Ngai, *Our Aesthetic Categories,* 82, emphasis added.
32. Ngai, 64.
33. Ngai, 96.
34. Ngai, 64.
35. Ngai, 64.
36. Ngai, 79.
37. Ngai, 96.
38. Ngai, 98.
39. Jamie Lorimer, "More-than-Human Visual Analysis: Witnessing and Evoking Affect in Human–Nonhuman Interactions," in *Deleuze and Research Methodologies,* ed. Rebecca Coleman and Jessica Ringrose (Edinburgh: Edinburgh University Press, 2013), 75.
40. Ngai, *Our Aesthetic Categories,* 54.
41. By this I do not mean to assert that there is only one "right" place for *D. farinosa* in the world. I am thinking about place and *D. farinosa* here especially through the work of Soren C. Larsen and Jay T. Johnson, *Being Together in Place: Indigenous Coexistence in a More than Human World* (Minneapolis: University of Minnesota Press, 2017). They write about place as a "call," "a summons to encounter, dialogue, and relationship among the humans and nonhumans who share the landscape" (1–2).
42. On these and other environmental aesthetics, see Emily Brady and Jonathan Prior, "Environmental Aesthetics: A Synthetic Review," *People and Nature* 2, no. 2 (2020): 254–66.
43. Collard, *Animal Traffic*; Nicole Shukin, *Animal Capital: Rendering Life in Biopolitical Times* (Minneapolis: Univeristy of Minnesota Press, 2009); Collard and Dempsey, "Life for Sale?"; Rosemary-Claire Collard and Jessica Dempsey, "Capitalist Natures in Five Orientations," *Capitalism Nature Socialism* 28, no. 1 (2017): 78–97.
44. Youatt, "Counting Species."
45. I draw this critique of actor-network theory and its uneasy fit with political ecology from Rebecca Lave, "Political Ecology and Actor-Network Theory,"

in *The Routledge Handbook of Political Ecology* (New York: Routledge, 2015), 231–23. And see Pohl, "Object-Disoriented Geographies."

46. Margulies, "Care for the Commodity?"

47. Email correspondence with the author, June 10, 2021. Used with permission.

48. The psychoanalytic concept of the gaze in Lacanaian thought is often misinterpreted as simply about how the gaze demonstrates dominance or power over the subject gazed upon. Instead, it is about how desire transforms the visual field. Lacan, *Four Fundamental Concepts,* 93.

49. McGowan, *Capitalism and Desire,* 79.

50. The gaze signifies what lies beyond the image (against popular misrepresentations of the Lacanian gaze in film studies, for example), manifest through the Other. This is explained well in Copjec, *Read My Desire,* 30–38.

51. Ngai, *Our Aesthetic Categories,* 91.

52. Maan Barua, "Affective Economies, Pandas, and the Atmospheric Politics of Lively Capital," *Transactions of the Institute of British Geographers* 45, no. 3 (2020): 678–92.

53. Robert J. Smith, Diogo Veríssimo, Nicholas J. B. Isaac, and Kate E. Jones, "Identifying Cinderella Species: Uncovering Mammals with Conservation Flagship Appeal," *Conservation Letters* 5, no. 3 (2012): 205–12.

54. Lorimer, "Nonhuman Charisma."

55. Meredith Root-Bernstein, L. Douglas, A. Smith, and D. Veríssimo, "Anthropomorphized Species as Tools for Conservation: Utility beyond Prosocial, Intelligent and Suffering Species," *Biodiversity and Conservation* 22, no. 8 (2013): 1577.

56. Ngai, *Our Aesthetic Categories,* 91.

57. Brock Bersaglio and Jared Margulies, "Extinctionscapes: Spatializing the Commodification of Animal Lives and Afterlives in Conservation Landscapes," *Social and Cultural Geography* 23, no. 1 (2022): 10–28; Barua, "Affective Economies."

58. Taylor Stephan, "14 Cute Succulents That Are Basically Impossible to Kill," *E! Online,* August 25, 2018, https://www.eonline.com/news/962983/14-cute-succulents-that-are-basically-impossible-to-kill.

59. Ngai, *Our Aesthetic Categories,* 65.

60. Lois Beckett, "'Crime against Nature': The Rise and Fall of the World's Most Notorious Succulent Thief," *Guardian,* March 20, 2022, https://www.theguardian.com/us-news/2022/mar/20/california-succulent-smuggling-dudleya.

61. Sentencing memorandum, entered January 6, 2022, USA v. Kim et al.

62. Plea agreement, entered June 25, 2019, USA v. Kim et al.

63. Complaint filed as to defendant Byungsu Kim, Youngin Back, and Bong Jun Kim in violation of 16:3372(a)(2)(B), (a)(4), entered January 4, 2019, USA v. Kim et al.

64. Government's sentencing position, no. CR 19-329-GW, January 6, 2022, 8, https://www.courthousenews.com/.

65. Exhibit G, USA v. Kim et al.

66. Rosaleen Duffy offers a similar word of warning about these "ethical and moral dilemmas" in *Security and Conservation,* xvii.

67. Sentencing memorandum, entered January 5, 2022, USA v. Kim et al.

68. Hillel Aron, "South Korean Man Sentenced to Two Years for Poaching Wild Succulents," *Courthouse News,* January 20, 2022, https://www.courthouse news.com/.

8. For a Flourishing Geography of Succulent Life

1. Some of the best writing on the relationships between time, death, and life is found in the work of Lynn Margulis and Dorian Sagan, *What Is Life?* (Berkeley: University of California Press, 2000).

2. Thom van Dooren, "Extinction," in *Critical Terms for Animal Studies,* ed. Lori Gruen (Chicago: University of Chicago Press, 2018), 169.

3. Puig de la Bellacasa, *Matters of Care,* 4.

4. Puig de la Bellacasa, 42.

5. Donna Haraway, "Awash in Urine: DES and Premarin® in Multispecies Response-Ability," *Women's Studies Quarterly* 40, no. 1/2 (2012): 302.

6. On the unthinkability of the Anthropocene from a psychoanalytic perspective, see Matviyenko and Roof's introduction to *Lacan and the Posthuman,* 6–7.

7. Anthony D. Barnosky, Nicholas Matzke, Susumu Tomiya, Guinevere O. U. Wogan, Brian Swartz, Tiago B. Quental, Charles Marshall et al., "Has the Earth's Sixth Mass Extinction Already Arrived?," *Nature* 471, no. 7336 (2011): 51–57.

8. Michael E. Soulé, "What Is Conservation Biology?," *BioScience* 35, no. 11 (1985): 727–34.

9. Richard J. Ladle and Paul Jepson, "Toward a Biocultural Theory of Avoided Extinction," *Conservation Letters* 1, no. 3 (2008): 111–18.

10. Richard Ladle, Ana Malhado, Paul R. Jepson, and Steve Jennings, "Perspective: The Causes and Biogeographical Significance of Species' Rediscovery," *Frontiers of Biogeography* 3, no. 3 (2011).

11. On this point, see a fascinating discussion of ethnobiology and taxonomies in Phillipe Descola, *The Ecology of Others* (Chicago: Prickly Paradigm Press, 2013), 45–54.

12. The chapter "Techniques, Time, and Geographic Space" offers a valuable review of key geographic works on space-time, as well as developing Santos's own important theorizing of hybrid geographic space. In Santos, *Nature of Space,* 13–33.

13. On the uses of species here, see Haraway, *When Species Meet,* 17.

14. On alternative taxonomic systems, see Marc Ereshefsky, *The Poverty of the Linnaean Hierarchy: A Philosophical Study of Biological Taxonomy* (Cambridge: Cambridge University Press, 2000).

15. Again, when we restrict our vision to the animal kingdom, this perspective is mostly sensible. A horse is a horse, of course. But plants are far more promiscuous beings.

16. Charles Darwin, *On the Origin of Species: By Means of Natural Selection or the*

Preservation of Favored Races in the Struggle for Life (1859; repr., New York: Cosimo Classics, 2007), 34.

17. Kirksey, "Species."
18. Taxonomic families evolve and diverge at dramatically different rates in evolutionary time. The cactus family represents a relatively young evolutionary branch, believed to be approximately 30–35 million years old. Cacti are understood to be rapidly speciating, with some of the highest diversification rates of any plants. Pablo C. Guerrero, Lucas C. Majure, Amelia Cornejo-Romero, and Tania Hernández-Hernández, "Phylogenetic Relationships and Evolutionary Trends in the Cactus Family," *Journal of Heredity* 110, no. 1 (2019): 4–21.
19. Hartigan, *Care of the Species,* 30.
20. Hartigan, xxiii.
21. Holmes Ralston III, "Duties to Endangered Species," *BioScience* 35, no. 11 (1985): 721.
22. "The crisis today is therefore not multiple but singular and manifold. It is not a crisis of capitalism and nature but of modernity-in-nature. That modernity is a capitalist world-ecology." Moore, *Capitalism in the Web of Life,* 4. On the politics of "we" and "our" and in the context of critical geographic writing, I frequently reflect on a point made by Juanita Sundberg, who writes about the Anglo-Eurocentric privileging of whom "we" is a referent in too much writing on human relations with nonhuman life and inattentions to social difference. Sundberg, "Decolonizing Posthumanist Geographies."
23. Dipesh Chakrabarty, "The Climate of History: Four Theses," *Critical Inquiry* 35, no. 2 (2009): 197–222; see also Sophie Chao, E. Kirksey, and K. Bolender, eds., *The Promise of Multispecies Justice* (Durham, N.C.: Duke University Press, 2022).
24. Ursula K. Heise, *Imagining Extinction: The Cultural Meanings of Endangered Species* (Chicago: University of Chicago Press, 2016), 13.
25. On the fetishization of the "last" of the species, see Dolly Jørgensen, "Endling, the Power of the Last in an Extinction-Prone World," *Environmental Philosophy* 14, no. 1 (2017): 119–38; see also van Dooren, *Flight Ways.*
26. Jessica Hernandez, *Fresh Banana Leaves: Healing Indigenous Landscapes through Indigenous Science* (Berkeley, Calif.: North Atlantic Books, 2022), 73–76.
27. Cuomo, *Feminism and Ecological Communities.*
28. Kimmerer, *Braiding Sweetgrass,* 15.
29. Franklin Ginn, Uli Beisel, and Maan Barua, "Flourishing with Awkward Creatures: Togetherness, Vulnerability, Killing," *Environmental Humanities* 4, no. 1 (2014): 115.
30. Cuomo writes that "nothing in a biotic community can flourish on its own." On the scalar and interdependences of flourishing, she writes that "individual and communal flourishing contribute to each other dialectically." Cuomo, *Feminism and Ecological Communities,* 74. On dynamic charms, see 71–73.
31. Holly Jean Buck, "On the Possibilities of a Charming Anthropocene," *Annals of the Association of American Geographers* 105, no. 2 (2015): 369–77.

32. Lacan, *Ethics of Psychoanalysis,* 319.

33. Ruti, "Why Some Things Matter More than Others," 207.

34. Pohl and Swyngedouw, "What Does Not Work in the World," 16–17.

35. Ruti, "Why Some Things Matter More than Others," 210. Specifically, see Ruti's engagement with why Lacan explains these ethics of desire through the story of Antigone.

36. Rose, "Multispecies Knots of Ethical Time," 139.

37. Jodi Dean, *The Communist Horizon* (London: Verso, 2012), 1.

38. Haraway might be "a creature of the mud, not the sky," but perhaps plants being creatures of both makes them especially generative teachers in learning "to be worldly from grappling with, rather than generalizing from, the ordinary." Haraway, *When Species Meet,* 3. As Karen Houle writes, "plants enjoy a relation to touch that we do not, by virtue of their slow straddling two elemental zones: the earth and the air. As air-breathers they connect up with anything in that sphere. As earth-touchers, they connect with anything in that sphere. And possibly enjoy qualities and freedoms of movements— passions—not available on the surface." Houle, "Animal, Vegetable, Mineral: Ethics as Extension or Becoming?," *Symposium* 19, no. 2 (2015): 53.

39. Pohl, "Object-Disoriented Geographies."

40. On hailing and interpellation, see Louis Althusser, *On the Reproduction of Capitalism: Ideology and Ideological State Apparatuses* (London: Verso, 2014), 264. Most germane to this discussion of interpellation here, Paul F. Robbins highlighted the theoretical power of interpellation in studies of political ecology and the capacity of nonhumans (namely, turfgrass) to "hail" human subjects. Robbins, *Lawn People: How Grasses, Weeds, and Chemicals Make Us Who We Are* (Philadelphia: Temple University Press, 2012), 14–16.

41. Kingsbury, "Extimacy of Space."

42. Pitt, "On Showing and Being Shown Plants," 50.

43. Wilson, "On Geography and Encounter," 464.

44. Ruti, "Why Some Things Matter More than Others."

45. McGowan, *Capitalism and Desire,* 114–19.

46. Roald Dahl, "The Sound Machine," in *The Collected Short Stories of Roald Dahl* (New York: Penguin, 1992), 567.

47. Katerine Wu, "Plants May Let Out Ultrasonic Squeals When Stressed," *Smithsonian Magazine,* December 9, 2019, https://www.smithsonianmag .com/smart-news/scientists-record-stressed-out-plants-emitting-ultrasonic -squeals-180973716/. For an in-depth and accessible overview of the contemporary science of plant sounds and communication, see Karen Bakker, *The Sounds of Life: How Digital Technology Is Bringing Us Closer to the Worlds of Animals and Plants* (Princeton, N.J.: Princeton University Press, 2022), 99–118.

48. See Michael Marder, "If Peas Can Talk, Should We Eat Them?," Opinionator, *New York Times,* April 28, 2012, and Marder and Gary Fancione, "Michael Marder and Gary Francione Debate Plant Ethics," *Columbia University Press Blog,* March 6, 2013, https://www.cupblog.org/.

49. See, for instance (among many), Stefano Mancuso and Alessandra Viola, *Brilliant Green: The Surprising History and Science of Plant Intelligence* (Washington, D.C.: Island Press, 2015), and Monica Gagliano, *Thus Spoke the Plant: A Remarkable Journey of Groundbreaking Scientific Discoveries and Personal Encounters with Plants* (Berkeley, Calif.: North Atlantic Books, 2018).

50. Olga Cielemęcka, Marianna Szczygielska, and Catriona Sandilands, "Thinking the Feminist Vegetal Turn in the Shadow of Douglas-Firs: An Interview with Catriona Sandilands," *Catalyst: Feminism, Theory, and Technoscience* 5, no. 2 (2019): 1–19.

51. Kimmerer, *Braiding Sweetgrass*; Hernandez, *Fresh Banana Leaves*; Myers, "How to Grow Livable Worlds."

52. There are examples of extremely rare succulent plants now guarded by armed security forces against the threat of poaching. For an extensive critique of these contemporary tendencies in conservation, see Duffy, *Security and Conservation*. On recent contributions to multispecies justice, see Chao et al., *Promise of Multispecies Justice*.

53. Shepherd, *Living Mountain*, 59.

Index

Page numbers in italics refer to illustrations.

371

Index

Blum, Virginia, 4
Boom, Boudewijn Karel, 1
botanists/botany, 10, 28, 34, 70, 87,
    90–93. *See also* taxonomies/taxonomy
Bourgon, Lyndsie, 196
Bowie, Malcolm, 153
Brazil: cacti and succulents in, 1–2, 9,
    61, 62, 73, 93–96, 155–87; colonialist
    violence against, 113–14; illegal seed
    collection in, 80–93; legislation
    regarding export of Brazilian cacti,
    84–85, 102; searching for cacti and
    succulents in, 44, 70–80, 97, 99, 111–13
British Cactus and Succulent Society
    (BCCS), 55–56
bugreiros, 352n10
Buining, Alfred, 70, 100, 102

Caatinga ecosystem (Brazil), 157
Cactaceae family, 3
cacti and succulents: areoles, 3, *40*;
    biodiversity of, 8, 164; collections of,
    30, 67, 89–90; commodification of,
    17, 260, 285, 292; conservation of,
    88–93, 159, 166; descriptions of, 1, 3–4;
    as desiring subjects, 13–20, 238–42;
    emotional connections to, 41–49, 65;
    evolution of, 4, 162, 165, 308, 368n18;
    fantasies of, 58, 298; flourishing of,
    66–67, 97, 152, 180, 359n68; illicit
    trade in, 6, 18–19, 35, 93–96; as objects
    of desire, 4, 160; organs, 59; poaching
    of, 2, 4, 6–7, 370n52; propagating,
    129–31; as signifiers, 15, 178–79, 180,
    182–83; spines, 1, 3, *40,* 57, 155, *288*;
    split natures of, 66; stems, 3, 165,
    250, 267, 273, 277, 323; stories about,
    9–11; survival of, 325; wild-harvesting,
    274, 279–80, 341n49. *See also* care;
    collecting/collectors; endangered
    species: cacti and succulents; flowers
cactoexplorers/cactoexploration, 44, *62,*
    63, 69, 77, 178
Cadena, Marisol de la, 182
California: *Dudleya* species from, 260, 261,
    266, 270, 294–95, 364n8; poaching
    incidents in, 189–91, 216–17, 220–21,
    229, 275–76, 299–305
California Native Plant Society (CNPS), 293

Čapek, Karel, 1, 36, 109, 121
capital/capitalism, 21, 129, 166, 183, 293;
    as cause of extinction, 313–17, 320;
    consumerism influenced by, 292, 321,
    354n38; desire highjacked by, 18, 159,
    298; extractive, 177, 236; global, 186,
    296, 314, 368n22; life ordered by, 67–68,
    103, 184. *See also* commodification/
    commodities: capitalist
Capitalocene, 181, 184, 185. *See also*
    Anthropocene
Cardinal, Roger, 43, 239, 251
care, for cacti and succulents, 10,
    28–31, 49–68, 159, 176–79, 180, 307;
    in multispecies registers, 324, 347n66;
    photography's contribution to, 56–64;
    politics of, 29, 184; practices of, 29,
    308–9, 310, 318, 347n63; as relation
    building, 313–14; species, 139–40, 168,
    171; tools of, *51. See also* more-than-
    human care; plants: care for; species:
    care for; vegetal life: care for
Carlson, Colin J., 279
cephalium rings, 165–66
Cephalocereus senilis, 113
Chao, Sophie, 182, 184
charisma, 8, 47, 152, 202, 216
China: collectors in, 34, 141, 261, 270, 275,
    276, 278–79; demand for endangered
    species, 282–84; *Dudleya* market in,
    280, 284; Euro-American sentiments
    against, 279, 281, 282; succulents in,
    266, 278, 283
Christmas cactus. See *Schlumbergera*
    orssichiana
Cipocereus bradei, 178
class/classicism, 101, 173. *See also* race;
    racism
climate change, 6–7, 8, 21, 182, 240. *See*
    also environment
Collard, Rosemary-Claire, 25, 259, 291
collecting/collectors, cacti and succulents,
    31–36, 342n12; building community,
    54–56, 132; caring in, 317–19;
    conservationists' affinity with, 69–70,
    82, 103, 171; culture of, 55, 67–68,
    88, 107–8, 240; desires of, 15–16,
    66, 69–70, 76, 79, 95, 131, 140, 180,
    206, 233, 235–36, 251–52, 271, 273,

Index

Dahl, Roald, "The Sound Machine," 323

Dang, Vu Hoai Nam, 282

Dark Mountain (Brazil). *See* Serra Escura

Darwin, Charles, 311

Dean, Jodi, 319

Debord, Guy, 357n50

Deleuze, Gilles, 76

de Man, Paul, 295

Dempsey, Jessica, 291

Descartes, René, 153

desire(s), 6, 49, 181–83, 187, 229, 240, 253, 311–12, 318; capitalism hijacking, 18, 159, 298; caring about, 186, 314–19; commodification and, 12, 139, 354n38; conceptualizing, 92–93; difference's relationship to, 90–100, 139; drive's relationship to, 66, 340n36; ethics of, 20, 79–80, 111; extinction anxiety and, 170–75, 307–8; fantasies of, 6, 15, 16, 160, 291; illicit intertwined with, 67–68; for immortality, 33, 43–44, 241; Lacanian theories of, 12, 153, 160–62, 316, 344n29, 355n7; objects of, 4, 14–18, 42–43, 48, 96; *objet a* structuring, 16–17, 182–82, 298, 311–12; political ecology of, 11–13, 20, 31, 108, 111, 150, 152, 244, 320–22; power of, 80, 152, 295; production of, 11, 99–108, 112, 132, 171–72, 184, 238, 255, 259, 286, 325; pyschoanalytic analysis of, 21; psychotopologies of, 131, 227; for species, 130–33, 159, 227, 228, 254–56; succulent, 238–42, 257–305; unconscious, 171, 179, 291; Western, 117–20, 125, 127–29. *See also* collecting/ collectors: desires of; lack: desire and; objects: of desire; Other, the: desires for; possession: desire for; subject(s): desiring

Dickinson, Hannah, 141–42

differences, 10, 102; between collections/ collectors, 27–28, 95; desire's relationship to, 90–100, 139; in plant ontology, 47, 61

Discocactus (genus), 7, 64

Discocactus zehntneri subspecies *boomianus*, 1–2, 7

drive(s), 49, 59, 60, 65, 161, 316; desire's relationship to, 66, 340n36; for

jouissance, 40–41, 75, 253, 316, 318, 319; Lacanian theory of, 12; satisfying, 14, 15–18

Dudley, William Russel, 229

Dudleya (genus), 228–29, 232, 240–41, 277; ability to resist their extraction, 235–36; aesthetics of, 264–75, 277, 289, 291, 296–97; from California, 260, 261, 266, 270, 294–95, 364n8; Chinee market, 280, 284; desires for, 284–85, 298; East Asian market, 213, 255, 262; poaching of, 254–55, 261–62, 281, 299–305; South Korean market, 250, 257–60, 264–66, 275

Dudleya brittonii, 228, *294*

Dudleya caespitosa: poaching of, 203

Dudleya farinosa, 22, *190, 224,* 227–38, *294*; colors of, 271–72, 273; conservation of, 230–31; demand for, 260, 264, 278; *Dudleya pachyphytum's* kinship with, 241, 255; encountering, 289–91; habitat, 229–30, 365n41; as houseplants, 236–38; leaves, 267–68, 272, 273, 277; poaching of, 189–206, 215, 216–17, 218, 221, 255, 263, 275–79; study of, 225, 227; survival of, 237–38, 254–55; trade in, 223; wild-collected, 267–68, 297

Dudleya gnoma, 228–29

Dudleya greenei, 264, 272

Dudleya pachyphytum, 206–21, *226, 243, 253, 261, 274*; colors, 273; commodification of, 291–92; descriptions of, 240–41, 247–52, 270–71; *Dudleya farinosa's* kinship with, 241, 255; encounters with, 242–54, 291; habitat of, *246,* 250; leaves, 272, 273; poaching of, 211–21, 284, 303, 360n10; pricing of, 271, 273; rarity of, 260; splitting heads, 272, 273; study of, 225, 227; threat of extinction, 238, 241, 242, 255, 308, 309; wild-collected, 267–68, 270, 277, 297. *See also individual regions and countries*

Duffy, Rosaleen, 215, 216, 217–18, 281–82

East Asia, 207, 275; *Dudleya* plants in, 213, 255, 262; interest in succulents, 221, 254, 259, 262, 277; legal and illegal

Index

Mexico: agaves case in, 312–13; ban on trade in cactus seeds from, 90, 124, 147–50, 245; biodiversity in, 91; *Dudleya* plants illegally collected in, 259–60, 261, 265, 268–69, 270, 364n8; Švejk's smuggling of cacti seeds from, 133–37; trade in cactus seeds, 83, 85–86. *See also* Isla de Cedros

Moore, Sarah A., 357n51

Moran, Reid, 240–41, 245, 247, 248, 252, 254

more-than-human care, 18–19, 28, 99, 111, 153, 175, 185–86. *See also* care; nonhuman life; vegetal life: care for

more-than-human endeavors, 255, 312

more-than-human relations, 238, 298. *See also* human–plant relations

more-than-human worlds, 12–13, 20, 92, 339n20. *See also* geography: more-than-human; vegetal worlds

Mottram, Roy, 105

mourning, 46, 48, 156, 314

multispecies justice, 314, 318, 325

Myers, Natasha, 66, 183, 225

Nagoya Protocol, 350n28

Ngai, Sianne, 260, 285–90, 291, 296, 298, 362n3

Nielsen, Martin Reinhardt, 282

nonhuman life, 21, 28, 137, 177, 235, 339n20, 357n51, 360n9; caring for, 49, 186, 297, 308; humans' relationship to, 10, 153, 315, 368n22, 369n40. *See also* human–plant relations; more-than-human relations

North America, 259, 279, 281; cacti and succulents in, 7, 191, 341n39; collectors in, 31, 91–92. *See also* Global North; Mexico; United States

nurseries, 303–4; CITES-registered, 124, 135, 148; commercial, 105, 114, 143, 149–50, 203, 257–58, 265, 269, 299–300. *See also* greenhouses

object(s): of desire, 4, 14–18, 42–43, 48, 96, 159, 160–61, 172, 183, 224, 228, 229; of a discipline, 355n54; elevating, 31–32, 75; fetish, 46, 58–59; species as, 101–3; subject's relationship to, 11, 238, 286, 289–99, 350n33, 356n26;

transitional, 41–42; unique, 240, 241. *See also* part-objects

object relations theory, 42, 59

objet a: anxieties through, 253, 357n51; desire structured by, 16–17, 182–83, 298, 311–12; inscribing species with, 130; Lacanian concept of, 15, 76–77, 160–62, 171–74; *petit,* 358n59

organized crime. *See* crimes: organized; illegal wildlife trade: as organized crime

Other, the: desires for, 16, 79, 132, 152–53, 179, 192, 295, 316–17, 340n33; desiring subject and, 159–60, 354n38; fantasies of, 192, 254, 286; fetish objects satisfying, 346n57; gaze manifest through, 366n50; Lacanian theory of, 355n7; of the unconscious, 192, 322; vegetal, 97–99, 325

Pachyphytum (genus), 240–41

Paraguay: colonialist violence against, 113–15; Frič's work in, 117, 352nn6–7

part-objects, 42, 59

Pearce, Susan, 31–32, 33, 92, 241, 244, 342n12, 343n19, 344n28, 349n26, 350n33

Penny, H. Glenn, 115

photography, 49, 53, 56–64; macroscale, *58*

phylogenetics: molecular, 165

Pile, Steve, 16–17, 19, 253, 254

Pilosocereus (genus), 178; flowering, *19, 58*

Pilosocereus aurisetus (hairy torch cactus), 71, 72, *73,* 77, 80–83, 88

Pilosocereus pachycladus, 60–61

Pires, Stephen F., 218

Pitt, Hannah, 49, 52, 55, 57, 320

plantiness, 61, 320, 347n67

plant neurobiology, 323–24. *See also* biology

plant people, 13–14

plants, 20, 61, 105, 175, 181, 311, 318, 348n13; care for, 49, 52–54, 183, 184, 298, 320; colors of, 271–72; commodification of, 255, 259; cute, 285, 292–93, 360n9; death of, 45, 46, 48; desirous, 227–38; differences in, 47, 61; endangered species, 69, 170–71, 203, 206; evolution of, 238, 287, 311, 323; extraction of, 3, 185, 211, 213,

Index

satisfaction: collectors seeking, 132; through desire, 8, 31, 160–61, 171–72; for drives, 14, 15–18; fantasies of, 318, 321–22. *See also* pleasure

Schlumbergera orssichiana (Christmas cactus), 9–10, 292

Schmeichel, Brandon, 33

Secor, Anna, 4

seeds, cacti and succulents, 147–52; catalogs of, *135*; cost of, 140, 354n41; germination of, 91, 129–30, 131; growing plants from, 93–94, 274; illegal trade in, 80–93

Serra Escura (Brazil), 177, 181, 182; *Arrojadoa marylanae* on, 162–70, *163*, *170*, 174, 184–85

Shepherd, Nan, 181, 307, 325

Shukin, Nicole, 291

slavery, 162, 314

Smith, Mick, 92, 150

Smith, Robert, 296

smugglers/smuggling, 11, 18, 25, 220, 278, 283; Czech, 117, 143–48; European, 133–36, 141, 150; South Korean, 192. *See also* illegal wildlife trade; poachers/ poaching; trade

social justice, 12, 338n13. *See also* multispecies justice

Sonoran Desert: saguaro poaching in, 2, 6, 20, 21, 137

South Africa: poaching incidents in, 53, 204, 302. *See also* Africa

South America: collectors in, 34, 97, 123, 252; Indigenous peoples of, 113–15, 182, 183, 290, 314. *See also* Brazil; Global South; Paraguay

South Korea: cacti and succulents in, 254, 256, 257–88, 292–93; collectors in, 141; cuteness concept in, 287, 293; *Dudleya* market in, 250, 257–60, 264–66, 275; smugglers in, 192. *See also* greenhouses: South Korean; growers: South Korean

sovereignty, 21, 91–92, 99, 150

species: anthropomorphizing, 296; care for, 96, 98, 139–40, 168, 171, 315, 316, 318, 319; conservation of, 20, 102, 107, 139, 145, 147; describing, 145, 155, 228; desire for, 130–33, 159, 227, 228, 254–56; as dynamic beings, 162,

231; endemic, 63, 143, 149, 192–93, 204, 209; epistemologies of, 175, 176; extinction of, 17, 18, 21, 71–72, 77–78, 90, 189, 308–14; flourishing of, 159, 165, 171, 180, 186, 307–25; knowledge of, 360n9, 360n11; Linnean taxonomy, 310–14; loss of, 17–18, 21, 70–80, 90, 98, 159, 174, 181, 311–12, 315; managed, 9–10; naming, 102, 139, 145, 228, 251; new, 93–94, 99–100, 130–33, 164–65, 355n1; propagating, 129–30, 131; trajectories of, 186–87. *See also* endangered species; illegal wildlife trade

species formation concept, 99–103, 175, 237–38, 310–14, 318

species thinking, 100–103

stereotypes, 22, 194, 259, 279–85

Strombocactus disciformis, 151

subject(s): cacti and succulents as, 13–20, 238–42; desiring, 43, 66, 101, 159–60, 171–74, 249, 289, 295, 316–19, 354n38, 358n59; drives of, 59; object's relationship to, 11, 238, 286, 289–99, 356n26, 362n10

sublimation, Lacanian theory of, 43, 75–76, 172, 345n36

succulents. *See* cacti and succulents

Sultana, Farhana, 21

Sundberg, Juanita, 368n22

sustainability, 52, 143, 169, 174, 206, 209, 233, 236, 279

Švejk, 111, 121–26, 138–39, 141–42, 353n22; similarities to Frič, 126, 133, 152, 353m22; smuggling activities, 133–37, 143, 147, 149–52

Swyngedouw, Erik, 317

taxonomies/taxonomy, 28, 70, 176; cacti, 138–42; collecting, 32; of *Dudleya*, 262–63; in evolution, 368n18; identifying new species, 102, 251, 313; Linnean system of, 103, 310–11; orders of, 3; work of, 227–28, 239. *See also* botanists/botany

terror management theory, 33, 43

Thailand: *Conophytum* popular in, 271

Thanksgiving cactus. See *Schlumbergera orssichiana*

Thing, the *(das Ding)*, 153, 317, 360n11;

380

Index

absence of, 40–41, 43, 161; aura of, 96, 286; centripetal pull of, 59–60; dignity of, 75–76, 172, 253–54; Lacanian concept of, 14–17, 40–41, 43, 340n28, 355n7
Tohono O'odham Nation, 6, 20, 21, 182
topology: Lacan's use of the term, 4. *See also* psychotopologies
trade, illegal and illicit, 13, 260–64, 266; causes of, 244, 259; Czech collectors engaging in, 121–26, 142–47; in *Dudleya* species, 299; geographic distribution of, 110, 259, 298–99; politics of, 279–86; seeds, 80–88; in South Africa, 53, 204, 302; transport, 94–95. *See also* black markets; gray markets; illegal wildlife trade; poachers/poaching; smugglers/smuggling
tramping, 128–29, 157, 353n33
Tronto, Joan, 28
Tsing, Anna, 13, 339n20
Turbinocarpus (genus), 135
Turbinocarpus alonsoi, 134, 136
Turbinicarpus nikolae, 124

Uebelmann, Werner J., 70, 100, 102
Uebelmannia (genus), 71, 96, 97, 99–100, 110
Uebelmannia buiningii, 73, 77, 79, 172; desire to possess, 96, 99; finding, 69–72, 74, 97, 99, 106; preserving, 103–6; threat of extinction, 95, 175, 309
Uebelmannia gummifera, 62
unconscious: conscious's relationship to, 107, 159, 172–73, 178–79; desires in, 108, 171, 179–80, 249, 253, 291; expressions of in the world, 13, 108; Lacanian theories of, 19, 152–53, 337n1, 359n68; language of, 15, 19; meaning shaped by, 320, 321; Other of, 192, 322; psychoanalytic theories of, 174, 177; psychotopologies of, 6, 248; role in shaping human–plant relations, 325; seeking the Other, 192; structure of, 4, 66

United Nations Convention against Transnational Organized Crime (UNTOC), 218–20
United States, 87, 183, 193; anti-Asian sentiments in, 279, 281, 282; cacti and succulents in, 137, 193; collectors in, 34–36, 54–55, 71–72, 91, 267, 270, 275, 343n20, 347n1; markets for IWT products in, 259–61, 278, 280–81; poaching incidents in, 203, 204, 205, 214, 216, 285. *See also* California
United States v. Byungsu Kim, 299–305

van Dooren, Thom, 162, 308
Van Schendel, Willem, 82
vegetal life, 47, 319, 325; care for, 49, 183–84; commodification of, 101–3; evolution of, 3, 186. *See also* cacti and succulents; Other, the: vegetal; plants
vegetal worlds, 3–4, 13, 29, 43, 64–68, 324. *See also* more-than-human worlds
videography, 60–62. *See also* photography
Vidon, Elizabeth, 249
Viguiera lanata (flowering shrub), 248
Viseu, Ana, 66
void, 14–15, 18, 48, 108, 161, 322

Whatmore, Sarah, 339n19
White, Kyle, 183
white supremacy. *See* racism
wildlife demand reduction campaigns, 281–85. *See also* conservation/conservationists
Wilson, Helen, 250–51
Wong, Rebecca, 281–82
Wyatt, Tanya, 141, 214–15, 218, 219

Yates, Donna, 88, 95
Youatt, Rafi, 235, 236, 291–92

Zehnter, Leo, 1
Zhu, Annah Lake, 282–83, 348n14, 364n8
Ziemann, Benjamin, 121
Žižek, Slavoj, 161

Jared D. Margulies is assistant professor in geography at the University of Alabama.